AQA
A-level

Economics

①

Ray Powell

James Powell

Approval message from AQA

This textbook has been approved by AQA for use with our qualification. This means that we have checked that it broadly covers the specification and we are satisfied with the overall quality. Full details of our approval process can be found on our website.

We approve textbooks because we know how important it is for teachers and students to have the right resources to support their teaching and learning. However, the publisher is ultimately responsible for the editorial control and quality of this book.

Please note that when teaching the **AQA A-level Economics** course, you must refer to AQA's specification as your definitive source of information. While this book has been written to match the specification, it does not provide complete coverage of every aspect of the course.

A wide range of other useful resources can be found on the relevant subject pages of our website: www.aqa.org.uk.

DYNAMIC LEARNING

HODDER EDUCATION
AN HACHETTE UK COMPANY

Hodder Education, an Hachette UK company, Carmelite House, 50 Victoria Embankment,
London EC4Y 0DZ

Orders

Bookpoint Ltd, 130 Milton Park, Abingdon, Oxfordshire OX14 4SB
tel: 01235 827827
fax: 01235 400401
e-mail: education@bookpoint.co.uk
Lines are open 9.00 a.m.–5.00 p.m., Monday to Saturday, with a 24-hour message answering service.
You can also order through the Hodder Education website: www.hoddereducation.co.uk

ISBN 978-1-4718-2978-9

Impression number	10	9	8	
Year	2020	2019	2018	2017

This textbook has been approved by AQA for use with our qualification. This means that we have
checked that it broadly covers the specification and we are satisfied with the overall quality. Full details
of our approval process can be found on our website.

We approve textbooks because we know how important it is for teachers and students to have the right
resources to support their teaching and learning. However, the publisher is ultimately responsible for the
editorial control and quality of this book.

Please note that when teaching the *AQA A-level Economics* course, you must refer to AQA's specification
as your definitive source of information. While this book has been written to match the specification, it
does not provide complete coverage of every aspect of the course.

A wide range of other useful resources can be found on the relevant subject pages of our website:
www.aqa.org.uk.

The publishers would like to thank the following for permission to reproduce photographs:

pp.1–2 Fotolia; **p.8** Fotolia; **p.24** Advertising Archives; **p.31** Fotolia; **p.59** Fotolia; **p.68** Fotolia; **p.80**
Jerome Eldorado/Alamy; **p.84** TopFoto; **p.85** Fotolia; **p.101** Fotolia; **p.103** Fotolia; **p.112** Advertising
Archives; **p.137–38** Fotolia; **p.141** Neil Fozzard; **p.142** TopFoto; **p.146** Richard Levine/Alamy; **p.150**
Fotolia; **p.156** Imagestate Media; **p.168** Fotolia; **p.172** Fotolia; **p.195** Fotolia; **p.201** Ingram Real Office;
p.214 Fotolia; **p.228** Fotolia; **p.236** Fotolia; **p.242** Stephen Bardens/Alamy; **p.245** Nathan King/Alamy.

All website addresses included in this book are correct at the time of going to press but may
subsequently change.

The front cover is reproduced by permission of Fotolia.

Typeset by 11/13 pt ITC Berkeley Oldstyle Std Book by Integra Software Services Pvt. Ltd.,
Pondicherry, India
Printed in Dubai

Hachette UK's policy is to use papers that are natural, renewable and recyclable products and made from
wood grown in sustainable forests. The logging and manufacturing processes are expected to conform to
the environmental regulations of the country of origin.

Get the most from this book

This textbook provides an introduction to economics. It has been tailored explicitly to cover the content of the AQA specification for the AS qualification and for the first year of the A-level course. The book is divided into two parts, each covering the sections that make up the AQA programme of study.

The text provides the foundation for studying AQA economics, but you will no doubt wish to keep up to date by referring to additional topical sources of information about economic events. This can be done by reading the serious newspapers, visiting key sites on the internet and reading such magazines as *Economic Review*.

Special features

Key terms
Clear, concise definitions of essential key terms where they first appear and a list at the end of each part.

Study tips
Short pieces of advice to help you present your ideas effectively and avoid potential pitfalls.

Learning objectives
A statement of the intended learning objectives for each chapter.

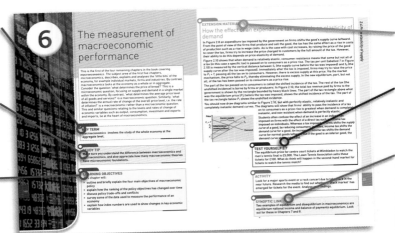

Extension material
Extension points to stretch your understanding.

Test yourself
Exercises to provide active engagement with economic analysis.

Synoptic links
Connections between different areas of economics are highlighted to help improve your overall understanding of the subject.

Case studies
Case studies to show economic concepts applied to real-world situations.

Quantitative skills
Worked examples of quantitative skills that you will need to develop.

A-level-only content
Sections of the book that apply only to A-level students are highlighted using a purple line.

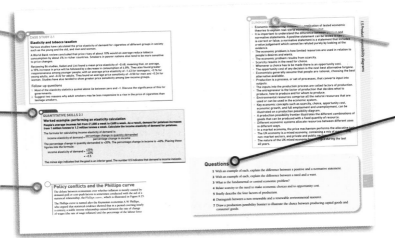

Summaries
Bulleted summaries of each topic that can be used as a revision tool.

Practice questions
Practice questions are provided at the end of each section to help you check your knowledge and understanding of the topics you have covered within each chapter.

Contents

08/08/19

Part 2   Macroeconomics

6   The measurement of macroeconomic performance

7   How the macroeconomy works

8   Economic performance

9   Macroeconomic policy

Introduction

For most of you, welcome to a new subject. Unless you have studied economics at GCSE, it is probably only in the last week or so that you have given thought to the nature of the economy in which you live, and to what you must learn about the economy in the next few months or years. This introduction aims to ease you into the subject so that you quickly build up a broad idea of what you are going to study in your economics course.

Starting from a position of ignorance

At the beginning of an economics course, you are not expected to know very much about the economy. For the last 2 years all your mental energy has been directed at the GCSE subjects you have been studying, and economics will probably not have been one of them.

It usually takes at least a term to settle into a new subject. This is certainly the case with economics, which is different in many important respects from other subjects you may have previously studied. We hope that by next February or March you will have settled, but if not, don't in the first instance blame yourself, blame the subject.

Economics is a current-affairs-related subject, so it will help if you can become interested in what is going on in the country you live in, and also in the wider world. However, you are not expected to possess this knowledge at the beginning of the course. Any relevant current affairs knowledge you already possess is a bonus, not a requirement.

Nevertheless, if you are not prepared to read about current affairs in newspapers or on web pages such as BBC News (**www.bbc.co.uk/news**), you are unlikely to enjoy economics or to do very well in the course. So start reading newspapers (getting advice on what to read from your teachers as you go), and don't switch off the television whenever the news or the BBC2 programme *Newsnight* starts.

Introducing microeconomics and macroeconomics

Economics divides into two parts: microeconomics and macroeconomics. Microeconomics, which is the part of economics concerned with economic behaviour in the *individual* markets that make up the economy, is the subject matter of Chapters 1–5. Essentially, microeconomics investigates the 'little bits' of the economy, namely individual consumers, firms, markets and industries.

By contrast, macroeconomics is the part of economics that attempts to explain how the whole economy works. Macroeconomics examines the *aggregates* rather than the little bits of the economy: the *aggregate* (total) levels of output, income, prices, employment and unemployment, and the trade flows that make up the balance of payments.

Economic problems and economic policies

One of the most interesting areas of economics lies in studying the economic problems facing governments and the economic policies that governments use to try to get rid of or reduce the problems. Economic problems can be microeconomic or macroeconomic, though some have both micro and macro elements.

At the micro level, the main problems lie in the field of market failure. As we shall see in Chapter 5, market failure occurs whenever markets do not perform very well — and in extreme cases fail to perform at all. Perhaps the best-known recent and current market failure stems from environmental pollution and subsequent global warming. We shall be examining a number of different government policies aimed at correcting market failures. These include taxation, subsidies and the use of regulations. We shall also explain how government failure results when government policies are ineffective or even downright damaging.

At the macro level, the main economic problems are unemployment, a failure to achieve and sustain a satisfactory rate of economic growth, inflation and an unsatisfactory trading and balance of payments position. Chapters 6–8 investigate these macroeconomic problems. Chapter 9 explains how fiscal policy, monetary policy and supply-side policy are used to try to tackle these problems.

How much maths do I need to know?

At the beginning of an economics course, students often seek advice about the amount of mathematics they need to know or must learn to help them with their studies. For AS and A-level economics, you don't need to learn any more maths skills over and above those that you learnt at GCSE, but you do need to develop analytical and quantitative skills in economics when '*selecting, interpreting and using appropriate data from a range of sources*'.

The quantitative skills you must possess are listed below, first for AS, then the additional A-level skills.

Quantitative skills requirements

At AS

In order to develop your skills, knowledge and understanding in economics, you need to have acquired competence in the quantitative skills that are relevant to the subject content and which are applied when answering an economics question at AS. These skills include:

- calculating, using and understanding ratios and fractions
- calculating, using and understanding percentages and percentage changes
- understanding and using the terms *mean*, and *median*
- constructing and interpreting a range of standard graphical forms
- calculating and interpreting index numbers

- calculating cost, revenue and profit (average and total)
- making calculations to convert from money to real terms
- making calculations of elasticity and interpreting the results
- interpreting, applying and analysing information in written, graphical and numerical forms

The assessment of quantitative skills will include at least Level 2 mathematical skills as a minimum of 15% of the overall AS marks. These skills may be assessed across the assessment objectives.

At A-level

The additional A-level skills, over and above the AS skills listed above, include:

- understanding and using the term *quantiles*
- calculating marginal cost, revenue and profit

The assessment of quantitative skills at the full A-level will include at least Level 2 mathematical skills as a minimum of 20% of the overall A-level marks. Again, these skills may be assessed across the assessment objectives.

You will be introduced to economics graphs and to the different ways of presenting and calculating statistics as you proceed through this book.

Although you don't need to learn any more mathematics, economics contains a large number of abstract ideas and concepts, similar to those employed in mathematics, summed up in the saying 'to an economist, real life is a special case'. A logical mind, capable of handling abstractions, will be of great help if you are to become a good economist.

Applying other skills from GCSE

For the most part, examination questions at both AS and A-level require written answers which vary in length from short definitions to long extended answers. This means that the writing skills you learnt when studying subjects such as English, history and geography at GCSE are essential for achieving high grades in economics. Particularly important are the skills of focusing an answer to address a set question, taking note of the total marks available for a question, and the ability to obey command words such as 'define', 'explain', 'analyse' and 'evaluate'.

Finally, for answers to case studies, test yourself questions etc. featured in this book, please visit **https://www.hoddereducation.co.uk/Product?Product=9781471829789** and click 'Download answers'.

Breakdown of the examinations

Scheme of assessment

The AS and A-level specifications are respectively designed to be studied over 1 year and 2 years, with all assessments taken at the end of the course. (Some schools may teach AS over 2 years.) Both qualifications are linear. In order to achieve the award, students must complete all exams in May/June in a single year. All assessments must be taken in the same series.

The assessment objectives and aims

The **assessment objectives (AOs)** are set by the GCE regulator, Ofqual, and are the same across all AS and A-level economics specifications and all exam boards.

The exams will measure how students have achieved the following assessment objectives:

- **AO1**: Demonstrate knowledge of terms/concepts and theories/models to show an understanding of the behaviour of economic agents and how they are affected by and respond to economic issues
- **AO2**: Apply knowledge and understanding to various economic contexts to show how economic agents are affected by and respond to economic issues
- **AO3**: Analyse issues within economics, showing an understanding of their impact on economic agents
- **AO4**: Evaluate economic arguments and use qualitative and quantitative evidence to support informed judgements relating to economic issues

The **assessment aims** are set by the GCE examining board, AQA. For both the AS and A-level courses, the assessment aims are to encourage students to:

- develop an interest in and enthusiasm for economics
- appreciate the contribution of economics to the understanding of the wider economic and social environment
- develop an understanding of a range of concepts and an ability to use those concepts in a variety of different contexts
- use an enquiring, critical and thoughtful approach to the study of economics and develop an ability to think as an economist
- understand that economic behaviour can be studied from a range of perspectives
- develop analytical and quantitative skills, together with qualities and attitudes which will equip economics students for the challenges, opportunities and responsibilities of adult and working life

During your course of study, you should develop a critical approach to economic models and methods of enquiry. You should build up a good knowledge of developments in the UK economy and government policies over the 15 years before you sit the exams. You should also have an awareness of earlier events where this helps to give recent developments a longer-term perspective.

The examination structure

The AS examination

If you are an AS student, you will be assessed through *two* examination papers.

Paper 1: The operation of markets and market failure will examine mainly microeconomic topics.

Paper 2: The national economy in a global context will examine mainly macroeconomic topics.

Both papers have to be answered in 1 hour and 30 minutes. In both Paper 1 and Paper 2, the question structure is the same. Section A of each exam contains 20 compulsory objective test questions, and Section B contains two data response questions, which are officially called Context questions. You should answer *either* Context 1 *or* Context 2, but not both.

Mark allocation

The mark allocation for the AS examination, Papers 1 and 2, is as follows.

- Section A: 1 mark per objective test question, with a maximum mark of 20 for the section
- Section B: 3, 4, 4, 4, 10 and 25 are the maximum marks for each of the six parts of the Context question, for which the maximum mark is 50

The maximum mark for each paper is 70.

The A-level examination

If you are an A-level student, you will be assessed through *three* examination papers, each of which is 2 hours long.

Paper 1: Markets and market failure will examine mainly microeconomic topics.

Paper 2: National and international economy will examine mainly macroeconomic topics.

However, the A-level specification states that '*students should appreciate that microeconomics and macroeconomics are not entirely distinct areas of study. For example, microeconomic principles often provide fundamental insights into understanding aspects of the macroeconomy. Similarly, economic issues and problems often contain both a microeconomic and macroeconomic dimension.*'

In both Paper 1 and Paper 2, the question structure is the same. Section A of each exam contains two data response questions, which are officially called Context questions. You should answer *either* Context 1 *or* Context 2, but not both. Section B contains three two-part essay questions, of which you should answer *one* two-part essay.

Paper 3: Economic principles and issues is different in coverage and structure from Papers 1 and 2. It includes topics from both microeconomic and the macroeconomic sections of the specification. Particularly when answering questions linked to the case study in the question, you will be expected to recognise when it is appropriate to use microeconomic and/or macroeconomic models.

Section A of Paper 3 contains 30 compulsory objective test questions, which are both microeconomic and macroeconomic. Section B contains a single compulsory case study question, which may overarch the whole A-level specification. The details of the case study are provided in a separate source booklet, which you read at the beginning of the exam. Typically, the source booklet will contain four extracts covering the theme of the case study. The extracts will be in both numerical and textual form. Candidates will be required to use the numerical data and be expected to demonstrate quantitative skills in their responses to questions. The exam paper itself will contain three questions, which you will answer in the style of an economist giving advice to a client. The client to whom you are providing economic advice could be a company, a government minister or a labour organisation, though there are other possibilities as well.

Mark allocation

The mark allocation for the A-level examination is as follows.

Papers 1 and 2:

- Section A: 2, 4, 9 and 25 are the maximum marks for each of the four parts of the Context question, for which the maximum mark is 40
- Section B: 15 and 25 are the maximum marks for each of the two parts of the Essay question, for which the maximum mark is 40

The maximum mark for Papers 1 and 2 is 80.

Paper 3:

- Section A: 1 mark per objective test question, with a maximum mark of 30 for the section
- Section B: 10, 15 and 25 are the maximum marks for each of the three parts of the investigation in the case study, for which the maximum mark is 50

The maximum mark for Paper 3 is 80.

For both the AS and A-level the papers are equally weighted:

- AS 50% + 50%
- A-level $33\frac{1}{3}$% + $33\frac{1}{3}$% + $33\frac{1}{3}$%

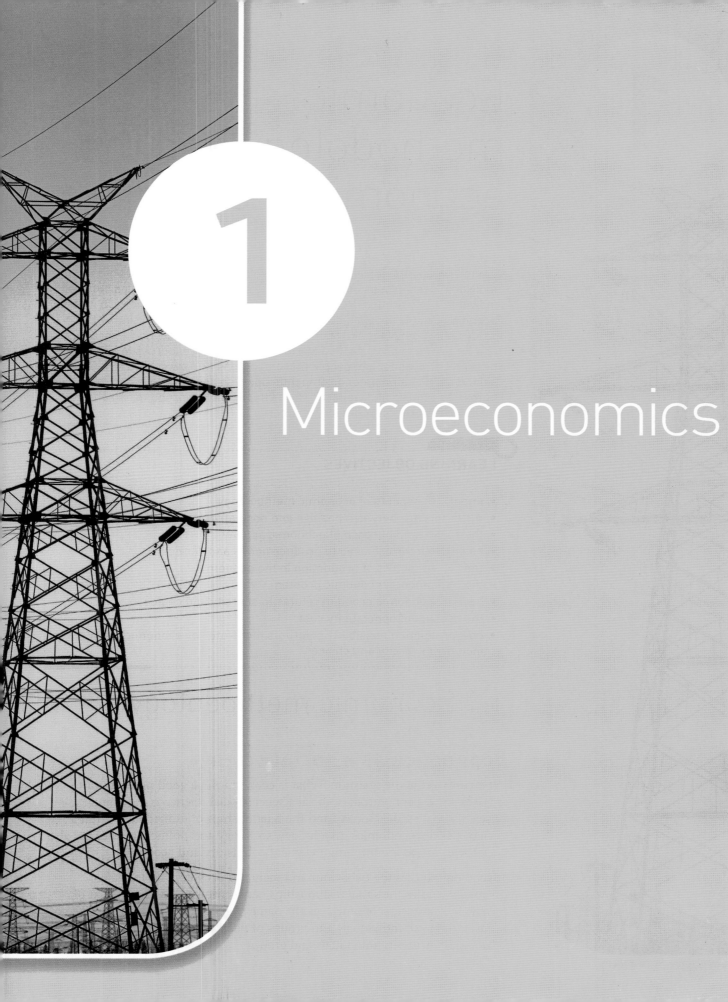

1

Microeconomics

1

Economic methodology and the economic problem

Economics is the study of choice and decision making in a world with limited resources. It tries to explain the economic behaviour of both individuals and groups of people, and the economic relationships between individuals and groups. Related to the noun 'economics', is the verb 'to economise'. In large part, economics is the study of economising — the study of how people make choices about what to produce, how to produce and for whom to produce, in a world in which most resources are limited or scarce. How best can people make decisions on how scarce resources should be allocated among competing uses, so as to improve and maximise human happiness and welfare? This is the economic problem, which is the main focus of this introductory chapter.

LEARNING OBJECTIVES
This chapter will explain:

- important aspects of economic methodology
- the difference between positive and normative statements
- the nature and purpose of economic activity
- how resources are used to produce goods and services
- the role of factors of production in the economy
- the fundamental economic problem
- how the economic problem relates to scarcity and choice
- the concept of opportunity cost
- how production possibility diagrams illustrate key economic concepts including scarcity and choice

1.1 Economic methodology

Economics as a social science

When answering the question 'What is economics?', a good point to start is the fact that economics is a social science. Social science is the branch of science that studies society and the relationships of individuals within a society. Besides economics, psychology, sociology and political science are also social sciences, as are important elements of history and geography.

Psychology studies the behaviour and mental processes of an *individual*. Sociology studies the *social* relationships between people in the context of *society*. By contrast, economics, as the name suggests, studies the *economic behaviour* of both individuals and groups of people, and the *economic relationships* between individuals and groups.

Let us give you two examples of what we mean. Our first example (about *individual behaviour*) is from an important part of economics known as demand theory, which is covered in Chapter 2. The theory addresses consumer behaviour, or how we behave when we go shopping. Why, for example, do people generally buy more strawberries as the price of strawberries falls?

Our second example introduces an important *economic relationship*. Having explained demand, we must go a stage further and look at how consumers interact with firms or producers. Firms supply and sell the goods that consumers buy, and economists call the 'place' in which goods are bought and sold a market. Indeed, before you started this economics course, you may well have heard the words 'supply and demand' and thought that is what economics is about. Well, in large measure that is true, particularly in the early chapters of this book, which cover Unit 1 of the specification.

Economics and scientific methodology

The essentials of scientific methodology, in the context of the demand theory we will look at in Chapter 2, are shown in the flowchart in Figure 1.1. Scientists start off by observing some aspect of the universe (in the natural sciences), or some aspect of human behaviour, in the case of the social sciences. In the case of demand theory, the starting-off point — shown in the uppermost box of Figure 1.1 — is observations of how individual consumers react to changes in the prices of the goods and services they buy. Demand theory then develops from the making of a tentative description, known as a *hypothesis*, of what has been observed. Hypothesis construction is depicted in the second box from the top in the flowchart. In the third box, predictions about human behaviour are deduced from the hypothesis, such as that an individual will always respond to a lower price by demanding more of the good in question.

This prediction is then tested against collected evidence about how individuals behave in the market place (the fourth box from the top). At this stage, the hypothesis becomes a *theory*. (The difference between the two is that whereas a hypothesis is a proposed explanation for something, a theory is when a hypothesis is tested and survives the test.)

At this stage, we are in the bottom left-hand box of Figure 1.1. However, this does not mean that the theory is true in all circumstances. All it says is that the hypothesis has survived the test or tests to which it has been exposed. It might not survive stronger tests, which may not yet have been devised. Scientific method is based on the possibility of *falsification* or *refutation* of a hypothesis.

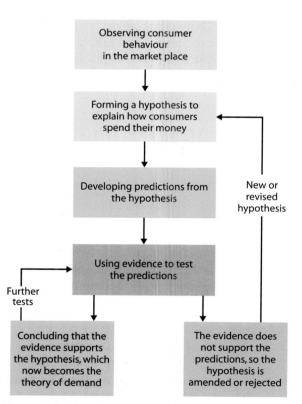

Figure 1.1 Scientific method

If a hypothesis fails to survive the tests to which it is exposed, one of two things can happen. The bottom right-hand box of Figure 1.1 shows the first possibility: outright rejection of the hypothesis. For example, a hypothesis that consumers *always* respond to price cuts by demanding *less* would surely be rejected (as would the hypothesis that consumers *always* respond to a price cut by demanding *more* of a good). The other possibility, which often occurs in economics, is that the hypothesis is changed, usually by watering it down, so as to make it less deterministic. In the case of demand theory, as the section on 'Exceptions to the "law" of demand' in Chapter 2 explains, watering down means that demand theory predicts that *in most but not all cases*, consumers respond to price cuts by demanding more of a good. Watered down in this way, the demand hypothesis survives the tests to which it is exposed, and becomes 'the first "law" of demand'.

Social sciences and natural sciences

In 1905, the world-famous physicist, Albert Einstein, developed a theory of gravitation which predicted, among other things, that as it approaches Earth, light from a distant star is 'bent' by the gravitational pull of the sun. However, Einstein's theory could not be tested until 1919 when there was a general eclipse of the sun. The theory survived the 1919 test, although much more recent tests have thrown doubt on parts of it. As is the case with Einstein's theory, natural science theories are usually much 'harder' than the theories associated with 'softer' social sciences such as economics. As we have noted, economic theories often survive only through allowing a significant number of exceptions to their central predictions, which, according to critics, turns the theories into little more than generalisations.

Very often economists respond to the criticism that their subject is 'soft' by arguing that they are only concerned with 'positive economics', which they claim is based on quite strict use of scientific methodology. Positive economics is concerned with 'what is' and 'what will happen' if a course of action is taken or not taken. In contrast, 'normative economics' is concerned with 'what *should* or *ought* to be'.

The difference between positive and normative statements

A lot of economics is concerned with what people *ought* to do. This is particularly true of the government. Ought the government try to reduce unemployment, control inflation and achieve a 'fair' distribution of income and wealth? Most people probably think that all these objectives are desirable. However, they all fall within the remit of normative economics. Normative economics is about value judgements and views, but because people have different views about what is right and wrong, **normative statements** cannot be scientifically tested.

By contrast, a **positive statement** can be tested to see if it is incorrect. If a positive statement does not pass the test, it is falsified. A positive statement does not have to be true, however. For example, the statement that the Earth is flat is a positive statement. Although once believed to be true, the statement was falsified with the growth of scientific evidence. The key point is that positive statements can in principle be tested and possibly falsified, while normative statements cannot. Normative statements include ethical, or moral, judgements. Words such as *ought*, *should*, *better* and *worse* often provide clues that a statement is normative.

To take an economic example, consider the statement 'If the state pension were to be abolished, a million older people would die of hypothermia.'

KEY TERMS

positive statement a statement of fact that can be scientifically tested to see if it is correct or incorrect.

normative statement a statement that includes a value judgement and cannot be refuted just by looking at the evidence.

4

This is a positive statement which could be tested, though few if any people would want to do this. By contrast, the statement 'The state pension ought to be abolished because it is a waste of scarce resources' is normative, containing an implicit value judgement about the meaning of the word 'waste'.

ACTIVITY

Get your fellow students to decide which of the following statements are positive and which are normative.

- Statement 1: More of a good is demanded at a higher price.
- Statement 2: The opportunity cost of spending an extra hour sleeping is always the same.
- Statement 3: Unemployment benefits should be cut to prevent idleness in society.
- Statement 4: If pensions are cut, more old people will die of hypothermia.
- Statement 5: The government must devote more resources to healthcare.

Compare your results.

STUDY TIP
Make sure you understand fully the difference between a positive and a normative statement.

EXTENSION MATERIAL

How value judgements influence economic decision making and policy

Economists emphasise the distinction between normative and positive economics, but they often forget that the decision to study one over the other is itself a value judgement, and therefore a normative decision. A value judgement is about whether something is desirable or not — if we believe it is more desirable to study what *is* happening in the economy rather than what *ought* to happen, we have made a value judgement. Economics necessarily requires that government ministers make value-based judgements when deciding on economic policies. Despite this, economists often wrongly insist that the subject is value-judgement free.

Several years ago, the then Chancellor of the Exchequer, the UK government minister in overall charge of economic policy, said: 'Rising unemployment and the recession have been the price that we have had to pay to get inflation down. That price is well worth paying.' Government ministers are seldom as frank as this, knowing that their political opponents and the media will immediately seize on the argument that those in power are uncaring and cynical people. However, the quote does serve to illustrate how decision makers make value judgements when making economic policy decisions.

On occasion, government ministers make decisions on issues such as where a new airport should be located or whether high-speed trains are worthwhile. Before making decisions on issues such as these, the policy-makers know in advance that large swathes of the population will strongly oppose whatever decision is eventually made. To ward off public hostility, government ministers usually create the illusion that the decision-making process is completely scientific and objective. To do this, they hire independent 'experts' to provide advice. But the choice of expert in itself involves a value judgement. Do you choose someone you know in advance is sympathetic to the government's cause, or are you more willing to go for an independent maverick? Whichever way you go, the so-called scientific processes used by the 'experts' to reach their conclusions may be riddled with value judgements. A classic case involved weighing up the costs and benefits of the location of a third London airport, which ultimately depended on putting money values on an hour of a business person's time, and an hour of a holidaymaker's time. It was quickly found that when different values were put on these, the airport location recommended by the experts would have 'lost out' under different costing criteria.

EXTENSION MATERIAL

The impact of moral and political judgements

Whatever decision is eventually made in the course of framing government economic policy, there will always be winners and losers who gain or suffer as a result of the decision. Governments often claim they have a moral right to make such decisions. They argue that their political manifesto published *before* the previous general election gives them the mandate, supported by the voters, to carry out their policies, regardless of the fact that among the electorate there would inevitably be some losers.

Consider, however, the position of the Liberal Democrats before and after the 2010 general election. Their party election manifesto contained a cast-iron commitment that, if elected to form the next government, the party would abolish university tuition fees. The Liberal Democrats did indeed form part of the next government, but the party's leader immediately abandoned his commitment to abolish tuition fees. He completely reversed his policy and the party immediately lost its moral authority over policy-making.

1.2 The nature and purpose of economic activity

Needs and wants

The central purpose of economic activity is the production of goods and services to satisfy people's needs and wants. A **need** is something people have to have, something that they cannot do without. Food provides an example. If people starve, they will eventually die. By contrast, a **want** is something people would *like* to have, but which is not essential for survival. It is not absolutely necessary, but it is a good thing to have. Books provide an example. Some people might argue that books are a need because they think they can't do without them. But they don't need literature to survive. They do need to eat. (It is worth noting that food can be both a need and a want, depending on the type of food. Protein, vitamins and minerals are needs, but bars of chocolate are wants. People don't need to eat chocolate to survive.)

Needs, wants and improving economic welfare

Satisfying people's needs and wants means improving **economic welfare**. Welfare is a concept bandied about a lot by economists, but often without a clear indication of what the concept means. Welfare basically means human happiness — anything which makes a person happier improves their economic welfare, though obviously we must ignore activities such as theft where one person becomes better off through stealing from other people. Short-term happiness may be at the expense of long-term happiness. The consumption of more material goods and services *usually* improves economic welfare, though consuming more and more food, and the wrong type of food, in the long term can lead to health problems.

There are also important elements of human happiness and welfare that have nothing to do with the consumption of material goods. These include quality of life factors, such as the pleasure gained from family and friends or from contemplating a beautiful view.

KEY TERMS

production a process, or set of processes, that converts inputs into output of goods.

capital good a good which is used in the production of other goods or services. Also known as a **producer good**.

consumer good a good which is consumed by individuals or households to satisfy their needs or wants.

1.3 Economic resources

Nevertheless, for most people, most of the time, increased consumption of material goods is an important part of improving economic welfare. Most of the goods we consume must first be produced. This requires the use of economic resources. These goods are scarce in relation to demand, which gives rise to the need for economising in their use.

The basic nature of **production** is shown in Figure 1.2. Production is a process, or set of processes, that converts inputs into outputs. The eventual outputs are the consumer goods and services that go to make up our standard of living, though inputs are of course also used to produce the **capital goods** that are necessary for the eventual production of **consumer goods**.

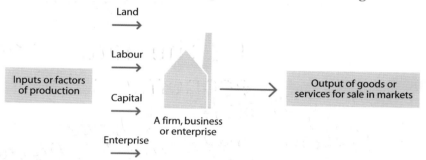

Figure 1.2 The basic nature of production

The factors of production

KEY TERM

factors of production inputs into the production process, such as land, labour, capital and enterprise.

Economists call the inputs into the production process, which are listed in Figure 1.2, the **factors of production**. Four factors of production are usually identified. These are land, labour, capital and enterprise, the last often being called the entrepreneurial input.

Entrepreneurs are different from the other factors of production. They are the people who address the issues introduced earlier, deciding what to produce, how to produce it and for whom to produce it. An entrepreneur decides how much of the other factors of production, including labour, to employ. The costs of employing land, labour and capital, together with the cost of the entrepreneur's own services, become the firm's costs of production. In essence, the entrepreneur is a financial risk taker and decision maker. Profit, which is the entrepreneur's financial reward, results from successful decision making. Entrepreneurial profit is the profit left over after the cost of employing the other factors of production is deducted from the sales revenue gained from the sale of the goods and services the entrepreneur decides to produce.

STUDY TIP

It is important to understand how factors of production are *inputs* used to produce *output* of goods and services.

The environment as a scarce resource

Environmental resources comprise all the natural resources that are used or can be used in the economic system. These are:

- physical resources, such as soil, water, forests, fisheries and minerals
- gases, such as hydrogen and oxygen
- abstract resources, such as solar energy, wind energy, the beauty of the landscape, good air and clear water

7

Wind energy is an abstract natural resource

KEY TERMS

finite resource a resource, such as oil, which is scarce and runs out as it is used. Also known as a **non-renewable resource**.

renewable resource a resource, such as timber, that with careful management can be renewed as it is used.

Environmental resources can be split into renewable and non-renewable resources, with the latter further divided into recyclable and non-recyclable resources. **Renewable resources**, which are reproducible and perpetually maintainable, include forests, animals and water. The availability of these resources depends, however, on their management by humans. By contrast, **non-renewable resources**, such as oil, gas and minerals, cannot be regenerated or regeneration is so slow that the stock of resources cannot meaningfully be increased. These are **finite resources**. Recyclable non-renewable resources such as minerals, paper and glass can be reused in the economic system. In theory, all of these resources can be recycled but it is not always possible and economic to recycle more than a small fraction. Non-recyclable resources such as coal, gas and oil are finite in the sense that once used, their stock is no more available for future use.

Environmental resources are part of the factor of production, land. Some environmental resources, such as the air we breathe and the water we drink, are often described as the 'free gifts of nature'. However, this view can be questioned. In most countries and regions where large numbers of people live, clean air and drinkable water are scarce commodities and not the 'free gifts of nature'. Resources which could be put to other uses are used instead to produce clean air and water. The need to get rid of the effects of pollution created by humankind means that clean air and water are scarce and not free. Production and consumption activities taking place in the economy affect and often damage the natural environment.

1.4 Scarcity, choice and the allocation of resources

The fundamental economic problem

The **fundamental economic problem** exists because both goods and the resources needed to produce goods are scarce. **Scarcity** also means that people (even the very rich) have limited incomes and face a budget constraint. If goods are scarce and incomes are limited, choices have to be made. Consider, for example, a family with a weekly income of £1,200. The family currently spends £350 on housing, £350 on food, £300 on other goods and services, including heating and lighting, and £100 on entertainment. The family's total weekly spending on goods and services is thus £1,100, meaning the family manages to save £100. Suddenly, the cost of housing rises to £400. To avoid getting into debt, and assuming that family income can't increase, one or more probably unpleasant choices will have to be made. An obvious possibility is to cut down on entertainment, such as visits to the cinema. Other possibilities could be spending less on home heating, buying cheaper food, cutting down on alcoholic drink and stopping saving. Something will have to be given up. Unless the family gets into debt or its income increases, it will have to economise even more on its spending and saving decisions.

You must also appreciate the fact that, even without an increase in house prices, scarcity means that individuals and households are constantly making choices on how to spend their limited incomes and how to make the best use of their time. A decision to spend more on a holiday, for example, means that a family chooses to spend less on other goods, or to save less.

A need for choice arises whenever an economic agent (for example, an individual, a household or a firm) has to choose between two or more alternatives which are mutually exclusive, in the sense that it is impossible or impractical to achieve both at the same time. In the jargon of economics, an opportunity cost is involved.

Opportunity cost

If you ask friends who haven't studied economics the meaning of the word 'cost', typically they will answer that cost is the money cost either of producing a good or of buying a good. Economists, by contrast, focus on opportunity cost. The **opportunity cost** of any choice, decision or course of action is measured in terms of the alternatives that have to be given up.

Economists generally assume that people behave rationally. Rational behaviour means people try to make decisions in their self-interest or to maximise their private benefit. When a choice has to be made, people always choose what they think at the time is the best alternative, which means that the second best or next best alternative is rejected. Providing people are rational, the opportunity cost of any decision or choice is the next best alternative sacrificed or foregone. For example, if you choose to spend half an hour watching *EastEnders* on TV, the opportunity cost is the lost opportunity to spend this time reading a magazine or book.

TEST YOURSELF 1.1
Can you think of one factor that in real life may prevent a person from making a rational decision?

STUDY TIP
Make sure you can link together the three concepts of scarcity, choice and opportunity cost.

EXTENSION MATERIAL

Rational behaviour and opportunity cost

Look carefully at the sentence in the previous paragraph about opportunity cost: *When a choice has to be made, people always choose what they think at the time is the best alternative, which means that the second best or next best alternative is rejected.* The words 'think at the time' are quite important. Suppose you decide to see a film, believing at the time you are going to enjoy the film. Two hours later, coming out of the cinema, you say 'that was a load of rubbish, I wish I hadn't bothered'. Nevertheless, at the time the decision was made, deciding to watch the film was a rational decision because you believed you would enjoy watching it. Having left the cinema, irrational behaviour would be going back to the box office and paying good money to see the film again.

Even if the film can be watched freely on television, there is still an opportunity cost, though in this case involving solely time. Time is scarce, and the two hours spent watching the film cannot be spent on some other activity such as reading a book. A choice has to be made between the two activities. Of course the way the choice is exercised will differ for different people, even if everyone enjoys both watching films and reading. People with plenty of time to spare, for example retired or unemployed people, value time less highly than a City trader working in a dealing room from 7.00 a.m. until 9.00 p.m.

Going to a cinema to watch a film is, of course, a consumer activity. People have to think carefully about how they spend their limited incomes. In economics this is known as a budget constraint. Money spent on one good cannot be spent on another good. There is always an opportunity cost when deciding to consume a good, involving time if not money.

Firms also have to make choices on what and how to produce. Consider a textile manufacturer who can produce either shirts or dresses from the same production line, but not both goods at the same time. In this situation, the opportunity cost of producing more shirts is the number of dresses sacrificed or foregone. Suppose also that both shirts and dresses can be produced using one of two different technologies. These are a labour-intensive technology involving lots of workers but very little capital equipment, and a capital-intensive technology in which there are very few workers but expensive automated capital equipment. Given the budget constraint facing the firm, the opportunity cost of choosing one method of production is the sacrificed opportunity to use the other method.

A further example of opportunity cost arises when a teenager makes a decision on whether to leave school and get a job, or whether to go to university. Very often this involves the choice between income now and income in the future. Economists call this inter-temporal choice, or choice over time.

ACTIVITY

Construct a questionnaire which lists five activities that you know interest most of the students in your class. These could be playing a video game, watching a popular TV show, visiting a coffee bar, reading a magazine on their favourite hobby, and going window shopping. Ask each of your fellow students to rank the activities in order from 1 to 5, with 1 being the most preferred, 2 the second preferred, and so on. Tell your classmates that all the activities are completely free, but that they can only take part in one activity. Compare the results with your fellow students, asking them to discuss how the results can be analysed using the concept of opportunity cost.

QUANTITATIVE SKILLS 1.1

Worked example: calculating an opportunity cost

A small electrical goods manufacturer can produce either TV sets or radio sets using all its available resources. Table 1.1 shows the different combinations of the two goods the firm can produce.

Table 1.1

TV sets	Radio sets
0	30
1	29
2	27
3	24
4	20
5	15
6	9
7	0

What happens to the opportunity cost of TV sets in terms of radios, as TV set production increases from zero to seven sets?

If the firm chooses to produce only one TV set, its opportunity cost is one radio set foregone (30 minus 29 radio sets). Performing a similar calculation when TV set production is increased by an extra unit, the opportunity cost of the second TV set is two radio sets. All the opportunity costs are set out in Table 1.2:

Table 1.2 Opportunity costs of producing an extra TV set

1st TV set	1 radio set (30 minus 29)
2nd TV set	2 radio sets (29 minus 27)
3rd TV set	3 radio sets (27 minus 24)
4th TV set	4 radio sets (24 minus 20)
5th TV set	5 radio sets (20 minus 15)
6th TV set	6 radio sets (15 minus 9)
7th TV set	9 radio sets (9 minus 0)

The data shows an increasing opportunity cost in terms of radio sets foregone as production of TV sets increases.

STUDY TIP
Make sure you understand and can distinguish between the words micro and macro. 'Micro' means small, whereas 'macro' means large. Microeconomics, which is covered in the first five chapters of this book, looks at the 'little bits' of the economy, for example individual markets, firms and consumers. By contrast, macroeconomics, covered in Chapters 6–9, looks at the 'aggregate economy' or the economy 'as a whole'.

1.5 Production possibility diagrams

So far, we have focused mainly on how scarcity and choice may affect firms, families and individuals at the microeconomic level. In much the same way, but on a far grander scale, the economy of the nation as a whole faces a similar need for choice. To explain how the economic problem affects the whole economy, we will use a diagram which you will come across again and again in your economics course — a production possibility diagram.

The key feature of a production possibility diagram is a **production possibility frontier (PPF)** or production possibility curve. A *PPF* curve illustrates the different combinations of two goods, or two sets of goods, that can be produced with a fixed quantity of resource, providing we assume that all available resources are being utilised to the full. The *PPF* curve in Figure 1.3 illustrates the different combinations of capital goods and consumer goods that the whole economy can produce when all the economy's resources are employed, with no spare capacity. To put it another way, the *PPF* curve shows what the economy can produce, assuming that all the labour, capital and land at the country's disposal are employed to the full, and assuming a given state of technical progress.

Given that resources and capacity are limited, a choice has to be made about the type of good to produce. Look closely at points *X* and *Y* on the diagram. Point *X* shows the maximum possible output of consumer goods, assuming that the economy only produces consumer goods (i.e. no capital goods are produced). Likewise, point *Y* shows the maximum possible output of capital goods, assuming that the economy only produces capital goods. In fact, points *X* and *Y* show the two extreme production possibilities, since all goods are either consumer goods or capital goods. Finally, the line drawn between points *X* and *Y* in Figure 1.3 is the economy's production possibility frontier. The *PPF* curve shows all the different combinations of consumer goods and capital goods that can be produced, given the assumptions mentioned earlier about full employment of available resources and the state of technical progress. Point *A*, for example, shows K_1 capital goods and C_1 consumer goods being produced. An increase in capital good production to K_2, shown at point *B*, means that consumer good production falls to C_2. C_1 minus C_2 is the opportunity cost of producing K_2 minus K_1 additional capital goods. Whichever combination of capital and consumer goods is actually chosen reflects decisions made in society about allocating scarce resources between competing uses.

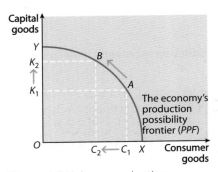

Figure 1.3 Using a production possibility frontier diagram to illustrate the economic problem

STUDY TIP

You must learn to draw and interpret production possibility diagrams, which are important in both microeconomics and macroeconomics. At the micro level they can be used to illustrate scarcity, choice, opportunity cost and productive efficiency. At the macro level, they can be used to illustrate economic growth, and full employment and unemployment.

SYNOPTIC LINK

As explained on the next page, production possibility diagrams can also be used to illustrate economic growth. This is revisited in Chapters 7 and 8. However, those chapters focus on another way of illustrating economic growth, in terms of aggregate demand and supply or AD/AS analysis.

EXTENSION MATERIAL

Macroeconomic *PPF* diagrams

The production possibility frontier in Figure 1.3 shows the economy *as a whole*, which means that the *PPF* curve depicts the macro economy. Before we look at some microeconomic production possibility frontiers, we shall explain two important ways in which macroeconomic *PPF* diagrams can be used.

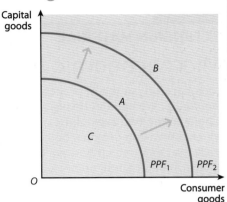

Figure 1.4 Long-run and short-run economic growth

Using a *PPF* diagram to show economic growth

Figure 1.4 shows how a *PPF* diagram can be used to illustrate economic growth. There are two forms of economic growth, which are explained in detail in Chapter 8. These are long-run economic growth and short-run economic growth.

Economic growth is defined as the increase in the *potential* level of real output the economy can produce over a period of time: for example, a year. Strictly, this is long-run economic growth, which is not the same as short-run economic growth. If the economy's production possibility frontier is PPF_1 initially, short-run economic

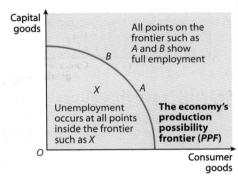

Figure 1.5 Using a production possibility curve diagram to show full employment and unemployment in the economy

growth is shown by the movement from point *C inside* the frontier to a point, such as point *A*, *on* the frontier. Long-run economic growth is shown by the *outward* movement of the frontier to PPF_2. The movement from point *A* to point *B* depicts long-run economic growth. Short-run growth makes use of spare capacity and takes up the slack in the economy, whereas long-run growth increases total productive capacity.

Using a *PPF* diagram to show full employment and unemployment

As mentioned earlier, all points on a production possibility frontier show full employment of available resources. For a macroeconomic production possibility frontier, this means **full employment** of labour as well as other resources that can be used in the course of production. Thus, points *A* and *B* in Figure 1.5 show full employment when the economy's production possibility frontier is in the position indicated. By contrast, a point *inside* the *PPF* curve, such as point *X*, shows that some resources, including labour, are not being employed. There is unused capacity in the economy. (Note that if long-run economic growth were to move the *PPF* curve outward to a new position, points *A* and *B* on the 'old' production possibility frontier would now be points of **unemployment**, as they would be located inside the new 'further out' frontier.)

13

SYNOPTIC LINK

Full employment and unemployment feature in all the chapters in Part 2, The national economy, particularly in Chapter 8.

EXTENSION MATERIAL

Microeconomic *PPF* diagrams

Look carefully at the microeconomic production possibility frontier in Figure 1.6. We can tell this is a *microeconomic* diagram because of the labels on the two axes of the graph. The diagram depicts a situation in which a firm can produce both mobile phones and laptop computers from the resources it has available. As in the first macroeconomic diagram (Figure 1.3), points X and Y show the extreme possibilities facing the firm. Point X on the horizontal axis shows the maximum possible output of laptop computers — providing no mobile phones are produced. This means that all available resources are devoted to the production of laptop computers. Conversely, point Y on the vertical axis shows the opposite situation: the maximum possible output of mobile phones when zero laptop computers are produced. As was the case in the macroeconomic production possibility diagrams, all points on the *PPF* curve *between* X and Y show different combinations of the two goods being produced between the two extreme possibilities.

We can use Figure 1.6 to explain a number of important economic relationships.

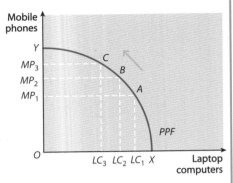

Figure 1.6 The production possibility frontier facing a firm producing mobile phones and laptop computers

Scarcity, resource allocation and choice

A *PPF* diagram such as Figure 1.6 shows different possible ways in which scarce resources can be allocated between competing uses. This involves **choice**. Compared to the **resource allocation** at point A, point B shows the effect of shifting more resources into the production of mobile phones, with fewer resources being allocated to laptop computer production.

Opportunity cost revisited

Production possibility diagrams provide a very good way of illustrating opportunity cost. Suppose, for example, that the firm in Figure 1.6 initially produces MP_1 mobile phones and LC_1 laptop computers. This combination of the two goods is shown at point A in the diagram. A decision by the manufacturer to increase production of mobile phones from MP_1 to MP_2 means that computer production falls by LC_1 minus LC_2. Moving from point A to point B on the curve, the fall in computer production is the opportunity cost of the increase in phone production.

Look now at the shape of the *PPF* curve in Figure 1.6. You can see that the slope of the curve falls, moving up the curve from point A to point B, and indeed to all other points further up the curve. There is a reason for this. The slope shows the opportunity cost of producing more mobile phones, in terms of the laptop computers that have to be sacrificed. When mobile phone production increases from MP_1 to MP_2 laptop computer production falls by LC_1 minus LC_2. This is the opportunity cost involved. But suppose mobile phone production increases again by the same amount as before (which means that MP_3 minus MP_2 is the same as MP_2 minus MP_1). In this situation, shown at point C on the curve, more laptop computers than before have to be given up. LC_3 minus LC_2 is larger than LC_2 minus LC_1. The slope of the curve of the production possibility frontier shows that the opportunity cost of producing mobile phones increases as more mobile phones are produced. A greater number of laptop computers have to be sacrificed whenever an extra mobile phone is produced.

1 ECONOMIC METHODOLOGY AND THE ECONOMIC PROBLEM

14

KEY TERMS

choice choosing between alternatives when making a decision on how to use scarce resources.

resource allocation the process through which the available factors of production are assigned to produce different goods and services, e.g. how many of the society's economic resources are devoted to supplying different products such as food, cars, healthcare and defence.

Productive efficiency and production possibility diagrams

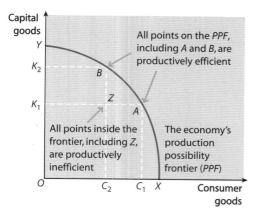

Figure 1.7 Productive efficiency and the economy's *PPF* curve

You will come across the concept of economic efficiency on numerous occasions as you proceed through the course. There are a number of different measures of economic efficiency, one of which is **productive efficiency**. Chapter 3 explains productive efficiency in terms of a firm minimising the average cost of producing a good. In this chapter, we focus on two other ways of explaining the concept, both of which are illustrated by the production possibility curve in Figure 1.7.

Productive efficiency occurs when output is maximised from available inputs. But we know already that a *PPF* curve shows maximisation of output from available inputs at every point on the curve, though the combination of the two goods (in this case capital goods and consumer goods) varies at different points on the curve. This means that all points *on* the economy's production possibility frontier shown in Figure 1.7, including points *A* and *B*, are productively efficient. By contrast, all points *inside* the *PPF* curve are productively *in*efficient, including point *Z*. Productive inefficiency occurs when output is not maximised from available inputs. At point *Z*, the economy is not employing all the available resources, including, of course, labour. Productive inefficiency is often associated with unemployment.

Consider now a movement *along* the *PPF* curve from point *A* to point *B*. The diagram is telling us that, when on the *PPF* curve, more capital goods can be produced only by giving up the production of some consumer goods. This is another way of explaining productive efficiency. Productive efficiency occurs when producing more of one good involves reducing production of other goods. By contrast, when the economy is productively inefficient at point *Z*, more capital goods *and* consumer goods can be produced by taking up the slack in the economy and making use of idle resources.

> **KEY TERM**
>
> **productive efficiency** for the economy as a whole occurs when it is impossible to produce more of one good without producing less of another. For a firm it occurs when the average total cost of production is minimised.

> **KEY TERM**
>
> **allocative efficiency** occurs when the available economic resources are used to produce the combination of goods and services that best matches people's tastes and preferences.

EXTENSION MATERIAL

Allocative efficiency

Another measure of economic efficiency is **allocative efficiency**. As is the case with productive efficiency, allocative efficiency can be explained in more than one way. In this chapter we define allocative efficiency as occurring when economic activity results in the best combination of goods and services being produced, and available to be consumed, taking into account consumers' preferences.

Production possibility curves show production possibilities, or the different goods people can choose to purchase when spending their limited incomes. The economy's production possibility frontier shows all productively efficient outcomes, but it does not identify an optimal allocation of resources. The allocatively efficient output is the point on the *PPF* curve that best meets people's tastes and preferences. However, this output does not necessarily optimise society's welfare because that also depends on the distribution of income and wealth and value judgements relating to fairness and justice.

QUANTITATIVE SKILLS 1.2

Worked example: drawing a production possibility curve from given data

Draw a production possibility frontier using the data below.

Table 1.3 Production possibility schedule for producing tanks and military aircraft

Tanks	Military aircraft
100	0
90	10
80	20
70	30
60	40
50	50
40	60
30	70
20	80
10	90
0	100

The production possibility curve drawn from this data is:

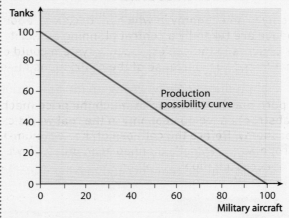

Figure 1.8 Production possibility curve or frontier for tanks and military aircraft

Unlike all the production possibility curves shown earlier in this chapter, this one shows a constant opportunity cost of ten military aircraft whenever 10 extra tanks are produced. This means that the production possibility curve is a straight line, positioned between the two production possibility extremes of zero tanks and 100 military aircraft, and 100 tanks and zero military aircraft.

TEST YOURSELF 1.2

Suppose the opportunity cost of producing one extra unit of a good in terms of another good sacrificed fell as more of the good is produced. In what way would the shape of the production possibility curve differ from those shown in this chapter?

CASE STUDY 1.1

Allocating resources through the price mechanism and the planning mechanism

There are a number of ways in which scarce resources can be allocated between competing uses. These include inheritance and other types of gift, theft and chance (such as winning a fortune on the National Lottery). However, the two main allocative mechanisms are the price mechanism (or market mechanism) and the planning mechanism (or command mechanism). An economic system in which goods and services are purchased through the price mechanism in a system of markets is called a market economy, whereas one in which government officials or planners allocate economic resources to firms and other productive enterprises is called a planned economy (or command economy).

In a pure market economy, the price mechanism performs the central economic task of allocating scarce resources among competing uses through the markets which make up the economy. Transport costs and lack of information may create barriers that separate or break up markets. In past centuries, such barriers often prevented markets from operating outside the relatively small geographical area of a single country or even a small region within a country.

However, while some markets exist in a particular geographical location — for example, a street market or until quite recently the London Stock Exchange — many markets do not. In recent years, modern developments have allowed goods to be transported more easily and at lower cost, and have helped in the transmission of market information via telephone and the internet. This has enabled many markets, especially commodity and raw material markets and markets in financial services, to become truly global or international markets functioning on a worldwide basis.

A complete command economy is an economy in which all decisions about what, how, how much, when, where and for whom to produce are taken by a central planning authority, issuing commands or directives to all the households and producers in the society. Such a system could only exist within a very rigid and probably totalitarian political framework because of the restrictions on individual decision making that are implied.

In much the same way as a pure market economy, in which the price mechanism alone allocates resources, is a theoretical abstraction, so no economy in the real world can properly be described as a complete or pure planned economy. Before the collapse of the communist political system around 1990, the countries of eastern Europe were centrally planned economies. However, they were not pure planned economies. Production but not consumption was planned. Consumers often had to queue to get consumer goods, whose prices were fixed by the planners. Shortages resulted, which, together with the generally inferior quality of consumer goods, contributed to the breakdown of the command economies. Some communist countries still exist, namely the People's Republic of China, North Korea, Vietnam and Cuba. However, all these countries, with the exception until recently of North Korea, have encouraged the growth of markets to a greater or lesser extent. They have communist political systems, but they have moved away from being pure command economies.

Follow-up questions

1 Distinguish between a pure market economy and the market sector of a mixed economy.
2 What is the other name of a planned economy?

The UK as a mixed economy

Many economies, particularly those of the developed countries of Western Europe such as the UK, are called mixed economies. A mixed economy contains both a large market sector and a large non-market sector in which the planning mechanism operates. Figure 1.9 illustrates mixed economies in relation to planned and market economies.

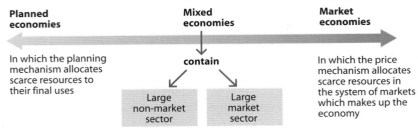

Figure 1.9 Planned economies, mixed economies and market economies

The UK economy developed into a mixed economy after the Second World War, when a number of important industries such as coal, rail and steel were nationalised and taken into public ownership. Previously, the 1944 Education Act had extended state provision of education, and the creation of the National Health Service in 1948 did the same for healthcare.

For about 30 years after the end of the Second World War, from the 1940s to the 1970s, the majority of UK citizens (and the major political parties) agreed that the mixed economy was working well. Most people believed that certain types of economic activity, particularly the production and distribution of consumer goods and services, were best suited to private enterprise and the market economy. But people also accepted that utility industries such as gas and electricity should be nationalised, and that important services such as education, healthcare and roads should be provided by government, outside the market, and financed through the tax system. In short, a consensus existed around the belief that the mixed economy was right for the UK.

However, from about 1980 onwards, many economists and politicians began to blame the mixed economy for the UK's deteriorating economic performance, relative to that of its main competitors in Western Europe and Japan. Critics argued that the public and non-market sectors of the economy were inefficient and wealth consuming rather than wealth creating. They had become too big and needed cutting down to size. Critics of the mixed economy argued that a concerted effort should be made to change fundamentally the nature of the UK economy by increasing private ownership and market production.

Successive governments implemented policies that changed the nature of the mix in favour of private ownership and market forces, at the expense of public ownership and state planning. The UK economy is now much closer to being a pure market and private enterprise economy than it was 40 years ago. The three main policies used to change the nature of the UK economy have been privatisation, marketisation and deregulation, polices which collectively can be called economic liberalisation.

Privatisation involved the sale of state-owned assets such as nationalised industries to private owners. This was often accompanied by marketisation (or commercialisation), whereby prices are charged for goods and services the state previously provided free of charge. Deregulation, the third aspect of liberalisation, attempts to remove barriers to entry and government red tape and bureaucracy from the operation of markets.

Follow-up questions

1 What is meant by private enterprise?
2 Distinguish between privatisation and marketisation.

SUMMARY

- Economic methodology involves the application of tested economic theories to explain real-world economic behaviour.
- It is important to understand the difference between positive and normative statements. A positive statement can be tested to see if it is correct or false; a normative statement is a statement that includes a value judgement which cannot be refuted purely by looking at the evidence.
- The economic problem is how limited resources are used in relation to people's desires and wants.
- The economic problem results from scarcity.
- Scarcity results in the need for choice.
- Whenever a choice has to be made there is an opportunity cost.
- The opportunity cost of any decision is the next best alternative forgone.
- Economists generally assume that people are rational, choosing the best alternative available.
- Production is a process, or set of processes, that converts input into outputs.
- The inputs into the production process are called factors of production.
- The entrepreneur is the factor of production that decides what to produce, how to produce and for whom to produce.
- Environmental resources comprise all the natural resources that are used or can be used in the economic system.
- Key economic concepts such as scarcity, choice, opportunity cost, economic growth, and full employment and unemployment, can be illustrated on a production possibility diagram.
- A production possibility frontier illustrates the different combinations of goods that can be produced with a fixed quantity of resource.
- Different economic systems allocate resources between different uses in different ways.
- In a market economy, the price mechanism performs the allocative task.
- The UK economy is a mixed economy, containing a mix of market and non-market sectors, and private and public sectors.
- The nature of the UK mixed economy has changed during the last 40 years.

Questions

1 With an example of each, explain the difference between a positive and a normative statement.

2 With an example of each, explain the difference between a need and a want.

3 What is the fundamental or central economic problem?

4 Relate scarcity to the need to make economic choices and to opportunity cost.

5 Briefly describe the four factors of production.

6 Distinguish between a non-renewable and a renewable environmental resource.

7 Draw a production possibility frontier to illustrate the choice between producing capital goods and consumer goods.

2

Price determination in a competitive market

Chapter 1 introduced you to one of the fundamental economic problems: how to allocate scarce resources between competing uses in conditions in which there are limited resources and unlimited wants. In a market economy, resource allocation is undertaken by the price mechanism operating in the system of markets that make up the economy. This is true also in the 'market sector' of a 'mixed economy'. However, in a mixed economy there is also a 'non-market sector' in which goods and services such as roads and police are produced and delivered to final users 'outside the market'. The UK is often said to be a 'mixed economy' though in recent decades the nature of the 'mix' has been shifting towards a pure market economy and away from non-market provision.

This chapter focuses on markets and the price mechanism, and looks only at **competitive markets**. Many of the markets in the UK economy are uncompetitive markets, but these are investigated in Chapter 4.

LEARNING OBJECTIVES
This chapter will:

- explain the nature of demand and supply in a competitive market
- differentiate between a movement along a demand or a supply curve and a shift of a demand or a supply curve
- introduce the concept of elasticity and explain the different elasticities you need to know
- bring demand and supply curves together in a supply and demand diagram
- distinguish between market equilibrium and disequilibrium in a supply and demand diagram
- investigate different ways in which markets are interrelated
- examine a number of real-world markets

What is a market?

A market is a voluntary meeting of buyers and sellers. Both buyer and seller have to be willing partners to the exchange. If, for example, a buyer uses violence or the threat of violence to 'persuade' a seller to supply goods at a price unfavourable to the seller, this is a forced transaction and not a market transaction.

Markets do not have to exist in a particular geographical location. Whenever a good or service is voluntarily bought and sold, a market transaction takes place. Over history, market transactions shifted away from open-air street markets to take place in shops. Shops have higher overhead costs, but they offer a permanent site of exchange and a continuing relationship between sellers and buyers. In recent years, the growth of the internet has allowed 24/7 e-commerce. As a result many markets, especially those in commodities, raw materials and financial services, have become truly global.

Competitive markets

A market is highly competitive when there are a large number of buyers and sellers all passively accepting the ruling market price that is set, not by individual decisions, but by the interaction of all those taking part in the market. The ruling market price (or **equilibrium price**) is set by **supply** and **demand** in the market as a whole. Highly competitive markets lack entry and exit barriers. This means that new buyers and sellers can easily enter the market without incurring costs. In the same way buyers and sellers can leave the market if they wish to. Competitive markets also exhibit a high degree of transparency — buyers and sellers can quickly find out what everyone else in the market is doing.

2.1 The determinants of demand for goods and services

Households and firms operate simultaneously in two sets of markets. The first of these contains the goods markets in which households demand and buy consumer goods and services produced and supplied by firms. But for household demand in the goods market to be an **effective demand** — that is, demand backed up by an ability to pay — households must first sell their labour, or possibly the services of any capital or land they own, in the markets for factors of production. These were briefly mentioned in Chapter 1. Households' roles are therefore reversed in goods markets and factor markets. In this chapter, we ignore factor markets and focus solely on the determinants of demand for consumer goods and services.

Market demand and individual demand

Normally when economists refer to demand, they mean **market demand**. This is the quantity of a good or service that all the consumers in the market wish to, and are able to, buy at different prices. By contrast, individual demand is the quantity that a particular individual, such as yourself, would like to buy. The relationship between market and individual demand is simple. Market demand is just the sum of the demand of all the consumers in the market.

The 'law' of demand

The 'law' of demand states that as a good's price falls, more is demanded. There is thus an inverse relationship between price and quantity demanded. Note that the word 'law' is in inverted commas. This is because a law in economics is not as strong or watertight as a law in a natural science subject such as physics. Whereas a law in physics will always hold, a social science

> **KEY TERMS**
>
> **equilibrium price** the price at which planned demand for a good or service exactly equals planned supply.
>
> **supply** the quantity of a good or service that firms are willing and able to sell at given prices in a given period of time.
>
> **demand** the quantity of a good or service that consumers are willing and able to buy at given prices in a given period of time. For economists, demand is always effective demand.

> **KEY TERM**
>
> **effective demand** the desire for a good or service backed by an ability to pay.

> **KEY TERM**
>
> **market demand** the quantity of a good or service that all the consumers in a market are willing and able to buy at different market prices.

law always has 'ifs' and 'buts' attached. More of a good is *usually* demanded as its price falls, but there are exceptions, which are explained on page 24.

The market demand curve

The market demand curve in Figure 2.1 illustrates the 'law' of demand. If the price starts off high, for example at P_1, household demand is Q_1. But if the price falls to P_2, demand increases to Q_2.

Demand for a good varies according to the time period being considered. For example, weekly demand is different from daily, monthly and annual demand. For this reason, the horizontal axis in Figure 2.1 is labelled 'Quantity demanded per period of time'. It is normal practice to use the label 'Quantity' on the horizontal axis of a demand curve diagram, as we do in the rest of this book, but this is an abbreviation. It always refers to a period of time.

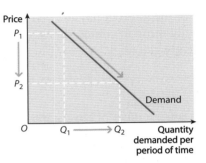

Figure 2.1 A market demand curve

> ### SYNOPTIC LINK
> Microeconomic demand curves look very similar to aggregate demand curves, which are explained in Chapter 7. It is vital that you don't confuse the two. Likewise, don't confuse demand with consumption, which is a component of aggregate demand, also explained in Chapter 7.

> ### ACTIVITY
> Construct a questionnaire containing the following question: 'How many litre bottles of cola would you buy each week if the price was £2, £1.50, £1.00, 50 pence, 25 pence?' Ask a sample of your friends to answer the question and analyse their answers. What are the problems with estimating demand curves in this way?

Movement along a demand curve and shifts of a demand curve

Students often confuse a movement *along* a demand curve and a *shift* of a demand curve. A *movement along a demand curve* takes place only when the good's price changes. Provided the demand curve slopes downwards, a *fall* in price results in *more* of the good being demanded. This is sometimes called an extension of demand. Likewise, a contraction of demand occurs when a *rise* in price leads to *less* being demanded.

When we draw a market demand curve to show how much of the good or service households plan to demand at various possible prices, we assume that all the other variables that may also influence demand are held unchanged or constant. This is the ceteris paribus assumption, which means 'other things being equal'. Among the variables whose values are held constant or unchanged when we draw a demand curve are disposable income and tastes or fashion. Collectively, the variables (other than the good's own price) whose values determine planned demand are often called the **conditions of demand**. A change in a condition of demand shifts the demand curve to a new position.

> ### STUDY TIP
> You must understand the difference between a movement along a demand or supply curve and a shift of the curve.

> ### KEY TERM
> **condition of demand** a determinant of demand, other than the good's own price, that fixes the position of the demand curve.

The conditions of demand

The main conditions of demand are:

- the prices of **substitute goods** or goods in competing demand (see section 2.6)
- the prices of goods in joint demand or **complementary goods** (see section 2.6)
- personal income (or more strictly personal disposable income, after tax and receipt of benefits)
- tastes and preferences
- population size, which influences total market size

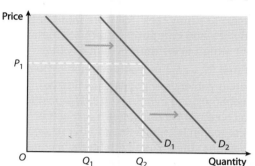

KEY TERMS

increase in demand a rightward shift of the demand curve.

decrease in demand a leftward shift of the demand curve

Figure 2.2 The effect of a rightward shift of demand

If any of the conditions of demand change, the position of the demand curve changes, shifting either rightward or leftward. Figure 2.2 illustrates a rightward shift of the demand curve, which is also called an **increase in demand**, and means more of the good is demanded at any given price. For example, at a price of P_1, the quantity demanded increases from Q_1 to Q_2. Conversely, a leftward shift of demand (known as a **decrease in demand**) causes the quantity demanded to fall at any given price.

Events that might cause a rightward shift of a demand curve include:

- an increase in the price of a substitute good or good in competing demand (see the section on the interrelationship between markets)
- a fall in the price of a complementary good or good in joint demand
- an increase in personal disposable income (but see the following section on normal goods and inferior goods)
- a successful advertising campaign making people think more favourably about the good
- an increase in population size

Normal goods and inferior goods

When disposable income increases, a demand curve shifts rightward, but only if the good is a **normal good**, for which demand increases as income increases. However, some goods are **inferior goods**, for which demand decreases as income increases, and an increase in income shifts the demand curve leftward.

To take an example, private car transport and bus travel are not just substitutes for each other. As people's incomes rise, demand for cars generally increases, while, at the same time, demand for bus travel usually falls. If people respond in this way to changes in income then private transport is a normal good, but certain forms of public transport are inferior goods. For an individual, whether a good is normal or inferior depends on personal income, tastes and, possibly, age. For young children, junk food such as sweets is usually a normal good. When parents increase small children's pocket money, they generally buy more sweets. But as children get older, tastes change, and sweets may very well become an inferior good.

By contrast, a change in a condition of demand shifts the demand curve to a new position. As already explained, a rightward shift of demand is often called an increase of demand while a decrease of demand occurs when the demand curve shifts leftward.

KEY TERMS

normal good a good for which demand increases as income rises and demand decreases as income falls.

inferior good a good for which demand decreases as income rises and demand increases as income falls.

Are there any exceptions to the 'law' of demand?

Demand curves don't have to slope downwards, though they usually do. However, there are circumstances in which a demand curve may be horizontal or vertical, or indeed slope upward, showing that more is demanded as the good's price increases.

There are a number of possible explanations for upward-sloping demand curves. Some of these are as follows:

1 **Speculative demand** If the price of a good such as housing, shares or a foreign currency starts to rise, people may speculate that in the near future the price will rise even further. In this situation, demand is likely to increase. In the case of rising house prices, young people who wish to become first-time buyers may scramble to buy houses, fearing that if they wait, they may never be able to afford to buy a house.

2 **Good for which consumers use price as an indicator of quality** Consumers may lack accurate information about the quality of some goods they want to buy, such as second-hand cars and computers. In this situation, a potential buyer may demand more as a good's price rises, believing that a high price means high quality.

3 **Veblen goods** Some companies try to sell their goods based on the fact that they cost more than those of their competitors. Veblen goods, named after the Norwegian economist Thornstein Veblen, are goods of exclusive or ostentatious consumption, or 'snob' goods. They are sometimes called positional goods, though strictly a positional good is so scarce that few people can ever acquire it. Some people wish to consume Veblen goods, such as Ferrari cars, as a signal of their wealth. The 'reassuringly expensive' advertising campaign for Stella Artois beer is a good example. A few years ago, Interbrew, the Belgian company (now called Inbev) that then owned the Stella brand, decided to sell its beer as a premium brand. Interbrew hoped that high prices would attract more customers. If you look at the prices of Stella beer, you will find that Inber has now changed tack, selling its beer on a 'stack 'em high, sell 'em fast' principle, at discounted prices.

Perhaps more could be done to justify Stella's ridiculous price.

Aaah the exquisite Stella taste.

Aargh the excruciating Stella price. Sadly, there's very little we can do about it.

Even offering small incentives like the one on the left is beyond our means.

Making Stella properly just costs far too much money.

We could, you might suppose, adulterate our premium barley with a few bags of a more questionable grain.

Substitute ordinary hops for the rare Czech Saaz variety.

Or hoist Stella out of the vat before the customary six weeks maturation.

While these expedients might produce a price that's not ridiculous, we're afraid the same could not be said of the beer.

Stella Artois. Reassuringly expensive.

Veblen goods are those that have high price as a selling point

2.2 Price, income and cross-elasticities of demand

The meaning of elasticity

Whenever a change in one variable (such as a good's price) causes a change to occur in a second variable (such as the quantity of the good that households are prepared to demand), an **elasticity** can be calculated. The elasticity measures the proportionate responsiveness of the second variable to the change in the first variable. For example, if a 5% increase in price were to cause households to reduce their demand by more than 5%, demand would be elastic. In this example, a change in price induces a more than proportionate response by consumers. But if the response were less than a reduction of 5%, demand would be inelastic. And if the change in price were to induce exactly the same proportionate change in demand, demand would be neither elastic nor inelastic — this is called unit elasticity of demand.

Elasticity is a useful descriptive statistic of the relationship between two variables because it is independent of the units, such as price and quantity units, in which the variables are measured.

Although, in principle, economists could calculate a great many elasticities for all the economic relationships in which they are interested, the three demand elasticities you must know are:

- price elasticity of demand
- income elasticity of demand
- cross-elasticity of demand

The following formulae are used for calculating these elasticities:

$$\text{price elasticity of demand} = \frac{\text{percentage change in quantity demanded}}{\text{percentage change in price}}$$

$$\text{income elasticity of demand} = \frac{\text{percentage change in quantity demanded}}{\text{percentage change in income}}$$

$$\text{cross-elasticity of demand} = \frac{\text{percentage change in quantity of A demanded}}{\text{percentage change in price of B}}$$

Price elasticity of demand

Price elasticity of demand measures consumers' responsiveness to a change in a good's price. (It is sometimes called an 'own price' elasticity of demand to distinguish it from cross-elasticity of demand for good A with respect to the price of B, which measures the responsiveness of demand for a particular good to a change in the price of a different good.)

EXTENSION MATERIAL

Infinite and zero price elasticity of demand

Horizontal and vertical demand curves have constant elasticities at all points on the curve. A horizontal demand curve, such as the demand curve in Figure 2.3(a), is infinitely elastic or perfectly elastic. At the other extreme, the vertical demand curve in Figure 2.3(b) is completely inelastic, displaying a zero price elasticity of demand at all points on the curve. When the price falls, for example from P_1 to P_2, the quantity demanded is unchanged.

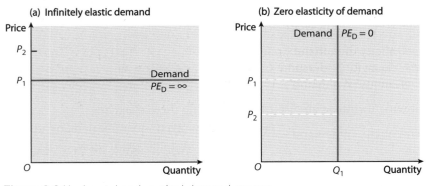

Figure 2.3 Horizontal and vertical demand curves

Figure 2.4 summarises the five demand curves you need to know

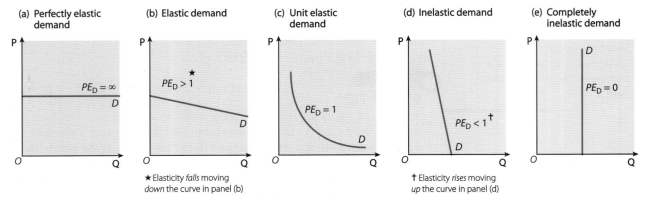

★ Elasticity *falls* moving down the curve in panel (b)

† Elasticity *rises* moving up the curve in panel (d)

Figure 2.4 Five demand curves you need to know

Factors determining price elasticity of demand

Substitutability

Substitutability, which is explained in section 2.6, is the most important determinant of price elasticity of demand. When a substitute exists for a product, consumers respond to a price rise by switching expenditure away from the good and buying a substitute whose price has not risen. When very close substitutes are available, demand for the product is highly elastic. Conversely, demand is likely to be inelastic when no substitutes or only poor substitutes are available.

Percentage of income

The demand curves for goods or services on which households spend a large proportion of their income tend to be more elastic than those of small items that account for only a small fraction of income. This is because for items on which only a very small fraction of income is spent, particularly for those which are rarely purchased, people hardly notice the effect of a change in price on their income. The same is not true for 'big-ticket' items such as a new car of a foreign holiday.

Necessities or luxuries

It is sometimes said that the demand for necessities is price inelastic, whereas demand for luxuries is elastic. This statement should be treated with caution. When no obvious substitute exists, demand for a luxury good may be inelastic, while at the other extreme, demand for particular types of basic foodstuff is likely to be elastic if other staple foods are available as substitutes. It is the existence of substitutes that really determines price elasticity of demand, not the issue of whether the good is a luxury or a necessity.

The 'width' of the market definition

The wider the definition of the market under consideration, the lower the price elasticity of demand. Thus the demand for the bread produced by a particular bakery is likely to be more elastic than the demand for bread produced by all bakeries. This is because the bread baked in other bakeries provides a number of close substitutes for the bread produced in just one bakery. And if we widen the possible market still further, the elasticity of demand for bread produced by all the bakeries will be greater than that for food as a whole.

Time

The time period in question will also affect the price elasticity of demand. For many goods and services, demand is more elastic in the long run than in the short run because it takes time to respond to a price change. For example, if the price of petrol rises relative to the price of diesel, it will take time for motorists to respond because they will be 'locked in' to their existing investment in petrol-engine cars.

In other circumstances, the response might be greater in the short run than in the long run. A sudden rise in the price of petrol might cause motorists to economise in its use for a few weeks before getting used to the price and drifting back to their old motoring habits.

CASE STUDY 2.1

Elasticity and tobacco taxation

Various studies have calculated the price elasticity of demand for cigarettes of different groups in society such as the young and the old, and men and women.

A World Bank review concluded that price rises of about 10% would on average reduce tobacco consumption by about 4% in richer countries. Smokers in poorer nations also tend to be more sensitive to price changes.

Reviewing 86 studies, Gallet and List found a mean price elasticity of −0.48, meaning that, on average, a 10% increase in price will be followed by a decrease in consumption of 4.8%. They also found greater responsiveness among younger people, with an average price elasticity of −1.43 for teenagers, −0.76 for young adults, and −0.32 for adults. They found an average price sensitivity of −0.50 for men and −0.34 for women. Studies have also tended to show greater price sensitivity among low-income groups.

Follow-up questions

1 Most of the elasticity statistics quoted above lie between zero and −1. Discuss the significance of this for governments.
2 Suggest two reasons why adult smokers may be less responsive to a rise in the price of cigarettes than teenage smokers.

A simple rule for detecting whether demand is price elastic or inelastic

As an alternative to using the formula to calculate price elasticity of demand between two points on a demand curve, a simple rule can be used to determine the general nature of the elasticity between the two points:

- if total consumer expenditure increases in response to a price fall, demand is elastic
- if total consumer expenditure decreases in response to a price fall, demand is inelastic
- if total consumer expenditure remains constant in response to a price fall, demand is neither elastic nor inelastic, i.e. elasticity = unity (or since the demand curve slopes downward, the elasticity is minus unity or −1)

Consider, for example, Figure 2.5, which shows an elastic demand curve D. At price P_1, total consumer expenditure is shown by the rectangle bounded by P_1, a, Q_1 and 0. When the price falls to P_2, the consumer expenditure rectangle changes to the area bounded by P_2, b, Q_2 and 0. Clearly, the second of these rectangles is larger than the first rectangle, so total consumer expenditure increases, following a fall in price, when the demand curve is elastic.

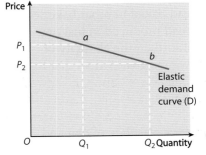

Figure 2.5 The effect of a price fall on total consumer expenditure when demand is elastic

TEST YOURSELF 2.2

Draw a diagram to illustrate what happens to total consumer expenditure in the event of a price fall when the demand curve is inelastic.

Income elasticity of demand

The nature of **income elasticity of demand** — which measures how demand responds to a change in income — depends on whether the good is a normal good or an inferior good. Income elasticity of demand is always negative for an inferior good and positive for a normal good. This is because the quantity demanded of an inferior good falls as income rises, whereas the quantity demanded of a normal good rises with income.

Normal goods can be further divided into superior goods or luxuries, for which the income elasticity of demand is greater than +1, and basic goods, with an income elasticity lying between 0 and +1. Although the quantity demanded of a normal good always rises with income, it rises more than proportionately for a superior good (such as a luxury car). Conversely, demand for a basic good such as shoe polish rises at a slower rate than income.

The size and sign (positive or negative) of income elasticity of demand affect how a good's demand curve shifts following a change in income.

TEST YOURSELF 2.3

The income elasticity of demand for foreign holidays in the UK is +1.6. What does this tell you about UK demand for foreign holidays?

QUANTITATIVE SKILLS 2.1

Worked example: performing an elasticity calculation

People's average incomes fall from £1,000 a week to £600 a week. As a result, demand for potatoes increases from 1 million tonnes to 1.2 million tonnes a week. Calculate the income elasticity of demand for potatoes.

The formula for calculating income elasticity of demand is:

$$\text{income elasticity of demand} = \frac{\text{percentage change in quantity demanded}}{\text{percentage change in income}}$$

The percentage change in quantity demanded is +20%. The percentage change in income is −40%. Placing these figures into the formula:

$$\text{income elasticity of demand} = \frac{+20\%}{-40\%}$$
$$= -0.5$$

The minus sign indicates that the good is an inferior good. The number 0.5 indicates that demand is income inelastic.

Cross-elasticity of demand

Cross-elasticity of demand measures how the demand for one good responds to changes in the price of another good. The cross-elasticity of demand between two goods or services indicates the nature of the demand relationship between the goods. There are three possibilities:

- complementary goods (or joint demand)
- substitutes (or competing demand)
- an absence of any discernible demand relationship

Cars and petrol or diesel fuel, for example, are complementary goods: they are in joint demand. A significant increase in fuel prices will have some effect on the demand for cars, though the effect may not be great. By contrast, private car travel and bus travel are substitute goods. A significant increase in the cost of running a car will cause some motorists to switch to public transport — provided its price does not rise by a similar amount as well.

KEY TERM

market supply the quantity of a good or service that all firms plan to sell at given prices in a given period of time.

KEY TERMS

profit the difference between total sales revenue and total costs of production.

total revenue the money a firm receives from selling its output, calculated by multiplying the price by the quantity sold.

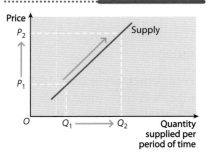
Figure 2.6 A market supply curve

As with the case with income elasticity of demand, the size and sign (positive or negative) of cross-elasticity of demand affect how a good's demand curve shifts following, in this case, a change in the price of another good. For example, a cross-elasticity of demand of +0.3 for bus travel with respect to the price of running a car indicates that a 10% increase in the cost of private motoring would cause the demand for bus travel to increase by just 3%. For most demand relationships between two goods, cross-elasticities of demand are inelastic rather than elastic, both when the goods are in joint demand and when they are substitutes.

2.3 The determinants of the supply of goods and services

Market supply

Normally when economists refer to **supply**, they mean market supply. **Market supply** is the quantity of a good or service that all the firms or producers in the market plan to sell at different prices. By contrast, supply by a single firm is the quantity that a particular firm within the market would like to sell. As with demand, the relationship between the two is simple. Market supply is just the sum of the supply of all the firms or producers in the market at different market prices.

The market supply curve

The market supply curve in Figure 2.6 illustrates the 'law' of supply, which states that as a good's price rises, more is supplied. If the price starts off low, for example at P_1, firms are willing to supply Q_1. But if the price rises to P_2, planned supply increases to Q_2.

The main reason for upward-sloping supply curves stems from the profit-maximising objective which economists assume firms have. If we assume that a firm always aims to make the biggest possible profit, it follows that a firm will only want to supply more of a good if it is profitable so to do.

For a firm, **profit** is the difference between the sales **revenue** the firm receives when selling the goods or services it produces and the costs of producing the goods. Assuming firms do not change their size or scale, the cost of producing extra units of a good generally increases as firms produce more of the good. As a result, it is unprofitable to produce and sell extra units of a good unless the price rises to compensate for the extra cost of production. The result is the upward-sloping market supply curve shown in Figure 2.6.

Firms only want to supply more of a good if it is profitable to do so

As with demand, the supply of a good varies according to the time period being considered. Hence the words 'Quantity supplied per period of time' on the horizontal axis in Figure 2.6. In later diagrams, this is shortened to 'Quantity'. But again, as with demand, remember that this is an abbreviation.

SYNOPTIC LINK
Microeconomic supply curves look very similar to aggregate supply curves which are explained in Chapter 7. Don't confuse the two.

TEST YOURSELF 2.5
Having set the price of bread at £3 a loaf, bread shops bake 10 million loaves which they then try to sell. However, 8 million of these loaves remain unsold. What is likely to happen next in the bread market?

Shifts of the supply curve

Earlier in the chapter, we saw that a market demand curve shows how much all the consumers in the market plan to buy at different prices of the good, assuming all the other factors that influence demand remain constant. These 'other factors' were called the conditions of demand and we explained how, if any of them change, the demand curve shifts to a new position.

KEY TERM
conditions of supply
determinants of supply, other than the good's own price, that fix the position of the supply curve.

In exactly the same way, a market supply curve shows the quantities of the good that all the firms in the market plan to supply at different possible prices, assuming the **conditions of supply** remain unchanged. Again, if the ceteris paribus assumption no longer holds, one or more of the conditions of supply change, and the supply curve shifts to a new position.

The conditions of supply

The main conditions of supply are:

- costs of production, including
  - wage costs
  - raw material costs
  - energy costs
  - costs of borrowing

31

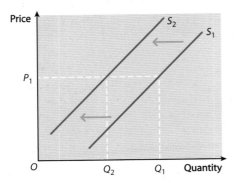

KEY TERMS

increase in supply a rightward shift of the supply curve.

decrease in supply a leftward shift of the supply curve.

- technical progress
- taxes imposed on firms, such as VAT, excise duties and the business rate
- subsidies granted by the government to firms

As we have noted, if any of the conditions of supply change, the supply curve shifts to a new position. As with demand, a rightward shift of supply is known as an **increase in supply**, whereas a leftward shift is known as a **decrease in supply**. An increase in wage costs, which for many firms are the most important cost of production, shifts the supply curve leftward (or upward). Firms reduce the quantity of the good they are prepared to supply because production costs have risen. For example, when the price is P_1 in Figure 2.7, a leftward shift of supply from S_1 to S_2 causes the quantity firms are prepared to supply to fall from Q_1 to Q_2.

Supply curves also tend to shift rightward when technical progress occurs, reducing production costs, or when firms enter the market. Conversely, the supply curve shifts leftward when costs rise or firms leave the market.

Figure 2.7 A leftward shift of the supply curve

EXTENSION MATERIAL

How expenditure taxes and subsidies shift supply curves

A supply curve shifts leftward (or upward) when the government imposes an expenditure tax such as customs and excise duties or VAT on firms. From a firm's point of view, the tax is similar to a rise in production costs. Firms try to pass the tax on to consumers by increasing the price of the good. For this reason, expenditure taxes provide examples of indirect taxes. The higher price charged means consumers indirectly pay the tax, even though the firms and not the consumers pay the tax to the government.

How the supply curve shifts depends on whether the tax firms are forced to pay is an *ad valorem* tax or a specific tax. In the case of an *ad valorem* tax such as VAT, which is levied at the same percentage rate (e.g. 20%) on the price, the new supply curve is steeper than the old supply curve. This is shown in Figure 2.8(a). If a good is priced at £1.00, 20% of the price without the tax is 20 pence. However, if the price of a good is £2.00, the government collects 40 pence of tax revenue for each unit of the good sold.

But in the case of a specific tax or unit tax, such as the excise duty levied on tobacco, alcohol or petrol, the tax levied does not depend on the good's price. Because of this, the new and old supply curves are parallel to each other, separated, as Figure 2.8(b) illustrates by the size of the tax levied on each unit of the good. When an indirect tax is imposed on a good, the supply curve shifts vertically upwards by the amount of the tax.

A subsidy given by the government to producers has the opposite effect to an expenditure tax; it shifts the supply curve to the right. In the case of a specific subsidy, which is illustrated in Figure 2.9, the sum of money paid to firms for each unit of the good produced is the same whatever the price of the good and hence the vertical distance between the two supply curves equals the subsidy per unit. By contrast, the size of the subsidy would vary if the subsidy were dependent on the price of the good.

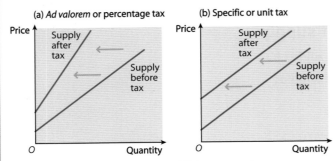

Figure 2.8 An expenditure tax shifting a supply curve

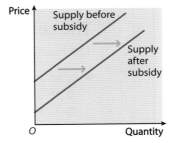

Figure 2.9 A specific or unit subsidy shifting a supply curve

EXTENSION MATERIAL

How the effect of an expenditure tax depends on elasticity of demand

In Figure 2.8 an expenditure tax imposed by the government on firms shifts the good's supply curve leftward. From the point of view of the firms that produce and sell the good, the tax has the same effect as a rise in costs of production such as a rise in wage costs. As is the case with cost increases, by raising the price of the good to cover the tax, firms try to increase the price charged to customers by the full amount of the tax. However, their ability to do this depends on price elasticity of demand.

Figure 2.10 shows that when demand is relatively elastic, consumer resistance means that some but not all of a tax (in this case a specific tax) is passed on to consumers as a price rise. The tax per unit (labelled T in Figure 2.10) is measured by the vertical distance between S_1 (the supply curve before the tax was imposed) and S_2 (the supply curve after the tax was imposed). Immediately after the tax is imposed, firms may try to raise the price to $P_1 + T$, passing all the tax on to consumers. However, there is excess supply at this price. Via the market mechanism, the price falls to P_2, thereby eliminating the excess supply. In the new equilibrium, part, but not all, of the tax has been passed on to consumers as a price rise.

The part of the tax passed on to consumers is called the shifted incidence of the tax. The rest of the tax (the unshifted incidence) is borne by firms or producers. In Figure 2.10, the total tax revenue paid by firms to the government is shown by the rectangle bounded by heavy black lines. The part of the tax rectangle above what was the equilibrium price (P_1) before the tax was imposed, shows the shifted incidence of the tax. The part of the tax rectangle below P_1 shows the unshifted incidence.

You should now draw diagrams similar to Figure 2.10, but with perfectly elastic, relatively inelastic and completely inelastic demand curves. The diagrams will show that firms' ability to pass the incidence of a tax on to consumers as a price rise is greatest when demand is completely inelastic, and non-existent when demand is perfectly elastic.

Students often confuse the effect of an increase in an indirect tax imposed on firms with the effect of a direct tax such as income tax imposed on individuals. Whereas a tax imposed on firms shifts the *supply curve* of a good, by reducing consumers' incomes, income tax shifts the *demand curve* for a good. An increase in income tax shifts the demand curve for normal goods leftward, but if the good is an inferior good, the demand curve shifts rightward.

Finally, note that subsidies granted to firms have the opposite effect to taxes imposed them. Subsidies shift the supply curve rightward or downward, showing that firms are prepared to supply more of the good at all prices.

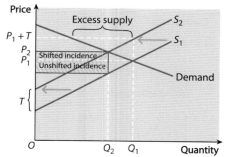

Figure 2.10 Shifting the incidence of a tax when demand is price elastic

2.4 Price elasticity of supply

KEY TERM
price elasticity of supply measures the extent to which the supply of a good changes in response to a change in the price of that good.

In contrast to demand elasticities explained earlier in the chapter, there is only one supply elasticity you need to know. This is **price elasticity of supply**, which measures how the supply of a good responds to an initial change in a good's price.

The formula for price elasticity of supply is:

$$\text{price elasticity of supply} = \frac{\text{percentage change in quantity supplied}}{\text{percentage change in price}}$$

Just as with demand curves, you must not confuse the *slope* of a supply curve with its *elasticity*. Upward-sloping *straight-line* (linear) supply curves display the following price elasticities:

- if the supply curve intersects the price axis, the curve is elastic at all points, though elasticity falls towards unity moving from point to point up the curve
- if the supply curve intersects the quantity axis, the curve is inelastic at all points, though elasticity rises towards unity moving from point to point up the curve
- if the supply curve passes through the origin, elasticity equals unity (+1) at all points on the curve

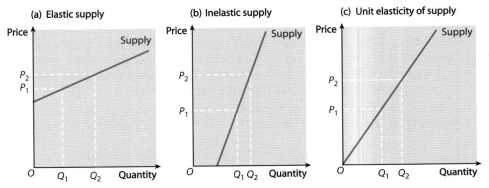

Figure 2.11 Price elasticity of supply and linear supply curves

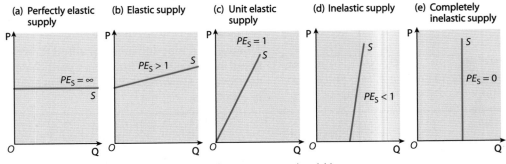

Figure 2.12 The five linear supply curves you should know

STUDY TIP

You should understand why price elasticity of supply is usually positive and why price elasticity of demand is usually negative.

TEST YOURSELF 2.6

If the price of a good with a price elasticity of supply of 2.5 increases by 10%, the quantity supplied will:

A fall by 25%

B rise by 25%

C fall by 40%

D rise by 0.4%

Which is the correct answer, and why?

The factors determining price elasticity of supply

The length of the production period

If firms can convert raw materials into finished goods very quickly (e.g. in just a few hours or days), supply will tend be more elastic than when several months are involved in production, as with many agricultural goods.

The availability of spare capacity

When a firm possesses spare capacity, and if labour and raw materials are readily available, production can generally be increased quickly in the short run.

The ease of accumulating stocks

When stocks of unsold finished goods are stored at low cost, firms can respond quickly to a sudden increase in demand. Alternatively, firms can respond to a price fall by diverting current production away from sales and into stock accumulation. The ease with which stocks of raw materials or components can be bought from outside suppliers and then stored has a similar effect.

The ease of switching between alternative methods of production

When firms can quickly alter the way they produce goods — for example, by switching between the use of capital and labour — supply tends to be more elastic than when there is little or no choice. In a similar way, if firms produce a range of products and can switch raw materials, labour or machines from one type of production to another, the supply of any one product tends to be elastic.

The number of firms in the market and the ease of entering the market

Generally, the more firms there are in the market, and the greater the ease with which a firm can enter or leave, the greater the elasticity of supply.

Time

We have already noted that demand is more elastic in the long run than in the short run because it takes time to respond to a price change. The same is true for supply. Figure 2.13 shows three supply curves of increasing elasticity, S_1, S_2 and S_3, which illustrate respectively market period supply, short-run supply and long-run supply.

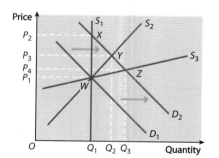

Figure 2.13 The effect of the time period upon price elasticity of supply

- **Market period supply** The market period supply curve S_1 is shown by a vertical line. S_1 depicts the situation facing firms following a sudden and unexpected rightward shift of demand from D_1 to D_2. When surprised by a sudden increase in demand, firms cannot immediately increase output. In the market period, supply is completely inelastic, and the price rises from P_1 to P_2 to eliminate the excess demand brought about by the rightward shift of the demand curve.

- **Short-run supply** The higher price means that higher profits can be made, creating the incentive for firms to increase output. In the short run, firms increase output by hiring more variable factors of production such as labour. The short-run increase in output is shown by the movement up the short-run supply curve, S_2. The short-run supply curve is more elastic than the market period supply curve, S_1. In the short run, supply increases to Q_2, and the price falls from P_2 to P_3.

● **Long-run supply** If firms believe the increase in demand will be long-lasting, and not just a temporary phenomenon, they may increase the scale of production by employing more capital and other factors of production that are fixed in the short run, but variable in the long run. When this happens, firms move along the long-run supply curve S_3. Output rises to Q_3, and the price falls once again, in this case to P_4.

In a competitive industry with low or non-existent barriers to entry, elasticity of supply is greater in the long run than in the short run, because in the long run firms can enter or leave the market. Short-run supply is less elastic because supply is restricted to the firms already in the industry.

> **STUDY TIP**
> You should understand why, for most goods, both the demand curve and the supply curve are more price elastic in the long run than in the short run.

CASE STUDY 2.2

Housing market elasticities in the UK

UK households have an income elasticity of demand for housing that exceeds +1. However, demand for housing is price inelastic. These demand elasticities, combined with a low price elasticity of supply for housing, push the UK's housing market towards long-term rising prices.

New housing would need to have a price elasticity of supply of +10 for supply to equal demand in the long term. But if the price elasticity of supply for new housing remains low, as Table 2.1 shows, house prices will never be stable in the UK when the demand for housing is increasing.

Table 2.1 Price elasticity of supply in the housing market for different countries

Country	Price elasticity of supply
Canada	+1.2
UK	+0.4
USA	+2.0
France	+0.3
Ireland	+0.6

Follow-up questions

1 Suggest why the price elasticity of supply of new houses is lower in the UK than in the USA.
2 'New housing would need to have a price elasticity of supply of +10 for supply to equal demand in the long term.' Explain this statement.

EXTENSION MATERIAL

A closer look at perfectly elastic demand and supply

Figure 2.14 shows a perfectly elastic demand curve and a perfectly elastic supply curve. (These can also be labelled infinitely elastic demand and infinitely elastic supply.) Although the two parts of Figure 2.14 appear to be identical (apart from the labels), this is misleading. The apparent similarity disguises a significant difference between perfectly elastic demand and perfectly elastic supply. In Figure 2.14(a), demand is infinitely elastic at all prices on or *below* the demand curve, though if the price rises *above* the demand curve (for example from P_1 to P_2), the amount demanded immediately falls to zero. This is because perfect substitutes are available when demand is perfectly price elastic. Customers cease to buy the good as soon as the price rises *above* the demand curve, switching spending to the perfect substitutes whose prices have not changed.

By contrast, in Figure 2.14(b), supply is infinitely elastic at *all* prices on or *above* the supply curve, though if the price falls *below* the supply curve (for example from P_1 to P_2), the amount supplied immediately drops to zero. P_1 is the minimum price acceptable to firms. If they are paid this price (or any higher price), firms stay in the market. The incentive to stay in the market disappears at any lower price and firms leave the market, unable to make sufficient profit.

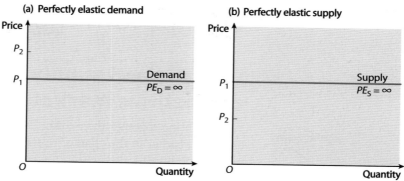

Figure 2.14 Perfectly price elastic demand and supply curves

Shifts of, and adjustments along, demand and supply curves

The extent to which price or the quantity bought and sold changes following a shift of demand or supply depends upon the slope and elasticity of the curve that has not shifted. Figure 2.15 shows a demand curve shifting rightward — along a gently sloping supply curve in (a) and along a much more steeply sloping supply curve in (b). Prior to the shift of demand, equilibrium occurs at point X in both (a) and (b). In each case, the rightward shift of demand induces an adjustment along the supply curve to a new equilibrium at point Z. With the elastic supply curve shown in (a), the quantity adjustment is greater than the price adjustment. The reverse is true in (b), where the supply curve is inelastic.

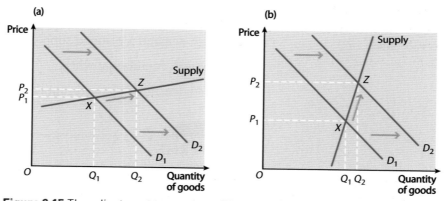

Figure 2.15 The adjustment to a new equilibrium following a shift of demand

> ## STUDY TIP
> You should apply elasticity analysis when answering questions on the effects of a shift of a demand or supply curve. The extent to which the good's price or equilibrium level of output changes depends on the price elasticity of the curve that has not shifted. For example, when the supply curve shifts leftward, the price elasticity of the demand curve determines the extent to which the good's price and quantity change.

2.5 The determination of equilibrium market prices

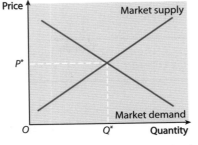

Figure 2.16 Market equilibrium in the tomato market

Demand and supply curves in a competitive market

We now bring together the market demand and market supply curves explained earlier in the chapter to see how the equilibrium price is achieved in a competitive market within the economy. The market we will look at is the tomato market. Its essential features are shown in Figure 2.16.

The market demand curve in Figure 2.16 shows how many tomatoes all the consumers in the market plan to purchase at different prices in a particular period of time. The market supply curve shows how many tomatoes all the farmers and firms in the market wish to supply at different prices in the same time period.

The equilibrium price

The concepts of **equilibrium** and its opposite, **disequilibrium**, are important in economic theory and analysis. You should think of equilibrium as a *state of rest* or a *state of balance between opposing forces*. In a market, the opposing forces are supply and demand. **Market equilibrium**, which is shown in Figure 2.16, occurs where the demand curve and the supply curve cross each other. At price P^*, households *plan* to demand exactly the same quantity of tomatoes that firms *plan* to supply. P^* therefore is the equilibrium price, with Q^* being the equilibrium quantity.

In summary:

A market is in disequilibrium when:

- planned demand < planned supply, in which case the price falls, or when
- planned demand > planned supply, in which case the price rises.

A market is in equilibrium when:

- planned demand = planned supply, in which case the price does not change.

KEY TERMS

equilibrium a state of rest or balance between opposing forces.

disequilibrium a situation in a market when there is excess supply or excess demand.

market equilibrium a market is in equilibrium when planned demand equals planned supply and the demand curve crosses the supply curve. In this situation there is no excess demand or excess supply in the market. Unless some event disturbs the equilibrium, there is no reason for the price to change.

market disequilibrium exists at any price other than the equilibrium price. When the market is in disequilibrium, either excess demand or excess supply exists in the market. Excess demand causes the price to rise until a new equilibrium is established. Conversely, excess supply causes the market price to fall until equilibrium is achieved.

Disequilibrium in a market

It is impossible at most prices for both households and firms to simultaneously fulfil their market plans. In Figure 2.17, P_1 is a disequilibrium price for tomatoes because the tomato growers and sellers cannot fulfil their plans at this price. When price is P_1 in Figure 2.17, firms would like to supply Q_2, but households are only willing to purchase Q_1.

To explain this further, it is useful to divide the market into two 'sides' — the short side and the long side. When the price is P_1, households, or the people wishing to buy tomatoes, are on the short side of the market, while tomato producers are on the long side. The economic agents on the short side can always fulfil their market plans, but those on the long side cannot. Thus, when the price is P_1, households can purchase exactly the quantity of tomatoes they wish to, namely Q_1. Farmers and other tomato producers, however, are in a different situation. They would like to sell Q_2, but can only sell Q_1, as long as the price remains at P_1. The difference between Q_2 and Q_1 is **excess supply** or unsold stock.

The market is also in disequilibrium at price P_2, because households are unable to buy as much as they wish to at this price. Households would like to buy Q_2 of tomatoes, but they can't, because at this price tomato producers are only willing to supply Q_1. The situation is now reversed compared to P_1. Tomato buyers are on the long side of the market and farmers and tomato sellers are on the short side. In this case, the difference between Q_2 and Q_1 is **excess demand** or unfulfilled demand. Households end up buying Q_1 of tomatoes because this is the maximum quantity tomato producers are prepared to sell at this price.

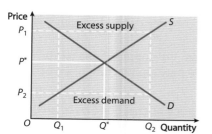

Figure 2.17 Disequilibrium and equilibrium in the tomato market

KEY TERMS
excess supply when firms wish to sell more than consumers wish to buy, with the price above the equilibrium price.

excess demand when consumers wish to buy more than firms wish to sell, with the price below the equilibrium price.

Worked example: calculating the equilibrium price of a good

Table 2.2 shows the demand and supply schedules for chocolate bars.

Table 2.2

Price per bar (£)	Quantity of bars demanded per week	Quantity of bars supplied per week
0.75	180	240
0.70	200	200
0.65	220	160
0.60	240	120

As a result of a fall in the price of cocoa beans, the supply of chocolate bars rises by 60 bars at all prices. What is the new equilibrium price of chocolate bars?

According to the table the initial equilibrium price of chocolate bars is 70 pence, at which demand and supply are equal at 200 chocolate bars. If 60 more chocolate bars are supplied at each price, following the fall in the cost of manufacturing the bars, 300 bars are supplied at a price of 75 pence, 260 bars at a price of 70 pence, and 220 bars at a price of 65 pence. This is the new equilibrium price. Demand equals supply at 220 bars at this price. The supply curve has shifted rightward by 60 at each price.

Incentives to change

We will now introduce an important assumption about economic behaviour which recurs throughout economic theory and analysis. This is the assumption that whenever an economic agent, such as a household or firm, fails to fulfil its market plans, it has an incentive to change its market behaviour. When excess supply exists in the market (as at P_1 in the tomato market, Figure 2.17), the market mechanism or price mechanism swings into action to get rid of unsold stocks. This moves the market toward equilibrium. Economists assume that firms react to stocks of unsold goods by accepting a lower price. Eventually the price falls until the amount that households wish to buy equals exactly the quantity that firms are prepared to supply. In the tomato market, equilibrium is reached at price P^*.

In the case of excess demand, it is useful to divide households into two groups of customers. In the tomato market, the first group, depicted by the distance from O to Q_1 in Figure 2.17, are *lucky* customers who buy the good at price P_1 before the available quantity runs out. By contrast, *unlucky* households, shown by the distance from Q_1 to Q_2, cannot buy the good at P_1, possibly because they turned up too late. However, in order to be able to purchase the good, unlucky consumers bid up the price until, once again, equilibrium is reached at P^*.

The equilibrium price, P^*, is the *only* price which satisfies both households and firms. Consequently, once this price is reached, neither group has reason to change their market plans. At P^*, planned demand equals planned supply and the market clears.

How a shift of supply disturbs market equilibrium

Once supply equals demand in a market, for example at point X in Figure 2.18, the market remains in equilibrium until an external event hits the market and causes either the market supply curve or the market demand curve to shift to a new position.

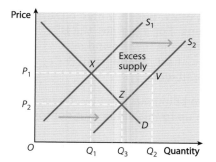

Figure 2.18 The effect of a rightward shift of the market supply curve of tomatoes

Figure 2.18 illustrates what happens in the tomato market when an event such as a bumper harvest causes the supply curve of tomatoes to shift rightward, from S_1 to S_2. Before the shift of the supply curve, P_1 was the equilibrium price of tomatoes. However, once the supply curve shifts, P_1 becomes a disequilibrium price. Too many tomatoes are offered for sale at this price, which means there is excess supply in the market. The excess supply is shown by the distance Q_2 minus Q_1, or between X and V.

To get rid of this unsold stock, tomato producers reduce the price they are prepared to accept. The market price falls from P_1 to P_2, which eliminates the excess supply. In the new equilibrium, planned supply once again equals planned demand, but at the lower equilibrium price of P_2.

How a shift of demand disturbs market equilibrium

Figure 2.19 shows what happens in the market for tomatoes following an increase in consumers' incomes. Tomatoes are usually considered a normal good: that is, a good for which demand increases as income increases. Before the increase in consumers' incomes, the equilibrium price of tomatoes was P_1, determined at the intersection of curves D_1 and S. At this price, planned demand equals planned supply. However, increased incomes shift the market demand curve rightward from D_1 to D_2. Immediately, disequilibrium replaces equilibrium in the market. The rightward shift of demand creates excess demand in the market, as long as the price remains at P_1. Excess demand is shown by Q_2 minus Q_1, or the distance between H and K.

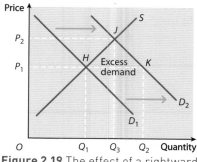

Figure 2.19 The effect of a rightward shift of the market demand curve for tomatoes

The market adjustment mechanism now swings into action to get rid of the excess demand. The price increases to P_2 to eliminate the excess demand, and the quantity of tomatoes bought and sold rises to Q_3. In response to the increase in demand from H to K, there is a movement along the supply curve between H and J (an extension of supply) to establish the new equilibrium (Note that there is also a movement along D_2 from K to J.)

41

TEST YOURSELF 2.8
There are 30 million customers and 1 million firms producing the good in a particular market in the UK. Explain why you would classify this market as being competitive or uncompetitive.

CASE STUDY 2.3

Auctions

In theory, an auction provides a quick and efficient method of establishing equilibrium in a market. Auctions have been brought into many people's everyday lives through sites such as eBay. But they also have a long history spanning many different domains. For example, the US government uses auctions to sell Treasury bills and timber and oil leases, Christie's and Sotheby's use them to sell art, and Morrell & Co. and the Chicago Wine Company use them to sell wine.

Each bidder has an intrinsic value for the item being auctioned — he or she is willing to purchase the item for a price up to this value, but not for any higher price.

Three types of auction at which a single item is sold are:

1 **Ascending-bid auctions**, also called English auctions. The seller gradually raises the price, bidders drop out until only one bidder remains, and that bidder wins the object at this final price.
2 **Descending-bid auctions**, also called Dutch auctions. The seller gradually lowers the price from a high initial value until the first moment when a bidder accepts and pays the current price. These auctions are called Dutch auctions because flowers have long been sold in the Netherlands using this procedure.
3 **First-price sealed-bid auctions.** In this kind of auction, bidders submit simultaneous 'sealed bids' to the seller. The terminology comes from the original format for such auctions, in which bids were written down and provided in sealed envelopes to the seller, who would open them all together. The highest bidder wins the object and pays the value of her bid.

Follow-up questions

1 eBay is the best-known and the largest internet-based auction. Give your views on the advantages and disadvantages of trading goods on eBay.
2 Explain how the use of the internet has affected the costs consumers incur when searching for goods they want to buy.

ACTIVITY
Watch an auction taking place on television, for example a house-price or antiques auction. Write a short report on the events taking place. (You may have to record the programme or do the activity in your holidays, as this type of programme tends to be broadcast during school hours.)

TEST YOURSELF 2.9
Describe how auctions on eBay take place.

2.6 The interrelationship between markets

So far in this chapter we have looked at how the price mechanism operates in a competitive market. We have seen how shifts of either the demand or supply curve for the good disturb market equilibrium and trigger an adjustment process to establish a new equilibrium.

Shifts of curves are often caused by events taking place in other markets in the economy. They can be caused by a change of price of a good in joint supply, or on the demand side, by a change in price of a good in joint demand, a substitute good, a good in composite demand, or a good in derived demand.

Joint supply and competing supply

Joint supply occurs when production of one good leads to the supply of a by-product. Suppose, for example, that the demand for beef increases, possibly because of rising incomes in developing countries. The slaughter of more cows to meet this demand leads to production of more cow hides, which increases the supply of leather. The interrelationship between the beef and leather markets is shown in Figure 2.20. Note that the price of beef *rises* following the rightward shift of the *demand* curve for beef, but the price of leather *falls* following the rightward shift of the *supply* curve of leather. A rise in the price of the first good leads to a shift of the supply curve of the other good in joint supply. In this example, beef is the main product and leather is the by-product, though the relationship could be reversed.

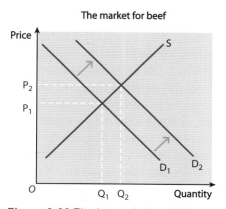
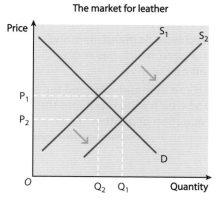

Figure 2.20 The interrelationship between two goods in joint supply

Now consider what happens if two goods are in **competing supply** rather than in joint supply. The relationship between food and biofuel provides a topical example. Increased demand for biofuels such as ethanol has diverted crop growing away from food supply to the supply of fuel for motor vehicles. Because farmers producing crops such as wheat, maize and sugar can earn a higher price by selling their produce to energy companies, the supply curve of crops for food is shifting leftward. We will leave it to you to draw appropriate diagrams to illustrate competing supply, and the four demand relationships between markets explained on the next page.

CASE STUDY 2.4

Competing supply: biofuels and food

Record-breaking food prices in 2011 led experts to warn of the danger of a global food crisis. Many factors contributed to the price rise, but the growth in production of biofuels was one of the most important. About 40% of US maize production goes into biofuels. In 2011, 18% of biofuels used in the UK were made from wheat and maize that are staple foods in the developing world. Yet just a year earlier, the UK hardly used either of these.

Increased demand for biofuels inevitably drives food prices higher. And biofuel use is set to grow. Less food is grown as biofuel production increases.

Follow-up questions

1 Explain how diverting crop production to meet the demand for biofuel is affecting world poverty.
2 Explain two causes, other than increased biofuel production, of recent changes in food prices.

Complementary and substitute goods

KEY TERMS

complementary good a good in joint demand, or a good which is demanded at the same time as the other good.

substitute good a good in competing demand, namely a good which can be used in place of the other good.

An increase in the price of a good in joint demand (or a **complementary good**) has the opposite effect to an increase in the price of a **substitute good** (or a good in competing demand). For example, Sony games consoles and Sony games cartridges are in joint demand, but Sony and Xbox consoles are in competing demand, so are substitute goods. Following a significant rise in the price of Sony consoles, demand for them falls, which in turn reduces the demand for Sony games cartridges. The demand curve for Sony cartridges shifts leftward. But the demand curve for Xbox consoles shifts rightward, assuming that consumers consider an Xbox console to be a good substitute for a Sony console.

Composite demand and derived demand

KEY TERMS

composite demand demand for a good which has more than one use.

derived demand demand for a good which is an input into the production of another good.

Students often confuse competing demand, which occurs in the case of substitutes, with composite demand and derived demand. **Composite demand** is demand for a good which has more than one use. An increase in demand for one use of the good reduces the supply of the good for an alternative use; for example, if more wheat is used for biofuel, less is available for food, unless wheat growing increases. By contrast, **derived demand** for a good occurs when a good is necessary for the production of other goods. The demand for capital goods such as machinery and raw materials is derived from the demand for consumer goods or finished goods. If the demand for cars falls, so does the demand for engines and gear boxes.

CASE STUDY 2.5

Digital downloads replace CDs and DVDs

In 2000, when the first MP3 players were hitting the market, no one anticipated that sales of music downloads would overtake CD and DVD sales. Even when the iTunes store opened in 2003, Apple was only vying for a small market share.

In 2012 sales of downloaded music overtook CD sales, reaching 55.9% of sales. Download sales went up 9.1% in 2012 while CD sales decreased by 10%, though music sales in general increased 3% after a decade of consistent decline.

What are we giving up by adopting the new technology? Booklets, posters and CDs we can hold in our hands, plus music quality (a CD holds far more information than an MP3 file). What are we gaining? Instant satisfaction, convenience, and mobile purchasing power. The debate is similar to that which accompanied the move from vinyl records to CDs a few decades ago.

As sales have moved online, music retail giants like HMV have closed. Now it seems that CDs could be phased out. How will our ways of consuming music evolve as time goes on?

Follow-up questions

1 Over the last 50 years, demand for recorded music has switched from vinyl records to CDs and then to downloads. Explain two reasons for these changes in demand.
2 How would you describe the demand relationship between CDs and MP3 files?

TEST YOURSELF 2.10

A farmer sells 100 sheep at a price of £20 per sheep. What is the farmer's total revenue and why is this not the same as the farmer's profit?

EXTENSION MATERIAL

Interrelated markets and cross-elasticity of demand

Complementary goods, such as computer games consoles and cartridges, have negative cross-elasticities of demand. A rise in the price of one good leads to a fall in demand for the other good.

By contrast, the cross-elasticity of demand between two goods which are substitutes for each other is positive. A rise in the price of one good causes demand to switch to the substitute good whose price has not risen. Demand for the substitute good increases.

If we select two minor items at random — for example, pencils and dustbins — the cross-elasticity of demand between the two goods is likely to be zero. When there is no discernible demand relationship between two goods, a rise in the price of one good will have no measurable effect upon the demand for the other.

2.7 Applications of demand and supply analysis to particular markets

This chapter has explained how a market for a good or service operates and how markets interrelate with each other. We now apply this analysis to a number of real-world markets, such as agricultural markets, commodity markets for raw materials and energy, the market for second-hand cars, housing markets and markets for healthcare.

Why prices are often unstable in agricultural markets

Over the years, agricultural markets for foodstuffs and primary products such as rubber have experienced two closely related problems:

- Until recently, there was a long-run trend for agricultural prices to fall relative to those of manufactured goods.
- Prices have fluctuated considerably from year to year.

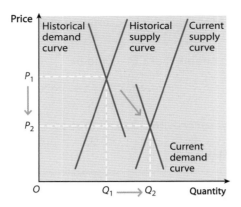

Figure 2.21 The long-run fall in the prices of agricultural products

Agricultural markets are prone to disequilibrium and random shifts of the supply curve from year to year, caused by climatic factors. This leads to unacceptable fluctuations in agricultural prices that, as Chapter 5 explains, require government intervention to stabilise the price.

The long-run fall in agricultural prices

The long-run downward trend can be explained by shifts of the demand and supply curves for agricultural products over extended periods of time. This is shown in Figure 2.21, where the equilibrium price for an agricultural product in an early historical period is P_1. Over time, both the demand and supply curves have shifted rightward. The shift in the demand curve was caused for example by rising incomes and population growth, while improved methods of farming increased supply. But for many farm products this shift of supply has greatly exceeded the shift of demand, resulting in a fall to the lower equilibrium price P_2.

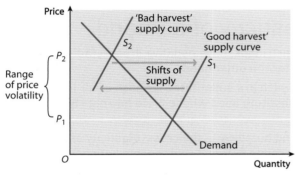

Figure 2.22 Fluctuating agricultural prices caused by shifts of supply

Short-run fluctuations in agricultural prices

Figure 2.22 provides another explanation of fluctuating farm prices. In the diagram, price volatility is caused by random shifts of the short-run supply curve in response to fluctuations in the harvest. Figure 2.22 shows two short-run supply curves: a 'good harvest' supply curve, S_1, and a 'bad harvest' supply curve, S_2. Weather conditions and other factors outside farmers' control shift the position of the supply curve from year to year between the limits set by S_1 and S_2. As a result, market prices fluctuate from year to year within the range of P_1 to P_2.

Commodity markets

The importance of speculative demand

Farm products are not the only goods whose prices fluctuate from year to year. The same is true for many primary products, especially metals such as copper and nickel. Part of the reason for this stems from the fact that it takes years to open new mines, with the result that sudden increases in demand cannot easily be met from supply.

Another reason is speculation. Many of the organisations that buy and sell commodities such as copper never intend to use the metal, or indeed to take delivery of the product. When speculators think the price of copper is going to rise, probably in conditions of increasing global demand and limited supply, they step into the market and buy copper. If speculative demand is large enough, the speculators themselves force the price up. In these circumstances, higher future prices become self-fulfilling. In a similar way, when speculators start to sell in the belief that copper prices are going to fall, the act of speculative selling forces down the price of copper.

CASE STUDY 2.6

Speculative demand and metal prices

Speculative demand has become increasingly important in driving up or down the prices of commodities such as copper and nickel. Mass buying or selling by international speculators is one of the factors causing commodity prices to be extremely volatile.

In 2011, the House of Commons Select Committee on Science and Technology became concerned by reports of financial institutions entering commodity markets and buying up significant quantities of strategic metals. The committee recommended that the UK government investigate

- whether there are increasing levels of speculation in the metals markets
- the contribution of these to price volatility
- whether markets that allow high levels of speculation, with associated price volatility, are an acceptable way to deliver strategic commodities to end users

Follow-up questions

1 What is meant by speculation?
2 Draw a supply and demand diagram to illustrate the effect of speculative demand on the price of a commodity such as copper.

The commodity price cycle

Global commodity prices move in long cycles or super cycles that last typically for 20–30 years. Between 1980 and 2000, there was a declining price trend over the whole period, which reversed at the turn of the millennium (Figure 2.23). After 2008, there was a significant fall in commodity prices, which partially corrected the earlier price increases.

The boom in commodity prices between 2004 and 2008 was caused by two factors: declining supply and increasing demand. The declining supply was caused by the earlier fall in commodity prices. Mining companies stopped investing on a large scale, and this put production under heavy pressure. The supply decline became evident when demand for commodities started picking up after 2000, with a huge spike in demand from emerging markets, especially China. At the time, China's economy was growing by more than 12% annually, much faster than growth in the developed world.

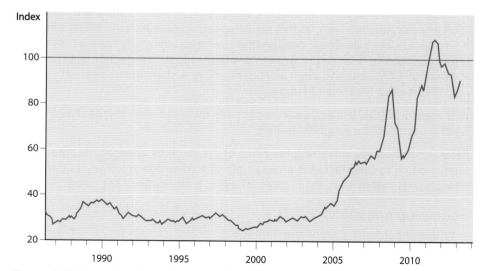

Figure 2.23 The index of world commodity prices, 1985-2013

Although China's growth slowed down immediately after the 2008 global financial crisis, the growth rate remained above 7% at all times — still a multiple of European and North American growth rates. Commodity prices fell in the aftermath of global recession, but, even at their lowest, prices were still far above the levels recorded at the turn of the century. At the time of writing in 2015, it is uncertain what will happen to commodity prices in the near future. The price of crude oil has begun to fall dramatically, but this may reflect a 'price war' in which Saudi Arabia tries to bankrupt American shale oil producers.

In the boom years of the early 2000s, China's investment in building infrastructure increased the demand for raw materials and energy, and hence their prices. If a second commodity price boom starts, the Chinese consumer will be a main contributor. In 2013, a Chinese employee earned close to 25,000 yuan per year, or about US$ 4,200, compared to 8,500 yuan per year, or about US$1,400, in 2004. This is still negligible compared to Western wages, but is a fourfold increase of disposable income in less than 10 years. It translates directly into Chinese consumer behaviour. The Chinese are spending like never before on goods which have to be produced using scarce commodities.

CASE STUDY 2.7

OPEC and the price of crude oil

Until recently the price of crude oil was rising rapidly. However, in 2014 and 2015 there was a dramatic fall in oil prices. Part of the reason for changing oil prices lies in the activities of OPEC, the Organization of Petroleum Exporting Countries.

OPEC was created in 1960 to protect the interests of oil-producing countries, in response to the efforts of Western oil companies to drive oil prices down. It allows oil-producing countries to guarantee their income by coordinating policies and prices.

Before recent discoveries of new oil resources, two-thirds of world oil reserves were believed to be located in OPEC countries and OPEC members were responsible for half of the world's oil exports.

OPEC's aim has been to keep crude oil prices within a particular range. OPEC countries attempt to control the amount of crude oil they export and avoid flooding or squeezing the international marketplace. But the oil market is notoriously difficult to balance, as demonstrated by sharp price swings in the years since OPEC was set up. OPEC members do not necessarily have identical interests, and often find it difficult to agree on their price and output strategies:

- Countries such as Saudi Arabia are completely reliant on income from oil. Their long-term interest is to prevent oil prices rising too high, as this would speed up research in industrialised countries for alternative fuels.
- Producers such as Dubai realise that they must diversify their economies before oil runs out. They are using oil revenues to finance the growth of other industries, particularly financial services and tourism.
- Other OPEC members, such as Nigeria, have a short-term interest in keeping oil prices as high as possible to finance the lifestyle of ruling elites.

In the early 2000s, the price range of crude oil was between about $25 and $30 a barrel. It then rose to over $100 a barrel, before rapidly falling.

OPEC's method of controlling the price of crude oil by altering the rate at which its members release or supply oil on to the market is an example of a retention scheme. It operates through shifting the supply curve of a product rather than through purchasing a stockpile of the good.

Follow-up questions

1 With the help of a supply and demand diagram, explain why in a free market the price of oil might be highly volatile.
2 Why can't OPEC completely control the world price of oil?

Markets for second-hand cars

A car is a consumer durable good, delivering a constant stream of consumer services throughout its life. Provided it is properly looked after and escapes a serious crash, a new car typically lasts about 15 years. However, unlike a house, which is the ultimate consumer durable good (with a much longer life than that of a person living in it), almost all new cars lose value or depreciate as soon as they have been driven off the showroom forecourt. This means that the prices of most second-hand cars fall throughout their lives.

At any time, the prices of second-hand cars depend on whether there has been excess supply or excess demand in the market for used cars. When the economy booms, demand for new cars is high, and a constant supply of second-hand cars is released onto the market as new-car owners replace their cars. In these conditions, excess supply may mean that second-hand car prices fall, relative to the prices of new cars. However, this is not inevitable, as a strong economy may also boost the demand for second-hand cars.

Likewise, in a recessionary period, new-car owners may hang on to their cars for longer before they sell them — which decreases the supply of second-hand cars — and/or the demand for second-hand cars may fall because people cannot afford them. There are all sorts of possibilities. Other factors to consider are: is a new car a 'superior good' and a second-hand car an 'inferior good'?; and are some second-hand cars 'superior goods' whereas others are 'inferior goods'?

Akerlof's 'lemons'

Another factor affecting the price of second-hand cars was first identified by George Akerlof, who was awarded the Nobel prize in economics for his research. Akerlof assumed that some second-hand cars have significant defects (he called these cars 'lemons'), whereas others are of high quality. If buyers could tell which cars are lemons and which are not, there would be two separate markets: a market for lemons and a market for high-quality cars. But there is often asymmetric information: buyers cannot tell which cars are lemons, but, of course, sellers know.

Fearing they will be buying lemons, car buyers in general offer lower prices than they would if they were certain they were buying high-quality cars. This lower price for all used cars discourages sellers of high-quality cars. Although some would be willing to sell their cars at the price that buyers of high-quality used cars would be willing to pay, they are not willing to sell at the lower price that reflects the risk that the buyer may end up with a lemon. Thus, exchanges that could benefit both buyer and seller fail to take place and market failure results. (See Chapter 5.)

49

CASE STUDY 2.8

Second-hand car prices in the recession

In 2009, in the depth of the recession which hit the UK economy, a Rolls-Royce limousine was auctioned in London. The car was only 2 years old, but it looked as good as a new model costing £270,000. Within a minute, it was sold for £140,000. All the cars that followed, including Mercedes and BMWs, also suffered the indignity of a collapse in used-car prices.

In 2009, sales of new luxury cars were significantly lower than in the boom years before the recession. Car manufacturers responded by closing factories, at least for short periods. The lack of readily available finance reduced the demand for luxury cars. Many car buyers traded down to purchase less expensive cars, or kept the cars they already owned. Some manufacturers offered discounts and incentives averaging more than £15,000 a car to attract buyers. With such big discounts available on new models, people expect to pay even less for second-hand ones. Second-hand prices did not improve until the surplus of new and used cars had been eliminated.

Follow-up questions

1 How might recovery from recession affect new car prices?

2 'A new Rolls-Royce car is a superior good, but a 15-year-old Ford car is an inferior good.' Explain this statement.

The housing market

The long-run rise in prices

There has been a long-run trend for house prices to rise in the UK, ignoring short-run booms and busts. Both the demand for and the supply of housing have increased (or shifted rightward), but unlike the case of agricultural goods described earlier, demand has increased faster.

There has been a long-run trend for house prices to rise in the UK

Supply has increased because the quantity of new houses added to the housing stock each year exceeds the number demolished or converted to other uses. The supply of housing for owner-occupancy increases fastest when landlords withdraw from the rental market and sell their properties. If, as in recent years, housing-market conditions are more favourable for private letting, the reverse happens. The main causes of the long-run rightward shift of demand have been: population growth, growth in the number of households, and real income growth. Also, until quite recently, people were switching to owner-occupancy, which they treat as a superior good (income elasticity of demand > +1) and away from the perceived inferior substitute, rented accommodation. This has now reversed and, as Figure 2.24 shows, rented accommodation has grown and owner-occupancy has fallen.

The level of activity in the national economy also affects the construction industry. Since the 1970s, the house-building industry has become dominated by a small number of 'volume' builders. They buy land and hold it in a 'land bank'. Houses are only built when the company expects to sell them during or shortly after construction. The process tends to be speculative — very few houses are built to meet customers' specific requirements. The construction process itself is sometimes contracted out to smaller builders, who depend on hired equipment and employ casual labour. In recessions or economic slow-downs, there is often a high level of bankruptcy among smaller subcontractors, and many building workers become unemployed.

Short-run fluctuations in prices

Short-run price fluctuations are explained primarily by the short-run demand curve shifting rightward or leftward along the near-vertical short-run supply curve. Figure 2.25 shows the demand curve increasing, shifting rightwards from D_1 to D_2, causing house prices to rise from P_1 to P_2, with a smaller resulting expansion of supply.

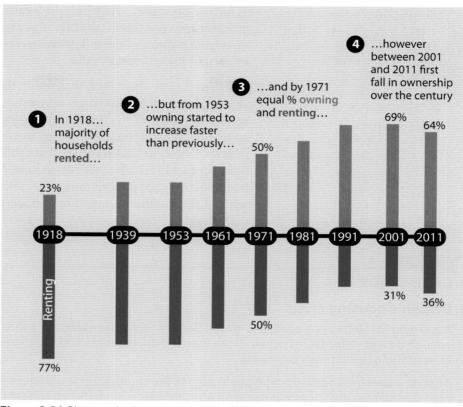

Figure 2.24 Changes in the proportion of UK homes owned or rented by their occupiers, 1918–2011

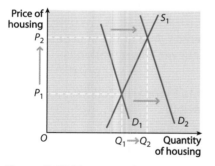

Figure 2.25 Short-run changes in the demand for housing

In the short run, as Figure 2.25 shows, the supply of housing is price inelastic or unresponsive to price changes. The factors that explain this include: the general shortage of land, the effect of planning controls that make it difficult to convert land from other uses, and the length of time taken to build a new house.

The demand for housing

As with all consumer goods, people demand housing for the utility or welfare derived from the consumer services that it provides. All houses provide basic shelter, but they each have a particular combination of other consumer attributes, such as location, view, garden, car parking and rooms suitable for work, leisure and hospitality.

The demand for housing is also affected by a number of special factors. Housing is a consumer durable good, delivering a stream of consumer services over a long period, often a century or more. Unlike most durable goods, such as cars and television sets, which lose value during their lives, most houses — or certainly the land on which they are built — gain value. This means that the demand for housing is determined not only by people's need for shelter, but by the fact it is a form of investment. Housing is an attractive wealth asset — indeed, the main wealth asset owned by many UK residents.

As a result, far from reducing demand, a rise in house prices can trigger a speculative bubble in the housing market. Rising prices drive up demand, causing a further rise in prices, with the process continuing until the bubble bursts. Owner-occupiers already on the 'housing ladder' have a vested interest in further price rises. They become wealthier because the value of their property rises but the value of their mortgages stays the same. They benefit from capital gains — the difference between the price paid for the house and its current higher market value.

In this situation, there is an increase in the number of first-time buyers, as young people, desperate to get on the housing ladder, try to buy houses before they become unaffordable. Existing owner-occupiers put their houses on the market and 'trade up' to buy larger properties or houses in more desirable locations. Both these events shift the demand curve for housing rightward and fuel a further rise in house prices. During housing-market booms activity soars, with increases in both the number of people trying to sell and the number trying to buy property. However, demand rises faster than supply.

CASE STUDY 2.9

Britain's housing crisis

According to the housing pressure-group Shelter, Britain is suffering a massive housing crisis. There aren't enough decent, affordable homes. More than 2 million people find their rent or mortgage a constant struggle or are falling behind with payments.

Against a background of mounting debt across the country, huge numbers of people are having their homes repossessed because they cannot keep up with their mortgage repayments. Second-home ownership is pricing local people out of rural areas. Over 1.7 million households are waiting for social housing.

Some homeless households — many with dependent children — wait for years in temporary accommodation. Families renting privately on low incomes have to put up with poor living conditions and little security.

The number of new households is increasing faster than the number of house builds. And at the sharpest end, many hundreds of people sleep rough on the streets every night. Shelter believes this situation is unacceptable.

Around 7.4 million homes in England fail to meet the government's Decent Homes Standard. Bad housing is closely linked to many wider social problems, such as crime and antisocial behaviour.

Shelter believes that the only solution to the current housing crisis is to build more homes. It claims that the government's proposal to build 150,000 affordable homes over 4 years is less than a third of what is needed.

Follow-up questions

1 Describe **three** causes of homelessness in the UK.
2 Evaluate **three** policies the government could use to reduce or eliminate the problem of homelessness in the UK.

Healthcare markets

Civitas, which is a pro-free market 'think-tank' with an interest in how healthcare should be provided, has looked at the advantages and disadvantages of markets for delivering healthcare services. Civitas's arguments start from the proposition that healthcare, due to its 'high upfront costs and centrality to humankind', is 'different' from most goods and services provided by markets. As a result, a popular view, particularly in the UK, is that healthcare is best provided outside the market.

Two arguments for providing healthcare through the market

In a market environment people can demonstrate their preferences for different goods and services by exercising choice. This generates precise information about their preferences, so providers are motivated to supply the services people want, improving **allocative efficiency**. Markets also create the incentive for providers to be as efficient as possible in order to undercut competitors. This improves **productive efficiency**.

In markets there is always the opportunity for people to come forward with new ideas to meet a need: a powerful incentive to experiment, innovate and focus squarely on service users.

Two arguments against providing healthcare through the market

Many economists argue that healthcare is a **merit good** (although, as Chapter 5 explains, not all economists agree). Assuming healthcare is a merit good, one person's 'consumption' of healthcare may well have beneficial effects for others — particularly where infectious diseases are concerned. Yet if, as markets typically assume, individuals and providers only have regard for themselves, there is likely to be both under-consumption and under-provision of services such as vaccinations.

Because healthcare costs are often high, most choose not to pay, or cannot afford to pay, for expensive services such as operations. Instead, they rely on third-party insurers to pay for operations. If people know more about their need for expensive healthcare services than insurers, insurers will want to raise premiums to all in order to guard against the costs of having unhealthy people on their books. High premiums mean that healthy people may choose not to buy insurance. And if people do choose to buy health insurance, they may choose to live less-healthy lifestyles because they no longer bear the full consequences of their decisions.

KEY TERMS

allocative efficiency occurs when the available economic resources are used to produce the combination of goods and services that best matches people's tastes and preferences.

productive efficiency for the economy as a whole occurs when it is impossible to produce more of one good without producing less of another. For a firm it occurs when the average total cost of production is minimised.

KEY TERM

merit good a good which when consumed leads to benefits which other people enjoy, or a good for which the long-term benefit of consumption exceeds the short-term benefit enjoyed by the person consuming the merit good. Whether a good should be regarded as a merit good, depends on the value judgements being made.

STUDY TIP

Make sure you understand fully the meaning of a merit good and are aware of examples of products that are generally agreed to be merit goods, e.g. healthcare and education.

TEST YOURSELF 2.11

Suppose that vaccination against measles is only available at a market price of £50. Why may this lead to an undesirable economic outcome?

SUMMARY

- Demand means effective demand, based on ability as well as willingness to pay.
- For most goods, demand curves slope downward.
- A market supply curve shows how much of a good all the firms in the market intend to supply at different prices.
- Supply curves usually slope upward because higher prices lead to higher profits, encouraging existing firms to produce more and attracting new firms into the market.
- The conditions of demand fix the position of the demand curve and the conditions of supply fix the position of the supply curve.

- If any of the conditions of demand (or supply) change, the demand curve (or the supply curve) shifts to a new position.
- Movements along a demand curve or a supply curve must not be confused with a shift in the position of the curve.
- There are four important elasticities: price, income and cross-elasticity of demand, and also price elasticity of supply.
- The slope of a demand or supply curve is not the same as price elasticity of demand or supply.
- It is important to understand the determinants of all the elasticities you need to know.
- Market equilibrium occurs at the price at which the demand curve crosses the supply curve, i.e. where demand equals supply.
- Disequilibrium occurs when there is either excess demand or excess supply in the market.
- In a competitive market, changes in the market price eliminate excess demand or excess supply; this is how the price mechanism helps to allocate scare resources.
- You must practise applying market theory to different real-world markets.

Questions

1 Explain the significance of the ceteris paribus assumption in microeconomic theory.

2 Evaluate the view that a fall in a good's price will inevitably lead to more demand for the good.

3 Explain how price elasticity of demand affects total consumer spending when a good's price changes.

4 Explain three reasons why a supply curve may shift rightward or downward.

5 Explain how the price elasticity of supply of new housing has affected UK house prices in recent decades.

6 With the help of an appropriate diagram, explain the effect of a government subsidy granted to producers of the good on the good's price.

3 Production, costs and revenue

Production was first mentioned in Chapter 1 — in the context of the role of production in trying to solve the fundamental economic problem of scarcity. This chapter begins by reminding you of the meaning of production, before introducing and explaining a number of production-related concepts. These are productivity, productive efficiency, the division of labour and specialisation. For specialisation and the division of labour to be worthwhile, the exchange of goods and services must be possible. Exchange can take place through barter, but in modern economies money is almost always used as the medium which allows exchange to take place. We complete the chapter by explaining the main features of a firm's average cost curve and then use average cost curves to illustrate economies and diseconomies of scale.

LEARNING OBJECTIVES
This chapter will:

- remind you of the meaning of production
- distinguish between production and productivity
- explain the various forms of productivity, including labour productivity
- introduce the concepts of specialisation and the division of labour
- explain why successful specialisation and division of labour require exchange to take place
- introduce average cost curves
- apply the concept of productive efficiency to average cost curves
- with the use of cost curves, explain economies and diseconomies of scale
- introduce and briefly explain the revenue curves facing a firm

3.1 Production and productivity

The meaning of production

Section 1.2 of Chapter 1 briefly explained the meaning of **production** and illustrated the basic nature of production in Figure 1.2. The chapter also mentioned the roles of factors of production such as labour and capital in the production process. Before proceeding any further with this chapter, refer back to Chapter 1 and read again what the chapter has to say on production. The key point to remember is that production converts inputs, or the services of factors of production such as capital and labour, into final outputs of goods and services.

> **KEY TERMS**
>
> **production** converts inputs or factor services into outputs of goods and services.
>
> **short-run production** occurs when a firm adds variable factors of production to fixed factors of production.
>
> **long-run production** occurs when a firm changes the *scale* of all the factors of production.

Productivity

Students often confuse productivity with production. While closely related, they do not have the same meaning. For most purposes, productivity usually means labour productivity, which is output per worker per period of time, e.g. per week. However, capital productivity and land productivity can also be measured, as can entrepreneurial productivity. In reality, of course, all the employed factors of production contribute to both a firm's current level of output and any increase in the level of output.

> **KEY TERMS**
>
> **productivity** output per unit of input.
>
> **labour productivity** output per worker.
>
> **capital productivity** output per unit of capital.

> **KEY TERM**
>
> **productivity gap** the difference between labour productivity in the UK and in other developed economies.

> **STUDY TIP**
>
> Productivity is a key concept in A-level economics. You must know the meaning of labour productivity, and also be aware of the meanings of other types of productivity. Be aware also of the UK's productivity gap, which is the difference in productivity levels between the UK and competitor countries.

Labour productivity or output per worker is extremely significant in manufacturing industries, such as the car industry. In the 1990s and early 2000s, the Rover Car Group (which has since been bankrupted) struggled to survive in the UK car industry. Rover was unable to compete with Japanese car makers such as Nissan and Toyota. Nissan had invested in a state-of-the-art factory near Sunderland. Labour productivity in the ramshackle Rover factories amounted to only 33 cars per worker per year. By contrast, Nissan produced 98 cars per worker in its brand new factory. Given these figures, it is not surprising that the Rover Group was forced to stop production.

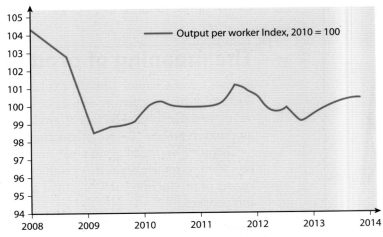

Figure 3.1 Output per worker index, UK, 2008–14

Source: ONS

> **STUDY TIP**
>
> Don't confuse productivity gaps with output gaps, which are explained in Chapter 8.

QUANTITATIVE SKILLS 3.1

Worked example: interpreting data presented in index number form

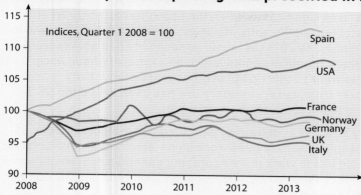

Figure 3.2 Changes in labour productivity per head across countries, 2008–13

Calculate the percentage change in labour productivity in the USA over the period shown in the data.

Students often confuse data presented in index number form (as in Figure 3.2) with data presented in percentages. The confusion may arise because percentages add up to 100, and the number 100 is the number generally used for the base year in an economic index. (Note: the plural of *index* is the word *indices*.) Between early 2008 and late 2013, US labour productivity changes by approximately 7.5 index points from the base index in Quarter 1 2008 of 100 to approximately 107.5. This is the one situation (when comparing with an index number of 100) that a percentage change is the same as the change in index points. The data changes by 7.5 index points and also by 7.5 percentage points. Now calculate the percentage change in US labour productivity between late 2008 and the end of the data period in 2013. Because the starting point for your calculation is approximately 98 index points (and not the Quarter 1 index of 100), you will find that the percentage change is not the same as the change in index points. If we calculate the percentage change in US labour productivity between the end of the last quarter of 2008 and the end of the last quarter of 2013, the starting point for the calculation is approximately 95 index points (and not the Quarter 1 index of 100). The change in index points over this period is approximately 12.5 index points. This means that the percentage change is an increase of approximately 13.2% (12.5 divided by 95 multiplied by 100).

SYNOPTIC LINK

Chapter 7 explains how index numbers are used as macroeconomic indicators, explaining how index numbers are calculated and interpreted, and the significance of the base year in an economic index.

TEST YOURSELF 3.1

Table 3.1

Number of workers	0	1	2	3	4	5	6	7	8	9
Total output of cars	0	1	4	9	16	25	32	35	36	34
Average output of cars										

The data in Table 3.1 shows the number of hand-built cars produced by a small specialist car manufacturer in a month. Calculate the average output of cars per worker at each size of labour force and use your figures to complete the bottom row of the table. Then plot the figures for the total and average output of cars on a graph.

The UK's productivity puzzle

In a recession, labour productivity falls, but it then rises significantly when the economy recovers. When the UK entered recession in 2008, labour productivity fell significantly. However, as Figure 3.2 shows, and in contrast to the experience of many developed economies, by 2014 UK labour productivity had not recovered to its pre-recessionary 2008 level, with British workers producing about a fifth less for every hour worked than other leading nations. In some years, there was weak recovery, but in other years productivity continued to fall. The failure of productivity to recover from its recessionary low has been called the UK's 'productivity puzzle'. Among the factors contributing to the productivity puzzle are:

- The UK's 'flexible' labour markets have been very effective in delivering part-time and temporary work, at low cost to employers. In 2014, up to 5.5 million people may have been working on 'zero hours' contracts. At the same time, underemployment (those who would like to work more hours, but cannot) has been at record levels. When faced with collapsing markets in the recession, employers — rather than reducing the number of people in work — cut the wages and hours of those working.
- This then led to labour 'hoarding' — keeping workers in employment even though they are in effect producing little or no output. Employers have been reluctant to fire skilled workers, believing that they will be difficult to re-recruit at a later point in the economic upturn. A 2012 survey of private-sector employers by the Chartered Institute of Personnel Development reported that close to a third of businesses had more staff than they needed to fulfil current orders. Most said they were anxious to retain their skills base. From an employer's point of view, it makes sense to let some workers stand idle if this cuts hiring and firing costs and avoids delays in training new workers when demand recovers.
- Following a recession, it takes time for firms facing declining demand to shed labour. It also takes time for new, fast-growing sectors to mop up the labour. During this period of flux, too many workers are concentrated in declining industries, with the result that economic output is less than it could be.
- Related to this, low labour productivity has been blamed on so-called 'zombie' firms. A 'zombie' firm is an under-performing company, with low labour productivity, which survives because it generates just enough sales revenue to enable interest to be paid on its debts. After previous recessions, banks and other creditors refused to rescue such poorly performing companies, which were allowed to go to the wall. However, this did not happen when the 2008 recession ended in 2009. Very low interest rates or easy credit, accompanied by government exhortations to banks to rescue struggling companies, meant that zombie firms survived. (In 2014, however, the Bank of England dismissed the view that zombie firms provided a significant explanation of low labour productivity.)

What are the consequences of the productivity puzzle? One possibility is that even greater sacrifices may be demanded from those in work, and from those looking for work. If productivity is not improving, reduced labour costs per hour could be achieved by cutting hourly pay. In a 'race to the bottom', UK workers would be pushed to match the lowest competing wages elsewhere in the world. Although the National Minimum Wage is meant to prevent this happening, there is plenty of evidence that rogue employers flout the law. A better possibility would be to boost productivity. This would require increased investment in newer, more efficient equipment and improved infrastructure. Investment spending on research and development (R&D) might lead to gains over time. However, none of this may happen. In 2014, investment in the UK economy was much lower than it had been in 2008.

Follow-up questions

1 What is a recession?
2 What is meant by a 'flexible' labour market?

SYNOPTIC LINK
You will learn about recessions when reading the section of Chapter 7 on measuring economic performance, in the context of the economic cycle and cyclical unemployment.

3.2 Specialisation, division of labour and exchange

Over 200 years ago, the great classical economist, Adam Smith, first explained how, within a single production unit or firm (he took the example of a pin factory), output could be increased if workers specialise at different tasks in the manufacturing process.

Smith had established one of the most fundamental of all economic principles: the benefits of **specialisation** or the **division of labour**. According to Adam Smith, there are three main reasons why a factory's total output can be increased if workers perform specialist tasks rather than if each worker attempts all the tasks himself or herself. These are as follows:

- A worker will not need to switch between tasks, so time will be saved.
- More and better machinery or capital can be employed. (Employing 'more of the same' capital is called capital widening, while investing in 'state-of-the-art' new technology is called capital deepening).
- The 'practice makes perfect' argument that workers become more efficient or productive at the task they are doing, the greater the time spent on the specialist task, although this advantage can easily become a disadvantage if it involves 'de-skilling' and the creation of boredom and alienation among workers.

Trade and exchange

For specialisation to be economically worthwhile for those taking part in the division of labour, a system of **trade** and **exchange** is necessary. This is because workers who completely specialise can't enjoy a reasonable standard of living if forced to consume only what they produce. The obvious solution is to produce more than what the worker actually needs, and then to trade the surplus for that produced by others.

Blacksmiths might exchange services with farmers

Until quite recently, people living in rural communities within the UK could specialise and then trade whatever they produced through barter. Thus a farmer might harvest wheat, part of which was then exchanged for services provided by local grain millers and village blacksmiths.

But successful barter requires a 'double coincidence of wants'. Not only must the farmer require the services of the blacksmith; the blacksmith must want the wheat produced by the farmer, and a rate of exchange must be agreed for the two products. As this example suggests, it is reasonably easy to achieve the double coincidence of wants in a small community where people live close to each other and where only a few goods and services are produced and exchanged. However, in modern economies in which a vast number of goods are produced, reliance on barter holds back the growth of the economy. In such economies, barter is an extremely inefficient method of exchange.

These days, when we buy or sell a good or a service, we almost always use money. For example, we finance the transaction either with cash or with a debit card or cheque drawn on a bank or building society deposit. Using money is much more efficient than bartering, as there is no need for a double coincidence of wants. Suppose I want to buy a television set and that I also have a second-hand car I wish to sell. Assuming you wish to buy a second-hand car and have an old TV set you want to get rid of, if we barter the goods, you must want my car and I must want your TV set. We must also agree that the two goods have the same value. But if we use money rather than barter, you pay for my car with money, which I can then use to buy a TV set or whatever I want from somebody else. I could also save the money rather than spend it. Used in this way, money enables the economy to achieve much greater specialisation and division of labour than is possible with barter.

STUDY TIP

Make sure you understand money's function as a medium of exchange or means of payment.

KEY TERMS

trade the buying and selling of goods and services.

exchange to give something in return for something else received. Money is a medium of exchange.

CASE STUDY 3.2

Adam Smith's pin factory

Adam Smith was an eighteenth-century Scottish philosophy professor, and later customs commissioner, who is often said to be the founder of modern economics. In his book *An Inquiry into the Nature and Causes of the Wealth of Nations*, which was published in 1776, Adam Smith used the example of a local pin factory to explain how the division of labour among workers greatly increases their ability to produce. Here is a slightly abridged version of what Adam Smith wrote:

A workman not educated in the business of pin making could scarce, perhaps, with his utmost industry, make one pin in a day, and certainly could not make twenty. But in the way in which this business is now carried on, one man draws out the wire, another straights it, a third cuts it, a fourth points it, a fifth grinds it at the top for receiving the pin head. The business of making a pin is divided into about eighteen distinct operations. Ten persons could make among them upwards of forty-eight thousand pins in a day. Each person, therefore, making a tenth part of forty-eight thousand pins, might be considered as making four thousand eight hundred pins in a day. But if they had all worked separately and independently, and without any of them having been educated to this peculiar business, they certainly could not each of them have made twenty, perhaps not one pin in a day.

This great increase in the quantity of work is a consequence of the division of labour. There are three different aspects of this: first, the increase of dexterity in every particular workman; secondly, the saving of the time which is commonly lost in passing from one species of work to another; and lastly, the invention of a great number of machines which enable one man to do the work of many.

Follow-up questions

1 What is meant by the division of labour?
2 What effects does the division of labour have on production and costs?

> **KEY TERM**
> The **short run** the time period in which at least one factor of production is fixed and cannot be varied.

3.3 Costs of production

Economics students often confuse production and costs. Production, as previously explained, simply converts inputs into outputs, without considering either the money cost of using inputs such as capital and labour, or the money or revenue received from selling the outputs produced. This section and the next section focus on costs; section 3.5 looks at certain aspects of the sales revenue that firms earn.

The difference between the short run and the long run

Cost curves, which measure the costs that firms have to pay to hire the inputs or factors of production needed to produce output, reflect the period of time being considered. Short-run cost curves differ from long-run cost curves.

In microeconomic theory, the **short run** is defined as the time period in which at least one of the factors of production is fixed and cannot be varied. This means that the only way in which a firm can produce more in the short run is by adding more variable factors to the fixed factors of production.

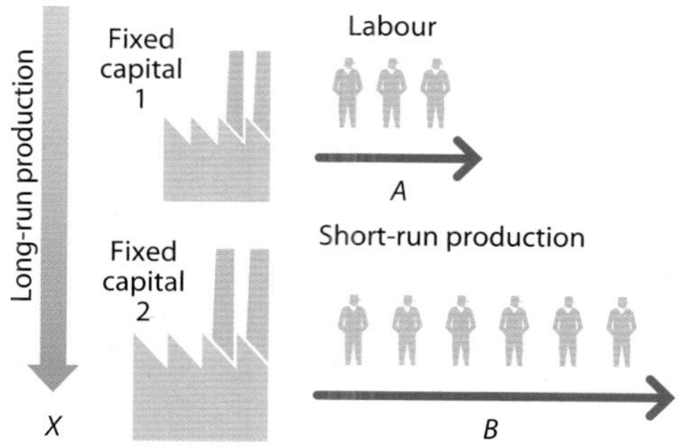

Figure 3.3 Short-run and long-run production

In Figure 3.3, the horizontal arrows labelled *A* and *B* show short-run production taking place.

By contrast, the movement along the vertical arrow *X* depicts the **long run**, defined as the time period in which the *scale* of *all* the factors of production can be changed.

> **KEY TERM**
> The **long run** the time period in which no factors of production are fixed and in which all the factors of production can be varied.

> **STUDY TIP**
> Make sure you know the differences between the short run and the long run and between fixed and variable costs.

The difference between fixed and variable costs

In the *short run*, when the inputs divide into fixed and variable factors of production, the costs of production can likewise be divided into fixed and variable costs. **Fixed costs** are the costs a firm incurs when hiring or paying for the fixed factors of production. In the short run, capital is usually assumed to be a fixed factor of production, giving rise to costs which are unchanged in the short run. These include the cost of maintaining a firm's buildings, as well as the initial cost of acquiring buildings such as factory space and offices. By contrast, as the name implies, **variable costs** change as the level of output changes. The costs of hiring labour and buying raw materials are usually regarded as variable costs of production. It is worth remembering that in the *long run*, all costs are variable because the long run is defined as the time period in which all the factors of production can be changed.

> **KEY TERMS**
> **fixed cost** cost of production which, in the short run, does not change with output.
>
> **variable cost** cost of production which changes with the amount that is produced, even in the short run.

The difference between average and total costs

When a firm increases its output, the variable and hence the **total cost** of production increases. At any level of output, the **average cost** (or unit cost) is calculated by dividing the firm's total cost of production by the size of output produced. Average costs for each level of output can be shown on an average total cost curve, such as the curve in Figure 3.4.

In Figure 3.4, the firm's average costs of production initially fall as the size of output increases. For example, when the firm produces output Q_1, average cost per unit of output is quite high at C_1; but when the firm increases output to Q_2, average cost per unit falls to C_2. However, for higher levels of output, average costs usually rise, for example to C_3 when output increases to Q_3.

In the short-run, average total cost curves, such as the curve in Figure 3.4, are assumed to be U-shaped, showing unit costs falling and then rising as the level of output increases. Point X, located above level of output Q_2, is the *average cost minimising level of output* and also the productively efficient level of output.

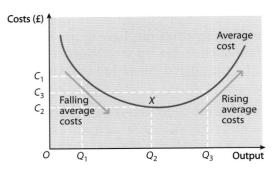

Figure 3.4 A firm's average total cost curve

Average costs of production can be divided into average fixed costs (*AFC*) and average variable costs (*AVC*):

$$ATC = AFC + AVC$$

The productively efficient level of output

In Chapter 1, we defined productive efficiency for the whole economy in terms of output being maximised from available inputs, and as a situation in which it is impossible to produce more of one good without giving up production of at least one other good. However, at the micro level, the productively efficient level of output for a single firm is the average cost minimising level of output.

The average fixed cost curve

Fixed costs of production are overheads, such as the rent on land and the maintenance costs of buildings, which a firm must pay in the short run. Suppose, for example, that a car manufacturing company incurs overheads of £1 million a year from an assembly plant it operates. If the plant only managed to produce one automobile a year, *AFC* per car would be £1 million — the single car would bear all the overheads. But if the company were to increase production, average fixed costs would fall to £500,000 when two cars are produced, £333,333 when three cars are produced and so on. The firm's average fixed costs per unit of output fall as output increases, since overheads are spread over a larger output. *AFC* curves *always* slope downwards to the right, as shown in Figure 3.5, with average fixed costs approaching zero at very high levels of output, but never quite equalling zero.

Figure 3.5 A downward-sloping *AFC* curve

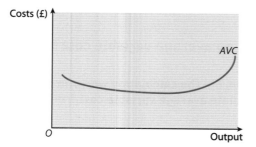

Figure 3.6 A firm's average variable cost curve

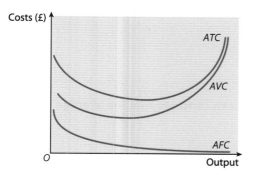

Figure 3.7 Adding the *AVC* curve to the *AFC* curve to form the *ATC* curve

The average variable cost curve

Variable costs are the costs that the firm incurs when it hires variable factors of production such as labour and raw materials. Assuming that labour is the only variable factor of production, variable costs are simply wage costs. Figure 3.6 has been drawn under the assumption that when a firm first employs workers, labour becomes more productive as more workers are employed. However, labour eventually becomes less productive as employment increases. Given these assumptions, the *AVC* curve is U-shaped, showing average variable costs of production first falling, and then rising, as output increases.

The average total cost curve

The average total cost (*ATC*) curve shown in Figure 3.7 is obtained by adding together at each level of output the *AFC* and *AVC* curves, respectively shown in Figures 3.5 and 3.6.

In summary:

average total cost = average fixed cost + average variable cost

or:

$$ATC = AFC + AVC$$

and:

average total cost = $\dfrac{\text{total cost}}{\text{output}}$ or: $ATC = \dfrac{TC}{Q}$

> ### STUDY TIP
> It is important to know that a firm's short-run average cost curve is assumed to be U-shaped.

QUANTITATIVE SKILLS 3.2

Objective test question: calculating average and total costs from given data

You should be able to calculate average and total costs from given data. This example takes the form of an objective test question in which the data is presented on a graph showing a firm's average variable costs (*AVC*) and average fixed costs (*AFC*) of production.

The total cost of producing four units is:

A £12   B £24
C £48   D £72

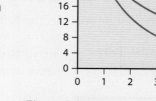

Figure 3.8

To arrive at the correct answer, which is D, two calculations are required. The first calculation involves adding *AVC* (£12) to *AFC* (£6) at an output of four units to arrive at average total cost (*ATC*), which is £18. The second calculation is multiplying *ATC* (£18) by output (4) to arrive at total cost, which is £72.

> ### STUDY TIP
> Make sure you practise calculating and plotting average and total costs from given data.

Objective test question: calculating average variable cost from given information on total cost

This is a similar objective test question, but the calculation works in the opposite direction, asking you to calculate average variable cost from given information on total cost.

Table 3.2 shows total cost at various outputs.

Table 3.2

Output	Total cost (£)
0	100
10	115
20	140
30	175
40	220

From the information in the table, we can conclude that the average variable cost at an output of 20 is:

A £2

B £7

C £14

D £120

Only the third and first rows of data are used in the calculation — the data in the other rows is irrelevant or 'background noise'. In row 3, we divide total cost (£140) by the output of 20, arriving at an average total cost of £7. The information in Row 1 tells us that total fixed cost is £100. This means average fixed cost is £5 when 20 units of output are produced. Finally, since $AVC = ATC - AFC$, average variable cost is £7 – £5, which is £2. A is therefore the correct answer.

Long-run average cost curves

In the long run, as already explained, a firm can change the scale of all its factors of production, moving from one size of plant to another. Figure 3.9 illustrates a U-shaped **long-run average cost** (*LRAC*) curve, showing a firm's average costs first falling and then rising as the firm moves to a larger scale of operation. On first sight, the *LRAC* curve appears identical to the short-run *ATC* curve in Figures 3.4 and 3.7. However, the reasons for the U shape of each curve are different. The shape of the *short-run ATC* curve is explained by the assumption that labour becomes more productive as it is added to fixed capital, before eventually becoming less productive. By contrast, the shape of the *long-run average cost* curve is explained by two long-run concepts which don't operate in the short run. These are economies and diseconomies of scale, which are explained in section 3.4.

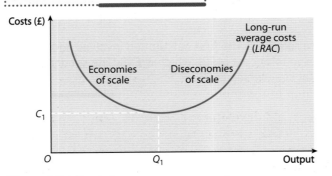

Figure 3.9 A firm's long-run average cost curve

3.4 Economies and diseconomies of scale

As a firm grows in size by investing in new plant or buildings, it can benefit from economies of scale. However, beyond a certain size, the firm may eventually suffer from diseconomies of scale. **Economies of scale** are defined as *falling* long-run average costs of production that result from an increase in the size or scale of the firm. Likewise, **diseconomies of scale** occur when an increase in output leads to *rising* long-run average costs of production.

EXTENSION MATERIAL

The 'L'-shaped *LRAC* curve

Figure 3.9, which shows a 'symmetrical' U-shaped *LRAC* curve, has been drawn assuming that economies of scale are followed symmetrically by diseconomies of scale. However, the shape of the *LRAC* curve may differ. Some industries, including many personal services such as hairdressing, exhibit economies of small-scale production. In such industries, diseconomies of scale may set in at a relatively small size of production plant or fixed capacity, resulting in a *LRAC* curve which, while U-shaped is skewed to the left.

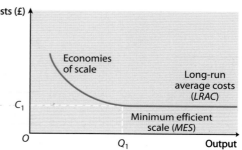

Another possibility is the L-shaped *LRAC* curve illustrated in Figure 3.10. This curve results from the assumption that there are substantial economies of scale, which eventually give way, not to diseconomies of scale, but to a 'flattening out' of long-run average costs. The size of firm at which this occurs is known as minimum efficient scale (MES). There is evidence of this type of *LRAC* curve in many manufacturing industries involving large-scale production.

Figure 3.10 An L-shaped *LRAC* curve, and minimum efficient scale (MES)

Reasons for economies of scale

Firms can benefit from various types or forms of economy of scale as they grow in size. These include technical economies of scale, managerial economies of scale, marketing economies of scale, financial or capital-raising economies of scale, risk-bearing economies of scale, and economies of scope.

Technical economies of scale

Technical economies of scale are generated through changes to the 'productive process' as the scale of production and the level of output increase.

The main types of **technical economy of scale** are listed below.

- **Indivisibilities** Many types of plant or machinery are indivisible in the sense that there is a certain minimum size below which they cannot efficiently operate.
- **The spreading of research and development costs** With large plants, research and development (R&D) costs can be spread over a much longer production run, reducing unit costs in the long run.
- **Volume economies** With many types of capital equipment, costs increase less rapidly than capacity. When a storage tank or boiler is doubled in dimension, its storage capacity increases eightfold. Volume economies are

important in industries such as transport, storage and warehousing, as well as in metal and chemical industries where an increase in the scale of plant provides scope for the conservation of heat and energy.

- **Economies of massed resources** The operation of a number of identical machines in a large plant means that proportionately fewer spare parts need to be kept than when fewer machines are involved.
- **Economies of vertically linked processes** Much manufacturing activity involves a large number of vertically related tasks and processes, from the initial purchase of raw materials, components and energy through to the completion and sale of the finished product. The linking of processes in a single plant can lead to a saving in time, transport costs and energy.

Managerial economies of scale

The larger the scale of a firm, the greater is its ability to benefit from specialisation and the division of labour within management as well as within the ordinary labour force. A large firm can benefit from a functional division of labour, namely the employment of specialist managers: for example, in the fields of production, personnel and sales. Detail can be delegated to junior managers and supervisors.

Marketing economies of scale

Marketing economies of scale are of two types: bulk-buying and bulk-marketing economies. Large firms may be able to use their market power both to buy supplies at lower prices and also to market their products on better terms negotiated with wholesalers and retailers.

Financial or capital-raising economies of scale

Financial or capital-raising economies of scale are similar to the bulk-buying economies just described, except that they relate to the 'bulk-buying' or bulk-borrowing of funds required to finance the business's expansion. Large firms can often borrow from banks and other financial institutions at a lower rate of interest and on better terms than those available to small firms.

Risk-bearing economies of scale

Large firms are usually less exposed to risk than small firms, because risks can be grouped and spread. Large firms can spread risks by diversifying their output, their markets, their sources of supply and finance and the processes by which they manufacture their output. Such economies of diversification or risk bearing can make the firm less vulnerable to sudden changes in demand or conditions of supply that might severely harm a smaller less-diversified business.

Economies of scope

Economies of scope are factors that make it cheaper to produce a range of products together than to produce each one of them on its own. An example is businesses sharing centralised functions, such as finance or marketing.

Reasons for diseconomies of scale

Firms can also suffer from various types or forms of diseconomy of scale as they grow in size. These include managerial diseconomies of scale, communication failure, and motivational diseconomies of scale.

Managerial diseconomies of scale

As a firm grows in size, administration of the firm becomes more difficult. Delegation of some of the managerial functions to people lower in the organisation may mean that personnel who lack appropriate experience make bad decisions. This may increase average costs of production.

Communication failure

Communication failure also contributes to managerial diseconomies of scale. In a large organisation there may be too many layers of management between the top managers and ordinary production workers, and staff can feel remote and unappreciated. When staff productivity begins to fall, unit costs begin to rise. As a result, the problems facing the business are not effectively addressed.

Motivational diseconomies of scale ☑

With large firms, it is often difficult to satisfy and motivate workers. Over-specialisation may lead to de-skilling and to a situation in which workers perform repetitive boring tasks and have little incentive to use personal initiative in ways which help their employer.

Internal and external economies and diseconomies of scale

KEY TERMS

internal economy of scale cost saving resulting from the growth of the firm itself.

external economy of scale cost saving resulting from the growth of the industry or market of which the firm is a part.

All the economies and diseconomies of scale so far described are examples of **internal economies and diseconomies of scale**. These occur when a firm grows and changes its scale and size.

By contrast, **external economies of scale** occur when a firm's average or unit costs of production fall, not because of the growth of the firm itself, but because of the growth of the industry or market of which the firm is a part. Very often, external economies of scale are produced by cluster effects, which occur when a lot of firms in the same industry are located close to each other, providing markets, sources of supply and a pool of trained labour for each other.

External *diseconomies* of scale occur in a similar way, with the growth of the whole market raising the average costs of all the firms in the industry. As with external economies of scale, external diseconomies can arise from cluster effects. When a large number of similar firms locate close to each other, not only do they create benefits which aid all the firms in the cluster; they may also get in each other's way. Competition for labour among the firms may raise local wages, which while being good for workers, increases the unit wage costs of their employers. There may also be an increase in local and regional traffic congestion, which lengthens delivery times and raises delivery costs both for firms and for their customers.

STUDY TIP
You should understand the difference between internal and external economies and diseconomies of scale.

Are economies of scale now less important in the car industry?

In the twentieth century, car manufacturing grew to become perhaps the most important industry in modern industrialised economies. Though car manufacture began in Germany and France, the main growth of car manufacturing in its early years took place in the USA. Henry Ford's adaptation of the <u>moving assembly line</u>, which allowed car factories to benefit from economies of scale, marked the beginning of <u>mass production</u>.

Garel Rhys, director of the Centre for Automotive Industry Research at Cardiff University, has calculated that economies of scale reach their peak at 250,000 cars a year in an assembly plant, although for the body panels the figure could be as high as 2 million.

However, economies of scale in car production are now not as important as they used to be. Reasons for this include: <u>market fragmentation</u>, leading to lower <u>production runs</u>; building cars to order rather than in large-scale batches of identical cars; and new ways of assembling finished cars in which manufacturers such as Toyota are outsourcing more and more of the car to outside suppliers. With car buyers demanding a wider choice of vehicles, production runs have to get smaller.

As car companies produce an ever-wider range of vehicles, so the way cars are made is changing. There is less need for huge, <u>capital-intensive factories</u>, and barriers to entry into the car industry are falling.

A modern car assembly line

Follow-up questions

1 Explain the meaning of each of the concepts underlined in the passage.
2 Describe some of the economies of scale that have contributed to lower average costs in the UK car industry.

How internal economies and diseconomies of scale affect particular industries

The following two case studies focus on two industries or markets that are affected by economies and diseconomies of scale.

CASE STUDY 3.4

The rise and fall of London's bendy buses

The end of London's bendy experiment has brought shouts of joy from some people. Motorists didn't like the long, low monsters getting stuck round narrow crossroads. Cyclists hated the crushing menace they seemed to present. Transport for London found too many fare-dodgers hopping on and off.

'Bendy buses' were used on 12 routes over the decade from 2002 to 2011 but Mayor Boris Johnson called them 'cumbersome machines' which were too big for narrow streets and encouraged fare-dodgers. Johnson has introduced nearly 500 new double-decker buses to replace the 'bendies'. But the 'bendies' could fit 120 on board, while their replacements take only 85. Even if there are plenty of seats available, well over half of them are usually upstairs. Many old people and young mothers with infants don't do stairs and can't reach the upper deck. They have to be downstairs. The 'bendies' were all downstairs, so with their replacement, there's been a massive loss of accessible seats. 'The most accessible bus in London' is now being missed by the old, wheelchair users and mothers with young children.

Follow-up question

1 Using the concepts of economies and diseconomies of scale, discuss the advantages and disadvantages of bendy buses (a) for Transport for London, the organisation that provided the buses, and (b) for members of the general public.

CASE STUDY 3.5

Super-tankers and volume economies of scale

The large super-tankers that are used to transport crude oil across seas and oceans from oil fields to industrial markets benefit significantly from volume economies of scale. However, super-tankers can also suffer from a diseconomy of scale. This is because large super-tankers cannot enter shallow ports. A wider tanker with a shallow draught does not yield as many economies of scale as a conventional super-tanker, but is more flexible and can enter more ports.

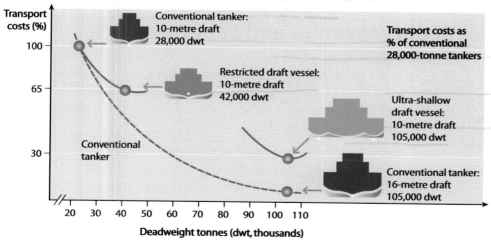

Figure 3.11 Economies of scale and oil tankers

Follow-up question

1 How could the oil tanker industry be organised to reduce the disadvantages of large super-tankers?

3.5 Average revenue, total revenue and profit

The difference between average revenue and total revenue

Revenue is the money that a firm earns when selling its output. It is important to avoid confusing total revenue and average revenue. **Total revenue** is all the money a firm earns from selling the total output of a product. It is cumulative. Selling one more unit of a product or good usually causes total revenue to rise. By contrast, at any level of output, **average revenue** is calculated by dividing total revenue by the size of output:

$$\text{average revenue} = \frac{\text{total revenue}}{\text{output}} \qquad \text{or:} \qquad AR = \frac{TR}{Q}$$

Average revenue and demand for a firm's output

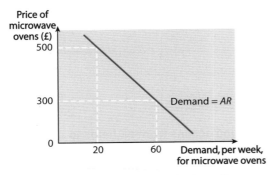

Figure 3.12 shows the demand conditions facing a high-street retailer of electrical goods in a particular week. If the firm sets the price of microwave ovens at £500, 20 customers want to buy an oven. Total sales revenue is £10,000 and average revenue per oven sold is £500. However, by reducing the price to £300, the retailer can sell 60 ovens. Total revenue is now £18,000 and average revenue is £300. The point to note is that at each level of sales, the average revenue the retailer earns is the same as the price charged. This is always the case when the price charged is the same for all the units of output being sold. Hence, in these conditions, the demand curve facing the firm is also its average revenue (AR) curve.

Figure 3.12 The demand curve facing a firm when it decides how much output to sell

Profit, revenue and costs

Students often confuse **profit** and revenue, mistakenly believing that the two terms have the same meaning. As we mentioned in Chapter 2, profit and revenue have different meanings. Profit is the difference between the sales revenue the firm receives when selling the goods or services it produces and the costs of producing the goods.

total profit = total revenue - total costs

In some circumstances, total costs of production may exceed total sales revenue, in which case there is a loss. Think of a loss as being *negative* profit.

QUANTITATIVE SKILLS 3.4

Objective test question: price elasticity of demand

This is an example of an objective test question synoptically testing your understanding of price elasticity of demand (see Chapter 2) and sales revenue (explained in this chapter).

Table 3.3 shows the demand schedule and total revenue for good X.

Table 3.3

£	Quantity demanded (000s)	Total revenue (£000s)
7.50	5	37.5
6.00	10	60.0
4.50	15	67.5
3.00	20	60.0
2.50	25	62.5
0	30	0.0

Between which prices is the price elasticity of demand unitary?

A £0 and £2.50
B £4.50 and £6.00
C £3.00 and £4.50
D £6.00 and £7.50

To answer this question, you should apply the rule set out in Chapter 2:

- if total consumer expenditure increases in response to a price fall, demand is elastic
- if total consumer expenditure decreases in response to a price fall, demand is inelastic
- if total consumer expenditure remains constant in response to a price fall, demand is neither elastic nor inelastic: i.e. elasticity = unity (or is unitary)

When the price falls from £7.50 to £6.00, and from £6.00 to £4.50, total sales revenue increases, so demand is elastic between these prices. Conversely, when the price falls from £3.00 to £2.50, and from £2.50 to zero, total revenue also falls, so demand is inelastic between these prices. This leaves C as the correct answer – total revenue remains constant at £67,500 when the price changes between £3.00 and £4.50.

TEST YOURSELF 3.2

Table 3.4 shows the number of ice creams a small shop sells each day at the different prices it may decide to charge. Calculate the total revenue and the average revenue the shop receives at each of the prices it may charge.

Table 3.4

Price charged for an ice cream	Quantity of ice creams sold per day	Total sales revenue per day	Average sales revenue per ice cream
£2.00	5		
£1.80	10		
£1.60	15		
£1.40	20		
£1.20	25		
£1.00	30		
£0.80	35		
£0.60	40		
£0.40	45		

On a piece of graph paper, use the data to plot the shop's daily average revenue curve.

SUMMARY

- Production is a process, or set of processes, that converts inputs into outputs.
- Productivity is measured by output per unit of input per period of time.
- Labour productivity, or output per worker, is the most commonly used measure of productivity.
- The division of labour means that different workers do different jobs.
- The division of labour and specialisation occur together, although specialisation can occur without division of labour.
- Specialisation and the division of labour require trade and exchange.
- Money is the main medium of exchange in modern economies, though barter still sometimes takes place.
- Average cost is cost per unit of output.
- A firm's short-run average cost curve is typically U-shaped, showing average costs first falling and then rising as output increases.
- A firm is productively efficient when producing the output that minimises its average cost of production.
- For the whole economy, all points on the economy's production possibility frontier are productively efficient.
- Economies of scale mean that a firm's average costs fall as the scale or size of the firm increases.
- There are a number of different types of economy of scale, such as technical economies.
- Diseconomies of scale mean that a firm's average costs rise as the scale or size of the firm increases.
- Economies and diseconomies of scale can be shown on a U-shaped long-run average cost curve, drawn to show average costs changing as the size of the firm increases.
- External economies and diseconomies of scale result from the growth of the industry rather than from the growth of a firm within the industry.
- Revenue is the money a firm receives from selling its output.
- Revenue must not be confused with profit; profit equals total revenue minus total cost.
- Providing all output is sold at the same price, average revenue is the same as price.

Questions

1 Using examples other than those mentioned in the chapter, explain three types of economy of scale.

2 Explain how economies and diseconomies of scale may affect the size of a firm.

3 Do you agree that large firms are always more productively efficient than small firms? Justify your answer.

4 'International competitiveness requires increased labour productivity and the closing of the economy's productivity gap.' Evaluate this statement.

5 Carefully distinguish between a firm's sales revenue and the profit it makes.

4

Competitive and concentrated markets

Markets, and how they operate, are central to a microeconomics course. In a pure market economy, resource allocation would take place solely in the markets which make up the economy (except in the case of events such as inheriting wealth, winning the lottery, and being the victim of theft). In the UK, which falls short of being a complete market economy, markets allocate scarce resources between competing uses in the market sector of the economy but not throughout the whole economy. The market sector dominates the UK economy, though the production and consumption of some goods and services, such as police and defence, lie largely 'outside the market'.

Markets vary considerably in the extent to which they are competitive, falling into one of two groups of market structure: competitive or concentrated. When economists talk of competition, they might be referring to forms of competition that are a part of the competitive market process in a modern economy, such as quality completion, competition in design and fashion, and after-sales service competition. However, in this chapter we focus on price competition, or the setting of prices in order to offer the best value for money.

Price competition involves a firm cutting the price (or prices) it charges for its goods, in order to sell more. Sometimes, however, cutting prices has an 'anti-competitive' motive. Prices are cut in order to drive rival firms out of the market. The end result is the creation of a concentrated market structure containing just a few surviving firms, or perhaps only one firm. The latter is a pure monopoly, the most extreme form of a concentrated market. In this chapter, we compare monopoly and other concentrated markets, with the polar opposite, perfect competition, which is the most extreme form of competitive market. We explain that while perfect competition does not actually exist in the real economy, it acts as a useful 'yardstick' for judging the desirable features of the competitive markets that do exist.

LEARNING OBJECTIVES
This chapter will explain:

- the meaning of a market structure
- different types of market structure
- the nature of competitive markets and perfect competition
- the nature of concentrated markets and monopoly
- profit maximisation and other objectives of firms
- price determination in competitive markets and monopoly
- monopoly and monopoly power
- how entry barriers affect market structure
- concentration ratios and market structure

4.1 Market structures

Market structures are usually defined by the number of firms in the market. However, this leads to other important aspects of market structure. These include competitiveness within the market (which involves the ways in which firms behave and conduct themselves), the extent to which the goods or services being produced are identical or different, and the ways in which barriers to entering the market affect the way the market operates.

KEY TERM

market structure the organisation of a market in terms of the number of firms in the market and the ways in which they behave.

The range of market structures

Perfect competition and monopoly are at the opposite extremes of the spectrum of market structure, as shown in Figure 4.1.

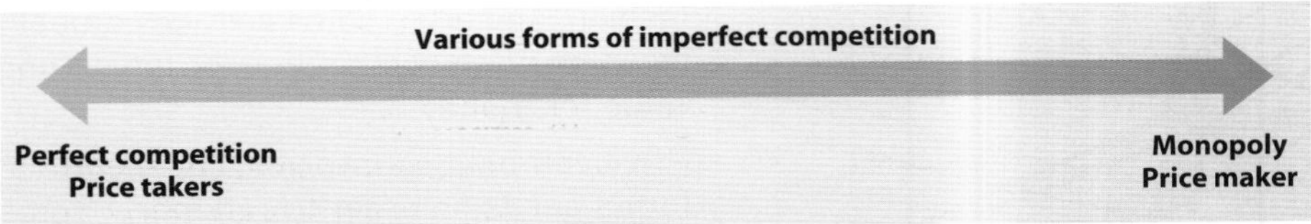

Figure 4.1 Perfect competition and monopoly as extreme forms of market structure

Figure 4.1 also introduces the distinction between a **price taker** and a **price maker**. A price taker lacks the market power to influence by its own action the ruling market price. By contrast, a price maker actively sets the price in the market. Sections 4.3 and 4.4 will explain the reasons for this in the context of competitive markets and monopoly.

KEY TERMS

price taker a firm which passively accepts the ruling market price set by market conditions outside its control.

price maker a firm possessing the power to set the price within the market.

A first look at perfect competition

Perfect competition is a form of market structure that requires six conditions to hold:

- There is a large number of both buyers and sellers in the market, namely consumers and producers or firms.
- Each buyer and seller possesses perfect information of what is happening in the market.
- Each consumer is able to buy, and each producer is able to sell, as much as they wish at the ruling market price.
- The market price is determined by the interaction of *all* the buyers and sellers in the market, but a single buyer or seller is unable to influence the ruling price by its own decisions.
- Only one good or service is being traded in the market and each item of the good is uniform or identical, i.e. firms produce uniform products.
- There are no barriers which might prevent new firms from entering the market in the long run, or prevent firms already in the market from leaving or exiting it.

KEY TERM

perfect competition a market that displays the six conditions of: a large number of buyers and sellers; perfect market information; the ability to buy or sell as much as is desired at the ruling market price; the inability of an individual buyer or seller to influence the market price; a uniform or homogeneous product; and no barriers to entry or exit in the long run.

Perfect competition is actually non-existent in the real world. It is best to regard perfect competition as an unreal or abstract economic model defined by the six conditions listed on the previous page. Real-world markets cannot display simultaneously all the conditions necessary for perfect competition. Since any violation of the conditions of perfect competition immediately renders a market imperfectly competitive, even the most **competitive markets** in the real economy are examples of imperfect competition rather than perfect competition.

A first look at concentrated markets

As the name implies, a **concentrated market** is a market containing very few firms. **Pure monopoly**, in which a single firm produces the whole of the output of a market or industry, is the most extreme example of a concentrated market. A pure monopolist supplies the whole market; there are no other firms to compete against. Usually, however, monopoly is a relative rather than an absolute concept. Until quite recently, the British Gas Corporation was the single producer of piped gas to households and most industrial customers in the UK, but it experienced competition from other sources of energy such as electricity and oil. Its **monopoly power** was further reduced in 1998 when other companies, including electricity companies, were allowed to sell gas to customers via the pipelines previously owned by British Gas.

In real life, dominant firms producing a large share of market output are more common than pure monopolies, the latter being quite rare. Firms with significant market power, or monopoly power, face competitive pressures from other firms which are also in the market. Competitive pressures also arise from substitute products and sometimes also from outside firms trying to enter the market to destroy the monopoly position enjoyed by the firm or firms already in the market.

Imperfect competition

Economists use the term **imperfect competition** to cover all the market structures lying between the two extremes of perfect competition and pure monopoly. Imperfect competition is a competitive market situation where there are many sellers, but they are selling heterogeneous (dissimilar) goods as opposed to the homogeneous or uniform goods produced in perfectly competitive markets. The term covers market structures ranging from those in which there are a large number of highly competitive firms approximating to perfect competition, to those which are highly concentrated, approximating to pure monopoly. Almost all real-world markets, certainly in developed economies such as the UK, are imperfectly competitive.

4.2 The objectives of firms

Profit maximisation

Economists generally assume that **profit maximisation** is a firm's ultimate business objective. If this is the case, then firms grow because their owners believe that growth leads to higher profits. Conversely, if the owners believe that growth reduces profits or indeed leads to losses, they will resist the temptation to pursue growth.

Short-run vs long-run profit maximisation

A complication that should be introduced at this point is the possible conflict between short-run and long-run profit maximisation. Long-run profits may require substantial investment in research and new capital. If a firm has a short time horizon, if it is worried about finance or about future risk and uncertainty, or if it fears that a lack of immediate profit will lower its share price and render it vulnerable to a hostile takeover raid, the firm may decide not to grow, even though it thinks that large profits could be made in the long run.

Sales maximisation

Sales maximisation is also known as revenue maximisation. Sales or revenue maximisation occurs at the level of output at which the sale of an extra unit of output would yield no extra revenue. Firms that attempt to maximise sales usually do so subject to a requirement or constraint that they must make a minimum or acceptable level of profit.

Other possible business objectives

These include growth maximisation, market share maximisation and survival.

- Growth maximisation occurs when the decision makers within a firm try to make the firm grow as fast as possible, even though this may conflict with profit maximisation. In an already large firm, these decisions tend to be made by the firm's managers, rather than by the shareholders who own the firm. This can lead to a conflict of interest: managers often favour fast growth because this increases their spheres of influence and salaries; the firm's owners, by contrast, may be more interested in maximising profit.

- **Market share maximisation**, which tends to accompany growth maximisation, involves increasing the percentage of market output which the firm produces. It often involves a firm trying to increase its market power and monopoly power.
- Finally, in a highly competitive market, firms may aim simply to survive. In such markets, firms are always threatened by the entry of new firms which may steal away their customers. 'Adapt or perish' is the choice facing such firms.

4.3 Competitive markets

The main characteristics of a perfectly competitive market

We listed the six main conditions or characteristics of a perfectly competitive market in section 4.1. Before reading further, go back and read through these conditions again.

Despite the lack of perfect markets in the real world, the theory of perfect competition is probably one of the most important and fundamental of all conventional economic theories. Critics attack this view and argue that economists pay undue attention to perfect competition as a market structure, and that this encourages a false belief that a perfect market is an attainable ideal.

Nevertheless, perfect competition performs a very useful function. It serves as a standard or benchmark against which we may judge the desirable or undesirable properties of the imperfectly competitive and monopolistic market structures of the world we live in.

Section 4.1 also mentioned that firms in perfectly competitive markets function as passive price takers.

Price determination in a competitive market

Figure 4.2 shows how the price facing each firm in a competitive market is determined by the interaction of demand and supply.

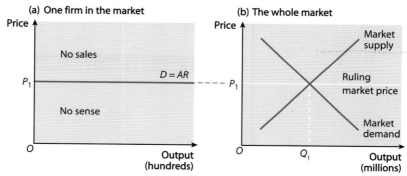

Figure 4.2 The determination of price in a competitive market

Figure 4.2(b) is very similar to the diagram we used in Chapter 2, Figure 2.16, to explain how the ruling market price is determined in a market. To recap, in a competitive market, the ruling market price is determined in the market as a whole by the interaction of demand and supply. The price is located where the market demand curve intersects or crosses over the market supply curve. However, Figure 4.2(a) shows how this affects each of the firms operating in the market. Look closely at the labels on the horizontal axes of the two diagrams. The axis in Figure 4.2(b) is labelled output in millions, whereas the label in Figure 4.2(a) is output in hundreds. This results from the assumption of there being a very large number of firms in a competitive market. This would certainly be the case in a perfectly competitive market.

The assumption that a perfectly competitive firm can sell whatever quantity it wishes at the ruling market price P_1, but that it cannot influence the ruling market price by its own action, means that the firm is a passive price taker.

The labels 'No sales' and 'No sense' that we have placed on Figure 4.2(a), respectively above and below the price line P_1, help to explain why each firm is a price taker. 'No sales' indicates that if the firm raises its selling price above the ruling market price, customers desert the firm to buy the identical products (perfect substitutes) available from other firms at the ruling market price. 'No sense' refers to the fact that although a perfectly competitive firm can sell its output below the price P_1, doing so is irrational. No extra sales can result, so selling below the ruling market price inevitably reduces both total sales revenue and profit. Such a pricing policy therefore conflicts with the profit-maximising objective that we have assumed firms to have.

Beaming the horizontal ruling market price line leftward into Figure 4.2(a), the price line is in fact the perfectly elastic demand curve for each firm's output. (Page 26 in Chapter 2 explains why a perfectly elastic demand curve is horizontal.) The horizontal price line and demand curve facing a competitive firm is also the firm's average revenue (AR) curve. (Go back to Chapter 3, where page 70 explains why the demand curve facing a firm is its AR curve.)

Suppose, for example, that the firm sells 100 units of a good, with each unit of the good priced at £1.00. The firm's total sales revenue (TR) is obviously £100.00. The firm's average revenue (TR/Q) is £1. If the firm increases sales to 110 units, the price does not change, so average revenue is still £1.

STUDY TIP

To properly understand the nature of competitive and concentrated markets, you need knowledge of price elasticity of demand.

TEST YOURSELF 4.1

The market demand and supply schedules in a highly competitive market are shown in Table 4.1. Using the data provided, plot the demand and supply curves on graph paper and calculate the average revenue of each of the competitive firms in the market.

Table 4.1

Price (£s)	Quantity demanded	Quantity supplied
1	3000	0
2	2800	400
3	2600	600
4	2400	1000
5	2200	1400
6	2000	2000
7	1800	2400
8	1600	2800
9	1400	3200
10	1200	3600

Why profits are likely to be lower in a competitive market than in a market dominated by a few large firms

In Chapter 3, we defined the short run as the time period in which at least one of a firm's factors of production, for example its buildings, is fixed and cannot be changed. This means that in the short run a firm cannot move into a new market. In the long run, by contrast, all the factors of production can be varied and firms can move between markets – *but only when barriers to entry or exit are not too high.*

Provided markets are competitive, there are few if any **entry and exit barriers**. (In perfect competition, there would be no barriers at all.) If, in the short run, firms in a competitive market are highly profitable, large profits act as a 'magnet' and attract new firms into the market. What happens next is shown in Figure 4.3, which has been developed from Figure 4.2.

KEY TERMS

entry barrier makes it difficult or impossible for new firms to enter a market.

exit barrier makes it difficult or impossible for firms to leave a market.

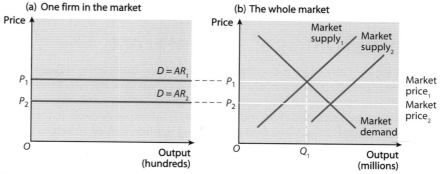

Figure 4.3 In a competitive market, the ruling market price falls when new firms enter the market

Initially the price is P_1, determined in Figure 4.3(b), where the market supply$_1$ curve intersects the market demand curve. In Figure 4.3(a), P_1 is the price facing *each* of the firms in the market. At this price, each firm makes large profits, which attract new firms into the market. The entry of new firms leads to a rightward shift of the market supply curve, to market supply$_2$. As a result, the ruling market price falls to P_2. In the new situation, the profits made by *all* the firms in the competitive market must be lower than they were at price P_1.

By contrast, the firms in markets containing just a few firms (including the extreme case of monopoly) are protected by substantial entry barriers. Under the assumption that, initially, the firms are highly profitable, the inability of new firms to enter the market means that both prices and profits are likely to remain high. However, in the long run and as a part of the competitive process, high profits provide an incentive for other firms to overcome any barriers to entry.

In summary, in highly competitive markets, the 'invisible hand' of the market acts as a mechanism for eliminating high profits — providing that there are few or no barriers to entry and exit. In markets dominated by a handful of firms, high entry and exit barriers may prevent the 'invisible hand' mechanism from operating in this way.

CASE STUDY 4.1

The 'invisible hand' of the market

In 1776, in his famous book *An Inquiry into the Nature and Causes of the Wealth of Nations*, the economist Adam Smith wrote:

> An individual neither intends to promote the public interest, nor know how much he is promoting it. ...He intends only his own gain, and he is in this, as in many other cases, led by an invisible hand to promote an end which was no part of his intention. ...It is not from the benevolence of the butcher, the brewer, or the baker that we expect our dinner, but from their regard to their own interest. We address ourselves, not to their humanity but to their self-love.

Smith was making the argument, repeated ever since by economists of a free-market persuasion, that the pursuit of individual self-interest in the market economy leads to outcomes which are in the common good or public interest — providing that the markets are free and competitive. Consumers benefit from individualistic behaviour in competitive markets because prices and profits end up being lower than would be the case if the markets were dominated by a few large firms.

Follow-up questions

1 Outline **one** way in which consumers can benefit from a lack of competition in a market.
2 Describe **one** circumstance, apart from when there is little or no competition in a market, in which the pursuit of self-interest may be undesirable in the economy.

The importance of self-interest

Economists generally regard competitive markets as desirable. However, the desirable properties of competitive markets (namely economic efficiency, welfare maximisation and consumer sovereignty) do not result from any assumption that business people or entrepreneurs in competitive industries are more highly motivated or public spirited than monopolists. Traditional economic theory assumes that everyone is motivated by self-interest and by self-interest alone. This applies just as much to firms in competitive markets as it does to monopolies. Entrepreneurs in competitive industries would very much like to become monopolists, both to gain an easier life and also to make bigger profits. Indeed, from a firm's point of view, successful competition means eliminating competition and becoming a monopoly. But in perfect markets, market forces (Adam Smith's invisible hand of the market) and the absence of barriers to entry and exit prevent this happening.

Imagine, for example, a situation in which a firm in a perfectly competitive industry makes a technical breakthrough which reduces production costs. For a short time the firm can make significant profits. But because, in highly competitive markets, market information is available to all firms, other firms within the market and new entrants attracted to the market can also enjoy the lower production costs.

Ultimately, of course, consumers benefit from lower prices brought about by technical progress and the forces of competition, but it is market forces, and not some socially benign motive or public spirit assumed on the part of entrepreneurs, that accounts for the optimality of a highly competitive market as a market structure.

CASE STUDY 4.2

To do with the price of fish

For a market to be competitive, buyers and sellers need accurate information about supply and demand. Before the use of mobile phones, fishermen in southern India lacked information about prices being charged for newly caught fish in other fishing villages along the coast. This lack of adequate information about conditions of supply and prices being charged led to small, separated and relatively uncompetitive fish markets.

If a fisherman made a good catch, other fishermen operating out of his home port and fishing in the same area would also catch a lot of fish. But when all the fishing vessels sailed back home, fish prices in the local village fish market would slump because of excess supply.

Another possibility was to sail down the coast after the catch was made, in the hope that in other villages fish catches were less bountiful and prices were therefore better. But, because of high fuel prices and uncertainty about what might be happening elsewhere, fishermen generally chose to return to their own village. This was wasteful because oversupply led to fish being thrown away, even though they might have been sold in slightly more distant fish markets. Another result was there were wide variations in fish prices in different fishing villages.

Mobile phones allow the fishermen to exchange information on fish prices

However, after mobile phones had been introduced in southern India, while they were still at sea fishermen began to call markets all along the coast to find out where prices were highest. Having obtained this information, fishermen were now prepared to market their fish further afield, despite the fuel costs involved. The number of unsold fish that previously had been thrown back into the sea fell dramatically. Fish prices also fell. The 'law of one price' was operating — there now being a single price along the coast for more or less identical fish. By improving the exchange of information between fishermen, mobile phone technology has therefore contributed to the growth of a larger and much more competitive market.

Follow-up questions

1 Explain how the case study illustrates how better information on the part of buyers or sellers improves the way a market functions.
2 Name two UK markets that have been made more competitive as a result of the growing use of mobile phones.

Consumer sovereignty and producer sovereignty

Arguably, competition has the advantage of promoting **consumer sovereignty**, in the sense that the goods and services produced are those that consumers have voted for when spending the pounds in their pockets. When consumer sovereignty exists, 'the consumer is king'. Firms and industries that produce goods other than those for which consumers are prepared to pay, do not survive in highly competitive markets.

By contrast, monopolies and firms producing in highly concentrated markets may enjoy and exploit their **producer sovereignty**. The goods and services available for consumers to buy are determined by the firms rather than by consumer preferences expressed in the market place. Even if producer sovereignty is not exercised on a 'take-it-or-leave-it' basis by a monopoly, the monopolist may still possess sufficient market power to manipulate consumer wants through such marketing devices as persuasive advertising. In these situations, 'the producer is king'.

> **KEY TERMS**
>
> **consumer sovereignty**
> through exercising their spending power, consumers collectively determine what is produced in a market. Consumer sovereignty is strongest in a perfectly competitive market.
>
> **producer sovereignty**
> producers or firms in a market determine what is produced and what prices are charged.

4.4 Monopoly and monopoly power

The difference between pure monopoly and monopoly power

Economics students often confuse monopoly power with monopoly. In economics, the word monopoly is used in two rather different ways: in terms of a *strict* definition and in terms of a rather *looser* definition. The strict definition refers to pure monopoly, which, as noted earlier, occurs when a single firm produces the whole of the output of a market. A pure monopolist faces no competition at all, since there are no other firms to compete against. The looser definition refers to a market in which there is a dominant firm, but there are also some other firms in the market. According to this second meaning, monopoly is a relative rather than an absolute concept.

We mentioned monopoly power in section 4.1, under the heading 'A first look at concentrated markets'. Virtually all firms in the real economy possess a degree of monopoly power, which is the power to act as a price maker rather than as a price taker.

Monopoly power is of course strongest when there is only one firm in the market, though, as we also mentioned earlier, the existence of substitute goods produced in other industries reduces monopoly power even in a pure monopoly. The Kodak and Microsoft/Apple case studies below show how technical progress can also erode monopoly power.

CASE STUDY 4.3

Kodak's decline and fall

For most of the twentieth century, Kodak was the dominant firm in the global photography industry. From the 1960s onwards, Kodak faced growing competition from Japanese firms in the film-using camera market, but the company still enjoyed significant market power in the markets for film and film chemicals.

More recently, however, Kodak has become a classic example of a company with significant monopoly power and market share declining as a result of changes in technology. From the 1990s onwards, digital cameras replaced film-using cameras and revolutionised the photography market. For a number of years Kodak still made a profit from manufacturing photographic films and paper used for printing photographs, but made no profit from manufacturing film-using cameras. But then the manufacture of photographic films and paper also went into sharp decline. This was because digital cameras do not require film, and digital camera users often do not transfer onto photographic paper the images they create. They prefer instead to keep the photographic images stored on their computers, or to print the images on non-photographic paper.

At the time, entry barriers were much lower in the digital camera market than in markets for film-using cameras and photographic film. Sony first made the successful transition from video technology to digital photography, quickly followed by computer makers and mobile phone manufacturers. Mobile phone handsets capable of taking digital pictures began to outsell both film-using cameras and ordinary digital cameras.

Despite attempts to diversify and to switch to digital photography, Kodak declared voluntary bankruptcy early in 2012. The bankruptcy ended in 2013 when, under new ownership, a slimmed-down Kodak re-emerged, specialising mostly in industrial photography.

Follow-up questions

1 Why did Kodak's market power decline, despite the fact that its traditional business was strongly protected by high entry barriers?
2 Name three other previously dominant firms which have suffered much the same fate as Kodak.

ACTIVITY

Construct a questionnaire to use with your friends on the ways in which they use their mobile phones. When taking photographs, do they prefer their phones to cameras, do they text messages to friends or do they make phone calls, do they gather most of the news they read from social media such as Facebook rather than from TV or printed newspapers? Analyse your results.

The US company Microsoft provides a good example of a monopoly in the second, looser, meaning of the word. Microsoft is the dominant producer in both the US and world markets of personal computer operating systems. Microsoft is also the largest producer of computer software applications. Its products, Word and Excel, dominate the word processor and spreadsheet markets. However, although Microsoft controls over 90% of the PC operating system market, it faces some competition: for example, from Linux and Apple.

CASE STUDY 4.4

Microsoft versus Apple: Nothing lasts forever

There was a time in the 1990s and early 2000s when Microsoft was at least as dominant as Apple now is in ICT markets. These days, Microsoft is still around, but it's an ailing giant — profitable but no longer innovative, trying (and so far failing) to get a foothold in the post-PC, mobile, cloud-based world.

Apple's current strength is that it makes iPods, iPhones and iPads that people are desperate to buy and on which the company makes huge profits. But the logic of the ICT hardware business is that those profits will decline as the competition increases, so Apple will become less profitable over the longer term. What will determine Apple's future is whether it can come up with new, market-creating products. If the company fails to do this, Apple may become a footnote in history. Just like Microsoft, in fact.

Follow-up questions

1 Explain how the passage illustrates how developments in technology erode monopoly power.
2 Do you agree that Microsoft is an 'ailing giant', and that Apple may eventually become one?

Sources of monopoly and monopoly power

There are various sources of monopoly and monopoly power which affect the behaviour and performance of firms. These include the following.

Natural monopoly

This occurs when there is only room in the market for one firm benefiting to the full from economies of scale. In the past, utility industries such as water, gas, electricity and the telephone industries were regarded as **natural monopolies**. Because of the nature of their product, utility industries experience a particular marketing problem. The industries produce a service that is delivered through a distribution network or grid of pipes and cables into millions of separate businesses and homes. Competition in the provision of distribution grids is extremely wasteful, since it requires the duplication of fixed capacity, therefore causing each supplier to incur unnecessarily high fixed costs.

> **KEY TERM**
>
> **natural monopoly** the term has two meanings, first when a country or firm has complete control of a natural resource, and second when there is only room in a market for one firm benefiting from economies of scale to the full.

Geographical causes of monopoly

A pure natural monopoly can occur when, for climatic or geological reasons, a particular country or location is the only source of supply of a raw material or foodstuff.

Geographical or spatial factors also give rise to another type of monopoly, for example a single grocery store in an isolated village. Entry to the market by a second store is restricted by the fact that the local market is too small. Monopoly does not exist in an absolute sense, since the villagers can travel to the nearest town to buy their groceries. Nevertheless, the grocery store can still exercise considerable market power, stemming from the fact that for many villagers it is both costly and inconvenient to shop elsewhere. Prices charged are likely to be higher than they would be if competition existed nearby.

Village shops exercise considerable market power

Government-created monopoly

Governments sometimes create monopoly, other than in utility industries or natural monopolies, in markets they believe are too important to leave to competition. In the UK, industries such as coal, rail and steel were nationalised in the 1940s by a Labour government and turned into state-owned monopolies. At the time, the government believed that these industries were the commanding heights of the economy, and were essential for the well-being and planning of the whole economy. It also believed that state ownership was required for the industries to operate in the public interest, rather than in the narrower interest of their previous private owners.

In other instances, governments may deliberately create a private monopoly. Examples include the granting of a broadcasting franchise to a commercial television company or a gambling franchise to a casino. Both these are examples of the state using monopoly to regulate the consumption of a good or service. In theory, at least, state monopolies can ensure standards of supply of goods such as public service broadcasting, or prevent the worst excesses of consumption of a good such as gambling.

Patent law provides another example of government-created monopoly. **Patents** and other forms of intellectual copyright give businesses, writers and musicians exclusive right to innovations or creative work (such as a novel or a piece of music) for several years and sometimes decades, though the right may be difficult or impossible to enforce.

> ### KEY TERM
>
> **patent** a strategic or man-made barrier to market entry caused by government legislation protecting the right of a firm to be the sole producer of a patented good, unless the firm grants royalties for other firms to produce the good.

Factors which influence monopoly power

Besides acting as a price maker or exercising the power to set prices, a firm's monopoly power is affected by a number of other factors. These include: the existence of barriers to entry, the number of competitors, advertising, and the degree of product differentiation.

Barriers to market entry

Barriers to market entry prevent new firms entering the market to share in the monopolist's profit both in the long run and in the short run. There are two main types of entry barrier: **natural barriers** and **artificial** or man-made **barriers**:

- **Natural barriers**, which are also known as innocent barriers, include economies of scale and indivisibilities. Economies of scale mean that established large firms produce at a lower long-run average cost, and are more productively efficient, than smaller new entrants, who become stranded on higher average cost curves. Indivisibilities prevent certain goods and services being produced in plants below a certain size. Indivisibilities occur in metal smelting and oil refining industries.
- **Artificial barriers** or **man-made entry barriers**, which are also known as strategic barriers, are the result of deliberate action by firms already in the market to prevent new firms from entering the market. Patents are used by firms as a strategic barrier to entry. Limit pricing and predatory pricing, which are explained on page 93, provide other examples of artificial barriers to market entry.

which are explained on page 93

KEY TERMS

natural barrier to entry a barrier to market entry which is not man-made.

artificial barrier to entry a barrier to market entry which is man-made.

STUDY TIP

Make sure you understand how entry barriers protect monopolists and firms in concentrated markets, and influence their behaviour.

CASE STUDY 4.5

Patents and drug companies

Pharmaceutical drug companies spend huge amounts of money on research and development (R&D) to give themselves a competitive advantage by marketing new drugs. They recoup much of this expenditure through the patent system, which allows them to charge high prices for drugs until their monopoly expires.

Without patents, drugs companies would be dead. When rivals try to breach those patents, multinational drug companies react ferociously. They bring in lobbyists. They bring in lawyers. Often — by their own admission — they bring in private detectives.

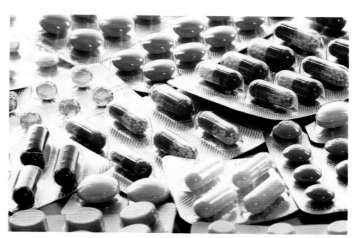

Patents allow drug companies to recoup their high expenditure on R&D

'Intellectual property protection is critical to an industry like ours,' said the chairman of Britain's largest drug company, GlaxoSmithKline. 'If someone can come along the next day and copy [your invention], then no one would ever put any money into R&D.'

He added: 'If we believe people are undermining our intellectual property we have to deal with it by getting the information. Of course we — and I'm sure all other companies — use professional people who work, within the law, to get that information.' Private detective agencies are often used. Pfizer admits to using private detectives: 'They know the loops in the law.' The 'loops' are many. Private detectives raid rubbish bins, track down former employees and prepare 'sting operations' by luring adversaries into doing business with fake companies.

In developed countries, the multinational drug companies are protected by strong patent laws. But in India, China and South America, where respect for intellectual property has never been engrained, the task facing drug companies in protecting their patents is far harder.

Follow-up questions

1 Governments in poor developing countries often claim that their citizens cannot afford the prices charged for medicines by companies such as GlaxoSmithKline and Pfizer. Do you agree that drug prices should be lower in poor countries? Justify your answer.
2 Describe how technical progress has been eroding the power of music industry companies to protect their intellectual property.

The number of competitors in a market

Generally, the larger the number of competitors in a market, the less scope is there for exercising monopoly power. However, there can be exceptions, for example when one very large dominant firm and a large number of small firms, possibly occupying niche positions, survive in the market.

CASE STUDY 4.6

The French book market

French law has long fixed book prices in France at levels set by book publishers. Readers pay the same price whether they buy online, from a big high-street chain or from a small bookseller. Extensive discounting is banned though 5% discounts are allowed. Result: there are between 2,500 and 3,000 independent bookshops in France, compared with less than 1,000 in the UK. Most small French towns have at least two bookshops and there is a wide choice of books on display.

The French government says that the banning of discounts of more than 5% has saved its independent bookstores from the ravages of free-market capitalism that hit the UK when it abandoned fixed prices. Nevertheless, the owners of French bookshops still argue they cannot compete with Amazon, even with Amazon's discounts limited to 5%, because the online retailer provides free postage and free fast delivery deals on top of the discount. Consumers can also bypass French law by ordering books online in countries such as Belgium.

The French culture minister recently said: 'Everyone has had enough of Amazon, which, by dumping practices, slashes prices to get a foothold in markets only to raise them as soon as they have established a virtual monopoly...the book and reading sector is facing competition from certain sites using every possible means to enter the French and European book market...it is destroying bookshops.'

Follow-up questions

1 UK bookshops are not protected from competition exercised by companies such as Amazon. State **one** advantage and **one** disadvantage for book buyers of competition in the book market.
2 Book authors claim that they are suffering from Amazon's marketing strategy. Why might this be the case?

Advertising and monopoly power

Advertising can be divided into informative advertising and persuasive advertising. As the name suggests, **informative advertising** increases competition because it provides consumers and producers with useful information about goods and services which are available to buy, and about the different goods that different firms are producing.

By making the demand curve for a product less price elastic, **persuasive advertising**, by contrast, often reduces competition. In effect, customers become 'captive customers' who are unwilling to buy a cheaper substitute good. Persuasive advertising tries to make people believe that a product is a 'must-have' product. Little information about the good itself is provided, for example its price. Instead, advertisements focus on how ownership or use of the product will improve the consumer's feelings of self-worth and/or the image portrayed to other people.

Persuasive advertising often goes hand in hand with **saturation advertising**. Monopolies and other large firms use saturation advertising to prevent small firms entering the market. The small firms are unable to enter the industry because they cannot afford the minimum level of advertising and other forms of promotion for their goods which are necessary to persuade retailers to stock their products. The mass-advertising, brand imaging and other marketing strategies of large established firms effectively crowd out newcomers from the

KEY TERMS
informative advertising provides consumers and producers with useful information about goods or services.

persuasive advertising attempts to persuade potential customers that a good or service possesses desirable characteristics that make it worth buying.

saturation advertising through flooding the market with information and persuasion about a firm's product, this functions as a man-made barrier to market entry by making it difficult for smaller firms to compete.

market place. Supermarkets are often unwilling to stock goods produced by new entrants to the market because their products are insufficiently advertised.

Product differentiation

Monopoly power is also influenced by **product differentiation**, which can have much the same effect on monopoly power as persuasive advertising.

Product differentiation means making a particular product different from other products, whether those produced by the firm itself or those produced by rival firms. The differentiation may result from the design of the product, from the method of producing the product, or from other characteristics of the product such as its ability to function properly. Along with persuasive advertising and other elements of a firm's marketing strategy, product differentiation can increase a firm's monopoly power.

Consider, for example, the market for cola drinks. Coca-Cola is the global brand leader. For many cola drinkers, successful product differentiation, resulting in part from persuasive advertising and brand imaging conducted over decades, means that Coca-Cola has become a 'must-have' drink, superior to its inferior substitutes. All these elements of Coca-Cola's marketing strategy have successfully shifted the demand curve for Coca-Cola's products to the right, while at the same time making the demand curve highly inelastic. This means that many consumers are prepared to pay more for Coca-Cola than for own-band supermarket colas.

Monopoly and market demand

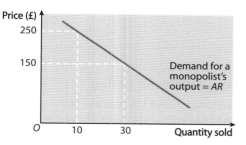

Figure 4.4 The demand curve for a monopolist's output

We noted earlier that the demand curve for the output of the most extreme form of a competitive market, namely perfect competition, is perfectly elastic and lies along the ruling market price set by market demand and supply in the market as a whole. By contrast, in pure monopoly, the demand curve for the monopolist's output *is* the market demand curve, which slopes downwards to the right. If there is only one firm in the market, demand for the monopolist's output and market demand are the same!

This is illustrated in Figure 4.4, which is basically the same diagram as Figure 3.12 in Chapter 3.

The downward-sloping demand curve affects the monopolist in one of two different ways. If the monopolist is a price maker, choosing to set the price at which the product is sold, the demand curve dictates the maximum output that can be sold at this price. For example, if the price is set at £150 in Figure 4.4, the maximum quantity that can be sold at this price is 30 units of the good. But if the monopolist raises the price to £250, sales fall to 10 units. Alternatively, if the monopolist is a **quantity setter** rather than a price maker, the demand curve dictates the maximum price at which the chosen quantity can be sold. The fact that the demand curve is downward-sloping means that the monopolist faces a trade-off. A monopoly cannot set price and quantity independently of each other.

In real life, monopolists and other imperfectly competitive firms try to escape from the choice of being either a price maker or a quantity setter by using advertising and other forms of marketing to shift the demand curve for their products to the right. However, the effectiveness of such a strategy may be limited by retaliatory advertising by rival firms.

Concentration ratios and market structure

Concentration ratios provide a good indicator of the degree of monopoly power in a market structure. For example, a five-firm concentration ratio shows the percentage of output in an industry produced by the five largest firms in the industry. In March 2013, the five-firm concentration ratio in the UK supermarket industry can be calculated from the market share data shown in Figure 4.5. The five-firm concentration ratio of 82.1% indicates that the supermarket industry is an **oligopoly**.

Of course, if the one-firm concentration ratio in an industry is 100%, the market is a pure monopoly. Concentration ratios are calculated by first ranking in descending order the market shares of the leading firms in the industry or market. The market shares are then added up, one by one, again in descending order. The five-firm concentration ratio is then the cumulative percentage market share of the five leading firms. Likewise the eight-firm concentration ratio is the cumulative market share of the eight leading firms.

Alternatively, concentration ratios can be calculated from the total output figures of the leading firms in the market. To calculate the five-firm concentration ratio in this way, first add together the total outputs of the five leading firms and then place the cumulative output of these firms as a ratio of the total output of all the firms that make up the market. Similar calculations can then be made, if required, to find the two-firm concentration ratio, the three-firm concentration ratio, and so on.

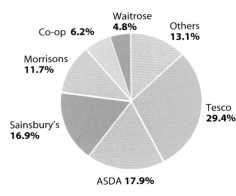

Figure 4.5 Market shares in the UK supermarket industry, 2013

The case against monopoly

Exploiting consumers by restricting output and raising the price

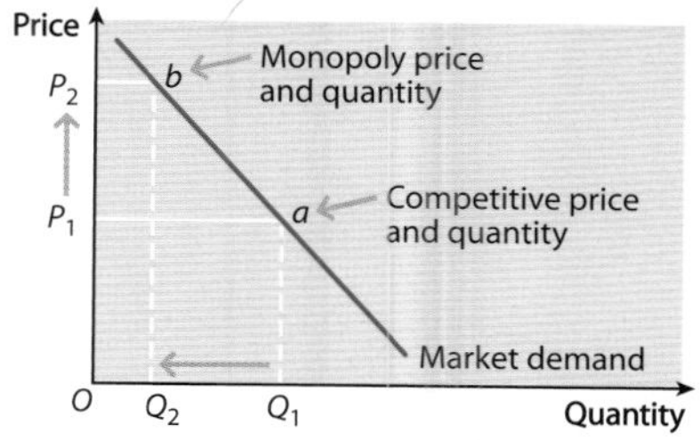

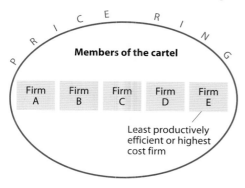

Figure 4.6 The case against monopoly: a monopoly may restrict output so as to raise the price

Figure 4.6 illustrates how a monopoly can increase its profit by reducing market output compared to the output that would be produced in a competitive market, which enables the monopoly to increase the price it charges. If the market is competitive, the combined output of all the firms in the market is output Q_1, which they sell at price P_1.

Suppose a monopoly now replaces the competitive firms. The monopoly uses its market power to restrict output to Q_2 and to hike the price up to P_2. Market failure and **resource misallocation** occur because, compared to the competitive market, output falls and the price rises. Higher prices mean that consumers buy less of the good than they would have, had the price remained lower. This is an example of resource misallocation: too little of the good is produced and consumed, at too high a price. Economic welfare is less than it could be. A recent example in the UK has been high gas and electricity prices charged by oligopoly energy companies. The firms benefit from higher profits, but many of their customers, particularly old people living on their own, reduce their consumption and end up in cold winters living in freezing houses.

A monopolist's ability to exercise producer sovereignty and exploit consumers by raising its price is greatest when demand for the product is inelastic. Persuasive advertising, brand imaging and other marketing strategies aim to reduce elasticity of demand and shift the demand curve to the right.

Productive inefficiency and monopoly

Monopoly may also be productively inefficient in comparison to firms in a competitive market. We saw earlier in the chapter how the entry of new firms reduces the price in a competitive market. This means that to remain profitable, competitive firms must reduce their costs of production by as much as they can. The pressure to do this is less powerful in monopoly — provided it is fully protected by barriers to market entry. The *threat* of entry by new firms can also exert pressure on monopolies to reduce costs. However, in the absence of economies of scale (see the section on the reasons for economies of scale on page 66), a monopolist's average costs may be higher than those of competitive firms, which would mean that the monopoly ends up being productively less efficient.

> **STUDY TIP**
> Productive efficiency is a key concept that can be used in the analysis of a wide range of economic topics, for example taxation and market failures studied later in the course.

> **KEY TERM**
> **resource misallocation** when resources are allocated in a way which does not maximise economic welfare.
>
> **collusion** co-operation between firms, for example to fix prices. Some forms of collusion may be in the public interest, for example joint research and labour training schemes.

Sometimes firms competing against each other in concentrated markets decide to reduce competition and give themselves an easier life by undertaking joint agreements and colluding together. A common form of **collusion** is the formation of a price ring or cartel agreement, though the fact that these are generally illegal means that they are generally undercover agreements.

In Figure 4.7, five firms jointly agree to charge a price to keep Firm E, which is the least productively efficient firm, in the market. In a competitive market, Firm E would have to reduce costs or go out of business. Cartel agreements enable inefficient firms to stay in business, while other more efficient members of the price ring enjoy high profits. By protecting inefficient firms and enabling firms to enjoy an easy life

Figure 4.7 A price ring resulting from a cartel agreement

protected from competition, cartels display the disadvantages of monopoly but generally without the benefits that monopoly can sometimes bring. (These benefits are explained in the next section.)

TEST YOURSELF 4.2
Calculating price elasticity of demand

Figure 4.8 shows the market demand curve for a product:

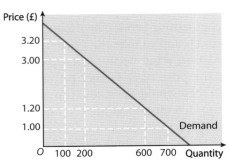

Figure 4.8 The market demand curve for a product

Calculate the price elasticity of demand for the product when

(a) the good's price falls from £3.20 to £3.00

(b) the good's price falls from £1.20 to £1.00

What do these figures tell you about the way price elasticity of demand changes, moving along a straight-line demand curve shown in Figure 4.8?

The potential benefits of monopoly
The benefits resulting from economies of scale

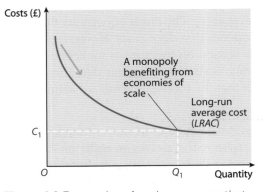

Figure 4.9 Economies of scale can mean that long-run average costs fall in monopoly

Consider now Figure 4.9. As we noted earlier, many markets are too small to allow more than one firm to benefit from internal economies of scale, which means that the firm is a natural monopoly.

In Figure 4.9, economies of scale are shown by the downward-sloping average cost curve. A monopoly, enjoying the benefits of economies of scale can produce output Q_1 at an average cost (or unit cost) of C_1. However, if there are a large number of competitive firms in the market, there is unlikely to be sufficient room in the market for each firm to reduce average costs by gaining the benefits of economies of scale. Achieving economies of scale would reduce the number of firms in the market, which would be likely to reduce competition.

STUDY TIP
Make sure you can link economies of scale to the growth of monopolies. Recap on how a U-shaped long-run average cost curve is used to illustrate economies and diseconomies of scale.

TEST YOURSELF 4.3

Table 4.3 shows a firm's long-run average cost schedule. From the data provided, draw a *LRAC* curve on graph paper.

Table 4.3

Output (thousands of units)	Average costs per unit (£)
5	500
10	400
15	300
20	200
25	100
30	200
35	300
40	400
50	500

1 Comment on the economies and diseconomies of scale the firm experiences at different levels of output.

2 Suppose that consumers only want 25,000 units of the good, however low the good's price. Comment on how this might affect the structure of the market in which the firm is selling the good.

KEY TERMS

invention creates new ideas for products or processes.

innovation converts the results of invention into marketable products or services.

STUDY TIP

Learn how to relate monopoly to market failure (see Chapter 5).

The benefits of invention and innovation

A monopoly may also benefit from another advantage possibly denied to firms in a competitive market. For example, protected by a patent that prevents competitors from free-riding on its success, a monopoly can use its high profits to finance product innovation. Monopoly profit can fund research and development (R&D), which leads to better ways of making existing products and to the development of completely new products.

Invention is about creating new ideas for products or processes. **Innovation**, by contrast, converts the results of invention into marketable products or services. Many inventions fail to see the light of day because they have no practical use. It is innovation, rather than invention, that is really important for the success of a firm.

ACTIVITY

Visit a local town centre shopping district. Calculate the number of coffee bars operated by companies such as Costa, Starbucks etc., and also local independent coffee bars and cafés. Then calculate the three-firm concentration ratio for neighbourhood coffee bars and cafés. What do your results tell you about this industry's market structure? How do the coffee bars and cafés you have observed compete with each other?

4.5 The competitive market process

Competition is a dynamic process which takes place over a period of time and is about much more than just price competition. Indeed, competition of various types is often extremely vigorous in highly concentrated markets.

What forms of competition would exist in perfect competition?

We mentioned earlier that the form of competition known as perfect competition does not actually exist. This is because no real-world market, however competitive, possesses the six characteristics or conditions necessary for perfect competition. The best that can be said about real-world markets is that some of them *approximate* to perfect competition, possessing some, but not all, of the required characteristics.

Although perfect competition is an abstract and unreal market structure, it is interesting to consider the forms competition might take in a perfectly competitive market economy. The first point to note is that price competition, in the form of price wars or price cutting by individual firms, would not take place. In perfect competition, all firms are passive price takers, able to sell all the output they produce at the ruling market price determined in the market as a whole. In this situation, firms cannot gain sales or market share by price cutting. Other forms of competition — involving the use of advertising, packaging, brand imaging or the provision of after-sales service to differentiate a firm's product from those of its competitors — simply destroy the conditions of perfect competition. These are the forms of competition which are prevalent, together with price competition, in the real economy in which we live.

So the only form of competition, both available to firms and also compatible with maintaining the conditions of perfect competition, is cost-cutting competition. Cost-cutting competition is likely in perfect competition because each firm has an incentive to reduce costs in order to make more profit. But even the existence of cost-cutting competition in a perfect market can be questioned. Why should firms finance research into cost-cutting technical progress when they know that other firms have instant access to all market information and that any extra profits resulting from successful cost-cutting can only be temporary?

Think also of the nature of competition in a perfect market from the perspective of a typical consumer. The choice is simultaneously very broad and very narrow. The consumer has the doubtful luxury of maximum choice in terms of the number of firms or suppliers from whom to purchase a product. Yet each firm is supplying an identical good or service at exactly the same price. In this sense, there would be no choice at all in perfect competition.

Real-world forms of competition

Various forms of competition take place in real-world markets. These include price competition, the use of persuasive advertising, product differentiation, marketing competition, brand imaging, packaging competition, the use of fashion, style and design, and quality competition, including the provision of point-of-sale service and after-sales service. By enabling firms to tell consumers that their products are superior to those offered by rival firms, innovation is also a significant part of the competitive process. Although some of these forms of competition may enhance a firm's monopoly power, many of them increase the degree of competition in the market by alerting consumers to the available choices and their features and creating products and services that best meet the needs of consumers.

Price competition

We now take a closer look at **price competition**. This takes place when a firm reduces prices in order to sell more of a good or service. Increased sales can occur in two different but interrelated ways. In the first, consumers switch from other markets where prices are higher and buy this good instead. In the second, consumers switch from buying similar goods from rival firms *within the same market* to buy the good from the firm that has cut its price.

It is sometimes argued, though without much evidence, that competitive firms do not like to use price competition because it leads to self-defeating price wars, which ultimately only benefit consumers. However, there are a number of ways in which firms undertake price competition, particularly in markets dominated by just a few firms. These include:

- **'Special offer' pricing** Firms introduce temporary 'special offer' prices on some of the goods they are selling. Supermarket pricing provides many examples of this, for example by offering certain goods for sale at discounted prices for a limited period of time.

- **Limit pricing** This is often linked to relatively short-lived price wars, which result from firms already in the market attempting to gain or to defend market share, or to 'kill off' new market entrants. With **limit pricing**, firms already in the market sacrifice short-run profit maximisation in order to maximise long-run profits, achieved through deterring the entry of new firms. They do this because they fear increased competition and loss of market power. For example, a large pest control company which dominates the UK market usually charges the same prices throughout the country. However, when new firms begin to enter local markets, the dominant firm (which is likely to have lower costs than potential entrants) responds by reducing its prices in these markets, in an attempt to deter market entry.
Should limit pricing be regarded as an example of a competitive pricing strategy, which reduces prices and the profits enjoyed by the established firms in the market? Or is limit pricing basically anti-competitive and unjustifiable? The answer probably depends on circumstances, but when limit pricing extends into predatory pricing, there is a much clearer case that such a pricing strategy is *anti*-competitive and against the consumers' interest.

- **Predatory pricing** Whereas limit pricing deters market entry, successful **predatory pricing** removes recent entrants to the market. Predatory pricing occurs when an established or incumbent firm deliberately sets prices below costs to force new market entrants out of business. Once the new entrants have left the market, the established firm may decide to restore prices to their previous levels. Both limit pricing and predatory pricing form barriers to market entry.

Though superficially they provide examples of large firms competing vigorously with each other, some forms of 'competition' such as the setting of predatory prices, are in fact anti-competitive, bolstering monopoly power, which in turn gives rise to consumer exploitation.

KEY TERMS

limit pricing reducing the price of a good to just above average cost to deter the entry of new firms into the market. Prices are set at levels which are likely to make it unprofitable for potential entrants who might consider coming into the market.

predatory pricing temporarily reducing the price of a good to below average cost to drive smaller firms or new market entrants out of the market.

STUDY TIP
Make sure you understand various forms of both price and non-price competition, and are able to describe and explain some of these practices, such as the use of persuasive advertising.

CASE STUDY 4.7

Newspapers and predatory pricing

Over 20 years ago, in 1993, Rupert Murdoch, owner of one Britain's most upmarket newspapers, *The Times*, and one of its most downmarket, the *Sun*, slashed the price of *The Times* from 45 pence to 30 pence, undercutting the prices charged by the UK's other 'quality' newspapers.

Journalists, media analysts, and especially the rival *Daily Telegraph*, the largest-selling upmarket newspaper in England, waited anxiously to see what would happen next. They soon found out. Murdoch's plan was simple: lower the price and people will buy. Sure enough, *The Times*' circulation began climbing and that of others began falling. The *Daily Telegraph*, panicking at seeing its circulation dip below 1 million for the first time since the 1950s, quickly cut its price from 48 pence to 30 pence.

The Times immediately responded by putting a 20 pence price tag on its paper, a move the *Daily Telegraph* could not afford to follow. In fact, *The Times* couldn't have afforded its price cut if it weren't subsidised by Murdoch's vast media empire.

What exactly was Murdoch trying to do? To some, it was simple: he hoped to kill off his rivals. In an editorial headlined, 'A Price War with Murder in its Sights', the *Daily Mirror* launched a full-page attack on Murdoch, asserting that Murdoch was practising nothing less than 'predatory pricing — selling his newspaper at a loss, at a figure that his rivals could not match'.

'Originally he wanted to prove that the newspaper market was price-sensitive,' said a spokesperson for Murdoch's UK publishing company. 'People were saying it wasn't true that people bought newspapers based on price.'

But the *Independent*, another quality newspaper, which initially resisted cutting its price, did not believe Murdoch's aims were so benign. The *Independent* filed two complaints with the government's competition authorities, arguing that *The Times*' price cuts were anti-competitive and amounted to predatory pricing. However, the authorities rejected both claims. Proof that even Murdoch couldn't maintain lower prices indefinitely was his decision a few months later to raise again the prices of both the *Sun* and *The Times*.

Follow-up questions

1 Explain the difference between predatory pricing and limit pricing.
2 Do you believe that Rupert Murdoch's price cuts were anti-competitive and against the public interest? Justify your answer.

SUMMARY

- Market structures are defined by the number of firms in the market and by other factors such as market concentration, entry barriers and the degree of product differentiation.
- Perfect competition is the extreme example of a competitive market structure, while pure monopoly is the most extreme example of a concentrated market structure.
- Economists usually assume that firms aim to maximise profits, but in the real world firms may have other objectives.
- The more competitive the market, the greater the likelihood that firms are price takers.
- The less competitive and the more concentrated the market, the greater the likelihood that firms are price makers.
- In the extreme, a price taker faces a perfectly elastic demand curve for its product, which is the ruling market price in the market as a whole. The curve is also the average revenue curve.
- By contrast, for a pure monopoly, the downward-sloping market demand curve is the demand curve for the monopolist's output, and also its average revenue curve.
- A monopolist may choose to be a quantity setter rather than a price maker.
- Monopoly must not be confused with monopoly power. Firms in every market except perfect competition can exercise a degree of monopoly power, which increases with market concentration.
- The existence of barriers to market entry is one of the main factors that increase monopoly power or market power.
- Barriers to market entry divide into natural or 'innocent' entry barriers and man-made or strategic entry barriers.
- Persuasive and saturation advertising are used as strategic entry barriers.
- Market concentration can be measured by concentration ratios.
- Monopolies and firms in concentrated markets can benefit from economies of scale and high levels of investment and product innovation financed by high profits.
- Monopolies use entry barriers to promote an 'easy life' and they are often productively inefficient.
- Forms of collusion such as cartels or price rings may lead to some of the worst forms of monopoly, restricting output, hiking up prices and promoting inefficiency.
- Firms with monopoly power, operating in concentrated markets, may try to use limit pricing to deter the entry of new firms into the market.
- If they are able to, they may also use predatory pricing to 'kill off' firms which have already entered the market.

Questions

1 Explain why the market for tomatoes is competitive whereas the market for tap water is uncompetitive.

2 Assess the role of markets in a mixed economy such as the UK economy.

3 Describe four different circumstances in which monopoly may occur.

4 State the circumstances in which monopoly may be (a) productively inefficient and (b) productively efficient.

5 Outline three different forms of competition that take place in markets.

6 'Since perfect competition does not exist in real-world markets, there are no lessons to learn from this market structure.' Critically evaluate this statement.

5

The market mechanism, market failure and government intervention in markets

Earlier chapters have explained how markets work. This chapter starts by adding another dimension by introducing and explaining the four functions that prices perform in a market economy, or in the market sector of a mixed economy. It then explains how, when one or more of these four functions breaks down, market failure occurs.

The next sections look in some detail at the main forms of market failure: public goods, merit and demerit goods, and externalities. This is followed by an explanation of how monopoly and imperfect markets — topics covered in Chapter 4 — are sources of market failure. We then go on to explain how income and wealth inequalities are a form of market failure.

In developed countries such as the UK, the existence of market failure leads to government intervention in the economy to make markets function better, and in some cases to replace the market with state provision of goods and services. In the final sections of the chapter, we explain and evaluate the methods of government intervention, and the government failure which arises when the intervention creates new problems.

LEARNING OBJECTIVES
This chapter will explain:

- the four functions that prices perform
- how markets and prices affect resource allocation
- the meaning of market failure, distinguishing between complete and partial market failure
- market failure in terms of the breakdown of the four functions of prices
- market failure in terms of the important economic concepts of efficiency and equity
- the difference between a private good and a public good
- the difference between a pure public good and a quasi-public good
- the difference between a merit good and a demerit good
- how externalities lead to market failure in the case of merit and demerit goods
- how under-consumption of merit goods and over-consumption of demerit goods may result from information problems
- how monopoly may lead to market failure and resource misallocation
- how income and wealth inequalities lead to market failure
- how government intervention in the economy tries to correct market failure
- how government intervention in markets may itself result in government failure

5.1 How markets and prices allocate resources

The functions of prices

Earlier chapters have provided lots of information about the role of prices in a market economy or in the market sector of a mixed economy. So far, however, we have not drawn attention to the precise functions that prices perform. These are:

- the signalling function
- the incentive function
- the rationing function
- the allocative function

Prices signal information

Prices provide information that allows buyers and sellers in a market to plan and coordinate their economic activities. This is the **signalling function of prices**. Here is an example. Most Friday afternoons, a woman visits a local street market to buy fruit and vegetables for her family. She wants to buy both strawberries and raspberries. On reaching the market, she looks at the prices displayed by the market vendors on white plastic tabs stuck into each tray of produce. The prices charged, which may not be the same at all the market stalls, provide vital information about what to buy.

Prices create incentives

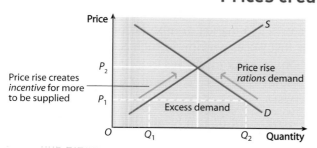

Figure 5.1 The incentive and rationing functions of prices

The information signalled by *relative* prices, such as the price of strawberries relative to the price of raspberries, creates incentives for people to alter their economic behaviour. A higher price in a market creates incentives for producers to supply more of a good or service because they believe that larger profits can be made. As Figure 5.1 shows, the incentive function of a price rise is shown by an extension of supply along the market supply curve, S, depicted by a movement up the left-hand arrow in the diagram. Likewise, falling prices reduce profits and thence the incentive to supply the product. Either way, this is the **incentive function of prices** in operation. Similarly, in labour markets, rising wages create the incentive for people to acquire new skills and supply their labour services, while falling wages reduce these incentives.

The rationing function of prices

Figure 5.1 also illustrates the **rationing function of prices**. At price P_1, the price rises to get rid of the excess demand shown in the diagram. The rising price, reflecting the strength of consumer preferences and consumers' ability to pay, rations demand for the good. The rationing function of prices is depicted by the movement up the right-hand arrow in the diagram, which shows a contraction of demand along the demand curve D. Demand contracts until excess demand is eliminated. In a similar way, rising wages in a labour market ration firms' demand for labour.

Prices and resource allocation

The rationing function of prices is related to, but not quite the same as, the **allocative function of prices**. The rationing function distributes scarce goods to those consumers who value them most highly. By contrast, the allocative function directs resources between markets, away from the markets in which prices are too high and in which there is excess supply, towards the markets where there is excess demand and price is too low.

5.2 The meaning of market failure

Market failure occurs whenever the market mechanism or price mechanism performs badly or unsatisfactorily, or fails to perform at all. It is useful to distinguish between complete market failure, when the market simply does not exist, and partial market failure, when the market functions, but produces the 'wrong' quantity of a good or service. In the former case, there is a '**missing market**'. In the latter case, the good or service may be provided too cheaply, in which case it is over-produced and over-consumed. Alternatively, as in monopoly, the good may be too expensive, in which case under-production and under-consumption results.

Market failure and the four functions prices perform in markets

In section 5.1, when explaining how the price mechanism distributes scarce resources between alternative uses in a market or mixed economy, we introduced the four functions that prices perform in such economies. To recap, these are: signalling information; creating incentives to influence people's behaviour; allocating scarce resources between competing uses; and rationing the demand for goods and services.

Ignoring the possibility that market failure can be associated with inequalities in the distribution of income, we can say that when all four of these functions perform well, markets also work well and market failure is either non-existent or trivial. However, when one or more of the four functions of prices significantly breaks down, market failure occurs. You will see in sections 5.3 and 5.4 how, in the case of pure public goods and externalities, the price mechanism breaks down completely. If an alternative method of provision does not exist, complete market breakdown means that markets fail completely and none of the public good is produced. A useful service is not provided — hence there is market failure. In the case of an externality such as pollution, firms (and indeed consumers) that generate pollution simply dump it on other people (whom we call third parties). There is no market in which the unwilling consumers of pollution can charge producers for the discomfort they suffer. The lack of a market means there is no incentive for the polluter to pollute less. Hence, again, there is market failure.

5.3 Public goods, private goods and quasi-public goods

Private goods

Most goods are **private goods** which possess two defining characteristics.

- The owners can exercise private property rights, preventing other people from using the good or consuming its benefits. This property is called excludability — for example, a shopkeeper can prevent people from consuming the goods on display in her shop, unless they are prepared to pay for them. (Shoplifters, of course, try to get round this exercise of private property rights!)
- The second property is called rivalry, which can be illustrated in the context of a good such as chocolate. If you eat a bar of chocolate, other people cannot eat it and gain its benefits. In this sense, people are rivals. (Rivalry is sometimes called diminishability. When one person consumes a private good, such as a sweet or a banana, the quantity available to others diminishes.)

Public goods

A **public good** exhibits the opposite characteristics of non-excludability and non-rivalry or non-diminishability. It is these characteristics that lead to market failure.

A lighthouse, or rather the beam of light provided by a lighthouse, is an example of a public good. Suppose an entrepreneur builds the lighthouse shown in Figure 5.2, and then tries to charge each ship that passes in the night and benefits from the beam of light. Providing ships pay up, the service can be provided commercially through the market.

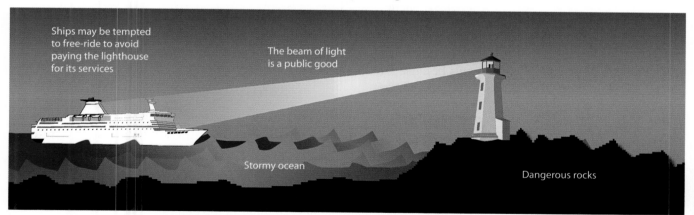

Ships may be tempted to free-ride to avoid paying the lighthouse for its services

The beam of light is a public good

Stormy ocean

Dangerous rocks

Figure 5.2 The beam of light provided by a lighthouse is a public good

However, the market is likely to fail. The appearance of one more ship near the lighthouse does not prevent other ships from sailing in the area. Non-rivalry thus occurs. It is also impossible to exclude free-riders (in this case, ships that benefit without paying). Because of non-excludability, it may be impossible to collect enough revenue to cover costs. If too many ships decide to 'free-ride', profits cannot be made and the incentive to provide the service through the market disappears. The market thus fails to provide a service for which there is an obvious need. There is then a need for alternative provision by the government in its public spending programme, or possibly by a charity (such as Trinity House in the UK).

Other examples of public goods

Other examples of public goods include national defence, police, street lighting, roads, and television and radio programmes. To take one of these, national defence is non-rival in the sense that receiving the benefits of national defence (for example, greater peace of mind) does not reduce the benefits available to other people. National defence is also non-excludable because providing the benefits for one means providing the benefits for all.

To explain this further, consider a situation in which the state does not provide national defence. Instead, the government lets individual citizens purchase in the market the defence or protection they want. But markets only provide defence when entrepreneurs can successfully charge prices for the services they supply. Suppose an aspiring citizen, who believes a fortune can be made in the defence industry, sets up a company, Nuclear Defence Services Ltd, with the aim of persuading the country's residents to purchase the services of nuclear missiles strategically located around the country. After estimating the money value of the defence received by each individual, Nuclear Defence Services bills each household accordingly and waits for the payments to flow in…

But the payments may never arrive. As long as the service is provided, every household can benefit without paying. Nuclear Defence Services Ltd cannot provide nuclear defence only to the country's inhabitants who are prepared to pay, while excluding the benefit from those who are not prepared to pay. Withdrawing the benefit from one means withdrawing it from all. But all individuals face the temptation to consume without paying, or to free-ride. If enough people choose to free-ride, Nuclear Defence Services Ltd makes a loss. The incentive to provide the service through the market thus disappears. Assuming, of course, that the majority of the country's inhabitants believe nuclear defence to be necessary (i.e. a good rather than a 'bad'), the market fails because it fails to provide a service for which there is a need. The result is a missing market.

TEST YOURSELF 5.1
Explain why D is the correct answer to the following objective test question, and why A, B and C are incorrect.

When applied to a public good, 'non-rival' means that:

A there is a single monopoly supplier of the good

B the resources used in the good's production could not have been used to produce other goods

C if the good is provided for one person, it must be provided for everybody else

D consumption of the good by one person does not reduce the amount of the good available to others

EXTENSION MATERIAL

'Goods' and 'bads'

A good such as a loaf of bread provides benefits to the person or persons who consume it. Consumer goods yield usefulness or utility, and sometimes pleasure and satisfaction. (Using economic jargon, we say that the consumption of consumer goods increases economic welfare.)

In everyday language, we generally use the word 'bad' as an adjective: for example, a bad film or a bad football match. However, economists also use the word as a noun. In this usage, an economic 'bad' is the opposite of a good, yielding disutility, dissatisfaction or displeasure. For most people, consumption of a bad such as rotten meat reduces rather than increases economic welfare.

Likewise, a 'public bad' is the opposite of a public good. An example of a public bad is rubbish or garbage. The production of public bads such as garbage leads to a free-rider problem, though the problem is subtly different from the one that occurs in the case of public goods. People are generally prepared to pay for the removal of garbage, to avoid the unpleasantness otherwise experienced. However, payment can be avoided by dumping the bad in a public place or on someone else's property.

In the UK, local authorities generally empty household dustbins without charging for each bin emptied. Suppose this service is not provided, and private contractors remove rubbish and charge households £1 for each dustbin emptied. To avoid paying £1, some households may decide to dump their waste in the road or in neighbours' dustbins. (Builders' skips provide a good example of this practice. A household hiring a skip is well advised to fill the skip as quickly as possible, before the rest of the street takes advantage of the facility.) If too many households free-ride, it is impossible for the private contractor to make a profit, and a service for which there is a need is no longer provided. Hence the case for free local authority provision, financed through taxation.

Free-riding can be a problem with public bads such as rubbish dumped in the street

CASE STUDY 5.1

The Seattle stomp

For several years some US local authorities have been charging households for emptying their dustbins, arguing that if rubbish disposal is free, people produce too much garbage. The obvious economic solution is to make households pay the cost of disposing of their waste. That will give them an incentive to throw out less and recycle more (assuming that local governments provide collection points for suitable materials). Several US cities have started charging households for generating rubbish. The common system is to sell tags which householders attach to rubbish bags or bins. In effect, the price of a tag is the price the household pays for creating another bag of rubbish.

In Charlottesville, Virginia, households were charged 80 cents for each tag they bought. Following the introduction of pricing, the number of garbage bags collected fell sharply, by 37% over the first 5 months. However, this was largely due to a practice nicknamed the 'Seattle stomp' — a frantic dance first noticed when Seattle introduced rubbish pricing. Rather than buy more tags, households simply crammed 40% more garbage into each bag. But this is inefficient as compacting or crushing is better done by machines at landfill sites than by households. The weight of rubbish collected at Charlottesville (a better indicator of disposal costs than volume) fell by a modest 14%, while in nearby cities with no pricing scheme, it fell by 3.5%.

More significantly, people resorted to illegal dumping rather than paying to have their rubbish removed. Illegal dumping may have accounted for 30–40% of the reduction in collected rubbish. There was a 15% increase in the weight of materials recycled, suggesting that people chose to recycle free rather than pay to have their refuse carted away. But cities with garbage-pricing policies are likely to have 'greener' citizens who recycle more in any case. Once this effect is removed, it appears that pricing rubbish collection has no significant effect on recycling. Also, in richer towns, people throw out more rubbish than in poorer ones. The rich not only have more trash to remove, but their time is too valuable to be spent recycling or dumping.

Follow-up questions

1 Why do most local councils in the UK empty household dustbins without charging a price for the service?
2 Evaluate the case for charging a price for emptying dustbins.

Quasi-public goods

> **KEY TERM**
> **quasi-public good** a good which is not fully non-rival and/or where it is possible to exclude people from consuming the product.

Public goods can be divided into pure public goods and **quasi-public goods**. National defence and police are examples of pure public goods — defined as public goods for which it is impossible to exclude free-riders. However, most public goods (street lighting, roads, television and radio programmes, and also lighthouses) are really quasi-public goods (also known as non-pure public goods).

Methods can be devised for converting the goods into private goods by excluding free-riders (e.g. electronic pricing of road use). Quasi-public goods can be provided by markets, but the second property of non-rivalry or non-diminishability means there is a case for providing all public goods free in order to encourage as much consumption as possible. Provided we assume the lack of a capacity restraint, for public goods and quasi-public goods, the optimal level of consumption occurs when they are available free of charge. (However, capacity constraints, resulting from factors such as the limited ability of roads to carry cars and the limited bandwidth of airwaves, means that there is also a case for charging for public goods such as roads and airwaves to deal with the problem of congestion.)

The significance of technological change

Roads provide one of the best examples of a good which has changed over the years from being regarded as a pure public good to now being thought of as a quasi-public good. Until quite recently, except in the case of motorways where limited points of access meant that toll gates could be installed, it was deemed impractical to charge motorists for the use of ordinary roads.

This has now changed. Technical change makes it feasible for the government or local authorities to use electronic pricing to charge *all* motorists for road use. The charges can also be varied at different times of day to create incentives for car drivers to shift their travel patterns from rush hour to non-rush hour. There is a case for *not* charging a price when roads are uncongested and thus largely non-rival, but for charging for road use as soon as the problem of congestion and road rivalry occurs. So why are there so few road pricing schemes? After all, we are happy to pay for most goods and to pay different prices at different times of day, for example for watching a movie at a cinema. The answer to this question probably lies in the political power of the motoring lobby. Politicians fear they will not get re-elected if they try to bring in road pricing schemes.

CASE STUDY 5.2

Twelve years of the London congestion charge

In February 2015, the London congestion charge was 12 years old. At the time of its introduction, many economists believed that the congestion charge marked the triumph of economic common sense over narrow self-interest. Economists confidently believed that many other cities, both in the UK and abroad, would rush to adopt London-style road pricing. In the event, this did not happen. In November 2008, Manchester voters were asked to approve the introduction of a city-centre congestion charge and they voted against it.

The congestion charge was introduced to London in 2003

What have been the possible benefits and costs of the London congestion charge? In 2003 the idea of charging car users to drive around the capital was met with near-apocalyptic warnings from motoring groups and newspapers such as the *Daily Mail*. The charge would 'destroy' the city's commercial heart and cause 'total gridlock', warned some. It would 'cause misery to thousands of commuters across the capital', said Conservative Greater London Authority's transport spokesman. 'Londoners will suffer conditions worse than cattle trucks on their morning commute into work,' she added. Motoring groups, such as the AA, say the cost to drivers has actually adversely affected the London economy by around £2.6 billion. For every £2 taken from drivers, more than £1 was spent on running the scheme. The AA also pointed out that traffic has been getting steadily slower. AA president Edmund King said: 'London drivers have paid a heavy price for slower journeys over the last decade'.

Since it was introduced in 2003, however, the charge, which has risen from £5 through £8 to its present level of £11.50, has not caused gridlock. Rather, it has resulted in a gradual reduction in traffic levels. The congestion charge has generated a net revenue of over £1 billion since 2003. The charge had an immediate environmental impact. Nitrous oxide fell 13.4% between 2002 and 2003, and there were similar falls for carbon dioxide and particulate matter. In terms of the effect the charge had on local businesses, despite the scaremongering which accompanied its introduction, certainly before 2009, business activity within the charge zone has been higher in both productivity and profitability since the charge was introduced. Transport for London claims that the charge had a 'broadly neutral impact' on the wider London economy. The charge is broadly supported by a majority of Londoners, with 45% for and 41% against. Boris Johnson, the Conservative mayor of London until at least 2016, has described the congestion charge a success which has benefited London.

Elliot Jacobs, managing director of office supplies firm UOE, says: 'Getting deliveries on time is really important and the congestion charge means we have a consistency of traffic flow and a reliability that we know where the traffic's going to be, and that's important. It means we can get there on time and that's worth £10 every day.' However, although the congestion charge — which was seen as a radical step a decade ago — has won over many of the original doubters, there are still those who claim it has not been a success.

Follow-up questions

1 Why have other cities, in Britain and the rest of the world, not rushed to follow London's example and introduce a congestion charge?
2 Do you agree that road use should be priced? Justify your answer.

5.4 Positive and negative externalities in production and consumption

An **externality** is a special type of public good or public 'bad' which is 'dumped' by those who produce it onto other people (third parties) who receive or consume it, whether or not they choose to. The key feature of an externality is that there is no market in which it can be bought or sold — externalities are produced and received outside the market, providing another example of a missing market.

As with the public goods, externalities provide examples of the free-rider problem. The provider of an external *benefit* (or **positive externality**), such as a beautiful view, cannot charge a market price to any willing free-riders who enjoy it, while conversely, the unwilling free-riders who receive or consume external *costs* (or **negative externalities**), such as pollution and noise, cannot charge a price to the polluter for the bad they reluctantly consume.

Externalities can be generated by firms in the course of producing the goods they eventually sell in a market, or they can be generated by households and individuals when they consume goods. The former are known as **production externalities**, with the latter being **consumption externalities**. We shall look at these in turn.

Production externalities

Negative production externalities

Consider the power station illustrated in Figure 5.3, which discharges pollution into the atmosphere in the course of producing electricity. We can view a negative production externality (or external cost) such as pollution as being that part of the true or real costs of production which the power station evades by dumping the bad on others: for example, the people living in the houses and the businesses in the commercial forestry industry. The price that the consumer pays for the good (electricity) reflects only the money costs of production, and not all the real costs, which include the external costs (including the eyesore or visual pollution also shown in the diagram). In a market situation, the power station's output of electricity is thus under-priced. The allocative function of prices has once again broken down — under-pricing encourages too much consumption of electricity, and therefore over-production of both electricity and the spin-off, pollution.

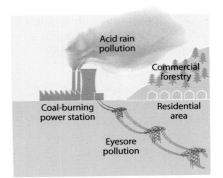

Figure 5.3 The discharge of negative production externalities by a power station

Positive production externalities

Figure 5.4 shows again the power station illustrated in Figure 5.3, but in this case the production of electricity yields positive production externalities (or external benefits) rather than negative externalities. We have assumed that the power station discharges warm (but clean) water into the lake adjacent to the power station. Warmer temperatures increase fish stocks, and commercial fishing boats and private anglers then benefit. Unless it owns the lake, the power station company cannot charge the fishermen for the benefits they are receiving. (You might, of course, query our assumption that the water discharge creates positive rather than negative externalities. In all likelihood, disruption of a local ecosystem might cause negative externalities, such as algae pollution.)

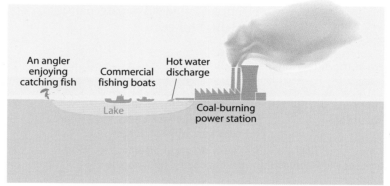

Figure 5.4 The discharge of positive production externalities by a power station

Consumption externalities

Negative consumption externalities

We are all probably familiar with the annoying experience of going to the cinema and having our pleasure disrupted by the ringing of mobile phones or the noisy eating of popcorn by the person sitting a few seats away. These are examples of negative consumption externalities, unwillingly received by a cinema goer as a result of consumption activities undertaken by other members of the audience. There are many examples of similarly annoying externalities — walking through litter and chewing gum dropped by pedestrians, being splashed by inconsiderate motorists, and reluctantly listening to 'head-banger' music discharged through open windows by 'boy racers' as they drive their souped-up BMWs too close to us on the pavement.

Positive consumption externalities

A good example of a positive consumption externality is the pleasure gained by a passer-by walking past beautiful buildings and household gardens in a residential area. At this point, it is also worth noting that a negative consumption externality suffered by one person may be a positive consumption externality for somebody else. For example, a few people, especially other 'head-bangers', enjoy the loud music and the throaty raw of the exhaust generated by our 'boy racer' in his souped-up BMW.

Consider also a situation when a person pays to watch a Premier League football match. If the stadium were empty, the football fan would gain less pleasure from watching the match than if soaking up the 'atmosphere' generated by other chanting fans in a packed stadium. Much the same happens in restaurants. Prospective diners walk past empty or nearly empty restaurants, preferring instead to queue for a table at an already full eatery. Maybe they think the food is better, but despite having to wait longer for their food, what they also enjoy is the 'atmosphere' generated by other diners.

Summary: different types of externalities

As we have explained, externalities divide into negative externalities and positive externalities (which are also known as external costs and benefits). Table 5.1 lists the possible types of externality and gives examples of negative externalities (costs) and positive externalities (benefits) for each.

Table 5.1 Examples of the different types of externality

Type of externality	Negative externalities	Positive externalities
Pure production externalities (*generated and received in production*)	Acid rain pollution discharged by a power station which harms a nearby commercially run forest	A farmer benefiting from drainage undertaken by a neighbouring farmer
Pure consumption externalities (*generated and received in consumption*)	Noisy music at a party disturbing neighbouring households	Households benefiting from the beauty of neighbouring gardens

How externalities lead to the 'wrong' quantity of a good being produced and consumed

We mentioned earlier that when negative externalities are generated in the course of production, part of the true or real costs of production are not borne by the producer, instead being dumped on others. This means that, even in competitive markets, if negative *production* externalities are generated, goods end up being too cheap or under-priced. The market has created the wrong incentives. Because prices under-reflect the true costs of production, which include the cost of the negative externalities, too much of the good ends up being produced and consumed.

The opposite happens when firms generate positive production externalities. Prices end up being too high, leading to the 'wrong' quantity of the good being produced and consumed. Once again, the market has created the wrong incentives, which discourages consumption. In this case, prices over-reflect the true costs of production. Not enough of the good ends up being produced and consumed.

In much the same way, when negative and positive *consumption* externalities are generated, markets are distorted and the wrong quantity of a good is produced and consumed. This is explained in section 5.5 on merit and demerit goods.

STUDY TIP
Students often fail to understand that externalities are generated and received outside the market. Remember that both public goods and externalities provide examples of missing markets.

QUANTITATIVE SKILLS 5.1

Worked example: calculating social costs and benefits

Table 5.2 shows the costs and benefits of building a new shopping mall.

Table 5.2

Private costs	£10 million
Private costs	£10 million
External costs	£20 million
Private benefits	£8 million
External benefits	£25 million

Calculate the social costs and the social benefits and then decide whether building the shopping mall is worthwhile, first for society, and second for the property developer.

social cost = private cost + external cost

and likewise:

social benefit = private benefit + external benefit.

Social cost is therefore £30 million, while **social benefit** is £33 million. Since the social benefit exceeds the social cost by £3 million, the shopping mall is worthwhile for society at large. However, it is not worthwhile for the property developer, whose private costs exceed private benefits by £2 million.

KEY TERM

social benefit the total benefit of an activity, including the external benefit as well as the private benefit. Expressed as an equation: social benefit = private benefit + external benefit.

TEST YOURSELF 5.2

Explain why B is the correct answer to the following objective test question, and why A, C, and D are incorrect.

Which one of the following creates an incentive for firms to reduce pollution?

A An increase in negative externalities when firms increase their output

B A tax levied on polluting firms

C Subsidies paid to firms that increase their levels of production

D The removal of regulations imposed on polluting firms

Using supply and demand diagrams to illustrate externalities

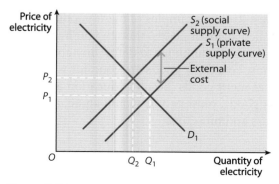

Figure 5.5 Negative external production externalities or external costs illustrated on a supply and demand diagram

Figure 5.5 illustrates a negative production externality, such as pollution, in the context of a supply and demand diagram for electricity generated by burning fossil fuels. The supply curve S_1 shows how much electricity power stations plan to supply, assuming that all the negative externalities they produce are dumped on third parties. Given this assumption, the 'private' equilibrium price of electricity is P_1, with Q_1 being the quantity bought and sold. However, the second supply curve, S_2, includes the external costs of generating electricity, which are shown by the vertical distance between the two supply curves for each unit of electricity. The 'social' equilibrium price is P_2, with Q_2 being the quantity of electricity bought and sold. The difference between these two equilibria comes from the upward shift of the supply curve when the negative external costs are added to the power station companies' private costs. By forcing the power companies to pay a pollution tax, equal

107

to the estimated value of the negative externalities they are discharging, the price of electricity could increase to P_2, which would cause electricity output to fall to the 'social' equilibrium quantity, Q_2. The diagram illustrates how market failure occurs through free markets producing too much of a good when negative external production externalities are generated.

The next diagram, Figure 5.6, illustrates a *positive* production externality, such as the improved quality of neighbouring land which can result when a farmer installs a drainage system on his own land. If the farmer invests £200,000 in the new drainage system, he gains most of the benefits, but not his neighbours. But if he invests an additional £100,000, most of the extra benefit goes to his neighbours, whose land also becomes better drained. However, the farmer may not spend the extra money because he gains little benefit from the investment. As a result, the farmer chooses to install Q_1 drainage, shown where the demand curve D_1 intersects supply curve S_1. The position of the second supply curve, S_2, reflects the external *benefits* enjoyed by others as a result of improved drainage on the farmer's land. The external benefits, per unit, are shown by the vertical distance between the two supply curves. Note that S_2 lies to the right of S_1. If governments were to give subsidies to farmers, with the subsidies equal to the estimated value of the positive production externalities, the 'social' equilibrium quantity Q_2 of drainage might result. The diagram illustrates how market failure occurs through free markets producing too little of a good when positive external production externalities are generated.

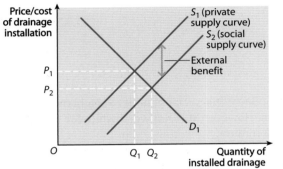

Figure 5.6 Positive external production externalities or external benefits illustrated on a supply and demand diagram

5.5 Merit and demerit goods

Merit goods

Merit goods are not the same as public goods. As we have seen, public goods are defined by two characteristics: they are non-excludable and non-diminishable. Because of these characteristics, a market may fail to provide a pure public good such as national defence. By contrast, markets can and do provide merit goods such as healthcare and education but, arguably, they under-provide. While public goods can result in a missing market or *complete* market failure, merit goods (and also their opposite, demerit goods) lead to *partial* market failure. As goods such as private healthcare and private education clearly show, markets provide merit goods, but they provide the 'wrong' quantity.

Education and healthcare are the best-known examples of merit goods. However, many goods can be classified as merit goods, though you must avoid the temptation that many students succumb to, to define any good that is 'good for you' as a merit good. Most consumer goods are good for you, but economists don't classify them as merit goods. Besides education and healthcare, other examples of merit goods, most people would argue, are car seatbelts, crash helmets, public parks and museums.

KEY TERM

merit good a good, such as healthcare, for which the social benefits of consumption exceed the private benefits. Value judgements are involved in deciding that a good is a merit good.

STUDY TIP
You should understand that merit goods are private goods, they are excludable and rival, even though they are often provided by the public sector.

Explain why C provides the correct answer to the following objective test question, and why A, B and D are incorrect.

A difference between a merit good and a public good is that:

A a merit good is always provided by the private sector whereas a public good is always provided by the government

B a merit good has a cost attached to it, whereas a public good is provided without cost to anybody

C consumption of a merit good reduces the amount available for others whereas an individual's consumption of a public good leaves unaffected the amount available for others

D a merit good is limited in supply whereas the supply of public goods is infinite

Positive consumption externalities and merit goods

A merit good, such as education or healthcare, is a good or service for which the social benefits of consumption enjoyed by the whole community exceed the private benefits received by the consumer. Consumption by an individual produces positive externalities that benefit the wider community. The community benefits from an educated (and civilised) population, and a healthy population means there are fewer people to catch diseases from.

If educational services were to be provided solely through the market, and at market prices, too few people would benefit from education. Figure 5.7 helps to explain why.

STUDY TIP

Make sure you practise drawing graphs such as the one in Figure 5.7.

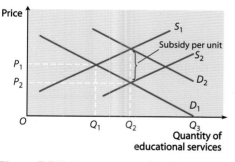

Figure 5.7 Under-consumption of a merit good in a free market and the effect of a subsidy

In Figure 5.7, the market supply curve of education is S_1. The curve shows the quantity of school places private schools are prepared to supply at different possible annual prices for education. The market demand curve D_1, which does not reflect the positive externalities enjoyed by society as a whole when children are educated, shows how much education parents are prepared to buy for their children at the different possible prices. In this situation, the market price of education is P_1, determined where the D_1 and S_1 curves intersect. At this price, Q_1 children are educated.

However, demand curve D_2, positioned to the right of D_1, includes the external benefits of education as well as the private benefits enjoyed by the children being educated. (D_2 is the social benefit curve, whereas D_1 is the private benefit curve.) Whereas Q_1 is the *privately optimal* level of education, Q_2, located immediately below the intersection of curves D_2 and S_1, is the *socially optimal* level of education.

The price of education would have to fall to P_2 to bring about equilibrium at Q_2. However, in a free market, schools would be unlikely to reduce the price they charge for education, largely because this would wipe out their profits. Free-market provision of merit goods therefore leads to under-consumption, and hence to their under-production. In a free market, too few scarce resources are allocated to the production and consumption of merit goods.

KEY TERM

subsidy a payment made by government or other authority, usually to producers, for each unit of the subsidised good that they produce. Consumers can also be subsidised: for example, bus passes given to children to enable them to travel on buses free or at a reduced price.

The solution could be a government **subsidy** granted to schools, which shifts the market supply curve to S_2. In Figure 5.7, the size of the subsidy per unit is shown by the vertical distance between the two supply curves, S_1 and S_2.

STUDY TIP

Students often assert that any good that is 'good for you' is a merit good. Make sure you can explain why this assertion is wrong.

CASE STUDY 5.3

Museums as merit goods

Museums perform the important cultural function of conserving, interpreting, researching and displaying heritage. Museums have a mix of ownership patterns. For example, over 40% of UK museums are governed by public authorities, with the rest privately owned, mostly on a non-profit basis. Museums cover a wide range of institutions of varying size and reputation, ranging from internationally renowned institutions such as the British Museum to a large number of relatively small, often locally focused museums.

The funding of museums remains a source of considerable debate. Government subsidy or provision may be justified on the basis that museums generate external benefits: for example, knowledge acquired by a visitor may be passed on to others. Museums may also be regarded as merit goods, generating a better educated and informed public and collective pride.

Government subsidy of museums may also be justified on the grounds that the subsidy would encourage consumption. The case against government subsidy is that it may encourage inefficiency, lead to government failure through favouring well-off visitors who can afford to pay. It is also a cost to the taxpayer.

Follow-up questions

1 Do you agree that a museum is a merit good? Justify your answer.
2 Some argue that if entry to museums is free, people will not value what museums have to offer. Explain why you agree or disagree.

KEY TERM

demerit good a good, such as tobacco, for which the social costs of consumption exceed the private costs. Value judgements are involved in deciding that a good is a demerit good.

Finally, remember that value judgements are being made when describing particular goods as merit goods (or demerit goods). It is also worth noting that under-provision of merit goods and over-provision of demerit goods may also result from the imperfect information that consumers possess, which can lead, for example in the case of demerit goods, to failure to give adequate weight to the long-term consequences of consuming a good such as tobacco. The effects of imperfect information are explored further later in this chapter.

Demerit goods

KEY TERM

social cost the total cost of an activity, including the external cost as well as the private cost. Expressed as an equation: social cost = private cost + external cost.

As their name suggests, **demerit goods** are the opposite of merit goods. The **social costs** to the whole community which result from the consumption of a demerit good, such as tobacco or alcohol, exceed the private costs incurred by the consumer. This is because consumption by an individual produces negative externalities that harm the wider community. The *private* cost can be measured by the money cost of purchasing the good, together with any health damage suffered by the person consuming the good. But the *social* costs of consumption also include the cost of the negative externalities. These include, for example, costs imposed on other people from passive smoking and road accidents caused by drunken drivers, together with the cost of taxes raised to pay for the care of victims of tobacco- and alcohol-related diseases.

Negative consumption externalities and demerit goods

In the same way as the consumption of merit goods generates positive externalities which benefit the wider community, the consumption of demerit goods leads to the dumping of negative externalities on others. An example is smoke breathed in by passive smokers, who don't enjoy the tobacco fumes they inhale.

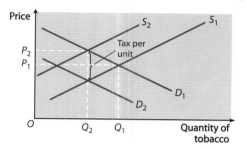

Figure 5.8 Over-consumption of a demerit good in a free market

Figure 5.8 shows too much tobacco being consumed when bought at market prices. At least in the short run, the privately optimal level of tobacco consumption is Q_1, located where demand curve D_1 intersects supply curve S_1. At this level of consumption, the price of a packet of cigarettes is P_1. However, because smokers generate negative consumption externalities, Q_1 is higher than the *socially optimal* level of consumption, which is Q_2. Free-market provision therefore leads to over-consumption, and hence over-production of tobacco products. In a free market, too many scarce resources are allocated to their production.

To explain this further, consider the demand curve D_2 in Figure 5.8. D_2 is positioned *below* curve D_1 because the social benefits to the whole community of smoking are less than the private benefits enjoyed by the smokers themselves. (D_2 is the social benefit curve, whereas D_1 is the private benefit curve.) Q_2, the socially optimal level of tobacco consumption, is located immediately below the intersection of curves D_2 and S_1.

One way of reducing tobacco consumption from the privately optimal level Q_1 to the socially optimal level, Q_2, is for the government to tax the sale of tobacco products. A tax per unit, set equal to the vertical distance between supply curves S_1 and S_2, shifts the supply curve up to S_2. This raises the price, to P_2, and consumption falls to the socially optimal level, Q_2.

Note that if the government were to deem the socially optimal level of tobacco consumption to be zero, a very large tax would be needed to achieve this end. Alternatively, the government might decide to ban the production, sale and consumption of tobacco products. However, as we shall shortly explain, both taxation and an outright ban are likely to lead to government failure.

SYNOPTIC LINK

Taxes and government spending are used in the government's fiscal policy. Along with monetary policy, fiscal policy is usually considered to be a macroeconomic topic. As such, fiscal policy is explained in some depth in Chapter 9, Macroeconomic policy. Nevertheless, taxes imposed on firms and subsidies, which are part of government spending, also have microeconomic dimensions.

CASE STUDY 5.4

Smoking yourself 'fit'

Strange as it seems, early cigarette ads, such as the Kensitas ad from 1929, often boasted the 'health benefits' of smoking, claiming 'relief' from asthma, wheezing, hay fever and obesity. In 1946 the American tobacco company Camel ran a series of adverts claiming that Camel were the 'doctor's choice'.

By the 1950s, research began to link smoking to cancer. Worldwide, tobacco use causes more than 5 million deaths per year, and current trends show that tobacco use will cause more than 8 million deaths annually by 2030, largely through the growth of smoking in developing countries.

1929 Kensitas magazine advert (left) and 1946 Camels magazine advert (right)

Follow-up questions

1 Most economists agree that tobacco is a demerit good. Why is this so?
2 Why do governments in countries such as the UK and USA now ban advertisements like these?

Cigarettes, and other tobacco products, and alcoholic drink are the two best-known examples of demerit goods. These days, governments in countries such as the UK either ban tobacco and drinks advertising, or severely regulate what the adverts can show. This has not always been the case, as the examples of advertisements for Kensitas and Camel cigarettes show.

Tobacco and drinks companies want to make their products appealing to young people, possibly in the hope that if teenagers develop the habit, they will be hooked on cigarettes and alcohol for the rest of their lives. To combat claims that the industry has been acting in an irresponsible way, the UK firms that produce alcoholic drinks have set up a public relations organisation, the Portman Group, to monitor adverts that might bring the drinks industry into disrepute. On the next page is an example of a recent drinks advert that was banned, not directly by the Portman Group, but by a local Trading Standards office.

CASE STUDY 5.5

Scratch-off label 'too sexy' for UK

Bottles of a Belgian lager whose labels showed a young lady wearing a swimsuit that could be scratched off have been banned in the UK. The 'Rubbel Sexy Lager' product breached the Portman Group's Code of Practice on the Naming, Packaging and Promotion of Alcoholic Drinks.

The Chief Executive of the Portman Group said: 'Some people might think this is harmless fun but there is a serious issue involved. Drinking excessively can affect people's judgement and behaviour, leading to them engaging in activity which they later regret. Our Code disallows drinks marketing being linked to sexual success.'

Follow-up question

1 Is self-regulation, by organisations such as the Portman Group, the best way of limiting consumption of a demerit good? Justify your answer.

Merit and demerit goods and value judgements

The left-hand and right-hand columns of Table 5.3 list a number of goods that are accepted by most people as clear-cut examples of merit goods or demerit goods. However, for the goods listed in the middle column — for example, contraception — the position is less clear. Because people have different values and ethics (often related to their religions), contraception is viewed by some people as a merit good, but by others as a demerit good. Whether a good is classified as a merit good or a demerit good, or indeed as neither, thus depends on the value judgements of the person making the classification. This provides an important example of the distinction between positive statements and normative statements, a distinction first explained in Chapter 1. A positive statement is a statement of fact or a statement that can be tested to see if it is right or wrong. For example, statements that the Earth is round and that the Earth is flat are both positive statements, though scientific evidence shows that the second statement is wrong. By contrast, a normative statement is a statement of opinion, involving a value judgement. Thus, a statement that the Earth *ought* to be flat is normative.

Table 5.3 Merit and demerit goods, and less clear-cut cases

Merit goods	Merit or demerit goods?	Demerit goods
Education	Contraception	Tobacco
Healthcare (e.g. vaccination, preventative dental care, AIDS testing)	Abortion	Alcohol
Crash helmets	Sterilisation	Narcotic drugs, such as heroin and crack cocaine
Car seatbelts		Pornography
Museums and public parks		Prostitution

Merit and demerit goods and the information problem

Some economists argue that under-consumption of merit goods and over-consumption of demerit goods stem not so much from the externalities that consumption generates, but from an **information problem**. Many people become addicted to demerit goods in their teenage years. Because of peer-group pressure and related factors, teenagers are heavily influenced by factors relating to lifestyle and personal circumstances, while at the same time

> **KEY TERM**
> **information problem** occurs when people make wrong decisions because they don't possess or they ignore relevant information. Very often they are myopic (short-sighted) about the future.

ignoring, downplaying or being myopic about how their addictions may affect them many years ahead. Individuals take account of *short-term* costs and benefits, but ignore or undervalue the *long-term* private costs and benefits.

For most merit goods, the long-term private benefit of consumption exceeds the short-term private benefit. But, as is the case with demerit goods, when deciding how much to consume, individuals often take account only of short-term costs and benefits. Preventative dentistry provides a good example. Many people ignore the long-term benefit of dental check-ups, and decide not to consume the service. Their decisions are influenced by factors such as the price charged by the dentist and the unpleasantness of the dental experience. Unfortunately, they may end up later in life with rotten teeth or gum disease, saying: 'If only I had visited the dentist more often when I was younger.'

ACTIVITY

Ask your classmates, friends or members of your family to answer a questionnaire about their consumption of demerit goods. Having ascertained whether your respondents smoke or drink, ask questions such as these:

● Do you know when you are consuming a good that economists call a demerit good?
● How may your consumption of the good affect other people?
● How may your consumption affect you in 20 years' time?
● Should the government tax your consumption of the good, and if so how high should the tax be?
● Should the government regulate your consumption of the good, and if so how?
● Should people be free to make their own decisions about whether or not to consume a good?

Analyse and report on your findings.

5.6 Market imperfections

Why the existence of monopoly may lead to market failure

We saw in Chapter 4 how, compared to competitive markets and in pursuit of excess profit, monopolies are likely to restrict market output and raise prices. The result is consumer exploitation. Prices end up being too high, with too few of society's scarce resources being allocated to the market in which the monopoly is producing. The outcome is illustrated in Figure 4.6. However, as Chapter 4 also explains, sometimes the benefits of monopoly can exceed the costs, in which case there is no market failure.

Why the immobility of factors of production can lead to market failure

An important cause of market failure is the immobility of factors of production, which can involve either geographical or occupational immobility.

STUDY TIP
Make sure you can link the analysis of market failure in Chapter 4 to the reasons why monopoly and market imperfections provide examples of market failure.

KEY TERMS

immobility of labour the inability of labour to move from one job to another, either for occupational reasons (e.g. the need for training) or for geographical reasons (e.g. the cost of moving to another part of the country).

geographical immobility of labour occurs when workers find it difficult or impossible to move to jobs in other parts of the country or in other countries for reasons such as higher housing costs in locations where the jobs exist.

occupational immobility of labour occurs when workers find it difficult or impossible to move between jobs because they lack or cannot develop the skills required for the new jobs.

Geographical immobility

Geographical immobility of labour occurs when barriers between markets prevent factors of production moving from one area to another to find employment. Land is obviously completely immobile and certain types of capital, for example factory buildings, can sometimes only be moved with extreme difficulty and cost. Usually, however, geographical mobility (and immobility) refers to the ease or difficulty of labour moving between different areas of the country, or between countries.

Reasons for this geographical immobility include: the financial costs involved in moving home, including the costs of selling a house and removal expenses; large regional variations in house prices which lead to a shortage of affordable housing in many areas; family and social ties, and differences in the general cost of living between regions and also between countries. Immigration controls and language differences also reduce the international mobility of labour.

Occupational immobility

Occupational immobility of labour arises when workers lack the skills to move between different types of employment, and because expensive and time-consuming training may be necessary if workers are to switch successfully between jobs. Sometimes the training is not available and some workers may lack the aptitudes to take on different types of employment. For example, workers made redundant in the coal-mining industry lack the specific skills that are needed in growing industries such as the provision of financial services. The need to gain recognised professional qualifications acts as an important cause of labour immobility, especially when workers want to move between different countries.

All these causes of **immobility of labour** lead to unemployment and a waste of scarce resources, and contribute to market failure in factor markets.

CASE STUDY 5.6

Taxi wars

Until quite recently, the London taxi market, in which cabs could be hailed or flagged down in the street, was dominated by black cabs. Entry into the black cab driving profession was strictly limited by the needs, first to spend several years gaining the 'knowledge' of all the streets in the centre ot the country's capital city, and second to be granted a cab-driver's licence, which were deliberately kept in short supply.

Competition first emerged from mini-cabs, but they had to be pre-booked by phoning or visiting a mini-cab company's office, and then hoping that the car would show up. But a new form of competition has now emerged which threatens to destroy the black cab market. Passengers are no longer subject to the availability of a black cab or a pre-booked mini-cab. They can now make use of a smartphone app that essentially puts a taxi in their pocket whenever they need one, in any major city in the world.

By reducing barriers to labour market entry, smartphone technology is destroying the monopoly power of black cab drivers. Since the launch of the Uber app in 2009, there has been a massive power shift in the cab market. Uber is a web-based cab booking service accessed via smartphones. The service connects passengers with vetted, private drivers who pick up their customers within minutes and take them to where they want to go. When the booking is made, the passenger's location is pinpointed with the GPS on their phone. The passenger chooses the kind of car they need, checks the estimated price of the journey, and is then told how long they will need to wait for their car to arrive. They see a photo of the driver, their name, and a contact phone number. When arriving at their destination, passengers don't need to hand over cash as payment automatically takes place via a credit card. Next day an e-mail is sent to the passenger with a breakdown of the costs, and passengers are not expected to tip their driver.

Follow-up questions

1 Explain the effect of the Uber app on labour mobility in the cab trade.
2 Describe one other example of smartphone technology improving labour market mobility.

5.7 An inequitable distribution of income and wealth

Equity means fairness or justness (though in other contexts, such as the housing market, equity has a very different meaning, namely wealth). **Inequity** means unfairness or unjustness. As soon as equitable considerations are introduced into economic analysis, normative or value judgements are made, which relate to what is a 'socially fair' **distribution of income and wealth**.

As the experience of many poor countries shows, unregulated market forces tend to produce highly unequal distributions of income and wealth. Some economists, usually of a free-market persuasion, dispute whether this is a market failure. They argue that the people who end up being rich deserve to be rich and that the people who end up being poor deserve to be poor. According to this view, the market has not failed — it merely creates incentives which, if followed, cause people to generate more income and wealth.

However, most economists reject as too extreme the view that the market contains its own morality with regard to the distribution of income and wealth. They argue that markets are 'value-neutral' with regard to the social and ethical desirability or undesirability of the distribution of income and wealth resulting from the way the market functions. It is also worth noting that if the initial distribution of income and wealth is deemed to be unfair, the allocation of resources, based on consumer preferences and effective demand, will also be suboptimal.

Few economists now believe that markets should be replaced by the planning or command mechanism. There is, however, much more agreement that, instead of *replacing* the market, governments should *modify* the market so that it operates in a more equitable way than would be the case without government intervention. Taxing the better-off and redistributing tax revenues as transfers to the less well-off is the obvious way of correcting the market failure to ensure an equitable distribution of income and wealth. (However, as section 5.9 explains, redistributive policies can promote new types of inefficiency and distortion within the economy.)

5.8 Government intervention in markets

The reasons against and for government intervention in markets

To understand why governments intervene in markets in economies such as the UK, it is useful to divide economists (and politicians) into two different groups: those who believe that unregulated markets generally work well, and those who argue that markets are prone to market failure. The former group are non-interventionists who want to leave as much as possible to market forces, while the latter group believe that government intervention can make markets work better.

- **Pro-free market economists** see a market economy as a calm and orderly place in which the market mechanism, working through incentives transmitted by price signals in competitive markets, achieves a better or more optimal outcome than can be attained through government intervention. In essence, risk-taking business men and women, who will gain or lose through the correctness of their decisions in the market place, know better what to produce than civil servants and planners cocooned by risk-free salaries and secured pensions. And providing that markets are sufficiently competitive, what is produced is ultimately decided by the wishes of consumers, who know better than governments what is good for them. According to this philosophy, the correct economic function of government is to act as 'night-watchman' by maintaining law and order, providing public goods and possibly merit goods when the market fails, and generally ensuring a suitable environment in which 'wealth-creating' firms can function in competitive markets, subject to minimum interference and regulation.

● **Interventionist economists**, by contrast, believe that all too often markets are uncompetitive, characterised by monopoly power and producer sovereignty, and prone to other forms of market failure. Additionally, uncertainty about the future and lack of correct market information are destabilising forces. By intervening in the economy, especially to correct market failures, the government 'knows better' than unregulated market forces. It can anticipate and counter the destabilising forces existent in markets, achieving a better outcome than is likely in an economy subject to market forces alone.

Correcting market failures

There are various methods open to a government for correcting, or at least reducing, market failures. At one extreme, the government can abolish the market, using instead the command or planning mechanism, financed from general taxation, for providing goods and services. At the other extreme, the government can try to influence market behaviour by providing information, and by exhorting and 'nudging' firms and consumers to behave in certain ways (e.g. not to use plastic bags). Between these extremes, governments can impose regulations to limit people's freedom of action in the market place, and use taxes and subsidies, price ceilings and price floors to alter prices in the market in order to change incentives and economic behaviour.

Government provision of public goods and merit goods

Because of the free-rider problem, markets may fail to provide pure public goods such as national defence and police services. When free-riding occurs, the incentive function of prices breaks down. If goods are provided by a market, people can free-ride rather than pay a price, so the firms that are trying to sell the goods can't make a profit. Given that there is a need for public goods, as we have seen, governments often step into the gap and provide the goods, financing the provision out of general taxation.

Just as governments discourage the production and consumption of negative externalities and demerit goods, in much the same way they try to encourage the production and consumption of positive externalities and merit goods. The government may choose to regulate or to try to change the prices of merit goods and other goods and activities which yield external benefits. In the latter case, subsidies are often used to encourage production and consumption.

KEY TERM

regulation involves the imposition of rules, controls and constraints, which restrict freedom of economic action in the market place.

Regulation, on the other hand, can force consumers to consume merit goods. The government may require people to be vaccinated against disease and to wear seatbelts in cars and crash helmets on motorbikes.

In the UK, education is both compulsory and completely subsidised, from 2015 at least for children between the ages of 5 and 18. Low-income families would be in an impossible situation if required to pay for education as well as to send their children to school. Subsidies can, of course, be paid to private providers of education and healthcare: namely, to private schools and private hospitals. However, in the UK, education and healthcare are also provided by the state, forming an important part of public spending. Nevertheless, private sector provision is growing. One reason for growing private sector provision of merit goods lies in the fact that state provision does not necessarily mean good-quality provision.

Forcing firms and consumers to generate positive externalities

The state can impose regulations that force firms and consumers to generate positive externalities. Local authority bylaws can require households to maintain the appearance of properties, and the state may order landowners to plant trees. In this situation, it is illegal *not* to provide external benefits for others.

Government intervention, negative externalities and demerit goods

There are two main ways in which governments can intervene to try to correct the market failures caused by negative externalities and demerit goods. As with positive externalities and merit goods, the government can use quantity controls or regulation. Alternatively or in addition, it can use taxation.

- **Regulation** directly influences the quantity of the externality that a firm or household can generate, and the level of consumption of a demerit good such as tobacco.
- **Taxation**, by contrast, adjusts the market price at which a good that generates the externality is sold, or the price of the demerit good. For example, taxing pollution discharged by power stations creates an incentive for less pollution to be generated and taxing tobacco and creates an incentive for less tobacco to be consumed.

In its most extreme form, regulation can be used to ban completely, or criminalise, the generation of negative externalities such as pollution or the sale and consumption of a demerit good such as heroin. However, it may be impossible to produce a good or service such as electricity in a coal-burning power station without generating at least some of a negative externality. In this situation, banning the externality has the perverse effect of preventing production of a good (e.g. electricity) as well as the bad (pollution). Because of this, quantity controls that fall short of a complete ban may be more appropriate. These include maximum emission limits and restrictions on the time of day or year during which the negative externality can legally be emitted. In the case of 'milder' demerit goods, smoking can be banned in public places, while shops would break the law by selling alcohol to younger teenagers.

Completely banning negative externalities and demerit goods is a form of market replacement rather than market adjustment. By contrast, because

KEY TERM

tax a compulsory levy imposed by the government to pay for its activities. Taxes can also be used to achieve other objectives, such as reduced consumption of demerit goods.

taxes placed on goods affect incentives which consumers and firms face, they provide a market-orientated solution to the problems posed by negative externalities and demerit goods. Taxation compensates for the fact that there is a missing market in the externality. In the case of pollution, the government calculates the money value of the negative externality, and imposes this on the firm as a pollution tax. This is known as the 'polluter must pay' principle. The pollution tax creates an incentive, which was previously lacking, for less of the bad to be dumped on others. By so doing, the tax internalises the externality. The polluting firm must now cover all the costs of production, including the cost of negative externalities, and include these in the price charged to customers. By setting the tax so that the price the consumer pays equals the social cost of producing another unit of the good generating the negative externality, resource allocation in the economy is improved. However, a pollution tax, like any tax, itself introduces new inefficiencies and distortions into the market, associated with the costs of collecting the tax and with creating incentives to evade the tax illegally: for example, by dumping pollution at night to escape detection. This is an example of government failure (see section 5.9).

Until recently, governments have been more likely to use regulation rather than taxation to reduce negative externalities such as pollution and congestion. Indeed, in the past, it was difficult to find examples of pollution taxes outside the pages of economics textbooks, possibly because politicians feared that pollution taxes would be too unpopular. But in recent years governments have become more prepared to use congestion and pollution taxes. This reflects growing concern, among governments and the public alike, of environmental issues such as global warming and the problems posed by fossil fuel emissions and other pollutants. It may also reflect both the growing influence of green or environment pressure groups, such as Friends of the Earth, and a growing preference to tackle environmental problems with market solutions rather than through regulation.

STUDY TIP

Make sure you can analyse the effects of taxes imposed on goods and subsidies by applying the concept of price elasticity of demand.

SYNOPTIC LINK

To analyse how the imposition of a tax on a demerit good such as tobacco affects consumption of the good, we must make use of the concept of price elasticity of demand. Figure 5.9 shows that imposing an expenditure tax on a good in fairly elastic demand is effective in reducing demand for the product. However, because of their addictive properties, the demand for demerit goods such as alcohol, tobacco and hard drugs can be inelastic. Taxing demerit goods can raise lots of revenue for the government, but does not do much to reduce consumption. And if the tax is set at a very high rate, it may lead to smuggling and to black market activity.

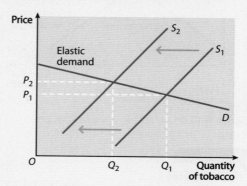

Figure 5.9 The effect of imposing a tax on tobacco when demand is elastic

119

EXTENSION MATERIAL

Pollution permits

Until quite recently, the main choice of policy for dealing with the problem of pollution was between regulation and taxation. As we have explained, the former is an interventionist solution whereas taxation, based on the principle that the polluter must pay, has been seen as a more market-orientated solution, but nevertheless one which required the government to levy and collect the pollution tax. In the 1990s, another market-orientated solution started in the USA, based on a trading market in permits or licences to pollute. More locally to the UK, the EU Emissions Trading Scheme is now the centrepiece of European efforts to cut emissions.

A permits to pollute scheme (for electricity) still involves regulation: for example, the imposition of maximum limits on the amount of pollution that coal-burning power stations are allowed to emit, followed by a steady reduction in these ceilings in each subsequent year (say, by 5%). But once this regulatory framework has been established, a market in traded pollution permits takes over, creating market-orientated incentives for the power station companies to reduce pollution because they can make money out of it.

A tradable market in permits to pollute works in the following way. Energy companies able to reduce pollution by more than the law requires sell their spare permits to other power stations that, for technical or other reasons, decide not to, or cannot, reduce pollution below the maximum limit. The latter still comply with the law, even when exceeding the maximum emission limit, because they buy the spare permits sold by the first group of power stations. But, in the long run, even power stations that find it difficult to comply with the law have an incentive to reduce pollution, so as to avoid the extra cost of production created by the need to buy pollution permits.

KEY TERM

price ceiling a price *above* which it is illegal to trade. Price ceilings, or maximum legal prices, can distort markets by creating excess demand.

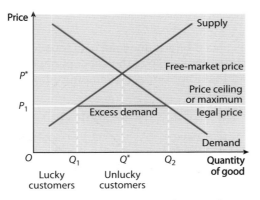

Figure 5.10 The effect of a maximum price control or price ceiling

KEY TERM

price floor a price *below* which it is illegal to trade. Price floors, or minimum legal prices, can distort markets by creating excess supply.

Price ceilings or maximum price laws

Perhaps the simplest ways in which a government can impose a price control is through the use of a **price ceiling** or a price floor. Suppose, for example, that in a particular market — say, the market for bread — the government imposes a price ceiling or maximum legal price, shown as P_1 in Figure 5.10. Because the price ceiling has been imposed below the free-market equilibrium price of P^*, it creates excess demand, shown by the distance between Q_1 and Q_2. In a free market, market forces would raise the price and eliminate the excess demand. But, because the price ceiling prevents this happening, there is no mechanism in the market for getting rid of excess demand. Rather than rationing by price, households are rationed by quantity. Queues and waiting lists occur, and possibly bribery and corruption, through which favoured customers buy the good but others do not. It is also worth noting that price ceilings interfere with the incentive function of prices, in the sense that the ceilings prevent prices from rising to attract new firms into the market.

The emergence of an informal or shadow market (sometimes called a black market) is also likely. Secondary markets emerge when primary markets (or free markets) are prevented from working properly. A secondary market is a meeting place for lucky and unlucky customers. In the secondary market, some lucky customers, who bought the good at price P_1, resell at a higher price to unlucky customers unable to purchase the good in the primary market. In the next section, we discuss the issue of whether a black market provides an example of government failure.

Price floors or minimum legal prices

Sometimes governments impose minimum price laws or **price floors**. For a minimum price law to affect a market, the price floor must be set above the free-market price. Figure 5.11 illustrates the possible effect of the national

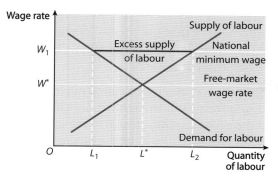

Figure 5.11 The possible effect of the UK national minimum wage

minimum wage imposed in UK labour markets. A national minimum wage rate set at W_1 (which is *above* the free-market wage rate of W^*) creates an excess supply of labour, thereby causing unemployment equal to the distance between L_1 and L_2. It may also cause rogue employers to break the law: for example, paying 'poverty wages' to vulnerable workers such as illegal immigrants. Note also that whereas a price ceiling imposed above the free-market price in Figure 5.10 would have no effect on the price at which bread is traded in the market, a national minimum wage set below the free-market wage rate in Figure 5.11 would have no effect on unemployment. This is the situation in many UK labour markets.

As with price ceilings, price floors interfere with the incentive function of prices. This is because falling prices cause inefficient or high-cost firms to leave the market. A price floor prevents this from happening.

○ **QUANTITATIVE SKILLS 5.2**

Worked example: calculating the effects of a price ceiling

Figure 5.12 shows how the imposition of a price ceiling distorts a market. Calculate the total amount spent on the good, first at market equilibrium price, and then when the price ceiling is in place.

At any price, the money value of the good bought and sold is calculated by multiplying price by quantity ($P \times Q$). At the good's equilibrium or market-clearing price of £10, 100 units of the good are bought and sold, so the amount spent on the good is £1,000. However, when a price ceiling of £6 is imposed, only 50 units of the good are bought and sold. The money spent on the good falls to £300, even though consumers would like to buy 150 units of the good at this price.

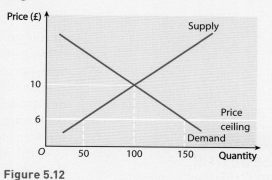

Figure 5.12

○ **STUDY TIP**

Make sure you can describe and explain at least three ways in which government intervention can affect the price of a good or service.

5.9 Government failure

When explaining market failure, we assumed that market failure can be reduced or completely eliminated, once identified, through appropriate government intervention: for example, by imposing taxes, controls or regulation. But there is another possibility. When the government intervenes in the economy to reduce or correct market failure, its intervention may lead to the appearance of other forms of resource misallocation. When this happens, **government failure** occurs.

121

We saw earlier that governments often provide free state education because they wish to increase consumption of what they perceive to be a merit good. If you refer back to Figure 5.7, you will see that the socially optimal level of provision of education, Q_2, is higher than Q_1, the amount of education which markets would probably provide. However, government intervention does not in itself ensure that Q_2 is eventually provided. Since it makes decisions on the basis of imperfect information, the government may not know what is the socially optimal level of education. Some people argue that free state education leads to over-provision, for example at Q_3 in

○ **KEY TERM**

government failure occurs when government intervention reduces economic welfare, leading to an allocation of resources that is worse than the free-market outcome.

Figure 5.7. If this is the case, governments may create, rather than remove, market distortions. Some people also believe that the quality of state education is poorer than that of private market-based education. If this is the case, it is a further example of government failure.

The pursuit of conflicting policy objectives can also lead to government failure. A good example is provided by government investment decisions. When governments wish to expand the economy, they may give the go-ahead to long-term investment projects such as the building of new roads, which they then cancel because of the perceived need to contract the economy. Very often government decisions can be criticised for favouring short-termism at the expense of long-termism.

There are also administrative costs to consider. Government intervention in the economy to correct market failure may create unnecessary layers of bureaucracy, which create costs which taxpayers have to pay. If so, this is a government failure. A recent example is the high costs the UK government incurred when deciding whether or not to permit the construction of a third runway at Heathrow airport, or to expand Gatwick or Stansted, or to build a completely new airport in the Thames estuary. Many free-market economists believe this is unnecessary government expenditure, but more interventionist economists believe the expenditure is fully justified because it leads to better eventual government decisions.

At this point, it is appropriate to introduce the 'law of unintended consequences'. This 'law', which has become very fashionable in recent years, predicts that, whenever the government intervenes in the market economy, effects will be unleashed which the policy-makers had not foreseen or intended. Sometimes the unintended effects may be advantageous to the economy, while in other instances they may be harmful but relatively innocuous. In either of these circumstances, government intervention can be justified on the grounds that the social benefits of intervention exceed the social costs and therefore contribute to a net gain in economic welfare. But if government activity — however well intentioned — triggers harmful consequences which are greater than the benefits that the government intervention is supposed to promote, then government failure results.

STUDY TIP
It is important to avoid confusing government failure with market failure.

ACTIVITY
UK local authorities provide facilities for waste and rubbish disposal. Here are a few research activities to undertake, possibly with your classmates and an organised division of labour.

1 Research details of your local authority's web page for waste collection and removal.
2 Summarise the authority's rules and policy for collection and disposal of waste.
   ● How often are dustbins emptied?
   ● Does waste have to be separated into categories such as general waste, recyclable waste and garden waste?
3 Visit your local authority's waste collection depot.
   ● Is the centre open to all or only to local residents?
   ● Does the authority charge a price for accepting waste for disposal?
   ● Is the waste separated into different categories?
   ● How does the authority deal with dangerous waste, such as batteries and refrigerators?
4 Research what happens to the waste. How much waste is recycled or composted? How much waste ends up in landfill or incineration?
5 Think of any other useful research questions you can investigate, e.g. is there any evidence of fly-tipping in your local area?
6 Write a group report summarising your findings.

Examples of possible government failure

Government price controls create black markets

In section 5.8, we explained how a price ceiling or maximum price law can create excess demand in a market, which is then relieved through trading in an informal or shadow market, in other words a black market. Price ceilings are normally put in place to protect consumers from high prices. However, the rising price of a product may simply reflect market forces and the changing nature of supply or demand in the market. A higher price might be needed to create incentives for consumers to economise and for firms to divert more scarce resources into producing the good. The price ceiling may prevent this happening. The controlled price can send out the wrong signals and create the wrong incentives, thus contributing to resource misallocation. And since it may be a criminal activity to break the price law, black markets are sometimes characterised by corruption and the threat of the use of illegal force.

However, economists of a free-market persuasion often justify black markets on the ground that they do the job that the primary market should do: that is, equate demand with supply. A price ceiling prevents the primary market from working properly. Arguably, the touts, spivs and dealers who act as middlemen in the black market or underground economy contribute to better resource allocation, although their contribution would not be needed if there were no price controls. A black market or secondary market only comes into existence because price controls distort the primary market.

Further side effects of government provision of merit and demerit goods

Various examples of government failure may occur when the state provides merit goods such as education at zero price for the consumer, or taxes or bans production and consumption of demerit goods. When education is provided free by the state, shortages emerge for places in so-called 'good' schools. Parents who are unable to get their children into these schools sometimes lie about where they live, in the hope of winning places in the 'post code lottery' through which the local education authority offers places to the children living nearest to the school.

In the case of demerit goods, the imposition of high taxes on goods such as alcohol and tobacco has encouraged 'booze cruise' trips to France to buy beer, wine, spirits and cigarettes at lower French prices. Not only does this erode the UK government's tax base, it also unnecessarily diverts productive resources into car and van journeys that would not otherwise take place, which in turn leads to unnecessary carbon pollution. And, however worthy it is, banning the production and consumption of demerit goods such as cocaine and heroin creates black markets characterised by crime and racketeering.

CASE STUDY 5.7

The landfill tax and government failure

Government policies that aim to reduce the discharge of negative externalities can also lead to government failure. Almost every economic activity produces waste: for example, household rubbish and the waste created by building and construction. A large fraction of UK waste is either incinerated (which discharges pollutants into the atmosphere) or collected by local government and placed in landfill sites. Landfill also causes pollution, and a further problem arises as all the available landfill sites fill up.

In 1996, the UK government imposed a landfill tax which it hoped would create jobs and reduce waste. But to evade the tax, rogue building contractors and some households began to fly-tip and to dump rubbish in public places and on other people's land. This was an unintended and adverse consequence of a tax that was intended to improve the environment.

Many blame the controversial landfill tax for the rise in organised unauthorised dumping. The tax increased the costs of taking waste to licensed sites by up to a third. The cost of getting rid of one truckload of rubble could be as high as £400. Finding alternative dumping grounds, where off-loading a lorry costs little or nothing, allows the unscrupulous to make a fortune. But the cost to the environment is immense.

Research published in 2011 by the Countryside Alliance uncovered the enormous scale of illegal fly-tipping in England and Wales. Figures obtained under the Freedom of Information Act reveal that illegal fly-tipping cost taxpayers over £40 million in 2010. At least 656,000 incidents of unlawful rubbish dumping were recorded in England and Wales between April 2010 and March 2011, which works out at 75 incidents of fly-tipping every hour — more than one per minute!

At the time, the cost of clearing the waste alone was just under £25 million, yet only one in 50 cases led to a prosecution. In cash-strapped rural local authorities, the rate of prosecutions dropped to just 3 in every 1,000. If waste is dumped on private land, the owners, irrespective of having no part in the fly-tip, have a duty of care and are bound by law to clear it up in their own time and at their expense.

The Chief Executive of the Countryside Alliance said, 'With the Coalition Government raising the landfill tax and with more cuts coming to council budgets, this problem is only going to get worse.'

Follow-up questions

1 Relate fly-tipping to the concept of negative externalities.
2 Do you agree that landfill illustrates both market failure and government failure? Justify your answer.

QUANTITATIVE SKILLS 5.3

Worked example: calculating price elasticity of demand

Between 2011 and 2015 a government increased its tax on waste disposal. Table 5.4 shows the changing price of waste disposal at a landfill site.

If the quantity of landfill space demanded fell by 10% between 2011 and 2015, calculate from the data the price elasticity of demand for landfill space.

If the quantity demanded fell by 10% and the price per tonne rose by 40%, the price elasticity of demand for landfill space was:

$$\frac{-10\%}{+40\%}$$

which is −0.25. According to the data, since the elasticity statistic (ignoring the minus sign) was less than 1 or unity, the demand for landfill space was inelastic with respect to the change in price.

Table 5.4

Year	£ per tonne of waste
2011	10
2012	11
2013	12
2014	13
2015	14

SUMMARY

- Prices perform four functions in markets: signalling information; creating economic incentives; and rationing scarce resources between competing uses, and allocation.
- Market failure, which occurs whenever markets don't perform very well, divides into complete market failure and partial market failure.
- Goods divide into private goods, such as a car, defined by the characteristics of excludability and rivalry, and public goods, such as national defence, defined by the characteristics of non-excludability and non-rivalry.
- In the case of a pure public good, people free-ride by benefiting without paying for the good.
- Governments often provide public goods directly, arguably because markets fail to supply them.
- Markets can provide quasi-public goods, such as roads, which are potentially excludable but non-rival, though governments also provide them.
- Externalities divide into production externalities and consumption externalities.
- A negative externality (external cost), such as pollution, is a public 'bad' dumped on others.
- A positive externality (external benefit), such as a beautiful view, is a public good that benefits others.
- Governments use regulations, including prohibition, and taxation to prevent or reduce production of negative externalities and to reduce consumption of demerit goods.
- Governments use regulations, including compulsory consumption, and subsidies to enforce or encourage production of positive externalities and the consumption of merit goods.
- Along with public goods, merit goods such as education are often provided by governments.
- Although both are often provided by the government, a merit good should not be confused with a public good.
- Merit goods are under-consumed in a free market because consumers ignore the positive externalities that consumption generates and/or downplay the long-term private benefits they will eventually enjoy.
- Demerit goods are over-consumed in a free market because consumers ignore the negative externalities that consumption generates and/or downplay the long-term private costs they will eventually suffer.
- Unlike public goods, merit goods are excludable and rival.
- Governments encourage consumption of merit goods through state provision and subsidy.
- Governments discourage consumption of demerit goods through regulation and taxation.
- Governments impose price ceilings or maximum legal prices to prevent prices rising above desired levels.
- A price ceiling imposed below the free-market price distorts the market and creates excess demand.
- In this situation, a secondary market or black market is likely to emerge.
- Black or informal markets can perform the useful economic function of dealing with shortages and equating demand with supply.
- Governments impose price floors or minimum legal prices, such as the national minimum wage, to prevent prices falling below desired levels.
- Government failure occurs when government intervention in markets fails to correct market failure and/or leads to outcomes worse than the intervention was meant to correct. Like market failure, government failure is associated with a misallocation of resources.
- Governments may create, rather than remove, market distortions.
- Government failure can result from government decisions made on the basis of inadequate information; as a result of conflicting objectives; and from the administrative costs of government intervention. It is also associated with the unintended consequences of government intervention in markets.

Questions

1 Do you agree that government policies which aim to correct market failure are always successful? Justify your answer.

2 Do you agree that governments should in all circumstances provide public goods? Justify your answer.

3 Evaluate different forms of government intervention to deal with the problems caused by negative externalities.

4 Evaluate the view that if merit goods are provided free by the state, the socially optimal level of consumption is always achieved.

5 Explain how monopoly may lead to market failure.

6 Do you agree that a highly unequal distribution of income is a market failure? Justify your answer.

7 Using the concept of elasticity, explain why taxing demerit goods may be relatively ineffective in reducing their consumption.

8 With the help of an appropriate diagram, explain how a maximum legal price may distort a market.

Microeconomic key terms

allocative efficiency occurs when the available economic resources are used to produce the combination of goods and services that best matches people's tastes and preferences.

allocative function of prices changing relative prices allocate scarce resources away from markets exhibiting excess supply and into markets in which there is excess demand.

artificial barrier to entry a barrier to market entry which is man-made.

average cost total cost of production divided by output.

average revenue total revenue divided by output; in a single-product firm, average revenue equals the price of the product.

capital good a good which is used in the production of other goods or services. Also known as a **producer good**.

capital productivity output per unit of capital.

choice choosing between alternatives when making a decision on how to use scarce resources.

collusion co-operation between firms, for example to fix prices. Some forms of collusion may be in the public interest, for example joint research and labour training schemes.

competing supply when raw materials are used to produce one good they cannot be used to produce another good.

competitive market a market in which the large number of buyers and sellers possess good market information and can easily enter or leave the market. A competitive market is one in which firms strive to outdo their rivals, but it does not necessarily meet all the conditions of perfect competition.

complementary good a good in joint demand, or a good which is demanded at the same time as the other good.

composite demand demand for a good which has more than one use.

concentrated market a market containing very few firms, in the extreme only one firm.

concentration ratio a ratio which indicates the total market share of a number of leading firms in a market, or the output of these firms as a percentage of total market output.

condition of demand a determinant of demand, other than the good's own price, that fixes the position of the demand curve.

conditions of supply determinants of supply, other than the good's own price, that fix the position of the supply curve.

consumer good a good which is consumed by individuals or households to satisfy their needs or wants.

consumer sovereignty through exercising their spending power, consumers collectively determine what is produced in a market. Consumer sovereignty is strongest in a perfectly competitive market.

consumption externality an externality (which may be positive or negative) generated in the course of consuming a good or service.

cross-elasticity of demand measures the extent to which the demand for a good changes in response to a change in the price of another good; it is calculated by dividing the percentage change in quantity demanded by the percentage change in the price of another good.

decrease in demand a leftward shift of the demand curve.

decrease in supply a leftward shift of the supply curve.

demand the quantity of a good or service that consumers are willing and able to buy at given prices in a given period of time. For economists, demand is always effective demand.

demerit good a good, such as tobacco, for which the social costs of consumption exceed the private costs. Value judgements are involved in deciding that a good is a demerit good.

derived demand demand for a good which is an input into the production of another good.

diseconomy of scale as output increases, long-run average cost rises.

disequilibrium a situation in a market when there is excess supply or excess demand.

distribution of income and wealth the way in which income and wealth are divided among the population.

division of labour this concept goes hand in hand with specialisation. Different workers perform different tasks in the course of producing a good or service.

economic growth the increase in the *potential* level of real output the economy can produce over a period of time.

economic welfare the economic well-being of an individual, a group within society, or an economy.

economy of scale as output increases, long-run average cost falls.

effective demand the desire for a good or service backed by an ability to pay.

elasticity the proportionate responsiveness of a second

variable to an initial proportionate change in the first variable.

entry barrier makes it difficult or impossible for new firms to enter a market.

equilibrium a state of rest or balance between opposing forces.

equilibrium price the price at which planned demand for a good or service exactly equals planned supply.

equity fairness or justness.

excess demand when consumers wish to buy more than firms wish to sell, with the price below the equilibrium price.

excess supply when firms wish to sell more than consumers wish to buy, with the price above the equilibrium price.

exchange to give something in return for something else received. Money is a medium of exchange.

exit barrier makes it difficult or impossible for firms to leave a market.

external economy of scale cost saving resulting from the growth of the industry or market of which the firm is a part.

externality a public good, in the case of an external benefit, or a public bad, in the case of an external cost, that is 'dumped' on third parties outside the market.

factors of production inputs into the production process, such as land, labour, capital and enterprise.

finite resource a resource, such as oil, which is scarce and runs out as it is used. Also known as a **non-renewable resource**.

fixed cost cost of production which, in the short run, does not change with output.

full employment when all who are able and willing to work are employed.

fundamental economic problem how best to make decisions about the allocation of scarce resources among competing uses so as to

improve and maximise human happiness and welfare.

geographical immobility of labour occurs when workers find it difficult or impossible to move to jobs in other parts of the country or in other countries for reasons such as higher housing costs in locations where the jobs exist.

government failure occurs when government intervention reduces economic welfare, leading to an allocation of resources that is worse than the free-market outcome.

immobility of labour the inability of labour to move from one job to another, either for occupational reasons (e.g. the need for training) or for geographical reasons (e.g. the cost of moving to another part of the country).

imperfect competition any market structure lying between the extremes of perfect competition and pure monopoly.

incentive function of prices prices create incentives for people to alter their economic behaviour; for example, a higher price creates an incentive for firms to supply more of a good or service.

income elasticity of demand measures the extent to which the demand for a good changes in response to a change in income; it is calculated by dividing the percentage change in quantity demanded by the percentage change in income.

increase in demand a rightward shift of the demand curve.

increase in supply a rightward shift of the supply curve.

inequity unfairness or unjustness.

inferior good a good for which demand decreases as income rises and demand increases as income falls.

information problem occurs when people make wrong decisions because they don't possess or they ignore relevant information. Very often they are myopic (short-sighted) about the future.

informative advertising provides consumers and producers with useful information about goods or services.

innovation converts the results of invention into marketable products or services.

internal economy of scale cost saving resulting from the growth of the firm itself.

invention creates new ideas for products or processes.

joint supply when one good is produced, another good is also produced from the same raw materials.

labour productivity output per worker.

limit pricing reducing the price of a good to just above average cost to deter the entry of new firms into the market. Prices are set at levels which are likely to make it unprofitable for potential entrants who might consider coming into the market.

long run the time period in which no factors of production are fixed and in which all the factors of production can be varied.

long-run average cost long-run total cost divided by output.

long-run production occurs when a firm changes the *scale* of all the factors of production.

market demand the quantity of a good or service that all the consumers in a market are willing and able to buy at different market prices.

market disequilibrium exists at any price other than the equilibrium price. When the market is in disequilibrium, either excess demand or excess supply exists in the market.

market equilibrium when planned demand equals planned supply in the market.

market failure when the market mechanism leads to a misallocation of resources in the economy, either completely failing to provide a good or service or providing the wrong quantity.

market share maximisation occurs when a firm maximises its percentage share of the market in which it sells its product.

market structure the organisation of a market in terms of the number of firms in the market and the ways in which they behave.

market supply the quantity of a good or service that all firms plan to sell at given prices in a given period of time.

merit good a good, such as healthcare, which when consumed leads to benefits which other people enjoy, or a good for which the long-term benefit of consumption exceeds the short-term benefit enjoyed by the person consuming the merit good. Value judgements are involved in deciding that a good is a merit good.

missing market a situation in which there is no market because the functions of prices have broken down.

monopoly power the power of a firm to act as a price maker rather than as a price taker.

natural barrier to entry a barrier to market entry which is not man-made.

natural monopoly the term has two meanings, first when a country or firm has complete control of a natural resource, and second when there is only room in a market for one firm benefiting from economies of scale to the full.

need something that is necessary for human survival, such as food, clothing, warmth or shelter.

negative externality, which is the same as an external cost, occurs when the consumption or production of a good causes costs to a third party, where the social cost is greater than the private cost.

normal good a good for which demand increases as income rises and demand decreases as income falls.

normative statement a statement that includes a value judgement and cannot be refuted just by looking at the evidence.

occupational immobility of labour occurs when workers find it difficult or impossible to move between jobs because they lack or cannot develop the skills required for the new jobs.

oligopoly a market dominated by a few firms.

opportunity cost the cost of giving up the next best alternative.

patent a strategic or man-made barrier to market entry caused by government legislation protecting the right of a firm to be the sole producer of a patented good, unless the firm grants royalties for other firms to produce the good.

perfect competition a market which displays the six conditions of: a large number of buyers and sellers; perfect market information; the ability to buy or sell as much as is desired at the ruling market price; the inability of an individual buyer or seller to influence the market price; a uniform or homogeneous product; and no barriers to entry or exit in the long run.

persuasive advertising attempts to persuade potential customers that a good or service possesses desirable characteristics that make it worth buying.

positive externality, which is the same as an external benefit, occurs when the consumption or production of a good causes a benefit to a third party, where the social benefit is greater than the private benefit.

positive statement a statement of fact that can be scientifically tested to see if it is correct or incorrect.

predatory pricing temporarily reducing the price of a good to below average cost to drive smaller firms or new market entrants out of the market.

price ceiling a price *above* which it is illegal to trade. Price ceilings, or maximum legal prices, can distort markets by creating excess demand.

price competition reducing the price of a good or service to gain sales by making it more attractive for consumers.

price elasticity of demand measures the extent to which the demand for a good changes in response to a change in the price of that good.

price elasticity of supply measures the extent to which the supply of a good changes in response to a change in the price of that good.

price floor a price *below* which it is illegal to trade. Price floors, or minimum legal prices, can distort markets by creating excess supply.

price maker a firm possessing the power to set the price within the market.

price taker a firm which passively accepts the ruling market price set by market conditions outside its control.

private good a good, such as an orange, that is excludable and rival.

producer sovereignty producers or firms in a market determine what is produced and what prices are charged.

product differentiation making a product different from other products through product design, the method of producing the product, or through its functionality.

production a process, or set of processes, that converts inputs into output of goods.

production externality an externality (which may be positive or negative) generated in the course of producing a good or service.

production possibility frontier a curve depicting the various combinations of two products (or types of products) that can be produced when all the available resources are fully and efficiently employed.

productive efficiency for the economy as a whole occurs when it is impossible to produce more of one good without producing less of another. For a firm this occurs when the average total cost of production is minimised.

productivity gap the difference between labour productivity in the UK and in other developed economies.

productivity output per unit of input.

profit the difference between total sales revenue and total costs of production.

profit maximisation occurs when a firm's total sales revenue is furthest above total cost of production.

public good a good, such as a radio programme, that is non-excludable and non-rival.

pure monopoly when there is only one firm in the market.

quantity setter a firm chooses the quantity of a good to sell, rather than its price. In monopoly, the market demand curve then dictates the maximum price that can be charged if the firm is to successfully sell its chosen quantity.

quasi-public good a good which is not fully non-rival and/or where it is possible to exclude people from consuming the product.

rationing function of prices rising prices ration demand for a product.

regulation involves the imposition of rules, controls and constraints, which restrict freedom of economic action in the market place.

renewable resource a resource, such as timber, that with careful management can be renewed as it is used.

resource allocation the process through which the available

factors of production are assigned to produce different goods and services, e.g. how many of the society's economic resources are devoted to supplying different products such as food, cars, healthcare and defence.

resource misallocation when resources are allocated in a way which does not maximise economic welfare.

sales maximisation occurs when sales revenue is maximised.

saturation advertising through flooding the market with information and persuasion about a firm's product, this functions as a man-made barrier to market entry by making it difficult for smaller firms to compete.

scarcity results from the fact that people have unlimited wants but resources to meet these wants are limited. In essence, people would like to consume more goods and services than the economy is able to produce with its limited resources.

short run the time period in which at least one factor of production is fixed and cannot be varied.

short-run production occurs when a firm adds variable factors of production to fixed factors of production.

signalling function of prices prices provide information to buyers and sellers.

social benefit the total benefit of an activity, including the external benefit as well as the private benefit. Expressed as an equation: social benefit = private benefit + external benefit.

social cost the total cost of an activity, including the external cost as well as the private cost. Expressed as an equation: social cost = private cost + external cost.

specialisation a worker only performing one task or a narrow range of tasks. Also, different firms specialising in producing different goods or services.

subsidy a payment made by government or another authority, usually to producers, for each unit of the subsidised good that they produce. Consumers can also be subsidised: for example, bus passes given to children to enable them to travel on buses free or at a reduced price.

substitute good a good in competing demand, namely a good which can be used in place of the other good.

supply the quantity of a good or service that firms are willing and able to sell at given prices and in a given period of time.

tax a compulsory levy imposed by the government to pay for its activities. Taxes can also be used to achieve other objectives, such as reduced consumption of demerit goods.

technical economy of scale a cost saving generated through changes to the 'productive process' as the scale of production and the level of output increase.

total cost the whole cost (fixed cost plus variable cost) of producing a particular level of output.

total revenue the money a firm receives from selling its output, calculated by multiplying the price by the quantity sold.

trade the buying and selling of goods and services.

unemployment when not all of those who are able and willing to work are employed.

variable cost cost of production which changes with the amount that is produced, even in the short run.

want something that is desirable, such as fashionable clothing, but is not necessary for human survival.

Microeconomic practice questions

In this section you will find a set of objective test questions, followed by a context question for AS.

Objective test questions

1 Which of the following represents a positive economic statement?

  A The recent increase in interest rates will help to reduce inflation.

  B Unemployment is a more serious economic problem than inflation.

  C Government expenditure on health and education should be raised.

  D The proportion of tax revenues raised from indirect as opposed to direct taxes is too high.

2 Which of the following is considered to be an essential characteristic of the price mechanism?

  A Resources are allocated in response to price changes.

  B Buyers and sellers set prices according to their preferences.

  C A socially optimum pattern of resource allocation is achieved.

  D Goods and services produced always reflect consumer sovereignty.

3 The diagram below represents the market for rail travel in country X.

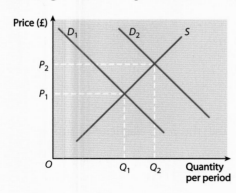

The shift of the demand curve from D_1 to D_2 could be explained by the government's decision to:

A expand its road-building programme

B abolish motorway tolls

C reduce rail subsidies

D impose a tax on car parking at work places

4 Cross-elasticity of demand measures the extent to which the:

A price of good X is affected by a change in the supply of good Y

B price of good X is affected by a change in the price of good Y

C demand for good X is affected by a change in the price of good Y

D demand for good X is affected by a change in the price of good X

5 The data below refer to the costs of a firm at various levels of output.

Output (units)	Total costs (£)
4	40
3	32
2	26
1	22
0	20

The average fixed cost of producing four units of output is:

A £5

B £10

C £20

D £40

6 The diagram below shows a supply curve.

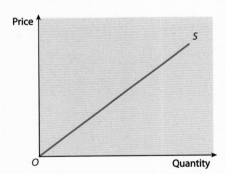

According to the diagram, as the price and the quantity increase, the price elasticity of supply:

A becomes elastic

B becomes inelastic

C remains unitary

D increases and then falls

7 Market failure occurs when:

   A firms in a particular market are forced out of business

   B market demand exceeds market supply

   C a good with a negative externality is overproduced

   D firms are unable to make adequate profits

8 The table below shows the weekly demand and supply schedules for a particular product.

Price (£)	Quantity demanded	Quantity supplied
20	100	200
18	120	170
16	140	140
14	160	110
12	180	80
10	200	50

A government decision to impose a minimum price of £12 would result in:

   A excess demand of 100

   B excess supply of 100

   C a fall in the equilibrium price to £12

   D no change in the equilibrium price or quantity

9 The table below shows price and total revenue (*TR*) for a given good.

Price (£)	TR (£)
1	12,000
2	18,000
3	18,000
4	12,000
5	0

From the information given, it may be concluded that the price elasticity of demand is inelastic over the price range:

   A £1.00 to £2.00

   B £2.00 to £3.00

   C £3.00 to £4.00

   D £4.00 to £5.00

10 Study the following diagram.

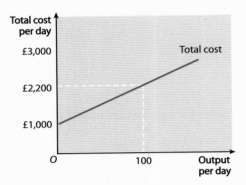

At 100 units of output per day, average variable cost is:

A £10

B £12

C £22

D £1,200

AS context question

Context 1

Total for this context: 50 marks

The provision of blood to health services

Study **Extracts A, B and C** and then answer **all** parts of Context 1 which follow.

Extract A: Stocks of blood units held by the NHS, 21 March to 19 August 2014

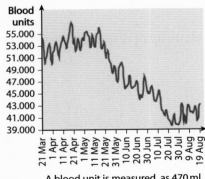

A blood unit is measured as 470 ml
(or just under a pint)

Extract B: The demand for and the supply of blood for hospital operations

1 The main purpose of economic activity is to improve people's welfare. Most of the goods that people consume are provided through markets, but others are not. At least in some countries, one such good is the blood used to treat hospital patients.

In recent years, the demand for blood has increased dramatically, due to, among other causes, an ageing population and new medical
10 and surgical procedures. Even though many individuals are eligible to donate blood and there are numerous awareness campaigns promoting its importance, only 4% of such individuals donate blood in the UK, and even fewer do so in developing countries. As a consequence, blood supply shortages are quite common throughout the world.

However, in the UK the donation system means that blood shortages are rare. On 19th August 2014, the blood stocks held in the UK by NHS Blood and Transplant (NHSBT) could meet medical demand for blood for periods ranging from four and a half days to eleven days for different blood types, assuming that no further blood donations were made. However, except in very special circumstances, the flow of new blood donations is generally sufficient to maintain an adequate stock of blood to meet medical demands.

Source: News reports, August 2014

Extract C: Donation versus market provision

1 In 1970, the British social scientist Professor Richard M. Titmuss contrasted the then American practice, in which recipients paid a market price for blood purchased from donors, with British practice, in which blood is freely given to patients.

Titmuss believed that the quality of life of the whole community is better when people are encouraged to give blood to strangers. In his
10 view, when blood becomes a commodity, the quality of the product becomes corrupted.

He argued that altruistic or charitable donors, who gave blood only to benefit others, had no incentive to give infected blood; whereas commercial donors who were in it mainly for the money, had an obvious financial incentive to give blood, even if the blood might harm the people receiving the blood.

Titmuss said that the cost to American
20 patients and their families of buying blood was sometimes so high that people who required very frequent blood transfusions could be bankrupted by the bills.

Professor Titmuss's opposition to a market for blood was part of his wider argument about the danger of using the market mechanism to provide merit goods such as health care. In the market for clothing, it is acceptable that cashmere wool is available for the rich and
30 cheap nylon for the poor. However, Titmuss believed that it was not acceptable to have a blood market in which safe blood is available for the rich, with potentially lethal blood only available for the poor.

Source: Academic research

01 Define the term 'welfare' (**Extract B**, line 2).   *(3 marks)*

02 Using the data in **Extract A**, calculate, to **one** decimal place, the percentage change in the stock of blood units held by the NHS between 21 March and 19 August 2014.   *(4 marks)*

03 Using **Extract A**, identify **two** significant features of the changes in the stocks of blood held by the NHS over the period shown.   *(4 marks)*

04 **Extract C** (lines 3–4) mentions that in the USA in 1970, the market mechanism was used for providing blood to hospital patients.

Draw a supply and demand diagram to illustrate how, in a country which relies on market provision rather than donation, the price of blood may be affected by an unexpected increase in the demand for blood.   *(4 marks)*

05 Lines 26–27 of **Extract C** mention that health care is usually considered to be a merit good. Explain why health care is generally regarded as a merit good.   *(10 marks)*

06 Professor Titmuss's opposition to a market for blood was part of his wider argument about the danger of using the market mechanism to provide services such as health care. (**Extract C**, lines 24–27).

Using the data and your economic knowledge, evaluate the case **for** and **against** using markets to provide health care.   *(25 marks)*

2

Macroeconomics

6

The measurement of macroeconomic performance

This is the first of the four remaining chapters in the book covering **macroeconomics**. The subject area of the first five chapters, microeconomics, describes, explains and analyses the 'little bits' of the economy, for example individual markets, firms and industries. By contrast, macroeconomics looks at the economy as a whole or in aggregate. Consider the question 'what determines the price of bread?' This is a microeconomic question, focusing on supply and demand in a single market *within* the economy. By contrast, 'what determines the average price level of *all* goods and services?' is a macroeconomic question. Similarly, 'what determines the annual rate of change of the overall price level, i.e. the rate of inflation?' is a macroeconomic rather than a microeconomic question. This and similar questions relating to the levels and rates of change of economic variables such as output, consumption, investment and exports and imports, lie at the heart of macroeconomics.

KEY TERM

macroeconomics involves the study of the whole economy at the aggregate level.

STUDY TIP

Make sure you understand the difference between macroeconomics and microeconomics, and also appreciate how many macroeconomic theories have microeconomic foundations.

LEARNING OBJECTIVES

This chapter will:

- outline and briefly explain the four main objectives of macroeconomic policy
- explain how the ranking of the policy objectives has changed over time
- discuss policy trade-offs and conflicts
- survey some of the data used to measure the performance of an economy
- explain how index numbers are used to show changes in key economic variables

6.1 The objectives of government economic policy

> **KEY TERM**
> **policy objective** a target or goal that policy-makers aim to 'hit'.

The four main objectives of a government's macroeconomic policy

A **policy objective** is a target or goal that a government wishes to achieve or 'hit'. Since the Second World War, governments in mixed economies such as the UK have generally had the same broad range of objectives. These are to:

- achieve economic growth and improve living standards and levels of economic welfare
  - create and maintain full employment or low unemployment
  - limit or control inflation, or to achieve some measure of price stability
  - attain a satisfactory balance of payments, usually defined as the avoidance of an external deficit which might create an exchange rate crisis

We shall now take a brief introductory look at each of the four policy objectives in turn, before examining them in greater detail in the final two chapters of the book.

Economic growth

You first came across economic growth in Chapter 1 when learning about production possibility curves. As a recap, Figure 6.1, which is much the same as Figure 1.4 in Chapter 1, will remind you of the distinction between short-run and long-run economic growth. **Short-run growth**, which occurs when there are unemployed resources (including labour) or 'slack' in the economy, is when there is a movement from a point *inside* the economy's production possibility frontier to a point *on* the frontier. Short-run growth is also called economic recovery. **Long-run growth**, by contrast, results from an outward movement of the production possibility frontier, from PPF_1 to PPF_2 in Figure 6.1.

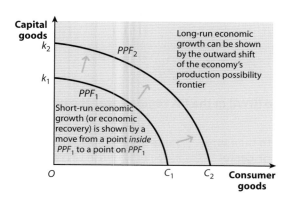

Figure 6.1 Short-run and long-run economic growth

> **KEY TERMS**
> **short-run economic growth** growth of real output resulting from using idle resources, including labour, thereby taking up the slack in the economy.
>
> **long-run economic growth** an increase in the economy's potential level of real output, and an outward shift of the economy's production possibility frontier.
>
> **gross domestic product (GDP)** the sum of all goods and services, or level of output, produced in the economy over a period of time, e.g. one year.
>
> **real GDP** A measure of all the goods and services produced in an economy, adjusted for price changes or inflation. The adjustment transforms changes in **nominal GDP**, which is measured in money terms, into a measure that reflects changes in the total output of the economy.
>
> **nominal GDP** GDP measured at the current market prices, without removing the effects of inflation.

Figure 6.2 shows what happened to UK growth between the first quarter of 2003 and the end of the first quarter of 2014. Note that the graph shows 'quarter-on-quarter' percentage growth rates of real **gross domestic product (GDP)** and not annual growth rates. The black bars show positive economic growth or increasing **real GDP**. By contrast, the red bars show negative economic growth or decreasing real GDP. In Figure 6.1, short-run negative economic growth could be depicted by a movement from a point on frontier PPF_1 to a point inside the frontier, or from an initial point inside the frontier to another point closer to the origin in the diagram. An inward movement of the production possibility frontier, for example from PPF_2 to PPF_1, would show long-run negative growth. A variety

STUDY TIP
Make sure you appreciate that economic growth is always measured in *real* rather than in *nominal* terms. You must understand the difference between real GDP and nominal GDP.

of events could be responsible for this. These include pollution degrading agricultural land within the economy and the destruction of buildings and other infrastructure in time of war.

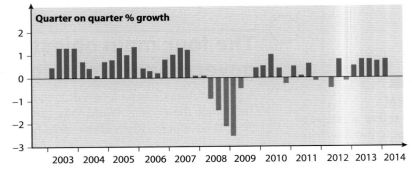

Figure 6.2 Quarter-on-quarter economic growth in the UK, Quarter 1 2003 to Quarter 1 2014

Source: ONS

QUANTITATIVE SKILLS 6.1

Worked example: calculating mean and median values

Calculate the mean and median values of nominal gross value added (GVA) in the UK regions over the period shown below.

Gross value added (GVA) is a term used in the UK's national accounts to measure the contribution to the economy of each individual producer, industry or sector in the United Kingdom. It is used in the estimation of GDP. Table 6.1 shows the percentage changes that occurred in *nominal* GVA for the 11 planning regions into which the UK is divided during recovery from recession in the years from 2009 to 2012. On first sight the percentage changes in the table may seem high. However, the table shows nominal rather than real changes in GVA. Both inflation and economic growth were occurring between 2009 and 2012 and these factors explain the percentage changes.

With a set of data such as this, the mean and the median are two measures of average values. The mean is the value obtained by dividing the sum of the percentage changes by the number of regions. Thus:

(11.1% + 10.5% + 7.2% +8.5% + 5.3% + 4.8% + 7.7% +3.6% + 8.2% + 4.5% + 3.4%) = 74.8%

74.8% ÷ 11 = 6.8%.

So 6.8 is the mean value.

By contrast, the median value is the 'middle number' in the sorted list of numbers. The sorted list, ranging from highest to lowest, is:

11.1%   10.5%   8.5%   8.2%   7.7%   7.2%   5.3%   4.8%   4.5%   3.6%   3.4%

As the sorted list contains 11 numbers (one for each of the UK's 11 planning regions), the middle number is the sixth number in the list, with five above and five below its value. Here 7.2% (East of England) is the median value.

Table 6.1 Percentage changes in regional GVA in UK regions, 2009–12

London	11.1%
South East	10.5%
East of England	7.2%
East Midlands	8.5%
South West	5.3%
North West	4.8%
North East	7.7%
Scotland	3.6%
Wales	8.2%
Yorkshire & Humber	4.5%
Northern Ireland	3.4%

Source: Regions and Countries of the UK Recovering from the Economic Downturn, ONS (July 2014)

CASE STUDY 6.1

Real and nominal GDP

It is important to avoid confusing real and nominal gross domestic product or GDP. (Nominal GDP is also called money GDP.) The difference between the two is that nominal GDP is real GDP multiplied by the average current price level for the year in question.

According to ONS data published in February 2014, while *nominal* GDP rose by 3.4% in the UK in 2013, *real* GDP rose by only 1.8%, the difference between the two reflecting the impact of the rate of inflation in 2013. It is the change in real GDP which measures the economy's rate of growth — the change in nominal GDP overstates the growth rate.

The approximate change in the real GDP can be calculated by subtracting the rate of inflation from the rate of change of nominal GDP.

The photograph shows some cheeses on display in a delicatessen in Oxfordshire at the end of 2014. The cheeses contributed in a small way to the UK's real national output in 2014 — a contribution made even smaller because all the cheeses on display were imported.

Two of the cheeses on display in the Oxfordshire delicatessen were priced at £1.80 and £1.99 per 100 grams. Estimates for the level of UK nominal national output in 2014 were based on information about the prices charged for all goods produced in the UK, including cheeses sold by market stalls, delis and supermarkets. However, with imports, only the contribution to output added in the UK is included in the real and nominal values of UK GDP.

Follow-up questions

1 Why do domestically produced cheeses such as British cheddar contribute more to UK national output than imported cheeses such as French brie?
2 Find out what has happened to real GDP in the UK in the years since 2014.

The Great Depression in the 1930s

These days, a **recession** is defined in the UK (though not in the USA) as a fall in real GDP which lasts for at least 6 months. However, a depression (or slump) is a vaguer term, best thought of as a very deep and long recession. (According to an old joke, a downturn is when your neighbour loses his job, a recession is when you lose your own job, and a depression is when economists lose their jobs!)

The 1920s was a period of growing national prosperity in the USA. Nevertheless, the Great Depression, when it arrived in 1929–30, was steeper and more protracted in the USA than in other industrial countries. The US unemployment rate rose higher and remained higher longer than in any other Western country. US real GDP fell by 9.4% in 1930 and the US unemployment rate climbed from 3.2% to 8.7%. In 1931, real GDP fell by another 8.5% and unemployment rose to 15.9%. But 1932 and 1933 were the worst years of the Great Depression. By 1932, real GDP had fallen in the USA by 31% since 1929 and over 13 million Americans had lost their jobs. The US economy began the first stage of a long recovery in 1934: real GDP rose by 7.7% and unemployment fell to 21.7%.

A soup kitchen in Chicago during the Great Depression

Follow-up questions

1 Find out how a recession is defined in the USA. See the article 'Economists who make the recession call' by Stephen Foley, 8 January 2008, **www.independent.co.uk**.
2 Research the details of the recession the UK experienced in 2008/09. When did recovery from recession start, and what is the state of the economy at the time you are reading this book?

KEY TERMS
recession a fall in real GDP for 6 months or more.

Full employment and unemployment

There are different definitions of **full employment**, two of which we briefly explain in this chapter. First is the so-called Beveridge definition. In 1944, a famous White Paper on employment policy, written by William Beveridge (an economist at the London School of Economics, who later became Lord Beveridge), effectively committed modern governments to achieving full employment. In the White Paper, Beveridge defined full employment as occurring when unemployment falls to 3% of the labour force.

Partly because they regard Beveridge's 3% definition as too arbitrary and lacking any theoretical underpinning, free-market economists favour a second definition of full employment. For them, full employment occurs in the economy's aggregate labour market at the market-clearing real-wage rate, where the number of workers willing to work equals the number of workers whom employers wish to hire. In Figure 6.3, this is shown where the aggregate supply curve of labour intersects the aggregate demand curve for labour. The full employment wage rate is w_{FE} and the full employment level of employment is E_{FE}.

Figure 6.3 could be interpreted as showing that when full employment occurs, there is absolutely no unemployment. However, as Figure 8.13 in Chapter 8 illustrates, in the real economy in which we live, this is not the case. Beveridge's definition of full employment accepts this fact. There will always be *some* unemployment, simply because the economy is constantly changing, with some jobs disappearing while new jobs are created. Chapter 8 describes and explains some of the main types of unemployment that economists recognise.

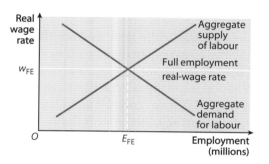

Figure 6.3 Full employment in the economy

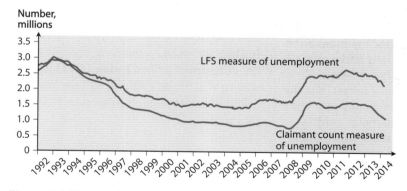

Figure 6.4 Changes in LFS unemployment and claimant count unemployment in the UK, 1992 to end of Quarter 1 2014

Two methods are used to measure unemployment in the UK. These are the **claimant count** measure and the **Labour Force Survey** (LFS) measure, which the UK government currently favours. The changes in UK unemployment, over a period starting in 1992 and ending at the beginning of the second quarter of 2014, using both measures of unemployment are shown in Figure 6.4.

143

SYNOPTIC LINK
Employment and unemployment are explained in further detail in section 8.2 in Chapter 8.

KEY TERMS

inflation a persistent or continuing rise in the average price level.

deflation a persistent or continuing fall in the average price level.

disinflation when the rate of inflation is falling, but still positive.

price index an index number showing the extent to which a price, or a 'basket' of prices, has changed over a month, quarter or year, in comparison with the price(s) in a base year.

consumer prices index (CPI) the official measure used to calculate the rate of consumer price inflation in the UK. The CPI calculates the average price increase of a basket of 700 different consumer goods and services.

retail prices index (RPI) the RPI is an older measure used to calculate the rate of consumer price inflation in the UK. Currently, the UK government uses the CPI for the **indexation** of state pensions and welfare benefits and for setting a monetary policy target, and the RPI for uprating each year the cost of TV and motor vehicle licences, together sometimes with taxes on goods such as alcoholic drinks.

indexation the automatic adjustment of items such as pensions and welfare benefits to changes in the price level, through the use of a price index.

Price stability

Inflation is a general rise in average prices (a rise in the price level) across the economy. This must not be confused with a change in the price of a particular good or service within the economy. Goods' prices rise and fall all the time in a market economy, reflecting consumer choices and preferences, and changing costs. If the price of one item — say, a particular model of car — increases because demand for it is high, this is not inflation. Inflation occurs when most prices are rising by some degree across the whole economy. A change in the price of one good may of course lead to a change in the measured rate of inflation, particularly if spending on the item makes up a significant fraction of total consumer spending.

Achieving absolutely stable prices is not necessarily the same as controlling the rate of inflation. Absolute price stability requires a zero annual rate of inflation, with the average price level neither rising nor falling from year to year. Although a zero rate of inflation has occasionally been achieved, it is extremely rare. Much more usually, in the UK at least, controlling inflation means achieving a low inflation rate rather than absolute price stability. For most of the last two decades, successive UK governments have aimed to achieve a 2% inflation rate. Usually, however, the inflation rate has been either a little above or a little below the 2% official target. On occasion, notably in the economic downturn in 2009, there were fears that the inflation rate would become negative. Negative inflation, which involves a falling average price level, is called **deflation**. Make sure you do not confuse deflation with **disinflation**, which occurs when the rate of inflation is falling but is still positive.

The changes that have taken place in the UK inflation rate between the start of 2000 and the end of the second quarter of 2014 are shown in Figure 6.5. The diagram introduces you to the fact that in the UK two different **price indices** are used to measure the rate of consumer price inflation. These are the **consumer prices index (CPI)** and the **retail prices index (RPI)**. The way in which the CPI and RPI are used to measure the rate of consumer price inflation are explained in section 6.3 of this chapter. (Note: *indices* is the plural of *index*.)

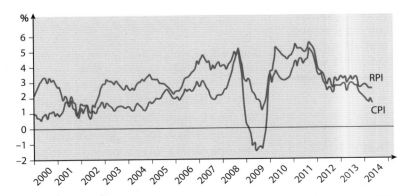

Figure 6.5 Changes in the RPI and the CPI inflation rates in the UK, 2000 to 2014
Source: ONS

QUANTITATIVE SKILLS 6.2

Worked example: calculating real values from nominal values

In Ruritania between 2014 and 2015, the rate of price inflation was 6% and the rate of increase of nominal GDP was 4%. What was the rate of increase of real GDP?

To answer this question, we use the equation:

rate of increase of real GDP = rate of increase of nominal GDP − rate of price inflation

Plugging the numbers given in the question into the equation, the rate of increase of real GDP = 4% − 6%, which equals −2%.

SYNOPTIC LINK

Inflation is explained in further detail in section 8.3 in Chapter 8.

STUDY TIP

You don't need to possess detailed technical knowledge of the construction of the CPI and the RPI, but you should appreciate the underlying features of the two price indices (see section 6.3).

KEY TERMS

balance of payments a record of all the currency flows into and out of a country in a particular time period.

current account of the balance of payments measures all the currency flows into and out of a country in a particular time period in payment for exports and imports, together with income and transfer flows.

exports domestically produced goods or services sold to residents of other countries.

imports goods or services produced in other countries and sold to residents of this country.

balance of trade the difference between the money value of a country's imports and its exports. Balance of trade is the largest component of a country's balance of payments on current account.

balance of trade deficit the money value of a country's imports exceeds the money value of its exports.

balance of trade surplus the money value of a country's exports exceeds the money value of its imports

---

TEST YOURSELF 6.1

Table 6.2 shows both the unemployment rate and inflation rate for an economy between 2013 and 2015.

Table 6.2

	Unemployment rate (%)	Inflation rate (%)
2013	5.4	3.3
2014	4.8	4.0
2015	4.0	4.5

What can you conclude from the data?

A satisfactory balance of payments

The **balance of payments** measures all the currency flows into and out of an economy in a particular time period, usually a month, quarter or year. An important part of the balance of payments is called the current account.

The **current account of the balance of payments** contains two main sections: the money value of **exports**, and the money value of **imports** (of both goods and services). Changes in these over a period extending from 1992 to 2012 are shown in Figure 6.6. Taken together, the money value of exports and imports make up the **balance of trade**. If the money value of imports exceeds the money value of exports, there is a **balance of trade deficit**; if the money value of imports is less than the money value of exports, there is a **balance of trade surplus**.

There are some other sections of the current account of the balance of payments, namely income flows and current transfers. These will be explained in Chapter 8.

The word 'satisfactory' can be interpreted in different ways. People sometimes assume that a satisfactory balance of payments only occurs when the government achieves the biggest possible current account surplus (i.e. the value of exports exceeding the value of imports by the greatest amount). However, a country can only enjoy a trading surplus if at least one other country suffers a trading deficit. It is mathematically impossible for all countries to have a current account surplus

145

at the same time. Therefore, most economists take the view that a 'satisfactory' balance of payments is a situation in which the current account is in equilibrium, or when there is a small surplus or a small but sustainable deficit.

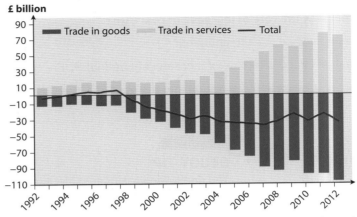

Figure 6.6 Changes in the UK's balances of trade in goods and services, 1992–2012

EXTENSION MATERIAL

The current account and capital flows

There are two main parts to the balance of payments: the current account and capital flows. The current account, which includes exports and imports, is so called because it measures *income* generated in the current time period flowing into and out of the economy. The second main section, capital flows, occur when residents of one country acquire *capital* assets located in other countries. Capital flows are of two types: direct capital flows and portfolio capital flows.

Direct capital flows and their links with the current account of the balance of payments are illustrated as follows. A few years ago, Sir Philip Greene's Arcadia Group (a British company) invested in Topman shops in the USA. The payments made when purchasing the US stores were a capital outflow. However, once Arcadia's investment was

The Topshop store in New York, part of the Arcadia Group

complete and the company's American shops were up and running, they began to generate profits which flowed back to Arcadia in the UK. The profits repatriated to Arcadia in the UK were an inward investment income flow (a current account item), generated by the outward capital flow that had taken place in previous years.

By contrast, the payments made several years ago by Toyota when building car plants in Derbyshire were a capital inflow from Japan to the UK. Toyota's investment is an example of inward investment or foreign direct investment (FDI) into the UK. In this case, subsequent to Toyota's investment, profits made by the company's UK factories flowed out of the UK to the Japanese owners of the company. To sum up, outward capital flows generate inward income flows, while inward capital flows usually lead eventually to outward income flows.

Portfolio overseas investment involves the purchase of financial assets (that is, pieces of paper laying claim to the ownership of real assets) rather than physical or directly productive assets. Typically, portfolio investment occurs when fund managers employed by financial institutions, such as insurance companies and pension funds, purchase shares issued by overseas companies or securities issued by foreign governments. The globalisation of world security markets or capital markets and the abolition of exchange controls between virtually all developed countries have made it easy for fund managers and other UK residents to purchase shares or bonds that are listed on overseas capital markets.

Other macroeconomic objectives

Governments may also have other objectives of macroeconomic policy, such as **balancing the budget** and achieving a more equitable or fairer distribution of income. Since the 2008/09 recession, the objective of balancing or at least reducing the government's **budget deficit** has become a very important macroeconomic objective. This will be explained in section 9.2 on fiscal policy in the final chapter of this book.

The opposite has been true in recent years in relation to achieving a more equitable distribution of income. During the recession and its aftermath, income inequalities have widened, which most people regard as inequitable.

STUDY TIP

Make sure you are aware that governments have policy objectives other than achieving economic growth, low unemployment, a low inflation rate and a satisfactory balance of payments.

SYNOPTIC LINK

Section 1.1 of Chapter 1 introduced you to the difference between positive and normative statements in economics. Section 5.7 of Chapter 5 explained how unequal and inequitable distributions of income illustrate the difference between positive and normative statements. At this stage, it will be useful to reread the two chapter sections.

A first look at policy conflicts

KEY TERMS

policy conflict occurs when two policy objectives cannot both be achieved at the same time: the better the performance in achieving one objective, the worse the performance in achieving the other.

trade-off between policy objectives although it may be impossible to achieve two desirable objectives at the same time, e.g. zero inflation and full employment, policy-makers may be able to choose an acceptable combination lying between the extremes, e.g. 2% inflation and 4% unemployment.

Economists often argue that it is difficult, if not impossible, for a government to 'hit' all its desired macroeconomic objectives at the same time. Believing they can't achieve the impossible, policy-makers often settle for the lesser goal of 'trading off' between policy objectives. A **trade-off** exists when two or more desirable objectives are mutually exclusive. Because the government thinks it cannot achieve, for example, full employment and zero inflation, it aims for less than full employment combined with an acceptably low and sustainable rate of inflation.

Over the years UK macroeconomic policy has been influenced and constrained by four significant conflicts between policy objectives. The main **policy conflicts** and their associated policy trade-offs are:

- between internal policy objectives of full employment and growth and the external objective of achieving a satisfactory balance of payments (or possibly supporting a particular exchange rate)

full employment and economic growth ← policy conflict and trade-off → satisfactory balance of payments or exchange rate

- between achieving full employment and controlling inflation

full employment and economic growth ← policy conflict and trade-off → control of inflation

- between increasing the rate of economic growth and achieving a more equal distribution of income and wealth

economic growth ← policy conflict and trade-off → greater income equality

- between higher living standards now and higher living standards in the future

current living standards ← policy conflict and trade-off → future living standards

Not all objectives conflict, however. Some economists believe that, with the 'right' policies, policy conflicts do not occur in the long run — i.e. they are compatible.

Most economists agree that these policy conflicts and trade-offs pose considerable problems for governments in the economic short run, defined as a period in macroeconomics extending just a few years into the future. However, there is much less agreement about whether they need be significant in the long run — a period extending many years into the future. Pro-free market economists often argue that if appropriate (and successful) supply-side policies are implemented, the main objectives of macroeconomic policy are compatible with each other and not in conflict in the long run. (Supply-side policies are explained in depth in Chapter 9.)

STUDY TIP
In microeconomics in Part 1 of this book, you learnt that the short run is the time period in which at least one factor of production is held fixed and the long run is the time period in which all factors of production are variable. However, in macroeconomics, economists tend generally to use the terms in a looser way. For example, the macroeconomic 'short run' may extend to about 3 years into the future, with the 'long run' being any period longer than that. To complicate things still further, a period known as the 'medium term' is sometimes identified. This could be a period of about 18 months to 3 years into the future, separating the short run and the long run.

SYNOPTIC LINK
Policy conflicts are explained in further detail in section 8.5 in Chapter 8.

How the importance attached to the different macroeconomic policy objectives has changed over time

The order in which the four main objectives of macroeconomic policy were listed at the beginning of this chapter shows a broadly **Keynesian** ranking of priorities. In the Keynesian era, which extended roughly from 1945 to 1979, UK governments implemented Keynesian macroeconomic policies. They believed that economic policy should be used to achieve full employment, economic growth and a generally acceptable or fair distribution of income and wealth. These were the prime policy objectives, which had to be achieved in order to increase human happiness and economic welfare — the ultimate policy objective. Controlling inflation and achieving a satisfactory balance of payments were regarded as intermediate objectives, or possibly as constraints, in the sense that an unsatisfactory performance in controlling inflation or the balance of payments could prevent the attainment of full employment and economic growth.

In the early 1980s, things changed. A new government in 1979, with Mrs Margaret Thatcher becoming prime minister, meant that UK governments were now **pro-free market** rather than Keynesian. In the 1970s inflation had threatened to escalate out of control, and in response UK governments placed control of inflation in pole position as a policy objective, relegating full employment to a lower position in the ranking of macroeconomic policy objectives.

KEY TERMS
Keynesian economists followers of the economist John Maynard Keynes, who generally believe that governments should manage the economy, particularly through the use of fiscal policy.

pro-free market economists opponents of Keynesian economists, who dislike government intervention in the economy and who much prefer the operation of free markets.

Since then, UK governments have continued to give much more attention to the need to control inflation. Indeed, in 1993, the Conservative chancellor Norman Lamont stated that high unemployment was a 'price well worth paying' for keeping inflation under control. This view was echoed in 1998 when, under a Labour government, the Governor of the Bank of England argued that 'job losses in the north were an acceptable price to pay for curbing inflation in the south'. These statements reflect the pro-free market view that, in order to maintain a high and sustainable level of employment, inflation must first be brought under control.

The long and deep recession, which hit the UK (and many other countries) in 2008, has led to a partial revision of this view. For various reasons, which are explained in section 8.3 of Chapter 8, inflation has generally been successfully controlled in the UK in recent years. Since 2009, UK governments have been more concerned with bringing about recovery from recession than with bringing the inflation rate down below 2%. Achieving faster economic growth and reducing unemployment have been reasserted as prime policy objectives. Chapter 9 explains how a combination of 'loose' **monetary policy**, i.e. very low interest rates, and 'tight' **fiscal** policy, i.e. cutting government spending in an effort to reduce the size of the budget deficit, have dominated recent UK macroeconomic policy.

It is also worth noting that, despite a rapid increase in the UK's balance of payments deficit on current account, achieving a satisfactory current account has not been viewed by recent governments as an important policy objective. All this may of course change.

6.2 Macroeconomic indicators

Performance indicators

A **performance indicator** provides policy-makers with information about the recent success or lack of success in achieving the target set for a particular type of economic policy such as monetary policy or fiscal policy. The size and rate of change of the money supply is a commonly used monetary performance indicator. Likewise the size and rate of change of the budget deficit is an indicator of fiscal policy performance. Performance indicators also provide information about whether current policy is on course to hit the future target set for the stated policy. Performance indicators, such as information about labour productivity and productivity gaps, can also be used to compare the performance of the UK economy with that of competitor countries.

Performance indicators can be divided into *lead* and *lag* indicators:

- **Lead indicators** provide information about the future state of the economy (stemming from the way people are currently forming their expectations). Surveys of consumer and business confidence and investment intentions indicate the existence of a feel-good or feel-bad factor and provide information about the likely state of aggregate demand a few months ahead. Statistics for house-building starts and the number of people who have booked expensive summer or skiing holidays several months in advance also provide information about future spending, while data on commodity and input prices can signal future changes in retail price inflation.

- **Lag indicators** provide information about past and possibly current economic performance and the extent to which policy objectives such as economic growth and control of inflation have been achieved. Data on the level of GDP, and current and recent employment and unemployment figures, provide examples of lag indicators giving information about current and recent economic performance.

The usefulness of a performance indicator depends on whether it provides accurate information about the state of the economy. Performance indicators are almost always presented in the form of statistical data, for example unemployment and growth figures in the case of lagged indicators, and projections about the number of house-building starts in the case of lead indicators. The accuracy of the information provided by performance indicators is thus highly dependent on the accuracy of the statistics available from the government and other sources.

CASE STUDY 6.3

David Smith's skip index and other confidence indicators

Every week David Smith, the economics editor of the *Sunday Times*, writes an Economic Outlook column. (You don't have to buy the *Sunday Times*; highlights of the Economic Outlook column can be accessed on David Smith's ECONOMICS UK.COM website on the internet.)

A few years ago, David Smith came up with the idea of a 'skip index', as an informal lead indicator of what might happen to the economy in the future. However, the accuracy of a skip index can be questioned. While an increase in the number of builder's skips might mean people are more affluent and spending the money on their houses, it might also mean that people cannot afford to move but their family is still growing and therefore they have to upgrade their house. A 'scaffolding index' might suffer from the same problem as a skip index.

Another possibility is a 'crane index'. This is a way to gauge prosperity by counting the cranes on the urban skyline. However, it is also possible to turn a crane index on its head. An increase in the number of tower cranes may indicate over-expansion or over-confidence — not necessarily economic growth. Another confidence indicator is frequency of receipt of unsolicited letters from estate agents, claiming for

A 'crane index' is a way to gauge prosperity by counting the cranes on the urban skyline

example that a 'Mr Jones' is desperate to buy a house in your road if you'll just give the agent a call.

Follow-up questions

1 Can you think of any other things that could be used to gauge the state of consumer or business confidence in the economy?
2 Questionnaires and surveys are sometimes used for finding out what people think will happen to the economy in the future. Why should the information provided by such surveys be treated with caution?

Introduction to index numbers

Earlier in this chapter, we mentioned the difference between nominal GDP (or money GDP) and real GDP. To recap, real GDP, or real gross domestic product, is a measure of the total quantity of goods and services produced by the economy over a period of time, having got rid of the distortive effects of price changes or inflation.

Changes in real GDP, along with other economic variables, are usually expressed using index numbers. Because index numbers frequently appear in the quantitative data you are expected to interpret in the course of your studies, it is especially important that you build up an understanding of how economic indices are constructed.

Economists frequently use index numbers when making comparisons over periods of time. An index starts in a given year, called the base year, which is given an index number of 100. In later years or months, an increase in the size of the variable causes the index number to rise above 100, while a fall in the size of the variable, compared to the base year, results in the index number falling to below 100. For example, an index number of 105 means a 5% rise from the base year, whereas an index number of 95 means a 5% fall.

QUANTITATIVE SKILLS 6.3

Objective test question: understanding data presented in index numbers, GDP per head

Table 6.3 shows index numbers for GDP per head for two countries, L and M, in 2010 and 2015.

Table 6.3

| | GDP per head | |
	2010	2015
Country L	100	115
Country M	100	108

From the data, it can be concluded that:

A GDP per head was the same in both countries in 2010
B GDP rose faster in country L than in country M
C the rate of increase in GDP per head was greater in country L than in country M
D GDP per head was higher in country L than in country M in 2015

To answer the question correctly, it is important to appreciate that the data shows GDP *per head of population*, and not the overall GDP figures for both countries. This means that although statement B could well be true, it cannot be concluded from the data, as the rate of population growth could be slower in country M than in country L. Statements A and D are wrong for a different reason, namely that there is insufficient information in the data to allow us to compare *across* the two data series. For statement A, the index number is the same in both countries, namely 100. The base year for both data series is probably 2010. The fact that both index numbers are 100 tells us nothing about whether GDP per head was the same in both countries in this year. For the same reason, we cannot conclude that GDP per head was higher in country L in 2015, simply because 115 is a larger number than 108. This means statement D is wrong. However, while we cannot compare *across* the two data series, we can compare *along* each series taken in isolation. The data allows us to conclude that GDP per head increased by 15% in country L between 2010 and 2015, but only by 8% in country M. This means that statement C is the correct answer.

QUANTITATIVE SKILLS 6.4

Objective test question: interpreting macroeconomic data

Table 6.4 shows figures for population and index numbers for inflation (CPI) and money national income (GDP at current prices) in the years 2014 and 2015.

Table 6.4

Year	GDP at current prices	Inflation index	Population size
2014	100	75	40 million
2015	106	125	42 million

In 2015, compared to 2014, which one of the following statements can be inferred from the data?

A Population grew by a slower rate than prices
B The inflation price index increased by 25%
C Money GDP per head rose by 6%
D Real GDP increased

Statement A provides the correct answer. The price level increased by nearly 67% (50/75 x 100) but population grew by only 5%. Statement B is wrong because the starting-off price index was 75 and not 100. Statement C is wrong: money GDP did indeed increase by 6%, but the population grew in size by 5%, so the increase in money GDP *per head* is less than 6%. Finally, statement D is also wrong: if money GDP increased by 6% but the price level increased by nearly 67%, *real* GDP must have fallen.

TEST YOURSELF 6.2

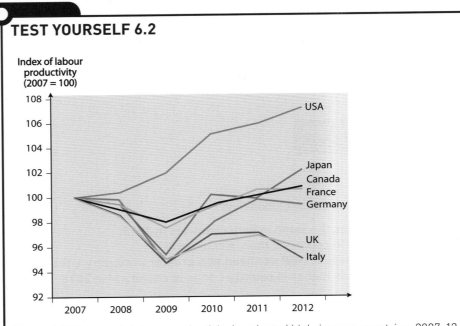

Figure 6.7 Changes in labour productivity in selected high-income countries, 2007–12

1 Identify two significant points of comparison in the labour productivity of the countries shown in Figure 6.7.

2 Find out what has happened to labour productivity in the UK since 2012.

An example of economic indices

To illustrate how index numbers are used (and also how data presented in index number form can be misused), we shall examine the changes that took place in labour productivity in the USA, the Euro Area and Japan between 1985 and 2011. These changes are shown in Figure 6.8.

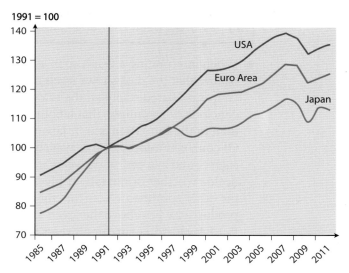

Figure 6.8 Changes in labour productivity (GDP per capita), 1985–2011

The blue, green and red lines in Figure 6.8 show the changes in labour productivity that occurred in the different countries over the 26-year period covered by the graph — though the Euro Area, or eurozone, is the group of countries that have replaced their national currencies with the euro, rather than a single country.

There are a number of points to be aware of when interpreting the graph. These are as follows:

● Providing you are comparing the index number for one of the years between 1992 and 2011 with the base year index number of 100 in 1991, the increase in the index number is the same as the percentage increase over the data period you are looking at. In 2011, for example, the index number for US labour productivity was approximately 135, compared to the base year index of 100. This represents a 35% increase in US labour productivity.

● However, a change in the index numbers is *not* the same as a percentage change when a comparison is made with a year other than the base year. Consider, for example, the change in US labour productivity between the end of 2009 and 2011. The index increased from approximately 133 to approximately 135, i.e. a 2-point increase. However, this does not mean that there was a 2% increase in labour productivity over the 2-year period. To calculate the percentage change over the 2-year period, we use the following formula:

$$\text{percentage increase} = \frac{\text{change in index points}}{\text{index number for 2009}} \times 100$$

or:
$$\frac{2}{133} \times 100 = 1.48\%$$

Likewise, the percentage change in US labour productivity between the beginning of the data series in 1985 and 1991 is *not* the same as the change in index points of approximately 9.5:

$$\text{percentage increase} = \frac{\text{change in index points}}{\text{index number for 1985}} \times 100$$

or:
$$\frac{9.5}{90.5} \times 100 = 10.49\%$$

- When interpreting a graph such as Figure 6.8, students often wrongly believe that the data shows *levels* of labour productivity in the different countries. Based solely on the information in the graph, it is wrong to conclude, for example, that labour productivity was higher in the USA than in the Euro Area and in Japan in every year between 1992 and 2011. Of course, if information is available on *levels* of labour productivity in each country in one of the years in the data series, it would be possible to decide whether or not labour productivity was higher in the USA than in the other countries. (Note that the blue line showing the US index of labour productivity lies above the green and red lines showing the indices for the Euro Area and Japan, for all years except the base year index number of 100 in all the countries. This means that if we can establish that the level of US labour productivity was higher in *one* year in the data series, it must also have been higher in *all* the years from 1985 to 2011.)

- An even sillier mistake would be to conclude that labour productivity was the same in all the countries shown in the graph in 1991, simply because the index number for all the countries was 100 in that year. 1991 is the chosen base year for all the countries, so the index number for each country is 100.

- Although, for the reason stated, index number data, taken on its own, does not permit a comparison of absolute levels of labour productivity, it does allow us to compare *relative* changes in labour productivity in the different countries. Figure 6.8 tells us, for example, that as labour productivity increased by just under 26% in the Euro Area between 1991 and 2011, but only by approximately 13% in Japan, the rate of growth of labour productivity was higher over the whole period in the Euro Area compared to Japan.

The consumer prices index (CPI) and the retail prices index (RPI)

Although economic indices are used to show changes taking place over a number of years of real economic variables such as real GDP and labour productivity, they are best known for showing changes in prices. The two price indices that you need to understand in some detail are the consumer prices index (CPI) and the retail prices index (RPI). For many years, the RPI was the measure of the average price level of consumer goods and services, and was used in the UK for calculating the rate of consumer price or retail price inflation. In recent years, the CPI has replaced the RPI, not only for measuring the average price level and the rate of consumer price inflation, but also when setting the government's target rate of inflation, and for purposes such as uprating pensions and other welfare benefits, and sometimes public sector pay.

CASE STUDY 6.4

The construction of the consumer prices index (CPI)

The following passages have been extracted from *A Brief Guide to Consumer Price Indices* published by the Office for National Statistics (ONS) in 2013 and accessible on the ONS website **www.ons.gov.uk**.

Consumer price inflation is the speed at which the prices of the goods and services bought by households rise or fall. Consumer price inflation is estimated by using price indices. The CPI measures price changes, **not** price levels. It is therefore expressed in terms of the comparison of prices relative to 2005, when the index is given a value of 100.

The national 'shopping basket'

A convenient way of thinking about the CPI is to imagine a very large 'shopping basket' full of goods and services on which people typically spend their money: from bread to ready-made meals, from the cost of a cinema seat to the price of a pint at the local pub, from a holiday in Spain to the cost of a bicycle. The content of the basket is fixed for a period of 12 months, however, as the prices of individual products vary, so does the total cost of the basket. The CPI, as a measure of that total cost, only measures price changes. If people spend more because they buy more goods this is not reflected in the index.

Considerable care is taken to ensure that the shopping basket is kept up-to-date and is representative of people's spending patterns: the places and shops we go to, the goods and services that we buy and the amounts we spend on them.

'Representative items'

It is impractical and unnecessary to monitor the price of every product sold in every single shop. The prices of similar items can reasonably be assumed to move in line with one another in response to market forces. It is therefore sufficient to compile the index using prices of a large and varied sample of products in selected locations. The goods and services for which prices are recorded are called 'representative items'.

The CPI is compiled using around 700 separate representative items. Their movements are taken to represent the price changes for all goods and services covered by the index, including those for which prices are not specifically monitored. There are, for example, several items in the basket covering purchases of bread — such as a large white sliced loaf and large wholemeal loaf — that are combined together to estimate the overall change in bread prices.

Collection of data and comparing 'like with like'

It is important that the index calculations are based on 'like for like' comparisons of prices each month for each of the items in the basket. Around the middle of each month, price collectors record about 100,000 prices for around 520 items consisting of specified types of goods and services. The price collectors visit a variety of shops in around 150 locations throughout the UK. Most local shops are visited in person to collect prices at first hand, although some work is done by telephone. The price collectors go to the same shops each month, noting the prices of the same products, so that over time they compare 'like with like'. For many goods and services it is more efficient to collect prices centrally at the ONS. Information on charges such as those for football admissions, water supply, newspapers and rail fares — about 80,000 prices for 190 items in all — are obtained from central sources and used in the CPI. Prices for some large chain stores that have national pricing policies are also collected centrally at ONS.

However, some brands or varieties of particular products priced at the start of the year may not be available in later months. This is common in markets where the rate of technological progress is high, as is the case with many electronic goods, or where consumer tastes change rapidly, for example in clothing. When particular products do disappear from the market, care is taken to ensure that replacements are of broadly comparable quality so that price comparisons are not distorted.

Explicit adjustments are made, for example, in the case of personal computers, where most replacement models are of higher quality than their predecessors. A rise in price might be accompanied by improvements in processing speed for example. In this case, an index which did not take account of improved quality would show higher inflation than an index that does adjust for quality change.

The system of 'weighting'

We spend more on some things than others, so we would expect, for example, a ten per cent increase in the price of petrol to have a much bigger impact on the CPI than a similar rise in the price of tea. For this reason, the components of the index are 'weighted' to ensure that it reflects the importance of the various items in the average shopping basket, and the amounts we spend in different regions of the country and in different types of shops.

It is important that the index is representative and kept up-to-date. The basket of goods and services is therefore reviewed every year, helping to ensure that the CPI calculations more accurately reflect UK shopping and purchasing patterns.

Follow-up questions

1 What is meant by 'weighting' in the construction of a price index such as the CPI?
2 Why may changes in a price index such as the CPI or the RPI not provide an accurate measure of the rate of inflation for an individual, for example a pensioner?

CASE STUDY 6.5

Recent changes to the CPI shopping basket

Currently, around 180,000 separate price quotations are used every month in compiling the consumer prices index, covering around 700 representative consumer goods and services. The 700 representative goods and services fall into the 12 commodity divisions shown in Table 6.5.

Table 6.5 Allocation of items to CPI divisions in 2014

	CPI weight (%)	Representative items (% of total)
1. Food & non-alcoholic beverages	11.2	23
2. Alcohol & tobacco	4.5	4
3. Clothing & footwear	7.2	11
4. Housing & household services	12.9	5
5. Furniture & household goods	6.0	10
6. Health	2.4	3
7. Transport	15.2	6
8. Communication	3.2	1
9. Recreation & culture	14.4	17
10. Education	2.2	1
11. Restaurants & hotels	12.0	8
12. Miscellaneous goods & services	8.8	11

The selection of the 700 representative items in the shopping basket is based on a number of factors, which include ease of finding and pricing the product; availability throughout the year; and the amount spent on a particular item or group of items.

The most notable entrant into the CPI shopping basket in 2014 was 'DVD rental/video on demand subscription services', reflecting the growth of products such as Amazon Instant Video or Netflix. Other notable additions included fruit snack pots, flavoured milk, mixer drinks and canvas shoes, while hardwood flooring and takeaway coffees have been removed (although takeaway lattes remain in the basket).

The ONS collects information on a 'shopping basket'

Follow-up questions

1 Why is it impractical to measure each month price changes for all the goods and services bought in the UK economy?
2 In 2014, manual car washes have replaced automatic car washes in the CPI shopping basket. Suggest reasons why manual car washes have grown at the expense of automatic car washes.

The average family

The goods and services in the CPI and RPI shopping baskets and the weights attached to them are meant to reflect the spending patterns of the 'average British family'. In so far that there is such a thing, the ONS calculated in 2013 that in 2012 the average British household spent £489 each week (see Figure 6.9). This was £7.70 less than it spent in 2011, reflecting the fact that with most people's wages and salaries rising at a slower rate than inflation, most families and households were poorer in real terms. The data, taken from a survey of over 5,000 households, also showed how an average family's money was spent. The largest single item of spending was on housing, fuel and power (£68 per week), followed by spending on transport (£64.10). 2012 was the first year since 2001 in which housing, fuel and power headed the list of family spending. Previously, transport topped the list. However, the fact that interest spending on mortgages was not included in the figures means that the data should be interpreted in a rather guarded way.

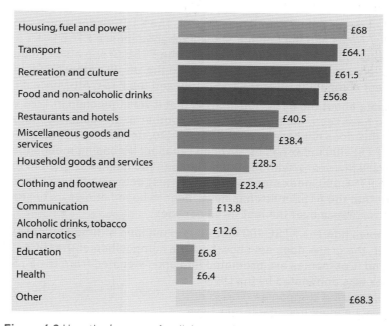

Figure 6.9 How the 'average family' spent £489 a week in 2012
Source: ONS

Other economic indices

The ONS publishes other economic indices besides the CPI and the RPI. The CPI and the RPI both look at the prices of hundreds of items people spend money on, such as food and cinema tickets, but they exclude housing costs and mortgage interest payments. In 2012, the ONS introduced a new price index to counteract criticisms that the main weakness of the CPI is that it does not reflect many of the costs of being a house owner, which make up about 10% of a typical family's average spending. The new index is called the CPIH where the letter 'H' stands for housing.

In recent years, as Figure 6.5 shows, the rate of inflation measured by changes in the RPI has been greater than the rate of inflation measured by the CPI.

The ONS also publishes a number of price indices which are not directly related to changes in consumer prices. These include *producer price indices (PPI)*, which measure changes in input and output prices of goods bought and sold by UK manufacturers. Input prices are prices of materials and fuels bought; output prices, also known as 'factory gate prices', are prices at which goods are sold.

Other indices constructed by the ONS measure changes in a range of economic variables including output per worker or labour productivity mentioned earlier in this chapter. The ONS also publishes the *Index of Production*, which measures the volume of production at base year prices for the manufacturing, mining and quarrying and energy supply industries.

The 'Footsie' index

Economic and financial indices are also published by non-government organisations. Perhaps the best known in the UK is the *FTSE 100 index*, often called the *'Footsie' index*. The FTSE 100 is an index composed of the 100 largest companies listed on the London Stock Exchange (LSE). The index is seen as a good indicator of the performance of major public companies (PLCs). The FTSE Group which produces the index is 50/50 owned by the *Financial Times* and the London Stock Exchange (hence FTSE — FT and SE). Although the FTSE 100 is the most famous index the company produces, the FTSE Group also calculates over 100,000 other indices, covering markets around the world, every day. In the UK, the other FTSE indices include the FTSE 250 (the next 250 largest companies after the FTSE 100) and the FTSE All-Share index.

One point to note about the FTSE 100 index is that it was launched in 1984 with a base year value of 1,000. Usually, as we have seen, the base year index number in an economic index is 100. However, as the FTSE 100 index shows, this does not have to be the case. Also, unlike most other indices, including those published by the ONS, the FTSE 100 index has never been rebased. (Rebasing means that the base year used in an index is changed every few years, with the index number 100 being assigned to the new base year.) On Monday 14 July 2014, the FTSE 100 index stood at 6746.1, or just below its then all-time peak of 6950.6 on 30 December 1999. The fact that the FTSE index has never been rebased allows us to see the index as a barometer of UK economic performance over the last three decades.

Figure 6.10 shows how the FTSE 100 index has risen (and at times fallen) over the years between 1985 and 2014. However, the graph does not show how the composition of the UK's 100 leading companies has changed over that period. Companies are promoted into and relegated from the FTSE index every 3 months. Back in 1984, the index was dominated by the UK's leading manufacturing companies. This is no longer the case. Leading manufacturers have either disappeared or have been taken over by foreign companies. To figure in the FTSE index, a company's shares have to be quoted on the London Stock Exchange. When a UK company is taken over and becomes a subsidiary of an overseas-based company, it disappears from the FTSE index. These days, the FTSE 100 companies are largely energy companies, retail companies and other service industry companies.

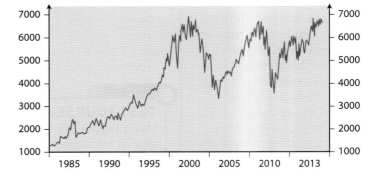

Figure 6.10 Changes in the FTSE 100 index between 1985 and 2014

SUMMARY

- A policy objective is a target or goal which a government aims to achieve or 'hit'.
- The main macroeconomic policy objectives are full employment, economic growth, a fair distribution of income and wealth, control of inflation and a satisfactory balance of payments on current account.
- Full employment and economic growth are the prime policy objectives, but many pro-free market economists place control of inflation in pole position.
- Whatever the ranking of policy objectives, improving economic welfare or human happiness is the ultimate policy objective.
- Sometimes governments have other policy objectives such as balancing the budget and achieving a more equitable distribution of income and wealth.
- As the name indicates, a performance indicator, such as changes in the level of unemployment, provides information on how the economy is performing.
- Economic indices are often used by economists to measure changes in economic variables occurring over time.
- Price indices are especially important in economics, particularly the consumer prices index (CPI) and the retail prices index (RPI).
- Inflation indices are used when measuring changes in real GDP.
- A representative sample of goods (sometimes call the national 'shopping basket') and a system of weights are used in the construction of the CPI and the RPI.

Questions

1 With the help of a *PPF* diagram, explain the difference between short-term and long-term economic growth.

2 Distinguish between an objective and an instrument of macroeconomic policy. Explain two macroeconomic policy objectives.

3 Explain two of the main conflicts affecting macroeconomic policy, and how a government might trade off between achieving these objectives.

4 Explain the differences between inflation, deflation and disinflation. When did deflation last occur in the UK economy?

5 What is the difference between a deficit and a surplus on the current account of the balance of payments? Which does the UK have today, and how large is it?

6 Briefly explain how a price index is constructed.

How the macroeconomy works

This chapter is about *macroeconomic theory*. The two main bodies of macroeconomic theory, or macroeconomic models, are explained in some detail. These are the circular flow and the aggregate demand/aggregate supply (*AD/AS*) models of the economy. The chapter then goes on to look at related macroeconomic concepts, such as the components of aggregate demand (consumption, investment etc.) and the multiplier concept. The final two chapters of the book will continue the task introduced in this chapter of applying macroeconomic theory to the analysis of current economic problems and the evaluation of government economic policies.

LEARNING OBJECTIVES

This chapter will:

- explain the meaning of national income and what it measures
- introduce and explain the circular flow macroeconomic model of how the economy works
- analyse the effect of changes in injections and withdrawals of demand on national income
- introduce and explain the aggregate demand/aggregate supply (*AD/AS*) macroeconomic model
- investigate aggregate demand and aggregate supply in greater detail
- explain the multiplier process

7.1 The circular flow of income

National income

Chapter 6 mentioned that gross domestic product (GDP) is perhaps the best known measure of national income or national output. This chapter starts by exploring the concept of national income in rather more detail.

National income, national output and national product

Economists use the terms **national income** and **national output** (also called **national product**) interchangeably. To produce the *flow* of national output, the economy must possess a *stock* of physical capital goods (the national capital stock) and a stock of human capital, together with stocks of the other factors of production: land and entrepreneurship.

STUDY TIP

Make sure you don't confuse *wealth*, which is a stock at a point in time, with *income*, which is a flow generated over a period of time. Wealth is the stock of assets, or things that have value, which people own.

national capital stock the stock of capital goods, such as buildings and machinery, in the economy that has accumulated over time and is measured at a point in time.

wealth the *stock* of assets which have value at a point in time, as distinct from income which is a *flow* generated over a period of time.

national wealth the stock of all goods that exist at a point in time that have value in the economy.

The **national capital stock** is part of the stock of **national wealth**, which comprises all physical assets owned by the nation's residents that have value. The national capital stock includes capital goods, together with social capital such as the roads, hospitals and schools which are owned by the state. However, the national capital stock excludes consumer goods, which are a part of national wealth but not part of national capital. All capital is wealth, but not all wealth is capital.

Figure 7.1 shows how we can relate a country's national income or output (e.g. in 2016) to the national capital stock and the human capital stock. In the figure, national income in 2016 is shown as the area contained by the three rectangles A, B and C. We will now assume that at the beginning of 2016, the economy operates on its production possibility frontier. This means there is no unemployed labour, and the economy is working at full capacity to produce the flow of national income shown by A + B + C.

STUDY TIP
Make sure you understand the difference between stocks and flows.

The national capital stock is the stock of capital goods that has accumulated over time in the economy. By contrast, national income is the flow of new output produced by the stocks of physical and human capital and other factors of production.

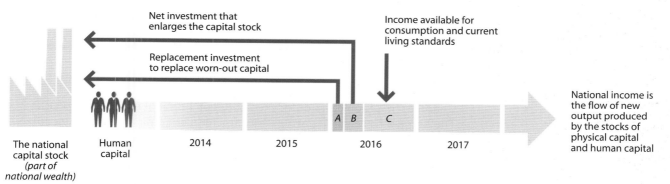

Figure 7.1 National income and the stocks of physical and human capital

national income the *flow* of new output produced by the economy in a particular period (e.g. a year).

national output the same as national income, namely the *flow* of new output produced by the economy in a particular period (e.g. a year).

national product another name for national income and national output.

However, part of the national capital stock wears out in the course of producing 2016's national income. Worn-out capital (or the *depreciation* of the national capital stock) reflects *capital consumption*. To maintain the size of the capital stock, so that (in the absence of population growth and technical progress) the stock is capable of producing exactly the same size of national income in 2016 as in 2015, part of 2016's national output must be replacement capital goods. The spending on replacement investment is shown by area A. If this investment doesn't take place, the national capital stock shrinks in size. Negative economic growth occurs and the economy's production possibility frontier shifts inward.

Positive economic growth generally requires that investment takes place, over and above the replacement investment shown by rectangle A in Figure 7.1. The extra investment needed to enlarge the capital stock is shown by rectangle B. This is called net investment. Gross investment (shown by A + B) is the sum of replacement investment and net investment. Only net investment increases the size of the capital stock, thereby facilitating long-run (positive) economic growth.

Rectangle *C* shows the fraction of national income available for **consumption** in 2016. A decision to sacrifice current consumption in favour of a higher level of future consumption means that more of society's scarce resources go into investment or the production of capital goods, enabling the national capital stock to increase in size. However, in the short term, the easiest way to increase living standards is to boost current consumption. This 'live now, pay later' approach sacrifices saving and investment, which ultimately reduces long-term economic growth.

EXTENSION MATERIAL

The difference between national income and GDP

Students often confuse gross national income (GNI) with GDP, though GDP is now the most commonly used measure of national income. Both reflect the national output and income of the economy. The word 'domestic' in gross domestic product indicates that GDP is the flow of output produced domestically *within* the economy. However, some British residents and companies receive income from assets they own in other countries. Likewise, some of the income produced within the UK flows out of the country to overseas owners of assets located within the UK. Gross national income takes account of these income flows; GDP does not.

ACTIVITY

Each year comprehensive details on national income for a recent year are published by the Office for National Statistics (ONS). To get a flavour of the details, access on the internet 'Chapter 01: National Accounts at a Glance' and then download and save the PDF document with the same title. At your leisure, scan-read the PDF document and paste and save any interesting tables or graphs.

SYNOPTIC LINK

Chapter 6 explained the difference between nominal GDP and real GDP. The same difference separates the concepts of nominal national income and real national income. Nominal national income measures national output at the current prices, but these usually rise each year in line with inflation. To get rid of the effects of rising prices, nominal national income must be converted into real national income. Real national income grows when more goods and services are produced, i.e. if economic growth is taking place, or when technical progress improves the quality of goods. Because the distortive effect of inflation has been removed, growth of real national income is a better measure of national economic performance than growth of nominal national income.

National income = national output = national expenditure

National income, national output and national expenditure measure the flow of new output produced in the economy in three different ways. National output measures the actual goods and services produced by the economy; national income measures the incomes received by labour and other factors of production when producing the goods and services; and national expenditure shows the spending of these incomes on the goods and services. Since they are three different ways of measuring the same things (the flow of new output), it follows that:

national income = national output = national expenditure

A simple circular flow model of the macroeconomy

The simple circular flow model, illustrated in Figure 7.2, assumes that there are just two sets of economic agents in the economy: households and firms. The model pretends that the government and foreign trade don't exist. This is a model of a two-sector economy, or a **closed economy** with no government sector. The dashed flow lines in the figure show the real flows occurring in the economy between households and firms. Households supply labour and other factor services in exchange for goods and services produced by the firms. These real flows generate money flows of income and expenditure, shown by the solid flow lines.

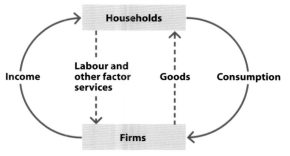

Figure 7.2 A simplified circular flow diagram of a two-sector economy

All the income received by households (shown by the left-hand flow curve of the diagram) is spent on consumption (shown by the right-hand flow curve).

Figure 7.3 is a more realistic version of Figure 7.2, because it shows households saving as well as consuming, and firms investing in capital goods. When households save part of their incomes, people are spending less than their incomes. **Saving**, which is an example of a leakage or **withdrawal** from the circular flow of income, is depicted by the upper of the two horizontal arrows in Figure 7.3. The lower of the two horizontal arrows shows **investment**, or spending on machinery and other capital goods, which is an **injection** of demand into the economy.

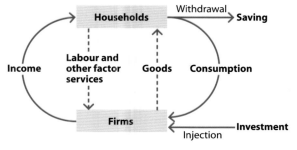

Figure 7.3 Introducing saving and investment into the circular flow of income

KEY TERM

closed economy an economy with no international trade.

saving income which is not spent.

withdrawal a leakage of spending power out of the circular flow of income into savings, taxation or imports.

investment total planned spending by firms on capital goods produced within the economy.

injection spending entering the circular flow of income as a result of investment, government spending and exports.

A first look at the concept of equilibrium national income

If planned saving (or the planned withdrawal of spending) equals planned investment (or the planned injection of spending into the flow), national income is in equilibrium, tending neither to rise nor to fall. However, if the withdrawal exceeds the injection, the resulting net leakage of spending from the circular flow causes output and income to fall. Likewise, if the withdrawal is less than the injection, the resulting net injection of spending into the economy causes output and income to rise.

Savings can be hoarded, or the funds being saved can be lent for others to spend. Hoarding — for example, keeping money under the mattress — means that a fraction of income is not spent. This can lead to deficient aggregate demand in the economy, which means there is too little demand to buy the output the economy is capable of producing. Because they cannot sell some of the goods and services they have produced, firms reduce their output and national income falls.

However, if all savings are lent, via financial intermediaries such as banks, for firms and other consumers to spend, planned saving may end up equalling planned investment. With this outcome, national income remains in equilibrium and there is no reason why the level of income should fall.

163

In the two-sector circular flow model, national income is in equilibrium when:

planned saving = planned investment

or:

$$S = I$$

However, because households and firms have different motives for making their respective saving and investment decisions, there is no reason why, initially, household saving should exactly equal the amount firms plan to spend on capital goods (i.e. investment). Consider, for example, a situation in which planned saving is greater than planned investment ($S > I$). In this situation, the national income or output circulating round the economy is in disequilibrium, with withdrawals out of the system exceeding injections of spending into the flow of income, and national income will fall.

> **EXTENSION MATERIAL**
>
> ## Keynes and deficient aggregate demand
>
> If planned saving by households exceeds planned investment by firms, there is a danger that deficient aggregate demand may cause the economy to sink into a recession. In the 1930s, during the Great Depression, John Maynard Keynes argued that if household savings are not lent to finance spending by others, particularly investment by firms, the level of income or output circulating round the economy falls. This reduces saving, until planned saving equals planned investment and equilibrium is restored, albeit at a significantly lower level of national income. The economy ends up in recession. Keynesian economists used the same analysis as part of their explanation of the 2008/09 recession, arguing that a liquidity crisis and an associated collapse of consumer and business confidence were responsible for the collapse in aggregate demand.
>
> Pro-free market economists, who generally reject Keynesian theory, believe that deficient aggregate demand only exists as a *temporary* and self-correcting phenomenon. They argue that when deficient aggregate demand occurs, the rate of interest, rather than the level of income or output, falls, quickly restoring equality between saving and investment intentions. When interest rates fall, people save less because saving becomes less attractive. At the same time, firms invest more in new capital goods because the cost of borrowing has fallen.
>
> Back in the 1930s, Keynes agreed that a fall in interest rates can bring about equality between saving and investment but he believed the process to be slow. In the very long run it may work, but, in Keynes's memorable phrase, 'in the long run we are all dead'. Keynes argued that when planned leakages of demand from the circular flow of income exceed planned injections of demand into the flow, the level of income or output falls to restore equilibrium. According to Keynes, deficient aggregate demand is the cause of recessions.

Bringing the government sector and the overseas sector into the circular flow model

The simple circular flow model we have looked at is unrealistic because it ignores how the domestic government and the rest of the world are sources of both injections of demand into, and withdrawals of demand from, the circular flow of income. Government spending is an injection of spending into the economy. Taxation, which takes spending power away from the people being taxed, is a withdrawal or leakage of spending. Exports and imports result from the fact that we live in an **open economy**, i.e. an economy open to international trade. Exports, which result from people living in other countries buying goods produced in Britain, are an injection into the circular flow. By contrast, imports, or spending by UK residents on goods produced overseas, are a withdrawal from the circular flow. Spending on imports stimulates the economies of other countries rather than the UK economy.

> **KEY TERM**
> **Open economy** an economy open to international trade.

Figure 7.4 shows the effect of bringing the activities of the government and overseas sectors into the circular flow model

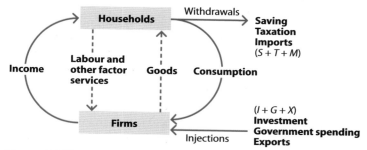

Figure 7.4 The circular flow of income in an economy with a government sector and an overseas sector

In this extended circular flow model, national income is in equilibrium, tending neither to rise nor to fall, when:

saving + taxation + imports = investment + government spending + exports

or:

$$S + T + M = I + G + X$$

However, whenever:

$$S + T + M > I + G + X$$

a net withdrawal or leakage of demand out of the circular flow occurs, which in Keynesian analysis causes the equilibrium level of national income to fall.

And when:

$$S + T + M < I + G + X$$

a net injection of demand into the circular flow occurs, which causes the equilibrium level of national income to rise.

STUDY TIP
Economists use the letters Y, C, S, I, G, T, X and M as shorthand, respectively for the macroeconomic variables income, consumption, saving, investment, government spending, taxation, exports and imports. Make sure you don't confuse S, used in the circular flow model as the shorthand for saving, with its microeconomic use as the shorthand for 'supply'. Section 7.2 below also introduces the concept of aggregate supply, for which the shorthand is AS.

ACTIVITY
Draw a circular flow diagram for a closed economy comprising households, firms and the government.

TEST YOURSELF 7.1
In an economy, savings are £10 billion, investment is £12 billion, taxes are £8 billion, imports are £13 billion, government spending is £6 billion, and exports are £11 billion. What is the net injection of demand into the circular flow of income, or the net withdrawal of demand from the circular flow?

Building and using economic models

Much of this chapter is about macroeconomic models: the circular flow model we have just explained, and the *AD/AS* macroeconomic model we are about to investigate. Model building is one of the most fundamental analytical techniques used by economists. Economic theory is based on developing economic models which describe particular aspects of the economic behaviour of individuals, groups of individuals and, in a macro context, the whole economy.

A model is a small-scale replica of real-world phenomena, often incorporating a number of simplifications. An economic model simplifies the real world in such a way that the essential features of an economic relationship or set of relationships are explained using diagrams, words and often algebra. Models are used by economists first to understand and explain the working of the economy, and second to predict what might happen in the future.

A good economic model simplifies reality sufficiently to allow important and often otherwise obscure economic relationships to be studied, away from irrelevant detail or 'background noise'. The danger is that reality can be oversimplified, with the resulting model failing to reflect in a useful way the world it seeks to explain. Economic modelling involves the art of making strong assumptions about human behaviour so as to concentrate attention and analysis on key economic relationships in a clear and tractable way, while avoiding an excessive oversimplification of the problem or relationship to be explained.

The ultimate purpose of model building is to derive predictions about economic behaviour, such as the prediction of demand theory that demand will increase when price falls. Economic controversy often exists when models generate conflicting predictions about what will happen in a given set of circumstances. For example, a model of the labour market which predicts that the supply of labour increases as wages rise carries the policy-making implication that a cut in income tax, being equivalent to a wage rise, creates an incentive to effort and hard work. Under alternative assumptions, the model could predict the opposite: that, as wages rise, workers begin to prefer leisure to work and react to the tax cut by working less.

It may often be possible to accept or dismiss a model of economic behaviour on the basis of common sense or casual observation of the world around us. Economists now usually go further, using sophisticated statistical tests to evaluate empirically the model's predictions. Good economic models or theories survive the process of empirical testing (which is part of a branch of the subject called 'econometrics'), whereas models or theories shown to be at odds with observed behaviour must be revised or discarded.

7.2 Aggregate demand and aggregate supply analysis

Introducing the *AD/AS* macroeconomic model of the economy

In recent years, the *AD/AS* model has become the preferred theoretical framework for the investigation of macroeconomic issues. The model is particularly useful for analysing the effect of an increase in aggregate demand on the economy. It does this by addressing the following question: will expansionary fiscal policy and expansionary monetary policy be **reflationary policies**, increasing real output and jobs, or will the price level increase instead (i.e. will the policy result in price **inflation**)? Before returning to this question in later sections of the chapter and in Chapter 9, we shall re-introduce the concept of **equilibrium national income** and take a close look at **aggregate demand**.

A second look at the concept of equilibrium national income

There are two ways of approaching the concept of equilibrium national income (or macroeconomic equilibrium). We have already seen how national income is in equilibrium when planned injections into the circular flow of income equal planned withdrawals of demand from the flow of income circulating round the economy. The second approach defines equilibrium national income in the aggregate demand/aggregate supply (AD/AS) model of the economy. Equilibrium national income occurs when the aggregate demand for real output equals the **aggregate supply** of real output, i.e. where $AD = AS$. This is illustrated in Figure 7.5 at point X, where the AD curve intersects the AS curve. The equilibrium level of real output is y_1, and the equilibrium price level is P_1.

> **KEY TERMS**
>
> **equilibrium national income** the level of real output at which aggregate demand equals aggregate supply ($AD = AS$). Alternatively, it is the level of income at which withdrawals from the circular flow of income equal injections into the flow. Also known as **macroeconomic equilibrium**.
>
> **aggregate demand** the total planned spending on real output produced within the economy.

> **KEY TERM**
>
> **aggregate supply** the level of real national output that producers are prepared to supply at different average price levels.

> **EXTENSION MATERIAL**
>
> ## The link between the two ways of defining equilibrium national income
>
> Equilibrium national income is a state of rest, or a situation in which, unless something changes to disturb the level of income circulating round the economy, once reached, the level of income remains at its equilibrium level. This can be expressed in two ways. First, as a situation in which injections into the circular flow of income match withdrawals or leakages out of the flow; or, second, as a situation in which total planned spending of all the economic agents in the economy (AD) exactly equals the level of real output that producers plan to supply (AS).

If either the AD curve or the AS curve shifts to a new position, the point of equilibrium national income will change. Figure 7.6(a) shows the effect of a rightward shift of the AD curve, with equilibrium national income moving from point X to point Z. By contrast, the Figure 7.6(b) shows the effect of a leftward movement of the AS curve, with equilibrium national income moving from point X to point V.

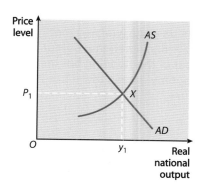

Figure 7.5 Equilibrium national income occurring when $AD = AS$

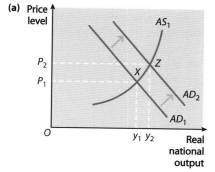
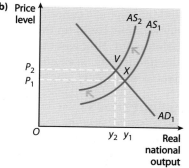

Figure 7.6 Shifts of, and adjustments along, AD and AS curves, showing movements to new points of equilibrium national income

167

Demand-side and supply-side economic shocks

An **economic shock** is a sudden unexpected event hitting the economy, disturbing either aggregate demand (a demand shock) or aggregate supply (a supply shock). In some cases, an outside shock may affect both aggregate demand and aggregate supply. Thus, looking at the UK economy, the outbreak of a war in the Middle East, for example, may affect demand by causing a sudden collapse in consumer and business confidence, and aggregate supply via its effect on the supply and price of crude oil.

> **KEY TERM**
>
> **economic shock** an unexpected event hitting the economy. Economic shocks can be demand-side or supply-side shocks (and sometimes both) and unfavourable or favourable.

> **STUDY TIP**
>
> You should build up knowledge of four or five economic shocks which have affected the UK economy in recent years.

CASE STUDY 7.1

Storms battering the UK could cost £15 billion and plunge the country back into recession

In February 2014 the Bank of England Governor Mark Carney declared that flooding would affect the UK's economic outlook. The storms could cost Britain £15 billion — and more bad weather could even plunge the UK back into recession. Mr Carney warned: 'There's a big human cost. There's the disruption to economic activity that we see just through transport, but farming clearly will be affected for some time.'

Flooding can cause economic shocks

Richard Holt, of Capital Economics, who calculated the potential £13.8 billion storm damage, warned that more heavy weather could tip the UK back into recession. Heavy snow caused a 0.5% dip in national output in 2010, he pointed out. Holt went on to say, 'It's too soon to estimate the economic cost of the flooding but the fact that the geographic area currently at risk accounts for perhaps 13% of our economy means there has to be an impact — especially since the UK's economic recovery is not completely secure.'

Follow-up questions

1 The winter storms that hit the UK in 2014 provide an example of a supply-side economic shock. Name two similar shocks originating from natural disasters.
2 Usually when we think of shocks hitting an economy, we think only of harmful adverse shocks. However, some shocks are favourable and have a good effect on the economy. Briefly describe one example.

7.3 The determinants of aggregate demand

The components of aggregate demand

Consumption, investment, government spending and net export demand (spending on UK exports by residents of other countries minus spending on imports by UK residents) form the components of aggregate demand. If any of the components change, aggregate demand increases or decreases. The four components of aggregate demand are often shown in the following equation:

aggregate demand = consumption + investment + government spending + exports (net of imports)

or:

$$AD = C + I + G + (X - M)$$

where C, I, G, X and M are the symbols used respectively for planned consumption, investment, government spending, exports and imports.

We shall now look at the first two of the components of aggregate demand — consumption and investment. We shall explain government spending's role as a component of aggregate demand in the section on fiscal policy in Chapter 9 and the role of exports and imports in the section on the balance of payments on current account in Chapter 8.

Consumption

Aggregate **consumption** is spending by all the households in the economy on consumer goods and services. Whenever members of households make decisions about whether or not to spend on consumer goods, they are simultaneously deciding whether or not to save. A determinant of consumption is also a determinant of household saving. If we assume a closed economy — pretending that there are no exports or imports — and that there is no taxation, then at any level of income, households can only do two things with their income: spend it or not spend it. Spending income is consumption, whereas not spending income is saving.

In the next paragraphs, we explain a number of factors influencing consumption and saving. These include interest rates (the reward for saving), the level of income, expected future income, wealth, consumer confidence and the availability of credit.

Interest rates

The **rate of interest** rewards savers for sacrificing current consumption, and the higher the rate of interest, the greater the reward. Thus, at any particular level of income, the amount saved will increase as the real rate of interest rises and the amount consumed will fall.

Level of income

An important, and perhaps the main, determinant of both consumption and saving is the level of income. This is often called the Keynesian theory of

---

consumption and saving. In 1936, in his explanation of the causes of the Great Depression, John Maynard Keynes wrote:

> The fundamental psychological law, upon which we are entitled to depend with great confidence…is that men are disposed, as a rule and on average, to increase their consumption as their income increases, but not by as much as the increase in their income.

In Keynes's view, as income rises, although absolute consumption rises, consumption falls as a fraction of total income, while the fraction saved increases. Therein lies the cause of recessions, according to Keynes: too much saving and too little spending.

Expected future income

The Keynesian consumption theory just explained is sometimes also called the 'absolute income' consumption theory because it assumes that the most important influence on consumption is the *current* level of income. However, the current level of income in a particular year may have less influence on a person's planned consumption than some notion of *expected* income over a much longer time period, perhaps extending over the individual's remaining lifetime or life cycle.

People plan a large part of their savings on the basis of a long-term view of their expected lifetime or permanent income, and of likely spending plans over the remaining length of an expected life cycle — this is the **life-cycle theory of consumption**. Temporary fluctuations in yearly income generally have little effect on forms of saving such as contributions to pension schemes and to the purchase of life insurance policies.

Wealth

The stock of personal wealth, as well as the flow of income, influences consumption and saving decisions. In countries such as the UK and the USA, houses and shares are the two main forms of wealth asset that people own. An increase in house prices usually causes homeowners to consume more and to save less from their current flow of income, partly because the wealth increase 'does their saving for them'. Rising house prices generally increase the amount of borrowing taking place in an economy, partly through house buyers taking out large mortgages to secure a house purchase. The additional borrowing finances extra consumption, not only on the houses themselves but on items such as furniture and new bathrooms and kitchens. Additionally, some owner-occupiers who do not wish to move house may take out a larger mortgage on the house they live in, and then spend what they borrow, for example on new cars and holidays. This is called equity withdrawal. In this context, the word 'equity' means 'wealth'. Borrowing against the value of a house reduces the amount of equity 'locked up' in people's houses.

Also, rising house prices induce a 'feel-good' factor among property owners, which leads to a consumer spending spree in the shops. Conversely, falling house prices have the opposite effect, increasing uncertainty and precautionary saving via a 'feel-bad' factor.

When share prices rise, share owners also become wealthier and may finance extra consumption by using borrowed funds. However, this effect is less noticeable in the UK, where houses rather than shares are the main household wealth asset. Stock market crashes have the opposite effect to booming share

KEY TERM

life-cycle theory of consumption a theory that explains consumption and saving in terms of how people expect their incomes to change over the whole of their life cycles.

prices, reducing the wealth of shareholders, and thence their consumption. In the summer of 2007, a dramatic fall in share prices occurred in the USA, and then in other countries, including the UK. A year later, in 2008, falling house and share prices, accompanied by a collapse in consumer and business confidence, ushered in recession in the USA and then in other countries such as the UK.

Consumer confidence

The state of consumer confidence is closely linked to people's views on expected income and to changes in personal wealth. When consumer optimism increases, households generally spend more and save less, whereas a fall in optimism (or a growth in pessimism) has the opposite effect.

Governments try to boost consumer (and business) optimism to ward off the fear of a collapse in confidence by 'talking the economy up' and by trying to enhance the credibility of government economic policy. If the government is optimistic about the future, and people believe there are good grounds for this optimism, then the general public will be optimistic and confident about the future. However, if people believe the government is pursuing the wrong policies, or if an adverse economic shock hits the economy in a way that the government can't control, confidence can quickly dissipate.

The availability of credit

Besides the rate of interest, other aspects of monetary policy, such as controls on bank lending, affect consumption. If credit is available easily and cheaply, consumption increases as people supplement current income by borrowing on credit created by the banking system. Conversely, a tight monetary policy reduces consumption. The financial crisis that occurred in 2007 and 2008, which arose from bad debts in the US sub-prime market, had this effect in the UK and the USA. In the so-called **credit crunch**, interest rates rose and the supply of credit dried up, with banks refusing to supply applicants with new credit cards or mortgages.

Distribution of income

Consumption and saving are also influenced by the **distribution of income** within an economy. Rich people save a greater proportion of their income than poor people; redistribution of income from rich to poor therefore increases consumption and reduces saving.

Expectations of future inflation

It is not easy to predict the impact of inflation on consumption. However, uncertainty caused by fears of rising inflation increases precautionary saving and reduces consumption. It may also, however, have the opposite effect. Households may decide to bring forward consumption decisions by spending now on consumer durables such as cars or television sets, thereby avoiding expected future price increases. People may also decide to borrow to finance the purchase of houses if they expect property prices to appreciate at a rate faster than general inflation. In this situation, and particularly if the real rate of interest is low or negative, people often decide to buy land, property and other physical assets such as fine art and antiques as a 'hedge' against inflation, in preference to saving through the purchase of financial assets.

> **KEY TERMS**
>
> **availability of credit** funds available for households and firms to borrow.
>
> **credit crunch** occurs when there is a lack of funds available in the credit market, making it difficult for borrowers to obtain financing, and leads to a rise in the cost of borrowing.
>
> **distribution of income** the spread of different incomes among individuals and different income groups in the economy.

Speculative demand for housing occurs because house prices rise faster than general inflation

ACTIVITY

Survey the other members of your economics class to find the proportions of their incomes they spend on consumption and save (a) in a typical week and (b) in the week before Christmas. Ask them how they save.

CASE STUDY 7.2

The 'credit crunch' and recession

The financial crisis which hit the world economy in 2007 started in the US housing market where banks had lent money to <u>sub-prime borrowers</u>. When these borrowers couldn't repay their loans, or even the interest on them, the banks were left with bad debts, as were other financial institutions that had bought 'packages' of bad debt from the banks.

This infected the entire financial system and meant that banks stopped lending to each other — creating the <u>credit crunch</u>. The first UK bank to be affected by the seizing up of financial markets was Northern Rock, which had to be rescued by the British government. (A few years later, the government sold the bank to Virgin Money.) A lack of mortgages meant the market began to stagnate and the properties that did change hands went for less than they would have done a few months previously. This increased the amount of <u>negative equity</u> in the economy.

Follow-up questions

1 Explain the underlined terms: sub-prime borrowers; credit crunch; negative equity.
2 Find out about how the UK housing market has fared since 2012.

The personal savings ratio and the household savings ratio

The personal savings ratio measures the *actual* or *realised* saving of the personal sector as a ratio of total personal sector disposal income:

$$\text{personal savings ratio} = \frac{\text{realised or actual personal saving}}{\text{personal disposable income}}$$

The household savings ratio is used in a similar way. It measures households' realised saving as a ratio of their disposable income. However, the personal savings ratio and the household savings ratio are not the same. The personal sector is more than just households, including unincorporated businesses such as partnerships and charitable organisations such as independent schools.

Economists and the government are interested in how much of their incomes people plan to save and to consume in the near future, as this provides important information about what lies ahead for the state of aggregate demand. Because it is difficult to measure people's plans accurately, the personal savings ratio calculated for the most recent past period is generally used as an indicator of what people wish to do in the future.

CASE STUDY 7.3

Changes in the UK household savings ratio

Figure 7.7 shows that the UK household savings ratio fell, though with some volatility, between 2010 and 2014, bottoming out at under 6% early in 2013 and again early in 2014. Annually for 2013, the household savings ratio was 6.4%, compared with 8.0% in 2012. As part of a general revision of official national income statistics published in September 2014, the household savings ratio was revised up across all periods as a result of changes being made in line with international standards adopted by all European Union countries. On average, the annual and quarterly savings ratio between 1997 and 2013 is 3.7% higher than previously published levels. The official statistics published before the 2014 revision had shown a negative savings ratio early in 2008, just before recession kicked in. Negative saving occurs if people borrow more than they save. This is called dissaving.

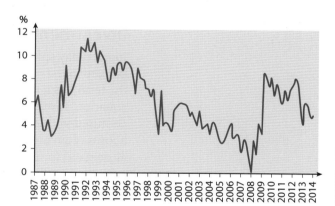

Figure 7.7 Changes in the UK household savings ratio, Quarter 1 1987 to Quarter 2 2014

Source: ONS

One of the factors affecting household savings is people's uncertainty about the future. People who fear job losses, or who expect to suffer a fall in future income, are likely to save more for precautionary reasons. They want a 'nest egg' to protect themselves from the loss of future income. This means that savings ratios generally rise in recessions, unless overridden by other factors such as the need to borrow more so as to maintain spending levels and current standards of living and lifestyles.

Follow-up questions

1 How have very low interest rates affected the savings ratio?
2 Research what has happened to UK savings ratios since 2014.

TEST YOURSELF 7.2

Figure 7.8 shows the personal savings ratio in the USA between 1970 and 2012.

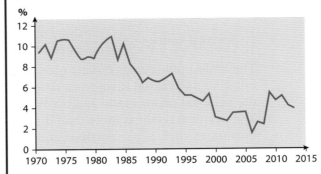

Figure 7.8

Which of the following can be concluded from the data?

A Total personal savings were lower in the USA in 2012 than in 1970.

B Personal savings and income both fell in the USA over the whole data period.

C The US personal sector saved a smaller percentage of its income in 2005 than in 2010.

Explain your answer.

Investment

In everyday speech, investment is often used to describe a situation in which a person 'invests' in stocks or shares, paintings or antiques. In economic theory, the term has a narrower and more specific meaning. In the aggregate demand equation, investment is *planned* demand for capital goods, which must not be confused with demand for financial assets such as shares and bonds, which is a form of saving. The latter is called financial investment, but is not the same as demand for physical capital needed for the production of other goods and services. Finally, by providing or improving education and training, firms and the government can invest in human capital.

It is important to remember that capital is a *stock* concept, but investment is a *flow*. We can measure the national capital stock at any particular point of time. It represents the total of all the nation's capital goods, of all types, which are still in existence and capable of production. By contrast, we measure the flow of investment over a period, usually a year.

A country's gross investment includes two parts: replacement investment (to make good depreciation or capital consumption), which simply maintains the size of the existing capital stock by replacing worn-out capital, and net investment, which adds to the capital stock, thereby increasing productive potential. Along with technical progress, net investment is one of the engines of economic growth.

The difference between saving and investment

Economists make a clear separation between saving and investment, even though in everyday language the two terms are often used interchangeably. Whereas saving is simply income that is not spent on consumption, investment is spending by firms on capital goods such as machines and office equipment.

STUDY TIP
Make sure you don't confuse investment with savings.

As a simplification, economists often assume that households make saving decisions, while firms make investment decisions. Firms invest when they buy capital goods such as machinery. However, firms also save, for example when they store profits in a bank account without spending them.

Factors influencing investment decisions

Investment in physical capital goods is of two types:

- investment in fixed capital, such as new factories or plant, and social capital such as roads and socially owned hospitals
- inventory investment in stocks of raw materials, semi-finished goods and finished goods

The new capital goods created by new fixed investment often have an economic life extending many years into the future. The future is always uncertain and the further we go into the future the greater the uncertainty. When deciding whether or not to go ahead with a fixed investment project in, for example, new machinery, firms need to form views on:

- expected future sales revenue attributable to the investment project
- expected future costs of production resulting both from the rate of interest paid for borrowing the funds to finance the initial investment, and from the future maintenance costs
- the future profit the investment is expected to yield, which is the expected future sales revenue stream minus the investment's expected future costs. Estimating expected future profit is complicated by the fact that a value has to be placed *now* on profits expected perhaps many years into the *future*.

Other factors that influence investment decisions, besides factors such as the rate of interest, include the following:

- The relative prices of capital and labour. When the price of capital rises (for example, when the prices of capital goods or rates of interest rise), in the long run firms adopt more labour-intensive methods of production, substituting labour for capital. A decrease in the relative prices of capital goods has the opposite effect. If the price of capital goods or interest rates falls, firms switch to capital-intensive methods of production, so investment increases.
- The nature of technical progress. Technical progress can make machinery obsolete or out of date. When this happens, a machine's business life becomes shorter than its technical life: that is, the number of years before the machine wears out. A sudden burst of technical progress may cause firms to replace capital goods early, long before the end of the equipment's technical life.
- The adequacy of financial institutions in the supply of investment funds. As mentioned, many investments in fixed capital goods are long-term investments that yield most of their expected income several years into the future. These investments may be difficult to finance because of the inadequacy of the financial institutions that provide investment funds. Banks have been criticised for favouring short-term investments and being reluctant to provide the finance for long-term investments. Likewise, the stock market may favour short-termism over long-termism, although in recent years the growth of new methods of lending to firms has provided an important source of medium- to longer-term finance. In recent years, private equity finance has emerged to provide an important source of medium- to longer-term finance.
- The impact of government policies and activities on investment by the private sector. Governments also provide funds for firms to borrow to

finance investment projects, though at the same time they tax firms, for example by levying corporation tax. Arguably, however, when choosing whether to invest in or support investment projects, governments may be better at 'picking losers' than 'picking winners'. In the past, UK governments have sometimes provided investment funds to rescue jobs in loss-making and uncompetitive industries that ought to be allowed to continue their decline. Government ministers and their civil servants may make bad investment decisions because, unlike entrepreneurs, they don't face the risk of being bankrupted as a result of poor decision making.

CASE STUDY 7.4

The emergence of private equity finance

Until quite recently, it was not usually possible for a private company to finance expansion by extending significantly its share capital or equity, while still remaining a private company. When an ambitious private company wanted to raise a large capital sum, there were normally only two options. The company could either borrow and increase its debt or extend its share capital by going public with a flotation on the stock exchange. However, this has now changed and a new financial services industry made up of private equity finance firms has come into existence.

Typically, a private equity finance firm invests a significant sum of money in a private company, in return for shares which are highly illiquid as long as the company receiving the funds remains private. Part of the deal might be that the company — having successfully grown as a result of the capital injection — eventually becomes a public company or PLC. The private equity finance provider could then sell its stake in the client company and take its profit. The funds released may be used by the private equity finance firm to invest in another start-up private company needing long-term funding.

The late 1990s and the early 2000s witnessed a massive growth of private equity finance in the USA and the UK. Most of this growth was fuelled by an activity very different from that just described of promoting the growth of small start-up private companies. Instead, the private equity companies borrowed money from institutional investors and used the borrowed funds to finance leveraged (and often hostile) takeovers of established public companies. Once ownership had been transferred to the private equity company, the victim company might be broken up. Its assets would be sold and its workers sacked, to release the funds needed to pay back the borrowed funds that had financed the takeover.

For some, this represented asset stripping, short-termism and the pursuit of private greed. But for others, private equity finance was simply a new and more efficient vehicle for engineering the restructuring of capitalism, that is: shifting productive assets from a less efficient to a more efficient use. Private equity finance suffered a decline 2008, as a result of the credit crunch, which decimated financial businesses that had relied for their success on borrowed funds. However, in the period of recovery following the 2008 recession, private equity finance began once again to experience rapid growth.

Follow-up questions

1 Find out the meaning of a leveraged hostile takeover bid.
2 What is 'asset stripping'?

The accelerator theory of investment

The accelerator theory stems from the assumption that firms wish to keep a relatively fixed ratio, known as the capital–output ratio, between the output they are currently producing and their existing stock of fixed capital assets. For example, if 4 units of capital are needed to produce 1 new unit of output, the capital–output ratio is 4 to 1. The capital–output ratio is the **accelerator coefficient**.

To understand why the theory is called the accelerator theory, consider the following:

● If national output grows by a constant amount each year, firms invest in exactly the same amount of new capital each year to enlarge their capital

stock so as to maintain the desired capital–output ratio. From year to year, the level of investment is therefore constant.
- If the rate of growth of output *accelerates, investment also increases* as firms take action to enlarge the stock of capital to a level sufficient to maintain the desired capital–output ratio.
- Conversely, when the rate of growth of national output *decelerates*, investment declines.

Aggregate demand affects the rate of growth of national income. As aggregate demand and national income change, firms adjust their stock of capital to maintain the capital–output ratio at 4 to 1. Relatively slight changes in the rate of growth of national income or output cause large absolute rises and falls in investment.

7.4 Aggregate demand and the level of economic activity

What is economic activity?

Economic activity can mean many things, but we shall think of it as centring on the production and consumption of goods and services in the economy, together with the employment of the labour, capital and other inputs that produce output.

Aggregate demand and economic activity

AD/AS diagrams can be used to illustrate how changes in aggregate demand affect the level of real output, but they don't directly show the employment levels at each level of real output. However, the main link between aggregate demand and employment is simple. When real output increases, firms generally have to employ more workers to produce the additional goods and services that the output increase involves. Conversely, when real output falls, less labour is required to produce the smaller amount of goods and services now being produced.

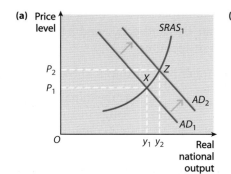
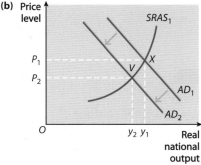

Figure 7.9 The effect of a change in aggregate demand on real output

Figure 7.9(a), which illustrates the effect of an increase of aggregate demand on real output, is the same as in Figure 7.6(a). Figure 7.9(b), by contrast, shows the how a leftward shift of the *AD* curve leads to a fall in real output. To put it another way, Figure 7.9(a) shows the expansionary effect of an increase in aggregate demand, while Figure 7.9(b) shows the contractionary effect of a decrease in aggregate demand. The expansionary effect is likely to increase employment; the contractionary effect is likely to lead to a fall in employment.

Two points to note about both diagrams:

● the greater the shift in aggregate demand, the greater the change in real output
● the extent to which real output changes also depends on the steepness of the *AS* curve

We shall explore the second of these issues in sections 7.5 and 7.6 on short-run and long-run aggregate supply.

Aggregate demand and the national income multiplier

The national income **multiplier** measures the relationship between an initial change in a component of aggregate demand, such as government spending or private-sector investment, and the resulting larger change in the level of national income.

Suppose, for example, that government spending increases by £10 billion, but tax revenue remains unchanged. The resulting budget deficit initially injects £10 billion of new spending into the circular flow of income. This spending increases people's incomes. If we assume that everybody in the economy saves a small fraction of any income increase and spends the rest, the £10 billion generates multiple and successively smaller further increases in income, until the next stage is so small that it can be ignored. Adding up the successive stages of income generation, the total increase in income is a multiple of the initial spending increase of £10 billion — hence the name multiplier theory. If the size of the multiplier is 2.5, an increase in consumption spending of £10 billion causes national income to increase by £25 billion.

Figure 7.10 illustrates the multiplier in an *AD/AS* diagram.

In Figure 7.10, an initial increase in government spending (*ΔG*) shifts the *AD* curve from AD_1 to AD_2. This then triggers the multiplier process, which leads to a further increase in aggregate demand to AD_3. If the size of the government spending multiplier is 2.5, then, as we have mentioned, the eventual increase in aggregate demand is two and a half times the size of the initial increase in government spending.

The multiplier relationship is shown in the following equation:

$$\text{multiplier} = \frac{\text{change in national income}}{\text{initial change in government spending}} \text{ or } \frac{\Delta Y}{\Delta G}$$

As the following quantitative skills example shows, the size of the multiplier can be worked out providing we possess knowledge of both the change in aggregate demand and the resulting change in national income.

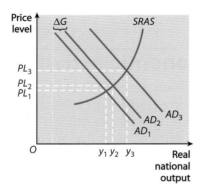

Figure 7.10 The national income multiplier illustrated on an *AD/AS* diagram

KEY TERM
multiplier the relationship between a change in aggregate demand and the resulting usually larger change in national income.

STUDY TIP
Make sure you don't confuse the multiplier with the accelerator.

QUANTITATIVE SKILLS 7.1

Worked example: calculating the size of the multiplier

In an economy, nominal national income is £2,000 billion in 2015. Government spending increases by £10 billion. The change in government spending causes nominal national income to increase to £2,050 billion in 2016.

What is the size of the government spending multiplier in relation to the change in *nominal* national income?

The increase in government spending of £10 billion causes nominal national income to increase by £50 billion between 2015 and 2016. The size of the multiplier in terms of the growth in nominal national income is thus £50 billion divided by £10 billion or 5. This is quite a large multiplier.

TEST YOURSELF 7.3

The multiplier can refer to the effect of a change in the level of:

A exports on national income

B national income on investment

C consumption on saving

D saving on imports

Which is the correct answer?

The different multipliers

Nested within the national income multiplier are a number of specific multipliers, each related to the particular component of aggregate demand that initially changes. Besides the government spending multiplier, there is an investment multiplier, a tax multiplier, an export multiplier and an import multiplier. Taken together, the government spending and tax multipliers are known as fiscal policy multipliers. Likewise the export and import multipliers are foreign trade multipliers. An increase in consumption spending can also trigger a multiplier process.

The multiplier process can also work in reverse, reducing rather than increasing national income. This happens when government spending, consumption, investment or exports fall. It also happens when taxation or imports increase. This is because taxation and imports are withdrawals from the circular flow of income, rather than injections. The tax and import multipliers are always negative, meaning that an increase in taxes or imports causes national income to fall (and a decrease in taxes or imports causes national income to rise).

STUDY TIP

Make sure you understand the government spending multiplier, the investment multiplier and the export multiplier.

KEY TERM

marginal propensity to consume the fraction of an increase in disposable income (income after tax) that people plan to spend on domestically produced consumer goods.

The marginal propensity to consume

The **marginal propensity to consume** (*MPC*) is the fraction of any increase in income which people plan to spend on the consumption of domestically produced goods, after allowing for the fraction of the increase in income which they pay in taxation to the government, and the fraction spent on imported goods. For example, if people, on average, plan to spend 20 pence of an income increase of £1.00 on consumption, the *MPC* is 0.2.

The multiplier formula

The formula you need to know for calculating the value of the multiplier is:

$$k = \frac{1}{1 - MPC} \text{ where } k \text{ is the multiplier}$$

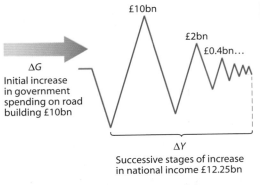

£10bn

£2bn

£0.4bn...

ΔG
Initial increase
in government
spending on road
building £10bn

ΔY
Successive stages of increase
in national income £12.25bn

Figure 7.11 The dynamic nature of the multiplier process

Thus, if the MPC is 0.2 (after allowing for the fractions of income that are paid in taxes and are spent on imports), the multiplier is 1 divided by 0.8, which is 1.25. If government spending (or some other component of aggregate demand such as investment) increases by £10 billion, national income eventually increases by £12.5 billion, i.e. by the increase in aggregate demand multiplied by the multiplier (k).

The multiplier as a dynamic process

The multiplier process, which is essentially dynamic, taking place over time, resembles ripples spreading over a pond after a stone has been thrown in the water. However, the ripples in a pond last only a few seconds, whereas the ripples spreading through the economy following a change in aggregate demand can last for months and even years. Figure 7.11 illustrates the ripple effect. The diagram, which shows the government spending multiplier, can easily be adapted to illustrate the investment multiplier or any other national income multiplier, such as the export multiplier.

Given the assumption we have made about the fraction of new income which is spent on domestically produced consumer goods at each stage of the multiplier process, each of the 'ripples' in Figure 7.11 is 0.2 in size of the previous 'ripple'.

QUANTITATIVE SKILLS 7.2

Worked example: using the *MPC*

Calculate the size of the multiplier when the size of the marginal propensity to consume (*MPC*) is (a) 0.6 and (b) 0.5.

The formula for the multiplier is $\dfrac{1}{1-MPC}$

(a) When the *MPC* is 0.6, the multiplier equals 1 divided by 1 – 0.6, which is 2.5.
(b) When the *MPC* is 0.5, the multiplier equals 1 divided by 1 – 0.5, which is 2.0.
The smaller the *MPC*, the smaller the multiplier.

Nominal national income, real national income and the size of the multiplier

It is important to understand the following relationship:

nominal national income = real national income × average price level

or, in shorthand:

$Y = Py$

The size of the multiplier depends on whether we are measuring the **nominal** national income multiplier or the **real** national income multiplier. In our numerical example, the size of the multiplier is 1.25, but this is the nominal national income multiplier. Provided the *SRAS* curve slopes upwards, as is the case in Figure 7.10, the size of the multiplier measured in real terms is always going to be smaller than the nominal national income multiplier. This is because part of the multiplier effect deflects into a rising price level. The growth of real income is restricted to the distance between y_1 and y_2, with the price level rising from P_1 to P_2. Indeed, if the *SRAS* curve were vertical rather than upward sloping, the size of the multiplier measured in real *income* terms would be zero. In this situation, the multiplier effect resulting from an increase in government spending would lead solely to inflation and **not** to rising real output.

7.5 The determinants of short-run aggregate supply

Economists identify two aggregate supply curves: the **short-run aggregate supply (SRAS)** curve and the **long-run aggregate supply (LRAS)** curve, both with different shapes. The *SRAS* curve is explained in this section of the chapter, while the final section of the chapter explains the *LRAS* curve.

All the *AS* curves drawn so far in this chapter are in fact short-run curves, though not labelled as such — earlier in the chapter, it was more important to introduce you to the *AD/AS* macroeconomic model than to distinguish between *SRAS* and *LRAS* curves.

A short-run *AS* curve is illustrated in Figure 7.12.

The upward-slope of the *SRAS* curve is explained by two microeconomic assumptions about the nature of firms. These are:

- all firms aim to maximise profits
- in the short run, the cost of producing extra units of output increases as firms produce more output

At the average price level P_1 in Figure 7.12, the level of real output that all the economy's firms are willing to produce and sell is y_1. To persuade the firms it is in their interest to produce the larger output of y_2, the price level must rise. This is because higher prices are needed to create the higher sales revenues needed to offset the higher production costs that firms incur as they increase output, so that profits do not fall. In Figure 7.12, the average price level has to rise to P_2 in order to create conditions in which profit-maximising firms are willing and able to supply more output. If prices don't rise, it is not profitable to increase supply. Without a higher price level, profit-maximising firms, taken in aggregate, will not temporarily increase the supply of real output.

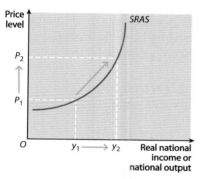

Figure 7.12 A short-run aggregate supply (*SRAS*) curve

Adjustments along a *SRAS* curve and shifts in the position of a *SRAS* curve

All the *SRAS* curves drawn in this book are 'curved curves' or non-linear curves, which become steeper moving up the curve. This has important implications for monetary and fiscal policy, which are further explained in Chapter 9. As the *AD* curve shifts to the right along a non-linear *SRAS* curve, such as the one in Figure 7.13, whether or not real income or the price level increases depends on the steepness of slope of the *SRAS* curve.

When the *AD* curve shifts to the right from AD_1 to AD_2, the resulting increase in real output is proportionately greater than the increase in the price level. Real income increases from y_1 to y_2 and the price level rises from P_1 to P_2. This is because the *AD* curve is shifting along the relatively shallow section of the *SRAS* curve. But when the *AD* curve shifts rightward from AD_3 to AD_4, it is shifting along a much steeper section of the *SRAS* curve. As a result, most of the effect of the increase in aggregate demand falls on the price level rather than on real output. The effect is

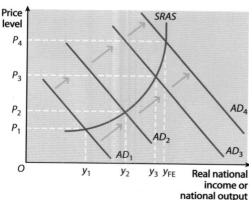

Figure 7.13 How an increase in aggregate demand affects real national income and the price level

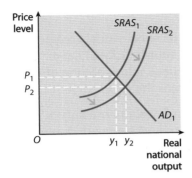

Figure 7.14 A rightward shift of the *SRAS* curve

inflationary rather than reflationary. Indeed, if the *AD* curve were to shift any further to the right beyond AD_4, only the price level, and not real output, would rise. In the diagram, y_{FE} is the full-employment level of real income. In this situation, any further increase in aggregate demand results solely in a rising price level, or inflation. At full employment, real income can't increase, at least in the short run, because the economy is producing at full capacity.

The *slope* of the *SRAS* curve must not be confused with a *shift* of the curve. The *SRAS* curve is constructed under the assumption that all the determinants of aggregate supply *other than the price level* remain unchanged. Should any of these determinants change, the *SRAS* curve shifts to a new position. The curve can shift either to the right (an increase in aggregate supply) or to the left (a decrease in aggregate supply). Figure 7.14 illustrates a rightward shift of the *SRAS* curve, or an increase in aggregate supply, which results in **deflation**, with the price level falling from P_1 to P_2.

Among the factors that cause a rightward shift of the *SRAS* curve are:

- a fall in businesses' costs of production; these include the costs of imported raw materials and energy
- a fall in unit labour costs, resulting from a fall in wage costs or an increase in labour productivity, the latter possibly caused by better labour training
- a reduction in indirect taxes such as VAT imposed on firms by the government
- an increase in subsidies granted to firms by the government
- **technical progress** which improves the quality and productivity of capital goods

KEY TERMS

deflation a continuing fall in the price level.

technical progress new and better ways of doing things.

Labour is a variable factor of production

7.6 The determinants of long-run aggregate supply

The meaning of long-run aggregate supply

In the short run, the aggregate supply of real output depends on the average price level in the economy, and the position of the *SRAS* curve is determined by business costs. Other things remaining constant, firms are only prepared to supply more output if the price level rises. However, in the long run, aggregate supply is *not* influenced by the price level. Long-run supply reflects the economy's production potential. The *LRAS* curve is located at the normal capacity level of output, which is the level of output at which the full production potential of the economy is being used. To put it another way, it is the maximum sustainable level of output that the economy can produce when the economy is on its production possibility frontier.

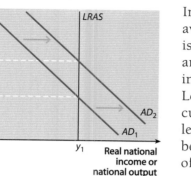

Figure 7.15 The vertical long-run aggregate supply (*LRAS*) curve

In Figure 7.15, y_1 is the normal capacity level of output. The next diagram, Figure 7.16, brings together the *SRAS* curve and the *LRAS* curve on the same graph. Note the similarity, but also the difference, between Figure 7.16 and an earlier diagram in this chapter, Figure 7 5. In the earlier diagram, although labelled simply as *AS*, the aggregate supply curve is a short-run aggregate supply curve. In Figure 7.16, the label is *SRAS*, and a vertical *LRAS* curve has been added, also passing through point *X* on the diagram. In the context of Figure 7.16, point *X* locates the long-run level of equilibrium national income, y_1, which, as indicated earlier, is the normal capacity level of output. (As is explained in the next chapter, the economy can temporarily produce a level of output greater than Y_1.)

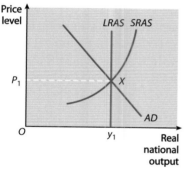

Figure 7.16 Bringing the *SRAS* and *LRAS* curves together

The position of the *LRAS* curve, shifts of the *LRAS* curve, and economic growth

The position of the vertical *LRAS* curve represents the normal capacity level of output of the economy, with the economy producing at full potential. The position is determined by the same factors that determine the position of the economy's production possibility frontier. These include:

- the state of technical progress
- the quantities of capital and labour and other factors of production in the economy
- the mobility of factors of production, particularly labour
- the productivity of the factors of production, particularly labour productivity
- people's attitudes to hard work
- personal enterprise, particularly among entrepreneurs. The emergence of a large number of risk-taking entrepreneurs is especially important for shifting the *LRAS* curve to the right
- related to this, the existence of appropriate economic incentives
- the institutional structure of the economy, involving such factors as the rule of law and the efficiency of the banking system

Earlier in this chapter, and also in Chapter 1, we explained how an *increase* in the quantity of available factors of production, and improvements in technology that increase the productivity of labour, capital or land, shift the economy's production possibility frontier outward. For the same reasons, the economy's *LRAS* curve shifts to the right. The shifts of the production possibility frontier and the *LRAS* curve to the right are both illustrated in Figure 7.17.

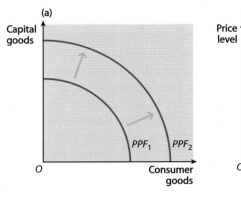

Figure 7.17 Linking an outward movement of the economy's production possibility frontier to a shift of the *LRAS* curve to the right

Remember that long-run economic growth involves an outward movement of the economy's production possibility frontier. This is shown in Figure 7.17(a). Meanwhile, Figure 7.17(b) depicts economic growth in terms of a shift of the economy's *LRAS* curve to the right. The shift from $LRAS_1$ to $LRAS_2$ increases the normal capacity level of real output, from y_1 to y_2.

The Keynesian aggregate supply curve

The vertical *LRAS* curve is sometimes called the free-market *LRAS* curve. This label reflects the view commonly expressed by free-market economists that, provided markets function competitively and efficiently, the economy always operates at or close to full capacity. In the short run, real output is influenced by the average price level, but in the long run, aggregate supply is determined by maximum normal production capacity, which determines the position of the *LRAS* curve.

These days, most economists agree that the *LRAS* curve is vertical. Some economists argue, however, that the *LRAS* curve has a different shape, the 'inverted L-shape' shown in Figure 7.18.

The inverted L-shaped *LRAS* curve is based on the explanation put forward by John Maynard Keynes of the Great Depression in the UK and US economies in the 1930s. Keynes argued that a depressed economy can settle into an under-full-employment equilibrium, shown for example by point *A* on the horizontal section of the *LRAS* curve. At point *A*, the level of real national output is y_1. Keynes believed that without purposeful intervention by the government, an economy could display more or less permanent demand deficiency. Market forces would fail to adjust automatically and achieve full employment. If the government could shift *AD* to the right along the horizontal section of the *LRAS* curve (mainly through expansionary fiscal policy), the existence of huge amounts of spare capacity would lead, in Keynes's view, to a growth in real output (and employment), without an increase in the price level. Eventually, when maximum normal capacity is achieved, the *LRAS* curve becomes vertical for the same reasons that the 'free-market' curve is vertical.

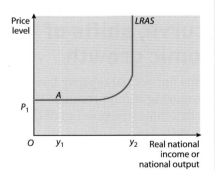

Figure 7.18 The Keynesian 'inverted L-shaped' *LRAS* curve

CASE STUDY 7.5

Keynes on 'Poverty in Plenty'

In 1934, in the depth of the Great Depression, and 2 years before he published his *General Theory of Employment, Interest and Money*, John Maynard Keynes gave a radio talk in which he expressed his view on the causes of unemployment. Keynes's talk was one of a series, entitled 'Poverty in Plenty', in which a number of economists and public figures gave their views on the title theme. At this time, the UK unemployment rate was 16.7%. Keynes started by summarising the common ground between himself and the other contributors. He then outlined what he saw as the main difference between the various contributors, before arguing that, in his view, the economic system was not self-adjusting. Here is what Keynes had to say.

Is the economic system self-adjusting?

We must not regard the conditions of supply, our ability to produce, as the fundamental source of our troubles. It is the conditions of demand which our diagnosis must search and probe for explanation. All the contributors to these talks meet to this extent on common ground. But every one of us has a somewhat different explanation of what is wrong with demand, and, consequently, a different idea of the right remedy.

Though we all start out in the same direction, we soon part company into two main groups. On one side are those who believe that the existing economic system is, in the long run, a self-adjusting system, though with creaks and groans and jerks, and interrupted by time lags, outside interference and mistakes.

On the other side of the gulf are those who reject the idea that the existing economic system is, in any significant sense, self-adjusting. They believe that the failure of effective demand to reach the full potential of supply, in spite of human psychological demand being far from satisfied for the vast majority of individuals, is due to much more fundamental causes.

The strength of the self-adjusting school depends on it having behind it almost the whole body of organised economic thinking and doctrine of the last hundred years. Now, I range myself with the heretics on the other side of the gulf. There is, I am convinced, a fatal flaw in that part of the orthodox reasoning which deals with the theory of what determines the level of effective demand and the volume of aggregate employment. The system is not self-adjusting, and, without purposive direction, it is incapable of translating our actual poverty into our potential plenty.

Follow-up questions

1 What is meant by 'effective aggregate demand'?
2 Suggest why there may be too little effective aggregate demand in an economy.

TEST YOURSELF 7.4

Write short answers to the following questions.

1 Is net national income the same as GDP?
2 What is the difference between nominal and real national income?
3 What is the difference between saving and investment?
4 List the components of aggregate demand.
5 What is deficient aggregate demand?
6 Why is the *LRAS* curve usually assumed to be vertical?

SUMMARY

- National income is the *flow* of new output produced in an economy in a particular time period.
- Changes in *real* national income must not be confused with changes in *nominal* national income.
- A circular flow model of the economy shows the flows of income and spending around the economy.
- The circular flow model can illustrate injections into and leakages (or withdrawals) from income circulating round the economy and equilibrium national income.
- The *AD/AS* model can be used as well as the circular flow model to show equilibrium national income (or macroeconomic equilibrium) in the economy.
- The *AD* curve shows total planned spending on real national output at different price levels.
- Aggregate demand is total *planned* spending on real output of all the economic agents in the economy. As an equation, $AD = C + I + G + (X - M)$.
- Consumption by households and investment by firms are two components of aggregate demand.
- Saving, or income which is not consumed, must not be confused with investment.
- Aggregate consumption and saving are determined by the rate of interest, the levels of current and future income, wealth, consumer confidence and the availability of credit.
- Investment is determined by factors such as the rate of interest, expected returns on capital, technical progress, the availability of finance, and the accelerator.
- The *SRAS* curve shows how much output producers are prepared to supply at different price levels.
- It is important to distinguish between a *shift* of an *AD* or *AS* curve and the resulting *movement along* the curve that doesn't shift.
- A shift of the *AD* curve to the right is known as an increase in aggregate demand, while a shift to the left is a decrease in aggregate demand.
- A shift of the *SRAS* curve to the right is known as an increase in aggregate supply, while a shift to the left is a decrease in aggregate supply.
- An increase or decrease in any of the components of aggregate demand, for example government spending, usually leads to a multiplier effect.
- It is important to distinguish between a short-run aggregate supply (*SRAS*) curve and a long-run aggregate supply (*LRAS*) curve.
- *SRAS* curves generally slope upwards, but the *LRAS* curve is generally assumed to be vertical with its position determined by the economy's normal capacity level of output.
- A rightward movement of the *LRAS* curve illustrates long-term economic growth.
- Some Keynesian economists have argued that the *LRAS* curve is horizontal to the left of the full-employment level of real output, becoming vertical at the full-employment level of output.

Questions

1 Explain the meaning of the circular flow of income.

2 What are the components of aggregate demand? Illustrate how an increase in exports affects the position of the *AD* curve and equilibrium national income.

3 Explain how changes in the rate of interest affect consumption and saving.

4 Explain how the multiplier process operates.

5 Explain the shape of the aggregate supply curve, both in the short run and in the long run.

6 Considering only the *SRAS* curve and not the *LRAS* curve, explain how an increase in aggregate demand may affect output and the price level.

8 Economic performance

This chapter returns to a number of topics mentioned briefly in Chapters 6 and 7. It focuses on the core macroeconomic topics of economic growth, unemployment, inflation and the balance of payments, explaining and exploring the topics in greater detail than was the case in the earlier chapters. In particular, the *AD/AS* macroeconomic model introduced in Chapter 7 is used to analyse various issues related to each of the topics.

The chapter is about **economic performance**. A country's macroeconomic performance can be judged by how successful the economy is at achieving the four main objectives of macroeconomic policy outlined in Chapter 6. Can the economy achieve and then sustain a satisfactory rate of economic growth, relatively full employment, relative price stability and control of inflation, and a degree of trading competitiveness in international markets?

> **KEY TERM**
> **economic performance** success or failure in achieving economic policy objectives.

> **LEARNING OBJECTIVES**
> This chapter will:
> - remind you of how economic growth, unemployment, inflation and the balance of payments are defined and measured
> - survey various demand-side and supply-side determinants of economic growth
> - explain the economic cycle and output gaps
> - examine the benefits and costs of economic growth
> - provide examples of the effects of economic shocks on the economy
> - explain some of the main types of unemployment
> - examine the demand-side and supply-side causes of unemployment
> - discuss how global events can impact on UK unemployment and inflation
> - explain demand-pull and cost-push inflation, and the monetarist theory of inflation
> - describe how changes in world commodity prices affect domestic inflation
> - discuss the effect of deflation on the economy
> - explain the different sections of the current account of the balance of payments
> - explain how current account deficits and surpluses affect economies
> - discuss how conflicts that arise from trying to achieve different macroeconomic policy objects affect economic performance in the short run and the long run
> - explain the Phillips curve relationship

8.1 Economic growth and the economic cycle

Definitions and measurement of economic growth

The definition and the measurement of economic growth are not the same thing. The *definition* of economic growth was first introduced to you on page 13 of Chapter 1, in the context of production possibility frontiers. Pages 139–40 of Chapter 6 extended the definition by explaining the difference between short-run and long-run economic growth. Short-run growth brings idle resources into production and takes up the slack in the economy. By contrast, long-run economic growth, depicted by an outward movement of the economy's production possibility frontier, increases the economy's production potential. In contrast to the definition, economic growth is *measured* by the percentage annual change in real GDP.

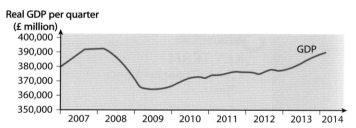

Figure 8.1 Quarterly changes in real GDP in the UK, 2007–2014

Figure 8.1 shows the level of UK GDP for each year from 2007 to the end of 2013. The graph reflects changes in GDP estimates which the ONS introduced recently. Clearly shown is the recession that hit the UK economy late in 2008/09. The UK economy moved out of the so-called 'great recession' in the third quarter of 2009. The revised data shows that the 2008/09 recession was not quite as long or as deep as previously thought, though it was still deeper than earlier recessions in the 1980s and 1990s. Another significant point to note from the graph is the long period of recovery and boom extending from 1992 to the onset of recession in 2008.

The years after late 2009 were a period of **economic recovery**. However, in the early years of recovery from late 2009 to 2012, the growth in output was hardly noticeable. Indeed, many people, especially low-paid workers and benefit claimants whose real incomes were falling, still believed the economy to be in recession. The recovery only really got going in 2013 and 2014, and even then, for most people, recovery was not accompanied by rising real household incomes. Things might be changing in 2015.

STUDY TIP
Remember that economic growth is always measured in *real* rather than in *nominal* terms. You must understand the difference between real national output and nominal national output.

KEY TERM
economic recovery when short-run economic growth takes place after a recession.

CASE STUDY 8.1

Recession: 'now you see it, now you don't'

The Office for National Statistics (ONS) regularly revises its published statistics. When this happens, the beginning, end and depth of recessions (and of periods of positive growth) can change. Before revised statistics were published in 2013, the official view was that the UK economy had entered the second dip of a 'double-dip' recession. Some economists were even predicting that a 'third dip' was on the cards. The revised statistics — if they can be trusted — show that the 'double dip' did not happen.

The new statistics led to newspaper headlines such as 'The recession that never was: the small change which makes a big difference' in the *Daily Mail*. The data in Figure 8.2, published by the ONS in June 2013, shows what 'apparently' happened to quarterly UK economic growth between January 2009 and the first quarter of 2013. The deep recession lasted from the second quarter of 2008 until the end of the second quarter of 2009 (i.e. five quarters in total).

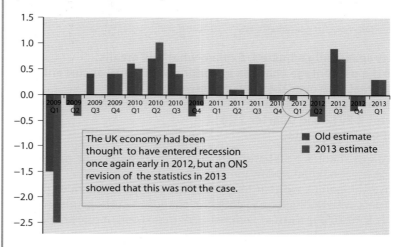

Figure 8.2 Real GDP, quarter-on-quarter growth, revised figures, 2013

Source: ONS

Figure 8.2 contains two sets of data. The blue bars in the graph show the ONS's estimate of quarterly growth published before June 2013. This data shows the 'second dip' of a 'double-dip' recession occurring between the fourth quarter of 2011 and the end of the second quarter of 2012. But according to the revised data, shown by the green bars, there was zero growth in the first quarter of 2012, i.e. neither positive nor negative. Hence the 'second dip' never happened and there was no 'double-dip' recession. However, the revised data also shows the 2008/09 recession being deeper than previously thought.

A conclusion you may draw from this story is never to trust economic data. The ONS follows the 'continuous revision' method of publishing economic statistics. When new information comes to light, the data is revised. Back in April 2013 the *Daily Telegraph* had published an article under the headline: 'Never mind the triple-dip recession, the double dip may have been an illusion too', which anticipated the data revision.

Follow-up questions

1 Research what has happened to UK economic growth since this book was published.
2 Find out how a recession is defined in other countries, including the USA.

Worked example: selected data on the growth of UK GDP

Study the data in Table 8.1 and then answer the questions that follow.

Table 8.1

	Index of nominal GDP at current market prices (2011 = 100)	Index of GDP in real terms (2011 = 100)
Q2 2012	101.2	100.3
Q3 2012	103.0	101.1
Q4 2012	103.0	100.8
Q1 2013	103.9	101.3
Q2 2013	105.1	102.0
Q3 2013	107.0	102.8
Q4 2013	107.7	103.5
Q1 2014	108.6	102.2
Q2 2014	110.7	105.2

Source: Quarterly National Accounts, Quarter 2 2014, ONS

1 **The data is seasonally adjusted. Explain what this means.**
2 **Calculate the percentage changes in nominal GDP (GDP at current market prices) and the percentage changes in real GDP over the periods between:**
   (a) 2011 and Quarter 2 2014
   (b) Quarter 2 2012 and Quarter 2 2014
3 **Comment on your results.**

1 Seasonal adjustment is a statistical technique that attempts to measure and remove the influences of predictable seasonal patterns in the data.
2 (a) Since 2011 is the base year for both data series, with an index number of 100, when comparing the Q2 2014 data with the base year data, the change in index points is the same as the percentage change. This is a 10.70% growth in nominal GDP measured at market prices and a 5.20% growth in real GDP.

   (b) The percentage growth in nominal GDP equals:

   $$\frac{110.7 - 101.2}{101.2} \times 100$$

   which is approximately 9.38%.
   The percentage growth in real GDP equals:

   $$\frac{105.2 - 100.3}{100.3} \times 100$$

   which is approximately 4.88%

3 In each year, the percentage change in the index of nominal GDP was larger than the percentage change in the index of real GDP. Thus, although the data does not tell us the absolute values of either GDP variable, we can conclude that the price level rose in every year in the data series, i.e. there was inflation in every year. The index numbers for real GDP tell us that there was also positive economic growth throughout the period. A recession cannot be detected.

STUDY TIP

It is important to understand the difference between short-run and long-run economic growth and the causes of the two forms of growth.

Demand-side and supply-side determinants of economic growth

Anything which shifts the position of the aggregate demand (AD) curve is a **demand-side** influence on the economy. Likewise, anything which shifts the position of the SRAS curve or the LRAS curve is a **supply-side** influence on the economy.

SYNOPTIC LINK
Chapter 7 explains the AD/AS macroeconomic model.

Shifts of aggregate demand

A good starting point for analysing the effects of a shift of aggregate demand is the aggregate demand equation first mentioned in section 7.3 of Chapter 7. The aggregate demand equation is:

$$AD = C + I + G + (X - M)$$

where C, I, G and $(X - M)$ are the symbols used for the components of aggregate demand: consumption, investment, government spending and net export demand (exports minus imports). $(X - M)$ is also known as net trade.

If any of these components of aggregate demand change, the AD curve shifts to a new position. An increase in consumption, investment, government spending or net export demand causes the AD curve to shift to the right, as shown in Figure 8.3. What then happens in the economy depends on the shape and slope of the aggregate supply curve. Figure 8.3 shows a SRAS curve which is horizontal at very low levels of real income, then slopes upward, and eventually intersects and crosses the economy's vertical LRAS curve.

If, initially, the level of real output is well below the normal capacity level of output (y_5 in Figure 8.3), a rightward shift of the AD curve from AD_1 to AD_2 increases real output, but has no effect on the price level. Real output increases from y_1 to y_2, but the price level stays the same at P_1. This is because the SRAS curve is horizontal at very low levels of real output and there is plenty of spare capacity throughout the economy.

However, as output rises, the SRAS curve begins to slope upward, which means that further increases of aggregate demand lead to inflation as well as rising real output. For example, when the AD curve shifts from AD_3 to AD_4, the price level rises from P_2 to P_3. And as the aggregate demand curve shifts closer to the full employment level of output, short-run economic growth is accompanied by higher rates of inflation. Short-run growth gradually absorbs the spare capacity in the economy until, when y_5 is reached (the normal capacity level of output), the economy is producing on the LRAS curve. Although output may temporarily be able to increase beyond y_5, at this point, for growth to continue, short-run growth must give way to long-run growth. However, long-run growth requires a rightward shift of the economy's LRAS curve, as depicted in Figure 8.4.

Shifts of aggregate supply

Once full capacity is reached at the level of real output y_1 (the initial normal capacity level of output), for sustainable economic growth to continue the LRAS curve must shift rightward from $LRAS_1$ to $LRAS_2$. As Chapter 7 has mentioned, the determinants of long-run growth include improvements in technology resulting from investment and technical progress, increases in the

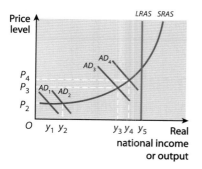

Figure 8.3 Comparing the effects on economic growth of rightward shifts of the AD curve

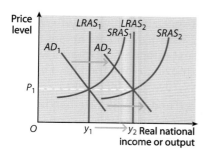

Figure 8.4 Long-run economic growth illustrated by a shift of the LRAS curve

size of the labour force, together with improvements in productivity, attitudes, enterprise, the mobility of factors of production and the economic incentives faced by entrepreneurs and the workers they employ.

An interaction between aggregate supply and aggregate demand

In summary, whereas the determinants of short-run economic growth lie in the demand-side of the economy, long-run economic growth is brought about by changes in the economy's supply side. However, aggregate demand still plays a role in bringing about long-run economic growth. For there to be just sufficient demand in the economy to absorb the extra real output enabled by the rightward shift of the *LRAS* curve, aggregate demand must increase to match the increase in aggregate supply. In Figure 8.4, this is shown by a rightward shift of the *AD* curve from AD_1 to AD_2. Note that the diagram has been drawn to show an eventual outcome in which the price level is unchanged at P_1. This depicts a situation in which just enough demand is created, no more and no less, to absorb the extra output the economy can now produce, without inducing inflation (a rising price level) or deflation (a falling price level). If aggregate demand were unable to keep up with *potential* aggregate supply, firms might decide not to produce the extra goods they are capable of producing. Deflation could then occur and the economy might slip into recession. A further burst of short-run growth would then be needed to eliminate demand deficiency and absorb spare capacity.

○ **KEY TERM**

trend growth rate the rate at which output can grow, on a sustained basis, without putting upward or downward pressure on inflation. It reflects the annual average percentage increase in the productive capacity of the economy.

The trend growth rate

The economy's **trend growth rate** (or potential growth rate) is the rate at which output can grow, on a sustained basis, without putting upward or downward pressure on inflation. The trend growth rate is measured over a period covering more than one (and preferably several) economic cycles.

What has happened to the UK's trend growth rate?

For several decades, the UK's trend growth rate had been judged to be about 2.25% a year. In 2002, the ONS estimated that the trend growth rate in the UK had increased from 2.25% to about 2.75%. At the time, this was explained by the impact of new technologies such as ICT and the internet improving labour productivity and causing structural change in the economy.

The UK government accepted this estimate, but was rather more cautious, building a 2.5% projected growth rate into its financial calculations. The government hoped that faster trend growth could deliver sufficient extra tax revenue to finance increased government spending on healthcare and education, without tax rates being raised. However, slower growth in 2007, followed by recession in 2008, meant that these hopes were over-optimistic.

At first sight, a growth rate in the range 2.5% to 3.0% appears low, especially when compared to higher trend growth rates in newly industrialising countries. Nevertheless, the UK's trend growth rate is similar to the long-run growth rates of other developed economies in Western Europe and North America. The absolute increase in real output delivered by a 2.75% growth rate may also exceed that delivered by a 10% growth rate in a much poorer country. Moreover, because of the compound interest effect, a 2.75% growth rate meant that average UK living standards doubled every 25½ years or so. (The compound interest effect also explains why the trend growth rate line shown in Figure 8.5 became steeper from year to year, moving along the line. For example, 2.75% of £1,000 billion is a larger absolute annual increase in GDP than 2.75% of £800 billion.)

In February 2013, Peter Dixon, a strategist at Commerzbank, argued that the UK's trend growth rate had fallen to 'more like 1%'. The effects of competition from newly industrialising economies and the destruction of productive capacity in the recession were two of the possible reasons for this. Two months later, however, the OECD reported that the UK was on track to return to its long-term growth rate later in 2013. A growth rate exceeding 3% in much of 2014 seems to have justified this optimism.

The economic cycle

Fluctuations in economic activity occur in two main ways: through **seasonal fluctuations**, and through cyclical fluctuations taking place over a number of years. Seasonal fluctuations are largely caused by changes in the weather. Examples include the effect of very cold winters closing down the building trade and seasonal employment in travel and tourism.

Upswings and downswings in economic activity which are longer than seasonal fluctuations are called the **economic cycle**. Economic cycles (also known as business cycles and trade cycles), which can be between approximately 4 and 12 years long, are caused primarily by fluctuations in aggregate demand. In recent years, supply-side factors such as supply shocks hitting the economy have also been recognised as causes of economic cycles.

Figure 8.5 shows two complete economic cycles, together with a line giving the economy's trend output, from which the economy's long-term growth rate can be calculated. **Actual output** rises and sometimes falls in the different phases of the economic cycle. Short-term growth, measured by the percentage change in real GDP over a 12-month period, also varies in the different phases of the economic cycle. In the cycle's upswing, growth is positive but, as Figure 8.5 shows, 'growth' becomes negative if and when a recession occurs in the cyclical downturn.

As explained below, a prolonged 'trough' is also known as a depression.

The phases of the economic cycle shown in Figure 8.5 are recovery, boom and the recessionary phase. Recovery occurs when real GDP begins to grow after the end of a recession, or at the end of the trough of the economic cycle. With continuing short-run growth in real output, recovery gives way to the boom phase of the economic cycle when the level of real output becomes greater than the trend level of output. The boom ends when the upswing of the economic cycle gives way to the next downswing, which is shown in Figure 8.5 by the economy entering a recession. (A severe recession lasting 2 years or more is sometimes called a depression. Unlike a recession, defined in the UK as real national output falling for 6 months or more, there is no generally accepted definition of a depression.)

However, Figure 8.6 paints a more accurate picture of how the UK economy performed in the years between 1993 and the recession which hit the economy in 2008. This diagram shows continuous *positive* economic growth with an absence of *negative* growth. This means there were no recessions (defined as two or more quarters of falling real GDP). In the downswings shown on the diagram, the rate of positive growth slows down but negative growth does not occur.

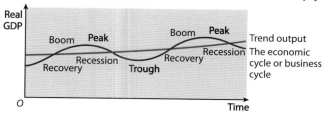

Figure 8.5 The phases of the economic cycle and the trend output line

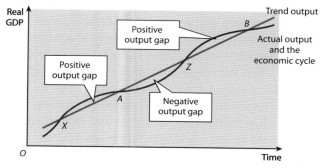

Figure 8.6 Upswings and downswings in the economic cycle, but no recessions

193

The causes of change in the phases of the economic cycle

- **Fluctuations in aggregate demand.** In the 1930s JoÚ Maynard Keynes argued that economic recessions are caused by fluctuations in aggregate demand, which are caused by consumer and business confidence giving way to pessimism, and vice versa.
- **Supply-side factors.** It is now recognised that supply-side factors can also trigger economic cycles. Edward Prescott and Finn Kydland, the 2004 Nobel Laureates in economics, have developed a theory of 'real business cycles', which argues that changes in tecÚology on the supply side of the economy might be as important as changes in aggregate demand in explaining economic cycles.

Other factors that may cause or contribute to cyclical changes include:

- **The role of speculative bubbles.** Rapid economic growth leads to a rapid rise and speculative bubble in asset prices. When people realise that house prices and/or share prices rise far above the assets' real values, asset selling replaces asset buying. This causes the speculative bubble to burst, which in turn destroys consumer and/or business confidence. People stop spending and the economy falls into recession. The resulting cyclical instability is made worse by the excessive growth in credit and levels of debt, and 'animal spirits' and 'herding'. These terms are used to describe how, in financial markets, share prices and asset prices tend to 'overshoot' when traders suffer a bout of 'irrational exuberance', and then to 'undershoot' when the 'pricking' of the speculative bubble causes asset prices to collapse.
- **Political business cycle theory.** In democratic countries, general elections usually have to take place every 4 or 5 years. As an election approaches, the political party in power may attempt to 'buy votes' by engineering a pre-election boom. After the election, the party in power deflates aggregate demand to prevent the economy from overheating, but when the next general election approaches, demand is once again expanded.
- **Outside shocks hitting the economy.** Economic shocks, which were mentioned in Chapter 7, divide into 'demand shocks', which affect aggregate demand, and 'supply shocks', which impact on aggregate supply. In some cases, an outside shock hitting the economy may affect both aggregate demand and aggregate supply. A commonly quoted example is the effect on other countries of a war in the Middle East. Not only might the war affect business confidence in a country such as the UK (a demand shock), it may lead to an oil shortage which increases businesses' costs of production. This would be a supply shock.
- **Changes in inventories.** Besides investing in fixed capital, firms also invest in stocks (inventories) of raw materials, and in stocks of finished goods waiting to be sold. This type of investment is called inventory investment or stock-building. Although this accounts for less than 1% of GDP in a typical year, swings in inventories are often the single most important determinant of recessions. Firms hold stocks of raw materials and finished goods in order to smooth production to cope with swings in demand. However, paradoxically, changes in these inventories tend to trigger and exacerbate economic cycles. Stocks of unsold finished goods build up when firms over-anticipate demand for finished goods. As the stocks accumulate, firms are forced to cut production by more than the original fall in demand. The resultant destocking turns a slowdown into a recession. In the USA, swings

in inventory investment account for about half of the fall in GDP in recent recessions. Destocking has also made UK recessions worse.

- **The Marxist explanation.** Marxist economists explain economic cycles as part of a restructuring process that increases the rate of profit in capitalist economies. Under normal production conditions, a fall in the rate of profit caused by competitive pressure threatens to bankrupt weaker capitalist firms. Marxists believe that recessions create conditions in which stronger firms either take over weaker competitors, or buy at rock-bottom prices the assets of rivals that have been forced out of business. Either way, restructuring by takeover or bankruptcy means that the 'fittest' capitalist firms survive. In Marxist analysis, economic cycles are deemed necessary for the regeneration and survival of capitalism.
- **Multiplier/accelerator interaction.** Keynesian economists have argued that business cycles may be caused by the interaction of two dynamic processes: the multiplier process, through which an increase in investment leads to multiple increases in national income; and the accelerator, through which the increase in income induces a change in the level of investment. Thus the relationship between investment and income is one of mutual interaction; investment affects income (via the investment multiplier), which in turn affects investment demand (via the accelerator process), and in this process income and employment fluctuate in a cyclical manner. (The accelerator is explained in Book 2.)
- **Climatic cycles.** Stanley Jevons was one of the first economists to recognise the economic cycle in the nineteenth century. Perhaps taking note of the Bible's reference to '7 years of plenty' followed by '7 years of famine', Jevons believed a connection exists between the timing of economic crises and the solar cycle. Variations in sunspots affect the power of the sun's rays, influencing the quality of harvests and thus the price of grain, which, in turn, affects business confidence and gives rise to trade cycles.

  Although Jevons's sunspot theory was never widely accepted, the effect named El Niño has renewed interest in Jevons's theory. El Niño is a severe atmospheric and oceanic disturbance in the Pacific Ocean, occurring every 7–14 years, which brings torrential rain, flooding and mud slides to the otherwise dry Pacific coastal areas of countries such as Chile and Peru. By contrast, droughts occur in much of Asia and in areas of Africa and central North America.

Climate changes can affect the economic cycle

195

The economic cycle and output gaps

Figure 8.6 introduces the concept of an **output gap**, which is a feature of the economic cycle. If the economy's *actual* level of output were always to equal *trend* output, there would be no output gap. (In this situation, there would also be no economic cycles.) Output gaps occur when the level of *actual* real output in the economy is greater or lower than the *trend* output level at a particular point in time. When actual output is above trend output, there is a **positive output gap**. Similarly, when actual output is below trend output, there is a **negative output gap**. (Positive and negative output gaps are illustrated in Figures 8.6 and 8.23, where the levels of actual output that the economy is producing are above and below the trend output line.) The UK government defines economic cycles as beginning and ending when there are no output gaps, whether or not a recession actually occurs. Thus, in Figure 8.6, an economic cycle beginning at point *X* would end at point *Z*. (Alternatively points *A* and *B* could be used to mark the beginning and end of an economic cycle.)

Output gaps and the UK economy

Figure 8.7 illustrates how the UK economy performed between 2002 and the end of the first quarter of 2014. The first half of the 12-year period, from 2002 to 2007, shows the tail-end of a long economic boom that had started in the 1990s. Despite continuous economic growth, mild economic cycles could still be identified.

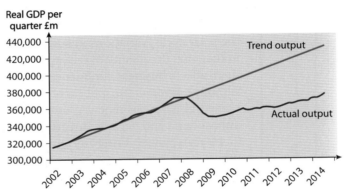

Figure 8.7 UK actual output and trend output, 2002–14
Source: ONS

However, as the years from 2008 to 2014 show, the mild cycles of most of the 1990s and the early 2000s ended in 2008. A recession, which arguably was the longest and deepest since the Great Depression of the 1930s, hit the UK economy (and many other economies throughout the world). According to the ONS, the UK recession began in the second quarter of 2008 and ended in the third quarter of 2009. The ONS estimates that the downturn in 2008 was 0.3% and in 2009 was 4.3%.

At the time of writing (in October 2014), there is plenty of evidence that by 2013 relatively fast economic recovery was kicking in. By the third quarter of 2013, real GDP had climbed back to the level achieved before the 2008/09 recession. Nevertheless, Figure 8.7 seems to show that despite the recovery, the UK economy continues to produce substantially below normal capacity. However, in this respect, the trend output line shown in Figure 8.7 may be misleading. A trend output line shows the *potential* output the economy is able to produce using normal capacity at different points in time. However, in the

2008/09 recession, normal capacity fell considerably due to the destructive impact of the recession. (This is an example of hysteresis, which is the name used for the effect of a disturbance on the course of the economy.) If this argument is accepted, from the recession onward, the trend output line, though still upward-sloping, should be drawn at a lower level than in Figure 8.7. This would considerably reduce the size of the negative output gap which the UK has experienced since the recession.

Also, for many people, particularly those on low incomes and those who live in the more depressed parts of the economy, despite positive economic growth, until recently real personal incomes have been falling. For them, economic recovery has not improved their standards of living.

Measures other than changing real GDP that can be used to identify economic cycles

Economic cycles are usually defined and measured in terms of changes in real output or real GDP. However, changes in other variables, including the rate of inflation, investment and unemployment, are also used to describe the phases of the economic cycle. In the upswing of the cycle, especially in the boom phase, excess aggregate demand begins to pull up the price level, a situation exacerbated by cost pressures when labour shortages lead to nominal wages and salaries rising faster than real wages. The reverse happens in the downswing. Business confidence is also higher in the upswing, leading to an increase in private sector investment. Conversely, a collapse of confidence in the cycle's downswing leads to investment projects being cancelled or postponed.

Employment rises and unemployment falls in the recovery and boom phases of the cycle, though, as noted, eventual labour shortages may lead to a higher rate of inflation. In past UK economic cycles, though less so recently, the employment cycle has tended to lag behind the output or GDP cycle. Because people have votes, political parties tend to be more influenced by what is happening to jobs than to what is happening to GDP. The fact that the two cycles are out of phase, as illustrated in Figure 8.8, can lead to governments expanding the economy to reduce unemployment, even when real GDP began its recovery several months beforehand. This can increase inflation. Likewise, governments have sometimes taken demand out of the economy to try to temper a 'frothy' job market, even though real GDP has already begun to decline.

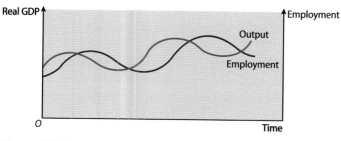

Figure 8.8 The output and employment cycles

> ### ACTIVITY
>
> Access the BBC Economy Tracker webpage on **www.bbc.co.uk/ news/10613201** and research the most recent information about the growth of UK GDP.

The benefits and costs of economic growth

For many people and most economists, achieving a satisfactory and sustained rate of economic growth is arguably the most important of all the macroeconomic objectives that governments wish to achieve. Without growth, other objectives, particularly full employment and competitive export industries, may be impossible to attain. And when growth becomes negative, as in the recession that started in the UK in 2008, people become all too aware of the rapid disappearance of the fruits of growth. For most people, standards of living fall, with the most unfortunate losing their jobs as the industries that used to employ them collapse or slim down.

However, as we hinted at in earlier parts of the chapter, including the last section, in the long run, high rates of economic growth may not be sustainable. This applies also to countries in the developing world, particularly the 'emerging-market' countries, recently growing at a far faster rate than richer developed economies. The rapid using-up of finite resources and the pollution and global warming that spin off from economic growth will result increasingly in desertification, water shortages, declining crop yields, famines and wars.

Some economists argue an opposite effect, namely that one of the benefits of growth, at least as far as advanced developed countries are concerned, is the development of environmentally friendly tecÚologies. These reduce the ratio of energy consumption to GDP. Nevertheless, rich developed economies, especially the USA, continue to be, at least for the time being, the world's biggest consumers of energy and the biggest polluters.

Benefits of economic growth

- Economic growth increases standards of living and people's welfare.
- Growth may lead to more civilised communities, who take action to improve the environment.
- Growth provides new and more environmentally friendly tecÚologies.
- Economic growth has increased the length of people's lives and has provided the means to reduce disease.
- Economic growth provides a route out of poverty for much of the world's population.
- Economic growth produces a 'fiscal dividend', namely the tax revenues that growth generates. Tax revenues can be used to correct market failures, to provide infrastructure, thereby increasing the economic welfare of the whole community.
- For a particular country, economic growth can generate a 'virtuous circle' of greater business confidence, increased investment in state-of-the-art tecÚology, greater international competitiveness, higher profits, even more growth, and so on.

Costs of economic growth

- Economic growth uses up finite resources such as oil and minerals that cannot be replaced.
- Economic growth leads to pollution and other forms of environmental degradation, with the Earth eventually reaching a tipping point, beyond which it cannot recover.
- Growth can destroy local cultures and communities and widen inequalities in the distribution of income and wealth.
- Economic growth leads to urbanisation and the spread of huge cities, which swallow up good agricultural land.
- In its early phases, economic growth leads to a rapid growth in population, more mouths to feed, and more people who are poor.

- Growth produces losers as well as winners. Countries suffering low growth may enter a vicious circle of declining business confidence, low profits, low investment, a lack of international competitiveness, even lower profits, zero growth, and so on.

The environment and the sustainability of economic growth

Over 40 years ago, the first oil crisis, in which the price of crude oil more than doubled, led to British people becoming aware of how the environment — in the guise of raw material and energy shortages — might severely limit a government's ability to achieve high employment levels and continuing economic growth.

Fuel shortages and increased energy prices drew people's attention to two publications of the new but fast-growing ecology or environmentalist movement. The first of these was a document called 'Blueprint for Survival', published in the January 1972 issue of the British journal *The Ecologist*. According to the authors:

> The principal defect of the industrial way of life with its ethos of expansion is that it is not sustainable. Its termination within the lifetime of someone born today is inevitable — unless it continues to be sustained for a while longer by an entrenched minority at the cost of imposing great suffering on the rest of mankind. Our task is to create a society which is sustainable and which will give the fullest possible satisfaction to its members. Such a society by definition would not depend on expansion but on stability.

The Limits to Growth: A Report for the Club of Rome's Project on the Predicament of Mankind, an influential book published a few months later in 1973, suggested that humanity would soon face a threefold dilemma:

- the impending exhaustion of the world's non-renewable natural resources
- the world's pollution problem becoming so acute that the capacity for self-cleaning and regeneration is exhausted
- continued population growth leading to humankind destroying itself through sheer weight of numbers

8.2 Employment and unemployment

We explained in Chapter 6 that full employment does not necessarily mean that every member of the working population has a job. Rather, it means a situation in which the number of people wishing to work at the going market real-wage rate equals the number of workers whom employers wish to hire at this real-wage rate.

However, even this definition needs qualifying since, in a dynamic economy, change is constantly taking place, with some industries declining and others growing. This leads to two types of unemployment known as frictional and structural unemployment. We shall now look at these and other types of unemployment.

STUDY TIP
Make sure you remember how unemployment is measured in the UK. You must be able to interpret claimant count or Labour Force Survey data.

The types and causes of unemployment

The four types of unemployment we shall consider in the next paragraphs are frictional, structural, cyclical and lastly seasonal unemployment, which is the least significant of the four, except of course for many of the workers who become seasonally unemployed.

Frictional unemployment

Frictional unemployment, also known as **transitional unemployment**, is 'between jobs' unemployment. As its name suggests, this type of unemployment results from frictions in the labour market which create a delay, or time lag, during which a worker is unemployed when moving from one job to another. Note that the definition of frictional unemployment assumes that a job vacancy exists and that a friction in the job market, caused by the immobility of labour, prevents an unemployed worker from filling the vacancy. It follows that the number of unfilled job vacancies in the economy can be used as a measure of the level of frictional unemployment. Frictional unemployment is usually short term; if it persists, it becomes structural unemployment.

Among the causes of frictional unemployment are geographical and occupational immobilities of labour, which prevent workers who are laid off from immediately filling job vacancies.

The **geographical immobility of labour** is caused by factors such as family ties and local friendships discouraging people from moving to other parts of the country, ignorance about whether job vacancies exist in other parts of the country, and above all, the cost of moving and difficulties of obtaining housing.

The **occupational immobility of labour** results from difficulties in training for jobs that require different skills, the effects of restrictive practices such as a requirement that new workers must possess unnecessary qualifications, and race, gender and age discrimination in labour markets.

KEY TERMS

frictional unemployment unemployment that is usually short term and occurs when a worker switches between jobs. Also known as **transitional unemployment**.

geographical immobility of labour when workers are unwilling or unable to move from one area to another in search of work.

occupational immobility of labour when workers are unwilling or unable to move from one type of job to another, for example because different skills are needed.

EXTENSION MATERIAL

The search theory of unemployment

The search theory of unemployment also helps to explain frictional unemployment. Consider the situation illustrated in Figure 8.9. A worker earning £1,000 a week in a skilled professional occupation loses her job. Although no vacancies apparently exist at present in her current line of work, there are plenty of vacancies for low-skilled office workers earning around £300 a week. Given this information, if on the day of her job loss, the newly unemployed worker sets the weekly wage she aspires to at £1,000, she will choose to be unemployed, at least to start with, because she doesn't wish to fill a lower-paid vacancy. The lower weekly wage on offer, and perhaps poorer conditions of work and status associated with the lower-paid job, fail to meet her aspirations. She may also realise that she possesses imperfect information about the state of the job market. This means she needs to search the labour market to find out whether better-paid and higher-status vacancies exist, but which she does not know about currently.

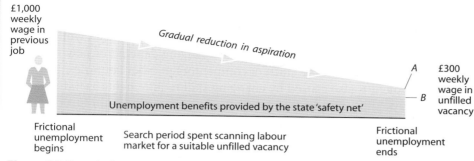

£1,000 weekly wage in previous job

Gradual reduction in aspiration

A £300 weekly wage in unfilled vacancy

B

Unemployment benefits provided by the state 'safety net'

Frictional unemployment begins

Search period spent scanning labour market for a suitable unfilled vacancy

Frictional unemployment ends

Figure 8.9 Search theory and frictional unemployment

Approached in this way, frictional unemployment can be viewed as a voluntary search period in which newly unemployed workers scan the labour market, searching for vacancies which meet their aspirations.

There are a number of ways in which a voluntary search period can end. First, in the example described above, the woman may eventually learn of a vacancy for which she is qualified, and which meets her initial aspiration. Indeed, the vacancy might have been there all the time but, until she searched the job market, she was unaware of its existence. Second, the vacancy may have arisen during her search period, perhaps because of a general improvement in the condition of labour markets. Third, she may end her voluntary unemployment if she decides, on the basis of her lack of success in getting a job, that her initial aspirations were unrealistically high and that she must settle for a lower-paid, less attractive job.

Skilled professionals are unlikely to want low-paid office jobs

Long search periods, which increase the amount of frictional unemployment in the economy, result in part from the welfare benefit system. Without the receipt of welfare benefits, search periods would have to be financed by running down stocks of saving, or through the charity of family and friends. In this situation, the threat of poverty creates an incentive to search the job market more vigorously and to reduce the aspirational wage levels of the unemployed.

The availability of a state safety net provided by unemployment benefits and other income-related welfare benefits, together in some cases with redundancy payments, enable unemployed workers to finance long voluntary search periods. Because of this, many free-market economists support a reduction in the real value of unemployment benefits, together with restricting benefits to those who can prove they are genuinely looking for work. Free-market economists believe these policies create incentives for the unemployed to reduce aspirations quickly, which shortens search periods.

Structural unemployment

Structural unemployment, which is more long term than frictional unemployment, results from the structural decline of industries which are unable to compete or adapt in the face of changing demand or new products, and the emergence of more efficient competitors in other countries. Structural unemployment is also caused by changing skill requirements as industries change ways of producing their products. In the latter case, the structural unemployment is often called technological unemployment. Technological unemployment results from the successful growth of new industries using labour-saving technology such as automation.

In contrast to mechanisation (workers operating machines), which has usually increased the overall demand for labour, automation can lessen the demand for labour because it means that machines (such as robots) rather than humans operate other machines. Whereas the growth of mechanised industry increases employment, automation of production can lead to the shedding of labour, even when industry output is expanding.

EXTENSION MATERIAL

International competition and structural unemployment

The growth of international competition has been a particularly important cause of structural unemployment. During the post-Second World War era from the 1950s to the 1970s, structural unemployment in the UK was regionally concentrated in areas where nineteenth-century staple industries such as textiles and shipbuilding were suffering structural decline. This regional unemployment, caused by the decline of 'sunset industries', was more than offset by the growth of employment elsewhere in the UK in 'sunrise industries'. However, in the severe recessions of the 1980s and 1990s, and also in the 2008/09 recession, structural unemployment affected almost all regions in the UK as the deindustrialisation process spread across the manufacturing base. Decline of manufacturing industries as a result of international competition can also lead to structural unemployment in industries which service the manufacturing sector, for example private security firms.

Although manufacturing output grew in the 'boom' years before the 2008/09 recession, employment in manufacturing industries often fell. Recession and the growth of cyclical unemployment caused a further fall in manufacturing employment. However, there is a danger of exaggerating the decline in employment in manufacturing, because many activities, ranging from cleaning to IT maintenance, which were previously undertaken 'in house' by manufacturing firms, have been outsourced to external service sector providers. Structural unemployment has occurred within the service sector as well as in manufacturing industries. For example, increasing use of ICT, automated services and the internet has meant that total employment has fallen in the travel agency industry. Call-centre employment has grown significantly in recent years, though much of this growth has been in low-wage economies such as India. However, a decline has been forecast, partly because companies employ automated communication software rather than human beings to provide customer service and to answer telephone and internet queries.

Cyclical unemployment

Cyclical unemployment is also known as **Keynesian unemployment** and **demand-deficient unemployment**. During the Great Depression in the 1930s, Keynes — but not his opponents — believed that deficient aggregate demand was a major cause of persistent mass unemployment. Free-market economists generally agree that temporary cyclical unemployment may be caused by a lack of demand in the downswing of the economic cycle. However, Keynes went further, arguing that the economy could settle into an under-full employment equilibrium, caused by a continuing lack of effective aggregate demand. In contrast to frictional unemployment, which is voluntary, Keynes believed that cyclical unemployment is involuntary: that is, not caused by the workers themselves. As a result, the unemployed should not be blamed for their idleness.

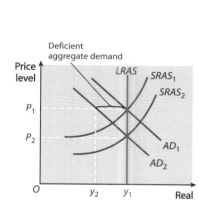

Figure 8.11 Cyclical unemployment caused by a leftward shift of aggregate demand

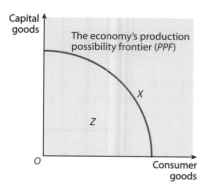

Figure 8.12 Cyclical unemployment and the economy's production possibility frontier

TEST YOURSELF 8.1

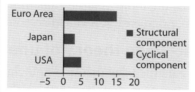

Figure 8.10

The bar graph in Figure 8.10, for a particular year, shows an estimate of the percentage of workers structurally and cyclically unemployed in the Euro Area (eurozone), Japan and the USA in that year. What can you conclude from the data?

Figure 8.11 illustrates cyclical unemployment in the context of the economy's *AD/AS* diagram. A collapse in business and consumer confidence causes the *AD* curve to shift left from AD_1 to AD_2. Keynesian economists argue that if prices and wages are 'sticky' (or inflexible), deficient aggregate demand and cyclical unemployment will persist, with the equilibrium level of national income falling from y_1 to y_2.

STUDY TIP

This is an example of applying *AD/AS* analysis to illustrate an important aspect of macroeconomics. There are many other economic problems and issues that can be analysed in similar ways.

However, anti-Keynesian or free-market economists reject this view. They assume that markets for both goods and labour are competitive; by reducing businesses' costs of production, falling wages shift the *SRAS* curve from $SRAS_1$ to $SRAS_2$. The price level falls to P_2 and output increases from y_2, back to the normal capacity level of output, y_1. According to the free-market view, cyclical unemployment is temporary and self-correcting — provided that markets are sufficiently competitive and prices and wages are both flexible.

Figure 8.12, which shows the economy's production possibility frontier (*PPF*), illustrates another way of showing cyclical unemployment. All points on the production possibility frontier, including point *X*, show the economy using all

its productive capacity, including labour. There is no demand deficiency and
thus no cyclical unemployment. By contrast, deficient aggregate demand can
lead to the economy producing inside its production possibility frontier: for
example, at point Z. When this is the case, cyclical unemployment exists in
the economy.

Seasonal unemployment

Seasonal unemployment is a special case of casual unemployment, which
occurs when workers are laid off on a short-term basis at certain times of the
year. It occurs in trades such as tourism, agriculture, catering and building.
When casual unemployment results from regular fluctuations in weather
conditions or demand, it is called seasonal unemployment.

The real-wage theory of unemployment

In recent years the view that unemployment is caused by too high a level of
real wages has been popular, particularly among free-market economists.
Figure 8.13 explains the theory. The diagram is similar to Figure 6.3 on page
143 in Chapter 6, except that it is now assumed that the average real-wage
rate in the economy is w_1 rather than w_{FE}. At this wage, employers wish to
hire E_1 workers, but a greater number of workers (E_2) wish to supply their
labour. An excess supply of labour then occurs in the labour market, equal on
the graph to the distance from point Z to point W. Free-market economists
believe that, as long as labour markets are highly competitive,
real-wage unemployment can only be temporary. Market forces
cure the problem, bidding down the real-wage rate to w_{FE} to get
rid of excess supply of labour. Full employment is then restored
at point X when the number of workers willing to work equals
the number whom firms wish to hire. On the graph, E_{FE} is the full
employment level of employment.

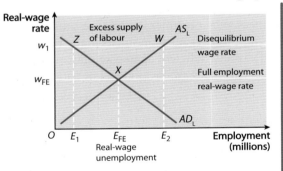

Figure 8.13 Real-wage unemployment

Suppose labour market rigidity, perhaps caused by trade unions,
prevents the real-wage rate falling below w_1. In this situation, the
market mechanism fails to work properly, the excess supply of
labour persists, and persistent real-wage unemployment occurs.

Keynesian economists believe real-wage unemployment to be involuntary
unemployment, caused by wage stickiness or wage inflexibility over which
workers have no control. By contrast, free-market economist argue that real-
wage unemployment is voluntary unemployment on the ground that workers
and their trade unions should be prepared to accept wage cuts.

At the beginning of this section (and also in Chapter 6) we stated that full employment does not necessarily mean that every single member of the working population is in work. Instead, it means a situation in which the number of people wishing to work at the going market real-wage rate equals the number of workers that employers wish to hire at this real-wage rate. We then stated that even this definition needs qualifying, since in a dynamic economy there is always some frictional and structural unemployment brought about by the changes that are constantly taking place in the economy.

Frictional and structural unemployment make up what is called equilibrium unemployment. Equilibrium unemployment, which is also called the natural *level* of unemployment, exists even with the real-wage rate at its market-clearing level. Expressed as a *rate* of unemployment, rather than as a level, this is the natural rate of unemployment (NRU).

The natural level of unemployment is illustrated in Figure 8.14, shown as E_1 minus E_{FE} (where E_{FE} is the 'full employment' level of employment) in the economy's aggregate labour market. It is the level of unemployment that occurs even when the aggregate labour market is in equilibrium, namely when the aggregate demand for labour equals the aggregate supply of labour ($AD_L = AS_L$). In the diagram, point X shows equilibrium *employment*, with the equilibrium wage rate or market-clearing real-wage rate at w_{FE}. Full employment occurs when E_{FE} workers are hired. The distance between AS_L and the curve AS_{LN} shows the amount of frictional and structural unemployment in the economy, namely the number of workers who are willing and able to work at different wage rates but who, for frictional and structural reasons, cannot get jobs. E_{FE} minus E_1 is the natural level of unemployment.

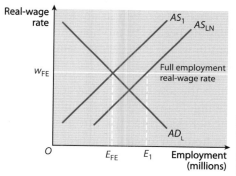

Figure 8.14 The natural level of unemployment, shown as the distance between E_{FE} and E_1.

The consequences of unemployment

Unemployment is bad for the economy as a whole, largely through the waste of human capital. When workers are unemployed, not all the economy's productive resources are used to produce output, which, if produced, could add to the material standards of living and economic welfare of the whole population. Instead, the economy produces inside its production possibility frontier and fails to operate to its potential.

Unemployment is also one of the factors that reduce an economy's international competitiveness. High unemployment can reduce incentives for firms to invest in new state-of-the-art tecÚologies that generally lead to increased export competitiveness. The under-investment associated with high unemployment also results from a reduced need to invest in capital-intensive tecÚologies when there are plenty of unemployed workers who are not only available but cheap to hire. In these circumstances, employers continue to use labour-intensive but antiquated tecÚologies, particularly when high unemployment accompanies a stagnant economy, low profits and a climate of business pessimism.

Under-investment can also be caused by the higher business taxes that firms may have to pay to help finance the welfare benefits paid to unemployed workers. While it is true that the Jobseeker's Allowance can be claimed only in the first months of unemployment, in the UK the state continues to pay Universal Credit to families in which there is no wage earner, in order to save family members, particularly children, from the effects of absolute poverty. However, in 2013, at the time of the introduction of the Universal Credit, which is replacing Income Support, the coalition government introduced a benefit cap, which limits to £26,000 a year all the benefits an out-of-work family can receive. The government justified the cap on the ground that families living solely on benefits should not receive welfare payments higher than the earnings of people on median incomes. The Conservative Party has promised to reduce the cap, if it forms the government after the 2015 general election.

Economies are particularly badly affected by long-term unemployment. A worker may become effectively unemployable the longer the period that he or she is out of work: for example, because of the erosion of job skills and work habits. Long-term unemployment is also made worse by the fact that employers, who might otherwise hire and retrain workers who have been economically inactive for several years, perceive that workers with more recent job experience present fewer risks and are more employable. When inactive workers are seen as unemployable, the economy begins to behave as if it is on its production possibility frontier, even though there are plenty of unemployed workers notionally available for work. An increase in aggregate demand can then lead to inflation rather than to an increase in output and jobs.

Nevertheless, despite the disadvantages of high unemployment for the economy, many free-market economists believe a certain amount of unemployment is necessary to make the economy function better. In particular, by providing downward pressure on wage rates, unemployment can reduce inflation. Unemployment also contributes to a widening of income differentials between better-paid and low-paid workers. Some free-market economists argue that this is a good thing, believing that differences in pay are needed to promote incentives, which then create the supply-side conditions in which the economy can prosper.

Unemployment is obviously bad for the unemployed themselves and for their families, largely because of the way in which the low incomes that accompany unemployment lead to low standards of living. However, the costs of unemployment for the unemployed go further than this. Apart from situations in which the unemployed enjoy having 24 hours of leisure time each and every day, or when the so-called 'unemployed' are engaged in black economy activity, unemployment destroys hope in the future. The unemployed become marginalised from normal economic and human activity, and their self-esteem is reduced. Families suffer increased health risks, greater stress, a reduction in the quality of diet, and an increased risk of marital break-up and social exclusion caused by loss of work and income.

> **STUDY TIP**
> Don't confuse the *causes* and *effects* of unemployment.

Government policies to reduce unemployment

When governments intervene to reduce unemployment, the appropriate policy depends on identifying correctly the underlying cause of unemployment. For example, if unemployment is incorrectly diagnosed in terms of demand deficiency, when the true cause is structural, a policy of fiscal or monetary expansion to stimulate aggregate demand will be ineffective and inappropriate. Indeed, reflation of demand in such circumstances would probably create excess demand, which raises the price level, with no lasting beneficial effects on employment.

Governments can try to reduce frictional unemployment by improving the geographical and occupational mobility of labour, and by reducing workers' search periods between jobs. Geographical mobility could be improved by making it easier for families to move house from one region to another, for example by subsidising removal costs. However, the widening difference in UK house prices between south and north are in fact reducing the geographical mobility of labour. Government spending on rented social housing in areas where there are ongoing labour shortages would perhaps be the most effective way of improving the geographical mobility of labour, though for cost and other reasons, this policy is unlikely to be adopted, at least on a scale sufficient to have a significant effect.

The introduction of the Jobseeker's Allowance (JSA) in 1996 was an attempt to reduce search periods between jobs. There have been two types of JSA, contribution based and income based, with the latter currently being merged into a new all-embracing benefit, Universal Benefit. The contributions-based allowance, based on having paid sufficient National Insurance contributions when working, can only be claimed for the first few months of unemployment providing the claimant is actively seeking work. The allowance creates an incentive for the newly unemployed to accept lower wage rates and to speed up the search for vacancies that meet their (now reduced) aspirations. However, the only really effective way to reduce frictional and structural unemployment is to achieve successful economic growth, which increases firms' demand for new employees.

Governments can improve the occupational mobility of labour by providing retraining schemes and introducing laws to ban professional and trade union restrictive practices that make it difficult for workers to move between jobs. Government retraining schemes are usually less effective than those run by private sector firms. But a problem is that employers in trades such as plumbing often prefer to avoid spending on training their employees, by poaching newly trained workers from the few employers who do invest in training their employees. As a result of this market failure, too few workers may end up being trained.

Supply-side policies (explained in Chapter 9) which try to improve the competitiveness and efficiency of markets are now used to reduce frictional and structural unemployment. In the past, deindustrialisation led to large-scale structural unemployment, concentrated in regions of decline such as coal fields and areas previously dominated by heavy industry.

Many traditional manufacturing industries and the coal industry have now largely disappeared in the UK, so there is less scope for further structural decline in these activities. The supply-side improvements of the 1980s and 1990s also created conditions in which service industries grew to replace manufacturing. As a result, more workers were able to move from declining industries into growing ones. However, as the recent and current financial services crisis shows, service industries such as banking have themselves become vulnerable to structural decline and to overseas location.

TEST YOURSELF 8.2

Table 8.2 shows changes in the UK index of production and total employment over the period from 2006 to the end of Quarter 3 2014.

Table 8.2

	2006 Q4	2007 Q4	2008 Q4	2009 Q4	2010 Q4	2011 Q4	2012 Q4	2013 Q4	2014 Q3
Index of production (2010 = 100)	110.3	111.0	102.7	97.3	100.0	98.0	94.8	96.9	102.1
Employment (millions)	28.01	28.31	28.17	27.68	27.79	27.82	28.26	28.51	28.95

With the help of the data, identify and explain **two** significant points of comparison between the changes in the index of production and employment over the period shown.

8.3 Inflation and deflation

UK inflation in recent decades

Inflation is a continuing rise in the average price level. For three decades from the 1960s to the early 1990s, unacceptably high rates of inflation were perhaps the most serious problem facing UK governments. The inflation rate crept up in the 1960s, before accelerating in the early 1970s to over 15% in each year between 1974 and 1977. Inflation peaked at its highest rate in modern UK history in the mid-1970s, when it hit 25–26%. A further surge, which took inflation to around 18% in 1980, ushered in the modern era in which, at least until 2008, control of inflation became arguably the most important single macroeconomic policy objective.

In 2008, the economic climate changed when recession hit the UK economy. During the recession, there were fears that the problems caused by inflation would be replaced by the problems caused by deflation, or a continually falling price level. Indeed, if you look back to Figure 6.5 in Chapter 6, you will see that according to the retail prices index (RPI), the UK price level did indeed fall during most of 2009 — though not according to the government's preferred measure of inflation, the consumer prices index (CPI).

Be that as it may, just before and just after 2009, there were two significant 'spikes' in the rate of inflation. Inflation had been more or less under control from around 1993 until 2008. However, in 2008 and then again in 2011, rising prices of commodities, ranging from crude oil to copper and wheat, together with the rising prices of manufactured goods produced in China, led to relatively severe but short bouts of imported inflation. Despite the recession, and because of its imported nature, UK inflation temporarily became difficult to control.

TEST YOURSELF 8.3

Table 8.3 indicates the percentage change in the price level in different years in a low-income country.

Table 8.3

Domestic prices (% change over 10-year periods)			
1985	1995	2005	2015
63.8	330.0	40.5	20.4

Over the whole period covered by the data, which of the following can be deduced from the data?

A There was a fall in the cost of living in the country throughout the data period.

B The annual rate of inflation fell in 2015.

C Between 1995 and 2015, a fall in the 10-year rate of inflation took place.

Explain your answer.

ACTIVITY

Access the BBC Economy Tracker webpage on **www.bbc.co.uk/news/10612209** and research the most recent information on inflation in the UK.

The causes of inflation

There are two basic causes of inflation: excess aggregate demand in the economy, and a general rise in costs of production. The former gives rise to demand-pull inflation (or demand inflation), while the latter is called cost-push inflation (or cost inflation). As the names imply, demand-pull inflation locates the cause of inflation in the demand side of the economy, whereas cost-push inflation has supply-side causes.

Demand-pull inflation

As its name indicates, **demand-pull inflation** is caused by an increase in aggregate demand. If the economy is initially producing on the economy's *SRAS* curve, but below the normal capacity level of output (which means to the left of the *LRAS* curve), the price level has to rise to persuade firms to produce more output to meet the extra demand. In part, this is because firms incur higher costs when they produce more goods. For firms to maximise profit, higher prices are needed to reward firms for producing more output. Once the *LRAS* curve is reached, higher prices can temporarily encourage firms to produce beyond this point, but the increase in output cannot be sustained. Instead, the quantity of goods and services produced falls back to the normal capacity level of output, in this case at y_2.

To remind you, the equation summarising the different elements of aggregate demand is:

$$AD = C + I + G + (X - M)$$

An increase in *any* of the components of aggregate demand, C, I, G or $(X - M)$, can lead to demand-pull inflation. Increases in consumption spending (C) by households or current government spending (G), for example on public sector pay, may create the extra demand which pulls up the price level.

Aggregate demand/aggregate supply (*AD/AS*) diagrams can illustrate the main features of both demand-pull and cost-push inflation. Figure 8.15 illustrates demand-pull inflation.

In the graph, we have assumed that equilibrium national income is initially at point X. The *AD* curve is in the position AD_1; real output is at level y_1 and the price level is P_1.

Given this initial situation, any event that shifts the *AD* curve to the right — for example, to AD_2 — causes the price level to rise, in this case to P_2. In this example, real income increases to its normal capacity level of y_2. At the price level P_1, the economy's firms are only prepared to produce an output of y_1. This means that a higher price level is needed to create the conditions in which firms increase output from y_1 to y_2.

STUDY TIP

Don't confuse the *causes* of inflation with the *effects* of inflation.

KEY TERM

demand-pull inflation a rising price level caused by an increase in aggregate demand, shown by a shift of the *AD* curve to the right. Also known as **demand inflation**.

STUDY TIP

Investment spending and government spending on capital goods shift the *LRAS* curve rightwards. In the *long run*, a shift of the *LRAS* curve to the right can offset demand-pull inflationary pressures.

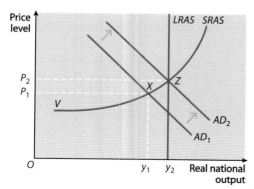

Figure 8.15 Demand-pull inflation illustrated by an *AD/AS* diagram

Figure 8.15 shows an economy initially producing below the normal capacity level of output, and then moving to normal capacity, once the *AD* curve has shifted right to AD_2. Following the increase in aggregate demand, equilibrium national income is at point Z, with the economy also on its long-run aggregate supply (*LRAS*) curve. In this situation, the economy is producing at full capacity or normal capacity, so any further shift of aggregate demand to the right would result solely in demand-pull inflation, with no increase in real output (except possibly on a temporary basis).

Contrast this outcome with what would happen had the *AD* curve initially been located substantially to the left of AD_1, for example at point V. The economy would be in deep recession, suffering severe demand-deficient or cyclical unemployment. Given this initial position, a shift of aggregate demand to the right would increase output and employment, but with relatively little effect on inflation. Arguably, the adverse effect of a rising price level would be less significant than the boost to output and employment brought about by an increase in aggregate demand. However, as the increasing slope of the *SRAS* curve suggests, as the *AD* curve shifts right and moves closer to the *LRAS* curve, increasingly, the *reflation* of real output (and employment) gives way to *inflation* of the price level.

Cost-push inflation

During the Keynesian era in the 1960s and 1970s, the rate of inflation increased even when there was little evidence of excess demand in the economy. This led to the development of the theory of **cost-push inflation**. Cost theories of inflation often locate the cause of inflation in structural and institutional conditions on the supply side of the economy, particularly in the labour market and the wage-bargaining process (known as wage-cost inflation), though rising prices of energy and/or commodities can also cause cost-push inflation (called import-cost inflation).

Cost-push theories generally argue that the growth of monopoly power in the economy's labour market and in its markets for goods and services is responsible for inflation. In labour markets, growing trade union strength in the Keynesian era enabled trade unions to bargain for money-wage increases in excess of any rise in labour productivity. Monopoly firms were prepared to pay these wage increases, partly because of the costs of disrupting production, and partly because they believed that they could pass on the increasing costs as price rises when they sold output in the markets for their goods.

The *AD/AS* diagram in Figure 8.16 illustrates cost-push inflation. Once again (as is the case in Figure 8.15, which illustrates demand-pull inflation), equilibrium national income is at point X, with real output and the price level respectively at y_1 and P_1. In this case, the money costs of production that firms incur when they produce output rise: for example, because money wages or the price of imported raw materials increase. The increase in production costs causes the *SRAS* curve to shift left and up from $SRAS_1$ to $SRAS_2$.

As a result of the shift of the *SRAS* curve to the left, the price level increases to P_2, but higher production costs have reduced the equilibrium level of output that firms are willing to produce to y_2. The new equilibrium national income is at point Z. The economy could be in recession, in which case recessionary effects may moderate the cost increases.

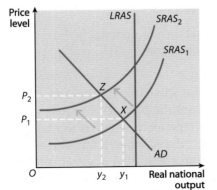

Figure 8.16 Cost-push inflation illustrated on an *AD/AS* diagram

How changes in world commodity prices affect domestic inflation

Forty years ago, it was generally assumed that rising wage costs were the main cause of cost-push inflation in the UK. More recently, there has been less evidence of **wage-cost inflation**. When it occurs, it may be largely restricted to the effect of salary increases among bankers, top business executives, premier league footballers and the like far exceeding the rise in their labour productivity. Additionally, trade unions representing public sector workers such as train drivers on the London Underground have contributed to cost-push inflation, though since 2008 the wages of most ordinary workers have risen at a slower rate than inflation, and in some cases not at all.

Cost-push inflation does still exist, but it is caused mainly by the rising prices of imported food, energy and raw materials, and to a lesser extent in recent years by rising prices of manufactured goods imported from China. The resulting **import-cost inflation** is caused by worldwide commodity price inflation. Figure 8.17 shows how world commodity prices changed between 1986 and 2013.

KEY TERMS

wage-cost inflation a rising price level caused by an increase in wages and salaries, shown by a shift of the *SRAS* curve to the left.

import-cost inflation a rising price level caused by an increase in the cost of imported energy, food, raw materials and manufactured goods, shown by a shift of the *SRAS* curve to the left.

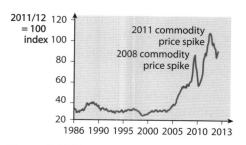

Figure 8.17 Changes in world commodity prices, 1986–2013

The message conveyed by the diagram is clear. Commodity prices were remarkably stable in the 1990s and early 2000s, thereby contributing to relatively low rates of consumer price inflation in those years. All this changed, however, after about 2004. Since then, in most years world commodity prices increased very rapidly, culminating in two highly significant price 'spikes' in 2008 and 2011. In 2013 and 2014, the UK inflation rate was brought down by falling prices of imported food, energy and raw materials. This is likely to be a short-lived lull. Many commentators believe that with faster economic growth in commodity-consuming countries, especially **emerging-market countries**, and limited natural resources, a third 'spike' in world commodity prices will soon occur. However, in 2014 and early 2015, commodity prices were generally falling. The fall was triggered by a collapse in oil and gas prices, party caused by the development of shale oil and gas in the USA.

How do changes in other countries affect UK inflation?

The answer to this question is partly provided by the information in the above paragraphs. However, other arguments can also be made.

KEY TERM

emerging-market country a country that is progressing towards becoming more economically advanced, by means of rapid growth and industrialisation.

First, the UK is now just a small part of a globalised economy in which it has very little power to influence the state of the world economy. When times are good in the world economy, with rising demand for commodities and hence rising prices, the UK tends to import inflation from booming economies in the rest of the world. The prices of imported food and raw materials increase, which leads to the UK suffering import-cost inflation. Conversely, when times are bad in the world economy, with other countries experiencing recession, pressure on UK inflation is reduced. In the extreme, falling worldwide demand for UK exports, and the associated leftward shift of the *AD* curve, could lead to falling prices or deflation. **Disinflation**, which is a fall in the rate of *positive* inflation, is, however, more likely to occur than *negative* inflation or deflation. Finally, a fall in the pound's exchange rate against other currencies contributes to imported cost-push inflation and this was a significant factor immediately after 2008.

KEY TERM

disinflation when the rate of inflation is falling and the price level is rising more slowly than previously.

Second, two countries, the USA and China, stand out in the way in which they can affect the UK price level. It was once said that when 'America sneezes, the rest of the world catches a cold'. The USA is so important for the UK as a source of export demand, inward investment, and business and consumer confidence, that an American downturn can exert downward pressure on the UK inflation rate.

China's influence on the UK inflation rate is a little different. For many decades, British consumers benefited from falling prices of manufactured goods imported from China. This reduced the UK's rate of inflation. However, more recently, costs of production have risen in China, partly as a result of increased wages paid to China's labour force. Rising prices of manufactured goods, imported from China and other emerging-market economies, are increasing retail prices in the UK. As yet, however, the effect has been mild.

Why it is important to diagnose correctly the causes of inflation

Just as a government must correctly diagnose the cause or causes of unemployment when implementing policies to reduce the level of unemployment, so it (and its central bank) must first determine whether inflation is caused by excess demand or by cost-push factors when deciding on the appropriate policies to reduce or control inflation.

In the early 2000s, the Bank of England, which is responsible for counter-inflation policy, generally assumed that UK inflation is caused by excess aggregate demand. More recently, the Bank has acknowledged that rising import prices are responsible for a temporary bout of cost-push inflation, though the Bank still views excess demand as the main cause of inflation. Before then, the increase in aggregate demand that occurred in the 1990s and early 2000s was accompanied by an absence of cost-push inflationary pressure. This was partly due to the success of the supply-side policies implemented in the 1980s and 1990s. These policies, which are explained in Chapter 9, improved labour market flexibility partly by attacking the power of trade unions. The UK economy was also benefiting from the benign effect of globalisation, which at the time reduced the prices of imported manufactured goods.

As long as the assumption holds that inflation is caused primarily by excess aggregate demand, raising or lowering interest rates (i.e. monetary policy) remains an appropriate policy for controlling inflation. The fact that interest rate policy kept the rate of inflation within the government's target range in virtually every month between 1997 and 2007 gave further support to the view held at the time that UK inflation had been primarily of the demand-pull kind.

However, until recently at least, cost-push inflationary pressures were becoming much more significant, particularly those stemming from the increased prices of imported energy and commodities such as copper. In this situation, raising interest rates to reduce aggregate demand can be an ineffective policy for tackling cost-push inflation, though raising interest rates can also reduce external cost pressures by strengthening the exchange rate in order to reduce the demand for imported oil, gas and industrial raw materials. If this argument is correct, UK governments now have to face up to the fact that they lack the tools, apart from interest rates (and other monetary instruments which are discussed in Chapter 9), for controlling the rate of inflation.

The monetarist theory of inflation

Around 40 years ago, a group of generally pro-free-market economists became known as monetarists. Monetarist economists subscribe to the demand-pull theory of inflation, but they go one stage further by arguing that excess aggregate demand for output is caused by a prior increase in the money supply. To quote the leading monetarist economist Milton Friedman, monetarists believe that 'inflation is always and everywhere a monetary phenomenon'.

A very old theory that originated hundreds of years ago, the quantity theory of money, lies at the heart of the monetarist theory of inflation. Suppose the government creates or condones an expansion of the money supply greater than the increase in real national output. As a result, according to the quantity theory, households and firms end up holding excess money balances which, when spent, pull up the price level — provided real output does not expand in line with the increase in spending power.

At its simplest, the quantity theory is sometimes described as too much money chasing too few goods. The starting point for developing the theory is the equation of exchange, devised by an American economist, Irving Fisher, early in the twentieth century:

> money supply (stock of money) × the velocity of circulation of money = price level × quantity of output

or:

$$MV = PQ$$

In the equation, for a particular time period, say a year, the stock of money in the economy (M) multiplied by the velocity of circulation of money (V) equals the price level (P) multiplied by the quantity of real output (Q) in the economy. On the left-hand side of the equation, the velocity of circulation (V) is the speed at which money circulates around the economy when people use money to buy goods. Monetarists argue that V is constant or at least stable. This means that, when M increases, it is spent on goods and services. If Q is unable to increase, the price level P is pulled up by excess demand. Keynesian economists, by contrast, believe that when M increases, it may be partially absorbed by a slowdown in V, which means that much of the extra money is not spent on consumer goods and services. (However, some of the extra money might be spent on investment in new capital goods, which would have a beneficial effect on aggregate demand and economic growth, stimulating Q rather than P.) In summary, PQ, on the right-hand side of the equation, can increase, either because real output increases or because the price level increases.

The effects of expectations on changes in the price level

It is now widely accepted by economists that people's expectations of *future* inflation can affect the *current* rate of inflation. Along with the quantity theory of money, expectations of future inflation are an important part of the monetarist theory of inflation. Milton Friedman was one of the first economists to draw attention to the role of expectations in the inflationary process.

Theories of expectation formation are complicated. However, the central idea is simple: if people expect that the rate of inflation next year is going to be high, they will behave in an inflationary way now, and their behaviour will deliver high inflation next year. Trade unions and workers bargain for higher wages, and

---

KEY TERM

quantity theory of money oldest theory of inflation, which states that inflation is caused by a persistent increase in the supply of money.

KEY TERM

equation of exchange the stock of money in the economy multiplied by the velocity of circulation of money equals the price level multiplied by the quantity of real output in the economy.

STUDY TIP

The velocity of circulation of money is the speed at which money circulates round the economy when money is spent.

STUDY TIP

The equation of exchange is often written as $MV = PT$, where T stands for total transactions taking place in the economy. A transaction occurs whenever a good or service is bought and sold. Total transactions include, for example, second-hand transactions as well as the exchange of new goods and services. Because of this PQ is a better measure than PT of expenditure on national output.

their employers then raise prices, in anticipation of tomorrow's higher expected inflation rate. Workers and firms try to 'get their retaliation in first', to avoid being left behind when the inflation rate they are expecting eventually materialises.

Homeowners expect to do well out of inflation

Likewise, when people expect the inflation rate to fall, they behave in a way that enables low inflation to be achieved. Governments therefore try to talk down the rate of inflation by convincing people that government policies are credible and that the government (and its central bank) know how to reduce inflation. The UK government's decision to make the Bank of England operationally independent in 1997 was part of an attempt to convince people (and financial markets) of the *credibility* of government policies and of its determination to keep the rate of inflation low. However, when the Bank fails to hit the 2% inflation rate target, credibility is eroded.

One of the factors that has made inflation difficult to control in the UK has been the existence, built up over decades, of an 'inflation psychology'. Over the years, many groups in British society, including house owners, wage earners in strong bargaining positions, and also governments, have done extremely well out of inflation. Home owners with large mortgages, and also the government, have a vested interest in allowing inflation to continue in order to reduce the real value of their accumulated debt. (Indeed, property owners do even better when house price inflation exceeds the general rate of inflation. In this situation, the real value of houses increases while the real value of mortgages falls.) Between 1997 and 2007 UK governments successfully cut through much of this inflation psychology by convincing people that inflation would remain low and around the target inflation rate of 2%. Because of this benign effect on people's behaviour and their expectations, it became much easier to control inflation. However, even in these years, some economists argued that circumstances could change quickly for the worse, and that inflationary dangers should be regarded as dormant rather than dead. In 2008 and 2011, inflation did indeed raise its ugly head once again and the same may be true in the future.

The consequences of inflation for the performance of the economy and for individuals

Inflation can impose serious costs on both the economy and on individuals, and the seriousness of these costs depends on whether individuals successfully anticipate the inflation rate. If inflation could be anticipated with complete certainty, some economists argue that it would pose few problems. Households and firms would simply build the expected rate of inflation into their economic decisions, which would not be distorted by wrong guesses.

When inflation is relatively low, with little variation from year to year, it is relatively easy to anticipate next year's inflation rate. Indeed, creeping inflation, which is associated with growing markets, healthy profits and a general climate of business optimism, greases the wheels of the economy. Viewed in this way, a low rate of inflation — and not absolute price stability or zero inflation — may be a necessary side-effect or cost of expansionary policies to reduce unemployment.

However, rather than greasing its wheels, inflation may throw sand in the wheels of the economy, making it less efficient and competitive. If the 'sand-in-the-wheels' effect is stronger than the 'greasing-the-wheels' effect, the costs or disadvantages of inflation exceed the benefits or advantages.

A low but stable inflation rate may also be necessary to make labour markets function efficiently. Even if average real-wage rates are rising, there will be some labour markets in which real wages must fall in order to maintain a low rate of unemployment. When prices are completely stable (i.e. when the inflation rate is zero), to cut real-wage rates, nominal wage rates have to fall. To save jobs, workers may be willing to accept falling real wages caused by money-wage rates rising at a slower rate than inflation. However, workers are much less willing to accept cuts in money-wage rates. Thus, with zero inflation, the changes required in relative real-wage rates, which are needed to make labour markets function efficiently, fail to take place. Labour markets function best when inflation is low but stable. By contrast, absolute price stability produces wage stickiness, which results in unnecessarily high unemployment.

Some of the costs or disadvantages of inflation are:

- **distributional effects.** Weaker social groups in society, living on fixed incomes, lose, while those in strong bargaining positions gain. Also, with rapid inflation, real rates of interest may be negative. In this situation, lenders are really paying borrowers for the doubtful privilege of lending to them, and inflation acts as a hidden tax, redistributing income and wealth from lenders to borrowers.
- **distortion of normal economic behaviour.** Inflation can distort consumer behaviour by causing households to bring forward purchases and hoard goods if they expect the rate of inflation to accelerate. Similarly, firms may divert funds out of productive investment in fixed investment projects into unproductive commodity hoarding and speculation. People are affected by *inflationary noise*. This occurs when changes in relative prices (i.e. a rise or fall in the price of *one* good) is confused with a change in the *general* price level or inflation.

215

- **breakdown in the functions of money.** In a severe inflation, money becomes less useful and efficient as a medium of exchange and store of value. In the most extreme form of inflation, a hyperinflation in which the rate of inflation accelerates to a minimum of several hundred per cent a year, less efficient barter replaces money and imposes extra costs on most transactions.
- **international uncompetitiveness.** When inflation is higher than in competitor countries, exports increase in price, putting pressure on a fixed exchange rate. Lower growth and rising unemployment are likely to result. With a floating exchange rate, the exchange rate falls to restore competitiveness, but rising import prices may fuel a further bout of inflation.
- **shoe leather and menu costs.** Consumers incur shoe leather costs, spending time and effort shopping around and checking which prices have or have not risen. By contrast, menu costs are incurred by firms having to adjust price lists more often.

The consequences of deflation for the performance of the economy and for individuals

Common sense might suggest that if inflation is generally seen to be bad, its opposite, deflation or a falling price level, must be good, both for the performance of the economy and for individuals. However, extended price deflation may bring its own problems. When people believe prices are going to fall, they postpone big-ticket consumption decisions, for example replacing their cars. This may erode business confidence and trigger recession or deepen and lengthen an already existing recession. However, this assumes that falling prices are the result of a *bad* or *malign* deflation rather than a *good* or *benign* deflation.

The difference between the two is illustrated in Figure 8.18. A good or benign deflation, shown in the left-hand panel of the diagram, results from improvements in the economy's supply side, which reduces business costs of production. Both the *SRAS* curve and the *LRAS* curve shift to the right and, assuming the *AD* curve does not itself shift, the price level falls, but output and employment rise. However, in the recessionary conditions existent in the UK economy in 2009, it was much more likely that a falling price level would signal a bad deflation. A bad or 'malign' deflation, shown in the right-hand panel of the diagram, is caused by a collapse of aggregate demand, negative multiplier effects, and possibly by a credit crunch.

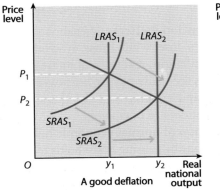
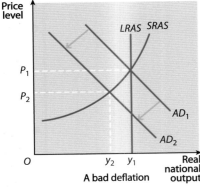

Figure 8.18 Good or benign and bad or malign deflations

Are lower prices a good thing? Not really

Deflation — if it gets out of control — can be just as bad as inflation. Like inflation, deflation is a form of monetary instability. It disrupts the price mechanism, so people become confused about the true value of things. Consumers see prices are going to fall, so they defer purchases and even procrastinate on other decisions, such as getting married, in the expectation it will be cheaper later. Pay rises are few and far between. Economic growth is almost non-existent.

In a deflation interest rates may appear to be low, but may actually be high. This is explained by the difference between nominal interest rates and real ones. For example, if the Bank of England's base rate is 2%, and prices are falling at 3%, real interest rates are actually 5%. The cost of borrowing is, therefore, actually higher than people think. Owing £10 is a heavier burden at the end of the year than it was at the beginning. A factory must sell more widgets, a farmer more milk and a shop more goods to meet those monthly interest payments.

When people wake up to this, they might take steps to remedy the situation quickly. For individuals, the key is the housing market. If it cracks and those with huge mortgages — secured on a dwindling asset — suddenly put their homes up for sale, a deflationary spiral could erupt. In a period of deflation, the real value of people's debt rises; this reduces net wealth and often leads to lower spending.

Follow-up questions

1 Who may benefit from deflation in an economy?
2 What is a 'deflationary spiral'?

8.4 The balance of payments on current account

The importance of international trade for an economy such as the UK

In Chapter 6, under the heading 'A satisfactory balance of payments' (pages 145–46), we mentioned exports and imports, which are the two main sections of the current account of the balance of payments. Before we examine the balance of payments in more detail, we shall introduce you to the general case for countries trading with each other in an open world economy.

Imagine a small country such as Iceland in a world without international trade. As a closed economy, Iceland's production possibilities are limited to the goods and services that its narrow resource base can produce. This means that Iceland's average costs of production are likely to be high because the small population and the absence of export markets mean that economies of scale and long production runs cannot be achieved. At the same time, the consumption possibilities of Iceland's inhabitants are restricted to the goods that the country can produce.

Compare this with Iceland's position in a world completely open to international trade. In an open economy, imports of raw materials and energy greatly boost Iceland's production possibilities. In theory at least, Iceland can now produce a much wider range of goods. In practice, however, Iceland produces the relatively few goods and services that it is good at producing, and imports all the rest. By gaining access to the much larger world market, Iceland's industries benefit from economies of scale and long production runs. Likewise, imports of food and other consumer goods present Iceland's inhabitants with a vast array of choice and the possibility of a much higher living standard and level of economic welfare than are possible in a world without trade.

While the UK is a much larger country than Iceland, it still has a relatively narrow resource base. The arguments outlined above about using trade to widen production and consumption possibilities help to explain the role of international trade in the British economy. The UK's economy is dependent on foreign trade. Successive British governments have supported free and unrestricted trade and the UK has few restrictions on foreign trade and investment.

The UK's balance of payments

The current account

The main sections of the current account, which are shown in Table 8.4, are the balance of trade in goods, the balance of trade in services, net income flows and net current transfers. The current account is usually regarded as the most important part of the balance of payments because it reflects an economy's international competitiveness and the extent to which the country is living within its means. If the currency outflows in the current account exceed the currency inflows, there is a **current account deficit**. If receipts exceed payments, there is a **current account surplus**.

Table 8.4 shows a revised estimate of the UK's current account for 2013, published by the ONS in September 2014. (In later publications, it is likely that the figures will change, as the ONS regularly revises its data.)

One very important point to note is that in September 2014 the ONS changed the way in which it presents the statistics for the current account of the balance of payments. The item 'Balance of primary income' in Table 8.4 used to be referred to as 'Income balance', and the item 'Balance of secondary income' used to be referred to as 'Current transfers balance'. The titles 'Balance of trade in goods' and 'Balance of trade in services' did not change.

Table 8.4

Sections of the current account, 2013 (£ million)	
Balance of trade in goods	−110,196
Balance of trade in services	+78,096
Balance of primary income	−13,133
Balance of secondary income	−27,162
Balance of payments on the current account	**−72,395**

Source: ONS Balance of Payments, Q2 2014, published 30 September 2014

For each of the sections of the current account, and for the current account itself shown in the bottom row of Table 8.4, a plus sign (+) indicates a credit item (net currency flowing into the UK), and a minus sign (−) indicates a debit item (net currency flowing out of the UK). The balance of trade in goods is sometimes called the balance of visible trade, and the balance of trade in services is part of the balance of invisible trade.

The story that can be read into the figures is quite worrying. On an annual basis, the current account deficit rose to about 4.4% of GDP, or over £72bn, in 2013, which was slightly narrower than the record deficit of 4.6% of GDP which occurred

KEY TERMS

current account deficit occurs when currency outflows in the current account exceed currency inflows. It is often shortened to 'exports less than imports'.

current account surplus occurs when currency inflows in the current account exceed currency outflows. It is often shortened to 'exports greater than imports'.

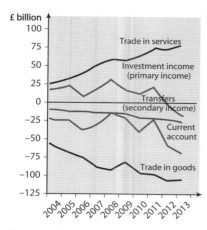

Figure 8.19 Changes in the current account of the UK balance of payments, 2004–13

> **KEY TERM**
>
> **balance of trade in goods** the part of the current account measuring payments for exports and imports of goods. The difference between the total value of exports and the total value of imports of goods is sometimes called the 'balance of visible trade'.

> **STUDY TIP**
>
> You must avoid confusing the balance of trade in goods with the whole of the current account, and the current account with the balance of payments as a whole.

in 1989. Figure 8.19 shows the changes in the four sections of the current account, and the current account itself, over the 10 years leading up to 2013.

The ONS's chief economist said the recent current account deficits were mainly being driven by a fall in income from investments earned abroad, rather than deteriorating net trade position. Britain's investment income deficit of £10.3bn in the fourth quarter of 2013 (part of the primary income account) was the largest on record. In many previous years, the UK had enjoyed a substantial surplus of investment income.

The consensus view among economists was that the size of the current account deficit is unlikely to cause a crisis in the near term, but was 'storing up big problems for the future'.

The main sections of the current account

We shall now take a closer look at each of the four sections of the current account.

The balance of trade in goods

The **balance of trade in goods** shows the extent to which the value of exports of goods exceeds the value of imports, and vice versa. Table 8.4 does not indicate the total value of exports and imports, which were respectively £306,810 million and £417,006 million in 2013. The balance of trade in goods was therefore in deficit to the tune of £110,196 million. This figure is shown in the bottom row of Table 8.5.

The balance of trade in goods can also be disaggregated (broken up) into different forms of trade in goods, such as the balances of trade in manufactured goods and non-manufactured goods. Some of the different ways of disaggregating the balance of trade in goods are shown in Table 8.5.

Table 8.5 Selected items from the UK balance of trade in goods, 2013 (£ million)

Balance of trade in food, drinks and tobacco	−18,388
Balance of trade in raw materials (basic goods)	−4,821
Balance of trade in oil	−10,013
Balance of trade in manufactured goods	−54,560
Balance of trade in all goods	**−110 196**

Source: ONS Balance of Payments, Q2 2014, published 30 September 2014

Data presentation

Take note of the word 'Selected' in the captions of Tables 8.5 and 8.6. The word tells you that not all the items in the balance of trade in goods and the balance of trade in services are in the tables. Selections such as these try to separate the most interesting items from the 'background noise' of other perhaps less interesting items.

Table 8.5 shows that the UK is a net importer of primary products (food and raw materials), and had also by 2013 become a large net importer of oil. Up until 2005, the UK enjoyed a balance of trade surplus in oil, as a result of the development of the North Sea oil and gas fields in the 1970s and 1980s. However, depletion of these fields means that the UK now imports much of the energy it uses, including coal and natural gas as well as oil.

The balance of payments deficit in manufactured goods is significant. Apart from the periods during and immediately following the First and Second World Wars, for over 200 years Britain was a net exporter of manufactured goods. In the mid-nineteenth century, Britain was the 'workshop of the world'. This has now changed. In the early 1980s, the UK became a net importer of manufactured goods. The manufactured goods deficit is now huge, reflecting loss of competitiveness, the resulting deindustrialisation of the UK, and the fact that most manufactured goods are now produced in emerging-market countries, particularly in China.

CASE STUDY 8.3

Has the UK once again become a net exporter of cars?

In 2011 it was estimated that rising exports to new markets such as Russia and China would increase the number of cars built in British factories in 2012 by 9%. The Society of Motor Manufacturers and Traders (SMMT) predicted that UK car manufacturing would continue to rise at the same rate for at least the next 4 years.

Eight out of ten cars currently built in the UK end up on foreign roads. British-made cars are now sold in more than 170 countries. And the UK is about to make more money from exporting cars than it spends on importing them. Jaguar Land Rover recorded its highest ever annual sales in 2012 with a 76% growth in China.

Dr Peter Wells of Cardiff University says: 'Overall, we're doing fantastically well at a bleak time for car manufacturing around the world. Prestige brands such as Jaguar seem to have come through better than we expected, while other companies have sought out new markets. In the Middle East and Africa, there's an appreciation of British culture and heritage. On its own, Britishness is not enough to sell cars but underpinned by quality and performance it gives us an edge. In China and Russia there are individuals with significant wealth who want British-made cars.'

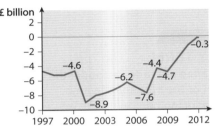

Figure 8.20 The UK's balance of trade in passenger cars, 1997–2012

Follow-up questions

1 'The recent success of the UK car industry reflects increased price and quality competitiveness.' Explain this statement.
2 How might the UK's membership of the European Union have affected the growth of the British car industry?

STUDY TIP
Make sure you have some knowledge of the balances of trade in items such as manufactured goods, oil and automobiles.

KEY TERM
balance of trade in services is part of the current account and is the difference between the payments for the exports of services and the payments for the imports of services.

The recent improvement in the balance of trade in automobiles, shown in Figure 8.20 in the case study, is an exception to the decline of manufactured exports and the growth of manufactured imports. As the case study predicted, after years of importing more cars than it exported, it was expected that the UK's trade balance vehicles would move into surplus in 2013. This seems to have happened. A report published in April 2014, written by the consultancy and accountancy firm KMPG and commissioned by the Society of Motor Manufacturers and Traders (SMMT), stated: '77% of vehicles produced in 2013 were exported. The average value of vehicles imported in 2013 was approximately £13,000 compared to an average of £20,600 for vehicles exported, meaning that the balance of trade for vehicles is £70 million net export.'

A large number of cars continue to be manufactured in the UK, albeit in the Japanese-owned plants created by foreign direct investment in the late 1980s and the 1990s. The UK plants owned by Nissan, Toyota and Honda are modern, incorporating state-of-the-art technology, and labour productivity is high. Following the closure of MG Rover's plants in 2005, the deindustrialisation of the UK car industry has for the moment come to an end. However, ownership of Jaguar and Land Rover has moved to India, raising fears that production may also eventually move there.

The balance of trade in services

The decline of manufacturing and the growth of service industries mean that the UK now has a post-industrial and service sector economy. This is reflected in the **balance of trade in services** shown in Table 8.6.

Table 8.6 Selected items from the UK balance of trade in services, 2013 (£ million)

Balance of trade in transport	+1,726
Balance of trade in travel	−7,497
Balance of trade in telecommunication, computer and information services	+5,206
Balance of trade in insurance and pension services	+20,362
Balance of trade in financial services	+38,127
Balance of trade in intellectual property	+2,795
Balance of trade in all services	**+78,096**

Source: ONS Balance of Payments, Q2 2014, published 30 September 2014

Whereas most manufactured goods are internationally tradable, the same is not generally true for services such as retailing, car repair and hairdressing. Services such as these are produced and consumed in the non-internationally traded economy, or sheltered economy. However, many services which were previously produced within the UK are now being imported. This is an important part of the globalisation process.

UK companies, which used to produce services 'in-house', now outsource or buy in the services from outside suppliers, often located in countries with cheap labour. UK-based companies are locating 'back-office' service activities overseas, including many financial and ICT-related services. Many call centres providing customer services and direct marketing services have moved to India.

Nevertheless, as Table 8.6 shows, the UK is still a significant net exporter of financial, insurance and ICT services. These industries illustrate the UK's competitive advantage in service sector industries, though the picture is not as rosy in industries such as travel and tourism, where Britons now spend much more in other countries than overseas residents spend in the UK.

STUDY TIP

Make sure you appreciate the importance of financial services in the balance of trade in services. You should also appreciate the significance of exports of financial services to the UK economy.

CASE STUDY 8.4

The UK financial services industry

This case study was written in the aftermath of the 2008/09 recession. Since then, with recovery under way, the future of the UK financial services industry may be more promising than was thought in 2010 and 2011 when the UK economy was 'flat-lining'.

The financial services sector is a significant contributor to UK income and employment. Over a million people in Britain are employed in financial services, of which two-thirds are based outside London. Financial services is also one of the largest export industries in the UK.

The financial crisis that began in the summer of 2007 has, however, highlighted the need for a more resilient and sustainable financial services industry to support the broader economy. In addition to being an important part of the economy in its own right, the financial services sector provides essential credit and financial services to businesses and households.

During the period after 2000 the expansion of the financial sector was a significant influence on the growth rate of the economy overall. But the recent growth of the sector has been reversed, reducing GDP permanently by about 1.9%. The country will suffer a further loss of income as a result of the losses that banks have made, giving a total fall in national income of about 2.4%, and reducing government revenue by about 1% of GDP.

Follow-up questions

1 Explain two reasons for the temporary decline of the UK financial services industry after 2007.
2 The growth of the financial services industry has led to an unbalanced economy. How might the UK economy be 'rebalanced'?

Investment income

Net investment income, which is the main component of net primary income flows shown in Table 8.4, is the income earned, mainly by UK companies, from assets owned abroad, minus a similar flow of income received by overseas multinational companies from the assets they own in the UK. Investment income divides into income from direct investments overseas, and income from portfolio investments overseas. BP investing in the construction of a new oil refinery in the US Gulf Coast region would be an example of overseas direct investment. Profits generated by the oil refinery and flowing back to the UK in future years would be inward investment income. But whereas direct investment involves spending on physical capital such as factories, shopping malls and oil refineries, portfolio investment is the acquisition by financial firms such as pension funds and insurance companies of financial assets such as shares and bonds issued by firms and governments outside the UK. Dividend income paid by overseas companies, and interest paid, for example, by overseas governments, which then flow into the UK are examples of inward flows of income generated by portfolio investments.

For many years, UK net investment income was strongly positive, the result of decades of outward investment which built up a huge stock of overseas-located assets owned by British companies and residents.

However, this has changed and the investment income account is now in deficit. Between 2012 and 2013, the investment income deficit for the UK increased from £4,841 million in 2012 to £12,337 million in 2013, according to the ONS's estimate published in September 2014. (Note: investment income is only one part, albeit the main part, of primary income, which, as Table 8.4 shows, was in deficit to the tune of £13,133 million in 2013.)

The large surplus in investment income in the pre-recession years was largely the result of the willingness of banks and companies to build up ownership of assets in other countries by taking risky, but high-yielding bets. In the more cautious post-crisis environment, rich people living in the rest of the world have invested heavily in the UK, which they see as a 'haven' safe from political turbulence in other countries. The rapid build-up of UK assets now owned by overseas-based companies and rich individuals has led to an investment income outflow. The fall in income earnt by UK investments overseas and persistent UK budget deficits financed by overseas borrowing have also been contributory factors.

Transfers

The deficit on current **transfers** or secondary income increased from £22,195 million in 2012 to £27,162 million in 2013, again according to the ONS's estimate published in September 2014. Britain has long had a negative secondary income balance, caused by the UK's net contributions to the EU budget, overseas aid and the cost of maintaining armed forces in countries such as Afghanistan.

'Balance', equilibrium and disequilibrium in the balance of payments

It is important to avoid confusing balance of payments *equilibrium* with the balance of payments *'balancing'*. Balance of payments equilibrium occurs when the current account more or less balances over a period of years, and is perfectly compatible with the occurrence of short-term current account deficits and surpluses. Fundamental disequilibrium exists when there is a persistent tendency for payments for imports to be significantly greater or less than payments for exports over a period of years.

The balance of payments must balance in the sense that all sections must sum to zero. In practice, however, the estimates of the items in the balance of payments never sum to zero. This is simply because trade flows, and other items in many of the sections of the balance of payments, are inaccurately measured and recorded. For example, a drug dealer flying a light aircraft into a remote landing strip in Essex is hardly likely to declare the value of the cocaine he is illegally importing. Hence, a balancing item (labelled as 'net errors and omissions') is included as a 'mistakes item' to make the balance of payments sum to zero.

As mentioned earlier, the statisticians who construct the UK balance of payments use a continuous revision method of measurement. When the estimates of the balance of payments for a particular year are first published soon after the end of the year in question, the balancing item is usually large. In this situation, the estimated figures should not be trusted completely. However, in subsequent months and years, the balancing item usually decreases. In the light of new and previously unavailable information, the statisticians whittle away the balancing item, allocating it to one or more of the real trade, investment income, or capital flows in the balance of payments.

Applying *AD/AS* analysis to the current account of the balance of payments

In section 8.1, and in Chapter 7, the meaning of aggregate demand in the economy was explained, together with the aggregate demand equation: $AD = C + I + G + (X - M)$. We showed how, in an *AD/AS* graph, an increase in *any* of the components of aggregate demand (C, I, G or $(X - M)$) causes the aggregate demand (AD) curve to shift rightward, leading to a new equilibrium national income.

We shall now apply *AD/AS* analysis to explain how a change in net exports, or $(X - M)$, affects the national economy. As mentioned earlier, the current account includes non-trade items (investment income and transfers) as well as exports and imports. However, for the rest of this section, we shall assume that exports and imports of goods and services are the only two sections of the current account of the balance of payments. Given this simplifying assumption, there is a current account surplus when net exports are positive (i.e. $X > M$), and a current account deficit when net exports are negative (i.e. $X < M$).

Exports are an injection of spending into the circular flow of income, whereas imports are a leakage or withdrawal of spending from the flow (refer to Figure 7.4 in Chapter 7, and to the accompanying explanation of the circular flow diagram).

Suppose initially that $X = M$, which means there is neither a surplus nor a deficit in the current account. Note also that in this situation, given

223

the assumption of no non-trade flows in the current account, foreign trade injections into the circular flow of income exactly equal foreign trade withdrawals from the flow. When $X = M$, the current account has a neutral effect on the state of aggregate demand and on the circular flow of income.

However, at the next stage, overseas demand for British exports increases, but UK demand for imports remains unchanged. This means there is a net injection of spending into the circular flow of income. The current account moves into surplus, with $X > M$.

In the *AD/AS* diagram in Figure 8.21, the increase in exports shifts the *AD* curve to the right. What happens next in the economy depends on the shape and slope of the *SRAS* curve around the initial point of equilibrium national income. In Figure 8.21, equilibrium national income is initially at point X, which shows the economy in deep recession, suffering from deficient aggregate demand. In this situation, any event that increases aggregate demand increases the level of real output in the economy and causes demand-deficient unemployment to fall. An increase in exports is just such an event, shifting the *AD* curve from AD_1 to AD_2. This causes real output to rise from y_1 to y_2, though at the cost of some inflation, since the price level rises from P_1 to P_2.

Following the rightward shift of the aggregate demand curve to AD_2, equilibrium national income is now shown at point Z. As the *SRAS* curve becomes steeper, moving up the curve, the diagram tells us that the main effect of a further shift of the *AD* curve from AD_2 to AD_3 falls on the price level rather than on output and jobs. Output increases, from y_2 to y_3, but the price level also increases to P_3. As full employment approaches, export demand becomes *inflationary* rather than *reflationary*.

Nevertheless, in this situation, the growth in export demand eliminates the demand deficiency previously existent in the economy. The economy ends up on its long-run aggregate supply (*LRAS*) curve, with equilibrium national income at point V.

At point V, what happens next in the economy depends on assumptions made about the nature of short-run and long-run aggregate supply. In Figure 8.21, when the economy produces on the vertical *LRAS* curve, any further increase in the demand for exports leads only to the price level rising above P_3, without any sustained increase in real output. However, there is another possibility. Foreign demand for a country's exports may be a response to favourable supply-side conditions in the domestic economy which shift the *LRAS* curve to the right. This means the economy can produce and supply the goods needed to meet the increase in export demand without generating inflation. This is the desired result of **export-led growth**. The German and Japanese economies enjoyed export-led growth from the 1960s to the 1980s, and China is now enjoying similar benefits. However, the worldwide growth of demand for Chinese exports has begun to cause inflation in the Chinese economy.

STUDY TIP
You must be able to use the *AD/AS* model and the circular flow of income to analyse how changes in exports and/or imports affect macroeconomic performance: that is, short-run growth, employment and inflation.

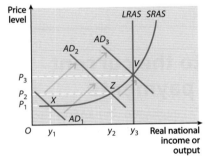

Figure 8.21 How an increase in exports can affect the national economy

KEY TERM
export-led growth in the short run, economic growth resulting from the increase in exports as a component of aggregate demand. In the long run, economic growth resulting from the growth and increased international competitiveness of exporting industries.

QUANTITATIVE SKILLS 8.2

Worked example: making calculations from balance of payments data

The following data shows the balance of payments on current account of a particular country:

Table 8.7

	2012	2013	2014	2015
Balance of trade in services (£)	+240bn	+120bn	+20bn	+30bn
Net primary income flows (£)	–30bn	–35bn	+10bn	–15bn
Net secondary income flows (current transfers) (£)	+5bn	–2bn	+12bn	–8bn
Current account balance (£)	+200bn	+100bn	+80bn	+100bn

Calculate the country's balance of trade in goods in each of the 4 years. Comment on your answers.

The calculations involve subtracting the balance of trade in services, net income (primary income) and current transfers (secondary income) from the current account balance in each of the 4 years.

2012: –£15 billion; **2013:** +£17 billion; **2014:** +£38 billion; **2015:** +£93 billion.

Over the 4-year period, the balance of trade in goods moved from a deficit of £15 billion in 2012 to a surplus of £93 billion. The current account as a whole and the balance of trade in services were in surplus throughout the period. Net income flows were in deficit throughout the period (except for 2014), which means that more profits and other income were flowing into the country than flowing out. Current transfers switched from being positive to negative, and then to positive and negative again, but the net transfer flows were generally smaller than the net trade and income flows.

TEST YOURSELF 8.4

Figure 8.22 shows a country's trade deficit in goods and its current account balance for the years 2009 to 2014. Suggest one possible reason which might explain why the trade deficit is smaller than the current account deficit.

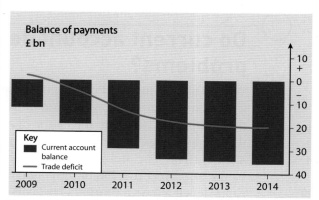

Figure 8.22 The balance of payments on current account and the trade deficit for a particular country, 2009–14

SYNOPTIC LINK

Supply-side policies, explained in Chapter 9, can be used to try to achieve export-led growth.

CASE STUDY 8.5

Export-led growth, the need to export to BRIC countries, and the 'march of the makers'

The pre-2008 UK boom resulted in large part from too much consumption and too little saving. For recovery from recession to lead into long-term growth, export-led growth is crucial. But achieving export-led growth is much easier said than done, requiring UK goods and services to be quality competitive as well as price competitive. Improved quality competitiveness, which involves good design and well-made products, may only be achievable in the long run if helped by improvements on the supply side of the economy.

Slow growth in many eurozone countries underlines just how important it is for the UK to diversify its export efforts to countries such as Brazil, Russia, India and China. But, it has been said, the UK exports more to Ireland than it does to all the BRIC countries combined. The new middle classes in emerging economies have significant spending power and growing demands for some of the high-end goods which the UK can provide. British products, talent and culture continue to command global appeal. If anything, the desirability of the 'Made in Britain' stamp is increasing — apparently in Japan it is more prestigious to own a Nissan car made in Sunderland than one made locally.

Despite its often maligned reputation, the UK manufacturing sector is in the top ten in the world and responsible for 70% of UK research and development. In 2011, Chancellor George Osborne said:

> We want the words: 'Made in Britain', 'Created in Britain', 'Designed in Britain', 'Invented in Britain' to drive our nation forward. A Britain carried aloft by the march of the makers. That is how we will create jobs and support families. We have put fuel into the tanks of the British economy.

In his rhetoric, the Chancellor was setting out the case for 'rebalancing' the UK economy in favour of manufacturing, partly because, compared to service industries, manufacturing contributes a lot more to UK exports. Together with other economists and politicians, Osborne wants Britain to 'reindustrialise'. He sees a resurgence of manufacturing as vital for export-led growth. But with an ever-burgeoning deficit in the balance of trade in goods, just how successful has been the 'march of the makers'?

Follow-up questions

1 The passage is generally optimistic about the possibility of export-led growth. Explain three reasons for being more cautious.
2 Assess whether in the UK economy today, a 'march of the makers' is in fact taking place.

KEY TERM

reindustrialise growth of manufacturing industries to replace industries which have disappeared or declined significantly in size. Reindustrialisation is the opposite of deindustrialisation.

Do current account deficits pose problems?

While a short-run deficit or surplus on current account does not pose a problem, a persistent or long-run imbalance indicates fundamental disequilibrium. However, the nature of any resulting problem depends on the size and cause of the deficit: the larger the deficit, the greater the problem is likely to be. The problem is also likely to be serious if the deficit is caused by the uncompetitiveness of the country's industries. Although in the short run a deficit allows a country's residents to enjoy living standards boosted by imports, and thus higher than would be possible from the consumption of the country's output alone, in the long run, the decline of the country's industries in the face of international competition lowers living standards.

In a poor country, a current account deficit can be justified because of the country's need to import capital goods on a large scale to modernise the country's infrastructure and to promote economic development. However, there is always a danger, as the experience of countries such as Nigeria has shown, that the deficit soon becomes the means for financing the 'champagne lifestyle' enjoyed by the country's ruling elite.

Do current account surpluses pose problems?

While many people agree that a persistent current account deficit can pose serious problems, few realise that a balance of payments surplus on current account can also lead to problems. Because a surplus is often seen as a sign of national economic virility and success, a popular view is that the bigger the surplus, the better must be the country's performance.

Insofar as the surplus measures the competitiveness of the country's exporting industries, this is obviously true. There are, nevertheless, reasons why a large payments surplus is undesirable, though a small surplus may be a justifiable objective of government policy.

Two arguments against a persistently large surplus

- **One country's surplus is another country's deficit.** Because the balance of payments must balance for the world as a whole, it is impossible for all countries to run surpluses simultaneously. Unless countries with persistently large surpluses agree to take action to reduce their surpluses, deficit countries cannot reduce their deficits. Deficit countries may then be forced to impose import controls from which all countries, including surplus countries, eventually suffer. In an extreme scenario, a world recession could be triggered by the resulting collapse of world trade. At various times since the 1970s, the current account surpluses of the oil-producing countries have led to this problem, as has Japan's and more recently China's payments surpluses, which have been the counterpart to the US trade deficit. On several occasions, the US government has faced pressure from US manufacturing and labour interests to introduce import controls and other forms of protectionism. When introduced, US protectionism undoubtedly harms world trade. Non-oil-exporting developing countries, almost without exception, also suffer chronic deficits, although these are very different from the US trade deficit. The imbalance of trade between more developed and less developed countries cannot be reduced without the industrialised countries of the 'North' taking action to reduce surpluses which have been gained at the expense of the developing economies of the 'South'.
- **A balance of payments surplus can be inflationary.** A balance of payments surplus can be an important cause of domestic inflation, because it is an injection of aggregate demand into the circular flow of income, which increases the equilibrium level of nominal or money national income. If there are substantial unemployed resources in the economy, this has the beneficial effect of reflating real output and jobs. However, if the economy is initially close to full capacity, demand-pull inflation results.

ACTIVITY

Access the ONS webpage **www.ons.gov.uk/ons/taxonomy/index.html?nscl=Balance+of+Payments** and find out the most recent information about the UK balance of payments.

The current account surplus of oil-producing countries can lead to problems

8.5 Possible conflicts between macroeconomic objectives

Revisiting the main conflicts

On pages 139–40 of Chapter 6 we outlined the main conflicts between macroeconomic objectives, and the resulting policy trade-offs that can face governments, particularly in the short run. Over the years, UK macro-policy has been influenced and constrained by four significant short-run conflicts between policy objectives. These conflicts have been between:

- the internal policy objectives of full employment and growth and the external objective of achieving a satisfactory balance of payments
- achieving low unemployment and controlling inflation
- increasing the rate of economic growth and achieving a more equal distribution of income and wealth
  By taxing the rich more and then transferring the tax revenues to the poor in the form of welfare benefits, UK governments have tried to reduce income

inequalities. However, free-market economists have argued that such policies reduce entrepreneurial and personal incentives in labour markets, which make the economy less competitive and the growth rate slower. In the free-market view, greater inequalities are necessary to promote the conditions in which rapid and sustainable economic growth can take place.

● between higher living standards now and higher living standards in the future
In the short term, the easiest way to increase living standards is to boost consumption. However, this 'live now, pay later' approach means sacrificing saving and investment, which reduces economic growth.

SYNOPTIC LINK

Chapter 9 investigates how monetary policy and fiscal policy attempt to resolve the conflicts arising when implementing macroeconomic policy.

EXTENSION MATERIAL

Revisiting output gaps

Positive and negative output gaps were introduced in section 8.1 in the context of describing the economic cycle. Figure 8.23 resembles Figure 8.5, except it shows negative and positive output gaps at particular points of time. The trend level of output is the volume of goods and services the economy can produce when it is working at its long-run, sustainable productive capacity. The distance from B to A shows a negative output gap, defined as the difference between trend output at point B and actual real output at point A, which is *below* trend output. Likewise, the distance from point D to point C illustrates a positive output gap, defined as the difference between trend output at point D and actual real output at point C, which is *above* trend output.

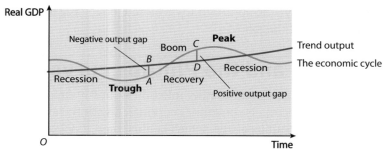

Figure 8.23 Negative and positive output gaps shown on an economic cycle diagram

The existence of a positive output gap means that the economy *temporarily* produces a level of real output which is higher than potential output at that point in time. However, partly due to inflationary pressures which emerge when there is a positive output gap, this level of output cannot be sustained. After the peak in the economic cycle has been reached, in the cycle's downswing real output begins to fall back towards trend output.

Negative and positive output gaps can also be shown on an *AD/AS* diagram as in Figure 8.24.

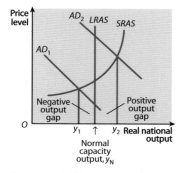

Figure 8.24 Negative and positive output gaps shown on an *AD/AS* diagram

To make sense of this diagram — and also economic cycle diagrams such as the one in Figure 8.23, you must again understand that the economy can produce *temporarily* a level of real output which is greater than potential output. To remind you, the *SRAS* curve in Figure 8.24 continues to the right of the *LRAS* curve and the normal capacity level of output. Again, this results from the assumption that the economy can *temporarily* produce a level of real output which is greater than sustainable potential output. On the diagram, a negative output gap is shown by the horizontal distance between y_1 and normal capacity level of output, and a positive output gap is shown by the horizontal distance between the normal capacity level of output and y_2.

Reconciling policy conflicts in the short run and the long run

When economic policy objectives are mutually exclusive, it is impossible for governments to achieve all their policy objectives at the same time — at least in the short run. The result of this is that governments often trade off between policy objectives, attempting for example to combine *relatively* low unemployment with *relatively* low inflation on the ground that full employment and absolute price stability cannot be achieved together.

Another possibility is that, over time, governments change their ranking of policy objectives. To win votes, a government may aim for low unemployment in the months before a general election, knowing that if the election is won, policy may have to be switched to the control of inflation. In the 5 years between the 2010 and 2015 UK general elections, the Conservative/Liberal coalition government started with policies of severe austerity which dampened growth and slowed down job creation. However, as the 2015 election approached, the austerity programme was replaced to a certain extent with more expansionary policies. Many commentators argued, however, that after the 2015 election, severe austerity policies would once again be resumed.

Pro-free market economists generally believe that successful supply-side policies, combined with supply-side reform in the private sector, facilitate the production of high-quality goods and services which people, in the UK and abroad, wish to buy. The recent success of car manufacturing in the UK is quoted as evidence. According to this supply-side view, in the long run the sustained economic growth which results resolves short-run conflicts between policy objectives. The supply-side approach to economic policy is explained in the next and final chapter of this book.

Policy conflicts and the Phillips curve

The debate between economists over whether inflation is mostly caused by demand-pull or cost-push factors is sometimes conducted with the aid of a statistical relationship, the Phillips curve, which is illustrated in Figure 8.25.

The Phillips curve is named after the Keynesian economist A.W. Phillips, who argued that statistical evidence showed that in a period covering nearly a century, a stable inverse relationship existed between the rate of change of wages (the rate of wage inflation) and the percentage of the labour force unemployed. Later versions of the Phillips curve, such as the one illustrated in Figure 8.25, measure the inverse relationship between unemployment and the rate of price inflation.

The Phillips curve is a purported statistical relationship between two variables, and not in itself a theory of inflation. However, both the demand-pull and the cost-push theories of inflation can be used to explain the apparent relationship. In the demand-pull explanation, the factor causing unemployment to fall, moving up the Phillips curve, is excess demand, which pulls up money wages and the average price level. By contrast, in the cost-push explanation, falling unemployment means that trade union power increases, enabling unions to use their growing monopoly power over the supply of labour to push for higher wages.

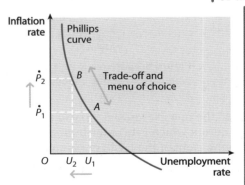

Figure 8.25 The policy choices indicated by the Phillips curve

Either way, the statistical evidence shown in the Phillips curve illustrates the conflict between full employment and control of inflation as policy objectives. It also suggests how the conflict can be dealt with. Suppose in Figure 8.25 unemployment initially is U_1 and the rate of inflation is $\dot{P}_1$ with the economy at point A on the Phillips curve. (Note the symbol $\dot{P}$ is used to show the rate of price inflation.) By increasing aggregate demand, the government can move the economy to point B. The unemployment rate falls to U_2, but at the cost of a higher rate of inflation at $\dot{P}_2$. By using demand management policies, it appears possible for governments to trade off between increasing the number of jobs in the economy and reducing inflation. Points such as A and B on the Phillips curve represent a menu of choice for governments when deciding an acceptable combination of unemployment and inflation.

The long-run Phillips curve

Economists now generally recognise that the Phillips curve in Figure 8.25 is a short-run Phillips curve (SRPC), representing the short-run relationship between inflation and unemployment. In the next diagram, Figure 8.26, a vertical **long-run Phillips curve (*LRPC*)** has been added to the graph, intersecting the short-run Phillips curve where the rate of inflation is zero. The rate of unemployment at this point is the natural *rate* of unemployment (NRU), depicted by the symbol U_N. (As we explained earlier in the chapter, when expressed as the unemployment level, it is called the natural *level* of unemployment.)

Free-market economists argue that it is impossible to reduce unemployment *below* the NRU, except at the cost of suffering an ever-accelerating unanticipated inflation. This would be likely to accelerate into a hyperinflation, which would then wreak severe damage on the economy. The explanation for this lies in the fact that the original Keynesian explanation of the (short-run) Phillips curve wrongly took into account only the *current* rate of inflation and ignored the important influence of the *expected* rate of inflation. If the government increases aggregate demand with the aim of reducing unemployment below the NRU, people revise upward their expectations of *future* inflation. This then leads to higher *current* inflation. Continuous upward revision of expected inflation of course leads to higher and higher rates of current inflation.

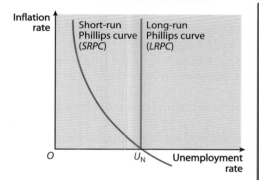

Figure 8.26 The long-run Phillips curve and the natural rate of unemployment

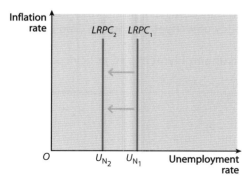

Figure 8.27 Successful supply-side policies shift the long-run Phillips curve to the left

The immediate solution, according to free-market economists, is for the government to respond to its mistake in trying to keep unemployment *below* the NRU, by reducing aggregate demand so as to take unemployment eventually back to its natural rate. However, the long-term solution is to reduce the natural rate itself. This can be done by implementing appropriate supply-side policies (see section 9.3 in Chapter 9), which shift the long-run Phillips curve to the left. In Figure 8.27, curve shifts from $LRPC_1$ to $LRPC_2$, and the natural rate of unemployment falls from U_{N1} to U_{N2}. In essence, supply-side economists argue that providing the 'correct' supply-side policies are implemented, the policy objectives of reducing unemployment and controlling inflation are compatible in the long run, though not necessarily in the short run.

SUMMARY

- Long-run economic growth is an increase in an economy's potential level of output, whereas short-term economic growth is a movement from a point inside the economy's production possibility frontier towards a point on the frontier.
- Economic growth is measured as a change in real GDP rather than as a change in nominal GDP.
- National income or output is the flow of new output produced by an economy in a year.
- Investment and technical progress are two of the causes of economic growth.
- The economic cycle or business cycle reflects actual output fluctuating around trend output.
- Economic cycles are often caused by changes in aggregate demand, though supply-side factors can also cause fluctuations in economic activity.
- An output gap is the difference between actual output and the trend level of output.
- Full employment exists when the number of workers whom firms wish to hire equals the number of workers wanting to work at current market wage rates.
- Frictional unemployment is transitional and 'between jobs' unemployment. It is also voluntary and short term.
- Structural unemployment is usually long term and results from the structural decline of industries and from changes in required job skills.
- Cyclical unemployment is also known as Keynesian and demand-deficient unemployment.
- Keynesian economists argue that cyclical unemployment is involuntary, which means that the people who are unemployed are willing to work at current wage rates but there aren't enough jobs available.
- Policies to reduce unemployment will only be effective if the causes of unemployment are correctly diagnosed.
- The costs of unemployment fall on the whole economy and on the unemployed and their families.
- Inflation is a continuing or persistent rise in the average price level.
- In the UK, the retail prices index (RPI) and the consumer prices index (CPI) are used for measuring inflation.
- The CPI is now used for the indexation of welfare benefits, as well as for setting the inflation rate target.
- Demand-pull inflation results from the fact that, when aggregate demand increases, firms are only prepared to produce and supply more output if prices increase.
- Cost-push inflation results from higher costs of production experienced by businesses.
- Demand-pull inflation and cost-push inflation can both be illustrated on *AD/AS* diagrams.
- It is important to diagnose correctly the cause(s) of inflation when selecting policies to reduce the rate of inflation.
- The balance of payments measures the currency flows into and out of an economy. It is a record of a country's financial transactions with the rest of the world.
- The main sections of the current account are exports and imports. Investment income and transfers are the other sections now part of the primary and secondary income balances.
- The balance of payments as a whole always 'balances'; deficits and surpluses relate to particular sections of the account, such as the current account.
- A change in any of the components of aggregate demand, including net export demand, shifts the *AD* curve rightward or leftward.
- An increase in exports or a fall in imports may be reflationary or inflationary, depending on circumstances.
- Other things being equal, a decrease in exports or an increase in imports will reduce aggregate demand.
- Current account deficits and surpluses both pose problems, though both may also have some advantages.
- The short-run Phillips curve illustrates a short-run conflict between policy objectives, but in the long run these conflicts may disappear.
- The Phillips curve shows the possible relationship between inflation and unemployment and policy conflicts and trade-offs that may exist.

Questions

1 Distinguish between short-run and long-run economic growth.

2 'Some economists argue that recessions are necessary for restructuring the economy.' Evaluate this view.

3 Explain the difference between frictional and structural unemployment.

4 Explain why it is important to identify correctly the cause of unemployment.

5 Do you agree that it is more important to reduce unemployment than to reduce inflation? Justify your answer.

6 Explain the difference between deflation and disinflation.

7 With the help of an *AD/AS* diagram, explain the difference between demand-pull and cost-push inflation.

8 Explain how a large increase in investment in new productive capacity in the UK by overseas firms may affect the UK current account of the balance of payments.

9 The UK has had a large current account deficit for several decades. Do you agree that a large balance of payments deficit on current account is bad for the UK economy?

10 Outline the possible conflicts that governments may experience when attempting to achieve their macroeconomic objectives. Do these conflicts exist in the long run as well as in the short run?

9 Macroeconomic policy

Early in our coverage of macroeconomics, Chapter 6 included a brief introduction to the objectives of macroeconomic policy. However, we didn't at that stage mention that governments use policy instruments to try to 'hit' one or more of the various objectives they wish to achieve. A **policy instrument** is a tool or set of tools used to try to achieve a policy objective.

This chapter explores the linkages between policy instruments and policy objectives, first in the context of monetary policy, and then in relation to fiscal policy. The chapter concludes by explaining the meaning of supply-side policies and the links between supply-side policy objectives and instruments.

Generally, monetary, fiscal and supply-side policies are used in combination rather than in isolation, with particular policies assigned to achieving particular policy objectives. In recent years, however, UK monetary policy rather than fiscal policy has been used to manage aggregate demand. With the exception of a brief period from 2008 to early 2010, when 'demand-side' fiscal policy was used to try to spend the economy out of the 'great recession', fiscal policy is nowadays mostly used as a supply-side policy — indeed arguably the most important form of supply-side policy. 'Supply-side' fiscal policy has largely replaced 'demand-side' fiscal policy, though there is a possibility that this could once again change if there is a change of government.

KEY TERM

policy instrument a tool or set of tools used to try to achieve a policy objective.

LEARNING OBJECTIVES

This chapter will:

- explain the meaning of monetary policy
- examine the objectives of monetary policy
- describe how monetary policy instruments are used to try to achieve these objectives
- explain the meaning of fiscal policy
- analyse the roles of the fiscal policy instruments of government spending, taxation and the budget in fiscal policy
- explain the difference between interventionist and anti-interventionist supply-side policies
- distinguish between demand-side and supply-side fiscal policy
- survey other supply-side policies such as deregulation and labour training policies

9.1 Monetary policy

The meaning of monetary policy

Monetary policy is the part of economic policy that uses monetary instruments to try to achieve policy objectives. The main monetary policy instrument is manipulation of interest rates. Other instruments include manipulation of the money supply and the exchange rate. Before 1997, UK monetary policy was implemented jointly by the Treasury (which is part of central government) and the **Bank of England**; these were known as the 'monetary authorities'. The Treasury abandoned its hands-on role in implementing monetary policy in 1997 when the government made the Bank of England operationally independent. These days, as we shall explain, the government sets the policy target, and then leaves the Bank of England free to decide how to achieve the target. Hence, unless it is 'leaned on' by the Treasury, there is now only one monetary authority, the Bank of England.

> **KEY TERM**
> **Bank of England** the central bank in the UK economy which is in charge of monetary policy.

The Bank of England and monetary policy

Most banks, such as Barclays and HSBC, are commercial banks, whose main aim is to make a profit for their owners. The most significant exception is the Bank of England, which is the UK's **central bank**.

The objectives and instruments of monetary policy

To understand monetary policy, it is useful to distinguish between its objectives and instruments.

- A monetary policy *objective* is the target or goal that the Bank of England aims to hit.
- A monetary policy *instrument* is the tool or technique of control used to achieve the objective.

Controlling inflation is the main monetary policy objective of the Bank of England, and the rate of interest has been the principal monetary policy instrument.

> **KEY TERM**
> **central bank** controls the banking system and implements monetary policy on behalf of the government.

> **KEY TERM**
> **money** an asset that can be used as a medium of exchange; it is used to buy things.

EXTENSION MATERIAL

What is money?

For most people, **money** is so desirable and so central to everyday life that what actually constitutes it hardly merits a second thought. For people living in England and Wales, money comprises coins and Bank of England notes, and any funds on deposit in banks such as HSBC and Barclays. Residents of Scotland and Northern Ireland would also include notes issued by local Scottish and Northern Irish banks. Building society deposits as well as bank deposits are now also regarded as money, although this has not always been the case.

Where do we draw the line as to what is money? Is a credit card money? Is a foreign currency such as the US dollar or the Indian rupee, given the fact that we may not be able to spend a foreign banknote or coin in the UK? Do we include financial assets such as National Savings Securities, which possess some, but not all, of the characteristics of money?

Consider also the social relationship that takes place whenever modern banknotes are spent on goods or services. Why, for example, are shopkeepers prepared to hand over new and valuable goods to strangers, in exchange for grubby and unhygienic pieces of paper with no apparent intrinsic value of their own? The answer lies in a single word: 'confidence'. In a modern economy, people are prepared to accept such tokens in settlement of a contract or debt, because they are confident that these notes and coins will also be accepted when they decide to spend them.

Is a credit card money?

KEY TERMS

inflation rate target the CPI inflation rate target set by the government for the Bank of England to try to achieve. The target is currently 2%.

Monetary Policy Committee (MPC) nine economists, chaired by the governor of the Bank of England, who meet once a month to set Bank Rate, the Bank of England's key interest rate, and also decide whether other aspects of monetary policy need changing.

The main monetary policy objective: controlling inflation

For the last 30 or so years, control of inflation has been the main objective of UK monetary policy. However, at a deeper level, control of inflation should be viewed not as an end in itself, but as the means of creating the 'sound money' deemed necessary for competitive markets to deliver improved economic welfare.

Since the 1990s, central government has set an **inflation rate target** for the Bank of England to achieve. Since 2003, the target set by the Treasury has been a 2% rate of inflation as measured by the rate of change of the consumer prices index (CPI). The Bank of England's **Monetary Policy Committee (MPC)** implements monetary policy to try to achieve the inflation rate target set by the government.

EXTENSION MATERIAL

Other monetary policy objectives

Until 1997, monetary policy was concerned only with getting the inflation rate at or below the target set by the government. Critics argued that the pre-1997 policy had a built-in deflationary bias (i.e. reducing inflation was favoured at the expense of achieving other possible macroeconomic objectives).

Since 1997, successive governments have asked the Bank of England to reduce interest rates to stimulate output and employment if the MPC believes that, on unchanged policies, an inflation rate below 2% will be accompanied by an undesirable fall in output and employment. In the government's words: 'The primary objective of monetary policy is price stability. But subject to that, the Bank of England must also support the government's economic policy objectives, including those for growth and employment.'

UK monetary policy has thus become symmetrical, in the sense that the MPC is just as prepared to use monetary policy to increase aggregate demand as it is to deflate the economy. Indeed, if the inflation rate falls below 1%, the Bank of England has to explain to the government why the inflation rate target has not been met, in the same way that the Bank's governor must write a letter of explanation when the inflation rate rises above 3%.

CASE STUDY 9.1

Regime change at the Bank of England

The government appoints Bank of England governors for terms of 5 years, subject to a maximum of two appointments. For most of the last 10 years, the governor was Mervyn King, a British economist and Bank of England 'insider'. In 2013, when his 10-year governorship ended, King was replaced by a surprise choice as new governor, the Canadian Mark carney, who had previously headed the Bank of Canada. At the time of his appointment, it was mooted that Carney would try to persuade the chancellor to change significantly the central thrust of UK monetary policy: namely, pursuit of the 2% CPI inflation rate target, with control of inflation by far the main monetary policy objective. At the time of writing (February 2015), this had not happened.

Follow-up questions

1 To what extent, if any, has UK monetary policy changed under Mark Carney?
2 In implementing monetary policy, the governor is assisted by eight members of the Monetary Policy Committee (MPC). Find out how the MPC members have changed in recent years.

Monetary policy instruments

To repeat, policy instruments are the tools used to achieve policy objectives. In this chapter, we have already noted that the Bank of England's interest rate, known as **Bank Rate**, is the UK's main monetary policy instrument.

Each month, the MPC either raises or lowers Bank Rate (usually by a quarter of 1%), or, more often, leaves the interest rate unchanged, to try to keep the inflation rate within a target range between 1% above and 1% below the 2% CPI target (i.e. between 3% and 1%). Indeed, for reasons explained later, from March 2009, in the midst of recession, until at least early 2015, Bank Rate remained unchanged at a low of 0.5%. This was the lowest rate ever set since the Bank of England was created in 1694. On the fifth anniversary of the 2009 decision, Mark Carney said that the recovery had 'some way to run' before a hike in interest rates would even be considered. Figure 9.1 shows the UK Bank Rate from 2000 to early 2015.

It is important to realise that interest rate policy acts on the demand for credit and loans. When interest rates are raised, people generally decide to borrow less, because the cost of loans becomes too high. Conversely, falling interest rates encourage people to borrow more and save less. As a result, interest rate policy affects aggregate demand.

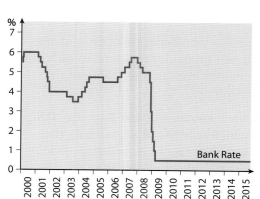

Figure 9.1 UK Bank Rate, 2000–14

How changes in the Bank of England's rate of interest affect lending and credit in the economy

In order to understand how a change in Bank Rate affects credit or loans provided by commercial banks and other financial institutions, it is necessary to understand how a commercial bank makes a profit. A bank such as Barclays or Lloyds is profitable because it 'borrows short and lends long'.

A bank 'borrows short', for example, by accepting deposits of money from people who have opened current accounts in the bank. The bank then lends this money to other people who wish to borrow from the bank. Many of the bank loans given to customers are long-term loans: for example, 25-year mortgage loans, or 5- or 10-year term loans. This type of banking business is profitable because the rate of interest that a bank pays when borrowing 'short' is lower than the rate of interest it charges when lending 'long'.

However, there is an element of risk in this. If customers who have lent 'short' to a bank suddenly decide to withdraw most or all of their funds, it might be difficult for the bank to repay them. If other customers then fear that the bank cannot honour its liabilities, they may also decide to withdraw their funds. In a worst-case scenario, there is a 'run' on the bank; the bank then crashes and goes out of business. In 2007 customers rushed to remove their money from the Northern Rock bank, which had to be rescued by the government before being sold to Virgin Money in 2011.

To maintain confidence in the commercial banking system, the Bank of England promises to lend to major banks in the event of large unexpected cash withdrawals, in order to preserve the **liquidity** in the banking system and to prevent runs on banks. The guarantee is part of the Bank of England's 'lender of last resort' function. Even in 'normal' times, when there is no fear of a run on a bank, the Bank deliberately keeps the commercial banks slightly short of cash. It does this in order to engineer a situation in which, as a matter of routine, commercial banks have to borrow from the Bank of England. However, Bank Rate, which is the rate of interest that the Bank of England pays to the commercial banks on their deposits, is normally about 0.15% lower than the rate of interest at which commercial banks such as Lloyds and NatWest lend to each other. This rate, which is called LIBOR (the London interbank offered rate), is the benchmark for short-term interest rates in the City of London.

At the next stage in the process, an increase in Bank Rate generally causes the commercial banks to increase the interest rates they charge their customers, because it now costs more for the banks to borrow from the Bank of England the funds they wish to lend on to their customers. With bank loans becoming more expensive, the banks' customers reduce their demand for credit and repay existing loans wherever possible. This reduces the **money supply**, or stock of money in the economy.

Conversely, when the Bank of England cuts Bank Rate, commercial banks generally follow by reducing their own interest rates. If a commercial bank did not reduce its own interest rate, it would lose business and make less profit.

KEY TERMS

liquidity measures the ease with which assets can be turned into cash quickly without a loss in value. Cash is the most liquid of all assets.

money supply the stock of money in the economy, made up of cash and bank deposits.

Bank Rate and the LIBOR

As well as paying interest to their customers who deposit money in savings accounts, commercial banks charge interest on money they lend to each other. The rate a bank pays when borrowing money from another bank is called the LIBOR rate (the London interbank offered rate).

In 'normal' times, the LIBOR rate hovers just above Bank Rate. In 2007, however, during the 'credit crunch' which ushered in a financial crisis lasting for several years, the gap between the two rates widened. One of the factors affecting interest rates is the risk attached to a loan. In the financial crisis, the increased possibility of a bank collapsing made interbank loans much riskier. As Figure 9.2 shows, this caused the LIBOR rate to drift away from Bank Rate. With Bank Rate being cut to 0.5% in

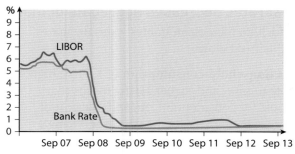

Figure 9.2 LIBOR and Bank Rate, 2007–13

2009, the fact that the interest rates that banks charge their customers are linked to LIBOR and not to Bank Rate undermined the effectiveness of the 0.5% Bank Rate in stimulating aggregate demand.

In 2012 and 2013 a financial scandal erupted when UK banks such as Barclays admitted they been had rigging the LIBOR. As a follow-up activity, try and find out about this and later scandals involving other banks and discuss how LIBOR rigging affected the cost of loans to households and firms.

Contractionary and expansionary monetary policy

In normal circumstances, monetary policy, rather than fiscal policy, is now used to manage the level of aggregate demand in the economy. To understand how monetary policy is used in this way, it is worth restating the aggregate demand equation:

$$AD = C + I + G + (X - M)$$

Whereas fiscal policy can affect aggregate demand by changing the level of government spending (G), monetary policy affects the other components of aggregate demand, C, I and ($X - M$).

> **STUDY TIP**
> Unlike modern fiscal policy, which is generally used in a supply-side way, monetary policy is not a supply-side policy. Some students wrongly assume that, because monetary policy can be used to control the growth of the money supply, it must therefore be a supply-side policy.

> **KEY TERM**
> **contractionary monetary policy** uses higher interest rates to decrease aggregate demand and to shift the AD curve to the left.

Contractionary monetary policy

In **contractionary monetary policy** interest rates are increased so as to take demand out of the economy. In Figure 9.3 higher interest rates shift the AD curve to the left. However, the extent to which the price level then falls (or, more realistically, the rate of inflation falls), and/or real output falls, depends on the shape of the economy's $SRAS$ curve. In Figure 9.3, the leftward shift of aggregate demand from AD_1 to AD_2 causes both real output and the price level to fall, respectively from P_1 to P_2, and from y_1 to y_2. This illustrates the possibility that a contractionary monetary policy, which aims to control the rate of inflation in the economy, might also cause the economy to sink into a recession. This is especially likely if the contractionary monetary policy triggers a multiplier effect that shifts the AD curve even further to the left. (See pages 179–80 for an explanation of the multiplier.)

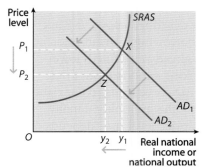

Figure 9.3 How an increase in the interest rate in a contractionary monetary policy causes the AD curve to shift to the left

> **STUDY TIP**
> Monetary policy shifts the AD curve in the economy rather than the AS curve. This reflects its role in the management of aggregate demand.

239

How an increase in interest rates decreases aggregate demand

There are three main ways in which an increase in interest rates decreases aggregate demand. These are explained below.

- **Higher interest rates reduce household consumption (C).** First, higher interest rates encourage people to save, and higher saving means that less income is therefore available for consumption. Second, the cost of household borrowing increases, which increases the cost of servicing a mortgage and credit card debt. Borrowers have less money to spend on consumption because more of their income is being used for interest payments. Third, higher interest rates may cause asset prices to fall, for example the prices of houses and shares. (An asset is something that has a value and can be sold for money.) These falling prices reduce personal wealth, which reduces consumption. Fourth, falling house and share prices reduce consumer confidence, which further deflates consumption.
- **Higher interest rates reduce business investment (I).** Investment is the purchase of capital goods such as machines by firms. Businesses postpone or cancel investment projects as they believe that higher borrowing costs make buying capital goods unprofitable. This is likely to be exacerbated by a fall in business confidence and increased business pessimism.
- **Changes in interest rates affect exports and imports via the exchange rate.** The third way in which an increase in interest rates leads to a decrease in aggregate demand works through the effect of higher interest rates on net export demand $(X - M)$. In the context of the UK balance of payments, a higher interest rate increases the demand for pounds by attracting capital flows into the currency. The increased demand for sterling causes the pound's **exchange rate** to rise, which makes UK exports less price competitive in world markets and imports more competitive in UK markets. The UK's balance of payments on current account worsens, which shifts the AD curve leftward.

By contrast, a fall in interest rates triggers a capital outflow in the balance of payments. The resulting increase in the supply of pounds on the foreign exchange market leads to a fall in the exchange rate. Exports become more price competitive, and the current account of the balance of payments improves. Aggregate demand increases and the AD curve shifts rightward.

Expansionary monetary policy

An **expansionary monetary policy**, the effect of which is illustrated in Figure 9.4, operates in the opposite way to that described above. A Bank Rate cut discourages saving, while stimulating borrowing, consumption and investment spending. Exports also increase. As already explained, lower interest rates cause the exchange rate to fall, making exports more price competitive and imports less competitive. The AD curve shifts to the right, with the size of the shift depending on the size of the multiplier. Finally, the extent to which real output increases or the price level rises depends on the shape and slope of the economy's SRAS curve, which in turn depends on the state of the economy. When the economy produces well below the normal capacity level of output, the SRAS curve is relatively 'flat'. In these circumstances, an expansionary monetary policy is likely to increase real output (and jobs), whereas the increasing 'steepness' of the SRAS curve as normal capacity utilisation approaches means that the stimulation of real output gives way to price inflation.

> **STUDY TIP**
> 'Sterling' is the word often used for the pound in the context of the currency's role in the international economy, for example, the sterling price of imports. Economists often write about the demand for sterling.

> **KEY TERM**
> **exchange rate** the price of a currency, e.g. the pound, measured in terms of another currency such as the US dollar or the euro.

> **KEY TERM**
> **expansionary monetary policy** uses lower interest rates to increase aggregate demand and to shift the AD curve to the right.

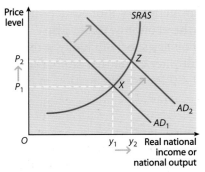

Figure 9.4 How a reduction in interest rate in an expansionary monetary policy causes the AD curve to shift to the right

Evaluating the success of recent UK monetary policy

In May 1997, Gordon Brown, the then incoming Labour chancellor of the exchequer, transferred to the newly independent Bank of England the task of using monetary policy to hit the government's inflation rate target, which then and more recently has been a CPI target of 2%.

Figure 9.5 shows that, for much of the time between 2000 and the end of the first quarter of 2008, the UK inflation rate was within its target range of 1% above and below the central target rate of 2%. Indeed, until early 2005, the inflation rate was always below 2%.

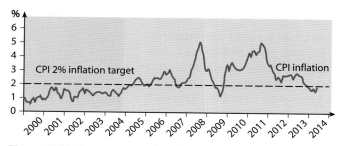

Figure 9.5 UK consumer prices index and the 2% CPI target, 2000–14

At the time, the Bank of England claimed that 'the proof of the pudding is in the eating'. Monetary policy had aimed to control inflation — inflation was low, therefore monetary policy was successful. The Bank's critics argued that, although monetary policy had been partly responsible for bringing down the rate of inflation, other factors also contributed in significant ways. First, there was the success of the supply-side reforms introduced by Mrs Margaret Thatcher's Conservative governments in the 1980s. When introduced, under the dictum 'first the pain and then the gain', supply-side policies contributed to high unemployment and a widening of income differentials. This was the 'pain'. From the mid-1990s onwards, the 'gain' arrived in the form of more competitive and efficient markets, which resulted in lower inflation rates.

Second, the policy-makers were 'lucky' in the last decade of the twentieth century and in the first few years of the twenty-first century. These were benign times, in which commodity, raw material and energy prices were generally falling, and when the ICT revolution increased productivity in manufacturing, communications and retailing.

But from 2008 onwards, times were much less benign. Despite the global recession, rising oil and commodity prices, agri-inflation (the rising prices of crops such as wheat and corn) and the beginnings of inflation in Chinese manufacturing industries triggered a severe bout of import-cost inflation in 2008, which UK monetary policy could not control. Indeed, at that time, monetary policy was also contributing to the build-up of inflationary pressures, mostly through Bank Rate cuts leading to a falling exchange rate, which was a further cause of rising import prices. A second bout of import-cost inflation occurred in 2011 after the recession was over. However, neither of the inflationary 'spikes' lasted very long. Partly because of this, the Bank of England resisted the temptation to raise interest rates to deal with inflation. As we have seen, Bank Rate was kept at the historical low of 0.5% to try to help 'spend the economy' into a sustained period of economic recovery.

241

CASE STUDY 9.2

'One-club golf' and macroeconomic policy

In recent years, UK governments have been accused of relying on the 'one-club golfer' approach to macroeconomic policy. The accusation is based on the following analogy.

Rory McIlroy is one of the greatest golfers in the world today. Imagine, however, Rory playing in the British Open golf championship with only one club in his golf bag. However great his talents as a golfer, Rory can't hope to win a major tournament playing under these conditions. Different golf clubs are needed for different shots: a driver for teeing off, a sand wedge for playing out of a bunker, and a putter for finishing off a hole on the putting green. So that Rory can show off his skills as a top-rate golf player, at the start of an 18-hole round, his caddy places ten or more different clubs in the golf bag to be carried round the greens. Part of Rory's skill then lies in selecting and using a particular club for a particular shot.

In the same way that Rory McIlroy selects different golf clubs for different shots, so the government needs different types of economic policy and policy instruments for achieving different policy objectives. Good government policy shouldn't rely just on changing Bank Rate. However sensible it is to raise interest rates in order to tackle demand-pull inflation, interest rates do not provide a panacea for all the macroeconomic problems that a government faces, particularly when policy conflicts and trade-offs are involved.

Rory McIlroy could not win a tournament with only one club

Follow-up questions

1 Name one other monetary policy instrument besides changing Bank Rate.
2 Explain how higher interest rates reduce demand-pull inflation.

Quantitative easing (QE)

In 2009, a new policy of quantitative easing (QE) was introduced to allow the Bank of England to escape from the 'one-club golfer' trap of solely using Bank Rate to implement monetary policy. QE, which is also known as the Asset Purchase Scheme (APS), is supposed to have the same effect as printing new money for people to spend. Of course, it is much more complicated than this. The Bank does indeed create new money, but it is electronic money with which the Bank purchases assets such as government bonds. By purchasing bonds from banks such as Barclays, and from other financial institutions, the Bank of England provides high-street banks with more money. In theory, the general public then borrow and spend the newly created money, which increases aggregate demand. By creating extra demand for bonds, QE also raises asset prices, which leads to a fall in long-term interest rates. Both of these factors — asset owners feeling wealthier and falling long-term interest rates — cause the *AD* curve to shift to the right.

By 2013, QE had been used three times: QE1 in 2009, QE2 in 2011 and QE3 in 2012.

Two important points to note are:

- The introduction and further use of QE marked the switching of monetary policy away from the control of inflation towards the deliberate boosting of aggregate demand. QE, combined with almost zero Bank Rate, was all about 'spending the economy out of recession', and, later, out of very slow growth.
- Critics of QE claim that it is leading to an erosion in the value of people's pensions and that it will eventually lead to inflation spinning out of control. Try and find out why this may be so. Nevertheless, the Bank of England argues that QE helped to prevent inflation falling much below the 2% CPI target. QE might be reintroduced if the Bank fears that deflation may occur.

STUDY TIP
QE was meant to support, but not to replace, Bank Rate policy.

How monetary policy fits in with fiscal policy

Figure 9.6 highlights the differences between monetary policy and fiscal policy, as they are currently implemented in the UK in early 2015.

STUDY TIP
The right-hand arrows in Figure 9.6 alert you to the fact that, as explained in sections 9.2 and 9.3, supply-side fiscal policy is an important part — perhaps the dominant part — of supply-side policies.

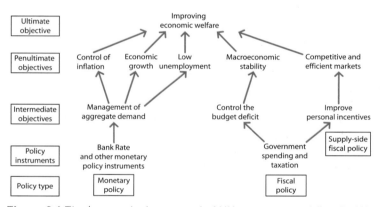

Figure 9.6 The 'transmission routes' of UK monetary and fiscal policy

As the upper row of the flowchart indicates, improved economic welfare or human happiness is considered by most people to be the ultimate objective of economic policy. Ranked below improving economic welfare are a number of policy objectives we consider to be *penultimate* rather than *ultimate*, in that they must be met in order to achieve sustainable improvements in human happiness.

The lower rows of the chart draw attention to some important aspects of recent and current UK macroeconomic policy. First, the chart shows that monetary policy, and not fiscal policy, is currently used to manage aggregate demand, which is an essential part of achieving the penultimate policy objectives of controlling inflation, achieving economic growth and reducing unemployment. Second — apart from during a short-lived period of fiscal stimulus, explained in section 9.2, from 2008 to 2010, when fiscal policy was also used to manage aggregate demand — modern fiscal policy tries to do two different things. These are to achieve macroeconomic stability as a result of controlling public finance and the government's budgetary position; and to achieve the supply-side objective of incentivising people to work harder and entrepreneurs to take more risks. (Take care when interpreting Figure 9.6. The flowchart is possibly over-simple. Other important aspects of monetary policy, and particularly fiscal policy and supply-side policy, are explained later in the chapter.)

QUANTITATIVE SKILLS 9.1

Worked example: calculating real Bank Rate

In June 2014, Bank Rate was 0.5% and CPI inflation was 1.9%. What was Bank Rate expressed in real terms?

The real rate of interest = the nominal rate of interest − the inflation rate.

Thus in June 2014, Bank Rate expressed in real terms was 0.5% minus 1.9%, which is −1.4%.

TEST YOURSELF 9.1

The following statements all relate to interest rates and to monetary policy. Explain why statement B is correct and why A, C and D are wrong.

A An increase in interest rates always reduces inflation.

B While reducing excess demand, an interest rate rise may increase cost-push inflation.

C Interest rate changes have no effect on the money supply.

D An increase in interest rates will always increase the level of investment.

KEY TERM

fiscal policy involves the use of taxation, public spending and the government's budgetary position to achieve the government's policy objectives.

ACTIVITY

Newspapers such as the *Sunday Times*, the *Observer* and the *Mail on Sunday* include details in their Business or Money sections of the rates of interest charged by banks when they lend to their customers, together with the rates they offer savers. Price comparison sites on the internet such as **www.moneysavingexpert.com** do the same. Research the Sunday newspapers or the comparison websites and find out what you can about the structure of interest rates.

KEY TERM

budget deficit occurs when government spending exceeds government revenue ($G > T$). This represents a net injection of demand into the circular flow of income and hence a budget deficit is expansionary.

9.2 Fiscal policy

The meaning of fiscal policy

Fiscal policy is the part of a government's overall economic policy that aims to achieve the government's economic objectives through the use of the fiscal instruments of taxation, public spending and the government's budgetary position. As an economic term, fiscal policy is often associated with Keynesian economic theory and policy. Between the 1950s and late 1970s, Keynesian governments used fiscal policy to manage the level of aggregate demand.

KEY TERM

balanced budget achieved when government spending equals government revenue ($G = T$).

The government's budgetary position

Using the symbols G for government spending and T for taxation and other sources of government revenue, the three possible budgetary positions a government can have are:

$G = T$: **balanced budget**

$G > T$: **budget deficit**

$G < T$: **budget surplus**

KEY TERM

budget surplus occurs when government spending is less than government revenue ($G < T$). This represents a net withdrawal from the circular flow of income and hence a budget surplus is contractionary.

A budget deficit occurs when public sector spending exceeds revenue. It is important not to confuse *financing* a budget deficit with *eliminating* a budget deficit. A budget deficit can be eliminated by cutting public spending or by raising taxation, both of which can balance the budget or move it into surplus. Assuming a budget deficit persists, the extent to which spending exceeds revenue must be financed by public sector borrowing.

From one year to another, it is the *change* in the budget deficit (or surplus) and not the absolute level that matters, though we shall explain later how a big budget deficit leads to a high level of government borrowing, which can lead to significant problems.

CASE STUDY 9.3

Budget day

The UK government's fiscal year runs for the 12 months starting on 1 April, for companies, and 6 April for individuals. A few weeks before, in March, the chancellor of the exchequer presents his budget to the House of Commons. Part of the budget speech, which is published in the 'Red Book' (formally called the Financial Statement and Budget Report (FSBR), but commonly named after the traditional colour of its cover), contains the chancellor's analysis of the state of the UK economy. This is the part of the budget which most interests economists.

Chancellor of the Exchequer George Osborne with his Treasury team on budget day 2014

By contrast, the general public is more interested in the announcement of tax changes, some of which come into effect within hours of the budget speech. Modern chancellors often use the trick of announcing tax *increases* a few months earlier, in the previous year's Autumn Statement (or Pre-Budget Report, as it used to be known). The chancellor hopes that taxpayers will not notice the announcement of these so-called stealth taxes because the higher tax rates will not be paid until a few months later. The extract below has been taken from the Treasury website.

History of the budget

The word 'budget' derives from the term 'bougette' — a wallet in which either documents or money could be kept. The longest Budget speech is believed to have been by William Gladstone on 18 April 1853, lasting four hours and forty-five minutes. The Budget box or 'Gladstone box' was used to carry the Chancellor's speech from Number 11 to the House for over 100 consecutive years. The wooden box was hand-crafted for Gladstone, lined in black satin and covered in scarlet leather.

Before going to Parliament to deliver the statement, the Chancellor holds up the red box outside Number 11 to waiting photographers. Chancellors are allowed to refresh themselves with alcoholic drinks during their Budget speech — no other Member of Parliament can do this! Traditionally, the Leader of the Opposition — rather than the Shadow Chancellor — replies to the Budget speech. This is usually followed by four days of debate on the Budget Resolutions (the basic parts of the Budget that renew taxes), covering different policy areas such as health, education and defence.

Follow-up questions

1 What is the purpose of budget day?
2 What is a 'stealth tax'? Why are stealth taxes unpopular?

The budget deficit and public sector borrowing

Various official terms are used by the Treasury for **public sector borrowing**, including the 'public sector's net cash requirement' and 'net public sector borrowing'. However, because the Treasury sometimes changes its terminology, the most important thing to learn is that public sector borrowing is 'the other side of the coin' to the budget deficit. Whenever there is a budget deficit, there is a positive borrowing requirement. Conversely, a budget surplus means the government can use the tax revenues it isn't spending to repay previous borrowing. In this case, the borrowing requirement is negative.

> **KEY TERM**
> **public sector borrowing** borrowing by the government and other parts of the public sector to finance a budget deficit.

Keynesian fiscal policy and the budget deficit

During the Keynesian era, a period which extended from around 1945 until the late 1970s, fiscal policy was used primarily to manage the level of aggregate demand in the economy. Keynesian fiscal policy, or **demand-side fiscal policy**, centred on the use of **deficit financing** to inject demand into the economy. Deficit financing describes a situation in which the government runs a budget deficit, usually for several years, deliberately setting public sector spending at a higher level than tax revenues and other sources of government revenue. For each of the years in which the government runs a budget deficit, the shortfall of tax revenue has to be financed through a positive borrowing requirement.

> **KEY TERMS**
> **demand-side fiscal policy** used to increase or decrease the level of aggregate demand (and to shift the *AD* curve right or left) through changes in government spending, taxation and the budget balance.
>
> **deficit financing** deliberately running a budget deficit and borrowing to finance the deficit.

> **EXTENSION MATERIAL**
> ## Deficit financing and Keynesian macroeconomic policy
>
> Before the Keynesian era, UK governments believed they had a moral duty to balance their budgets. This has been called sound finance or fiscal orthodoxy. The orthodox view was that a budget surplus placed the government in the moral position of a thief, stealing from taxpayers. If the government ran a budget deficit, it would be in the moral position of a bankrupt, perceived as not being able to manage its finances. Since both these budgetary positions were regarded as wrong or undesirable, the government's fiscal duty was to aim for a balanced budget.
>
> However, in the 1930s, John Maynard Keynes established a new orthodoxy that legitimised deficit financing and overturned the view that a government should always aim to balance its budget. The new Keynesian orthodoxy lasted until the late 1970s, when Keynesianism was replaced by a return to pro-free market economics and a belief in balanced budgets.
>
> Keynes argued that mass unemployment in the Great Depression was caused by deficient aggregate demand. He believed that, in the economy as a whole, too little spending was taking place because households and firms in the private sector were saving too much and spending too little.
>
> In the 1950s and 1960s, Keynes's followers, the Keynesians, argued that, in this situation, if the government deliberately runs a budget deficit, the deficit can be financed by the government, first borrowing and then, in its public spending programme, spending the private sector's excess savings. This injects spending into the economy and (in Keynesian theory, at least) gets rid of demand-deficient unemployment.

Using *AD/AS* diagrams to illustrate demand-side fiscal policy

Demand-side fiscal policy, also known as Keynesian fiscal policy, is the use of government spending, taxation and the budgetary position to manage the level of aggregate demand in the economy.

To understand demand-side fiscal policy, it is worth reminding ourselves of the aggregate demand equation:

$$AD = C + I + G + (X - M)$$

Government spending (G) is one of the components of aggregate demand. An increase in government spending, and/or a cut in taxation, increases the size of the budget deficit (or reduces the size of the budget surplus). Either way, an injection into the circular flow of income occurs and the effect on aggregate demand is expansionary.

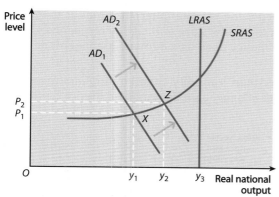

Figure 9.7 Keynesian or demand-side fiscal policy

Figure 9.7 illustrates the effect of such a reflationary or **expansionary fiscal policy**. Initially, with the aggregate demand curve in position AD_1, equilibrium national income occurs at point X. Real income or output is y_1, and the price level is P_1.

To eliminate demand-deficient (cyclical or Keynesian) unemployment, the government increases the budget deficit by raising the level of government spending and/or by cutting taxes. The expansionary fiscal policy shifts the *AD* curve right, from AD_1 to AD_2, and the economy moves to a new equilibrium national income or output at point Z.

However, the extent to which expansionary fiscal policy reflates real output (in this case, from y_1 to y_2), or creates excess demand that leads to demand-pull inflation (in this case, an increase in the price level from P_1 to P_2), depends on the shape of the *SRAS* curve, which in turn depends on how close, initially, the economy was to its normal capacity level of output (y_3 in Figure 9.7). The nearer the economy gets to its normal capacity level of output, depicted by the position of the *LRAS* curve in Figure 9.7, the greater the inflationary effect of expansionary fiscal policy and the smaller the reflationary effect. Once the normal capacity level of output is reached at y_3, a further increase in government spending or a tax cut solely inflates the price level. In this situation, real output cannot grow (except possibly temporarily), because there is no spare capacity. The economy is producing on its production possibility frontier.

Figure 9.7 can be adapted to illustrate the effect of a deflationary or **contractionary fiscal policy**. In this case, a cut in government spending and/or an increase in taxation shifts the *AD* curve to the left. The extent to which the demand deflation results in the price level or real income or output falling again depends on the shape and slope of the *SRAS* curve.

KEY TERMS

expansionary fiscal policy uses fiscal policy to increase aggregate demand and to shift the *AD* curve to the right.

contractionary fiscal policy uses fiscal policy to decrease aggregate demand and to shift the *AD* curve to the left.

The multiplier and Keynesian fiscal policy

During the Keynesian era from the 1950s to the late 1970s, governments in many industrialised mixed economies, including the UK, based macroeconomic policy on the use of fiscal policy to manage the level of aggregate demand. This became known as **discretionary fiscal policy**. To achieve full employment, governments deliberately ran budget deficits (setting $G > T$). This expanded aggregate demand, but sometimes too much demand 'overheated' the economy. Excess demand pulled up the price level in a demand-pull inflation, or pulled imports into the country and caused a balance of payments crisis. In these circumstances, governments were forced to reverse the thrust of fiscal policy, cutting public spending or raising taxes to reduce the level of demand in the economy. The Keynesians used demand-side fiscal policy in a discrete way (supplemented at times by monetary policy), to 'fine-tune' the level of aggregate demand in the economy. Government spending and/or taxes were changed in order to stabilise fluctuations in the economic cycle, and to try to achieve the macroeconomic objectives of full employment and economic growth, without excessive inflation or an unsustainable deterioration in the balance of payments.

The larger the government spending multiplier, the smaller the increase in public spending needed to bring about a desired increase in national income. Similarly, the larger the tax multiplier, the smaller the required tax cut. It follows that if the government spending and tax multipliers are sufficiently large, and if the multipliers affect real output more than the price level, fiscal policy used as a demand management instrument can be an effective way of controlling the economy.

Unfortunately, real-world multipliers are unlikely to be much larger than 1 or unity. Small multipliers mean that demand-side fiscal policy has relatively little effect on the level of aggregate demand and thence on the economy.

A process known as **crowding out** may provide one reason for a small government spending multiplier. It is, of course, impossible to employ real resources simultaneously in both the private and the public sectors of the economy. This means that if more of the available factors of production are employed in the public sector, private sector output must fall, assuming the economy is producing on its production possibility frontier. Employing more capital and labour in the public sector involves sacrificing the opportunity to use the same resources in private employment. The production possibility frontier in Figure 9.8 shows maximum levels of output that can be produced with various combinations of public sector and private sector spending and output. Assuming there is full employment and the economy is initially at point A, an increase in public sector spending from Pu_1 to Pu_2 crowds out or displaces private sector spending, which falls from Pr_1 to Pr_2, shown at point B. Given these assumptions, the size of the multiplier with respect to real output is therefore zero. However, if the economy was initially producing at point C, inside the production possibility frontier, the multiplier is likely to be larger with respect to real output. In this situation, the increase in public sector spending from Pu_1 to Pu_2 absorbs idle or spare capacity in the economy, without reducing the resources available for the private sector to use. (Back in the 1930s, Keynes recommended fiscal expansion when the economy was in recession, or depression, but he did not advocate its use if the economy was already fully employed or operating at full capacity.)

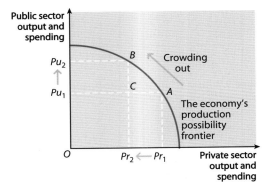

Figure 9.8 The crowding-out process

248

EXTENSION MATERIAL

The 'fiscal stimulus', the 'sovereign debt problem' and 'fiscal austerity'

In 2008 when recession began, Keynesian fiscal policy suddenly, but temporarily, came back into fashion. Barack Obama in the USA and the then Labour government in the UK justified the use of an expansionary demand-side fiscal policy, which became known as the fiscal stimulus. For a time, both monetary policy and fiscal policy were used in conjunction in the demand-side management of aggregate demand. The Labour government implemented tax cuts (the rate of VAT was cut temporarily to 15%), public spending increases and a burgeoning budget deficit to 'spend the economy out of recession'.

For a few months, the rebirth of Keynesian fiscal policy seemed to work, preventing the economy from slumping into a deep recession and triggering a weak recovery.

However, as in other EU countries such as Greece and Ireland, the massive increase in government borrowing that resulted from the fiscal stimulus led to a new problem: the sovereign debt problem. Put simply, the rest of the world was not prepared to lend to the UK government to help finance its budget deficit, except at ever-higher interest rates which the country could not afford. As in other deficit countries, Britain's 'Triple A' credit rating was threatened.

In May 2010, however, the newly elected coalition government, dominated by the Conservatives, was ideologically opposed to Keynesian economic policies. Under Chancellor George Osborne, the Conservatives immediately abandoned the fiscal stimulus and introduced a new fiscal policy based on public spending cuts and, for a time, higher taxes (VAT was increased to 20% on 4 January 2011). The Labour government's Keynesian-inspired fiscal stimulus was replaced by a policy of fiscal austerity (known also as fiscal consolidation or fiscal restraint).

KEY TERM

sovereign debt problem
sovereign debt is the part of the national debt owned by people or institutions outside the country that has sold the debt to them. The sovereign debt problem stems from the difficulties governments face when trying to finance budget deficits by borrowing on international financial markets.

KEY TERM

supply-side fiscal policy used to increase the economy's ability to produce and supply goods, through creating incentives to work, save, invest, and be entrepreneurial. Interventionist supply-side fiscal policies, such as the financing of retraining schemes for unemployed workers, are also designed to improve supply-side performance.

Supply-side fiscal policy

It is misleading to associate fiscal policy exclusively with Keynesian demand management. After 1979, with the exception of the 2 years from 2008 to 2010, demand-side fiscal policy gave way to **supply-side fiscal policy**.

In demand-side fiscal policy, income tax cuts stimulate aggregate demand through shifting the *AD* curve to the right. In supply-side fiscal policy, by contrast, income tax cuts increase aggregate supply via their effects on economic incentives. Supply-side fiscal policy aims to increase the economy's ability to produce and supply goods, through creating incentives to work, save, invest and to be entrepreneurial. (There are other important elements to supply-side fiscal policy, which include such interventionist policies as government spending on retraining schemes.)

STUDY TIP

Make sure you don't confuse demand-side fiscal policy and supply-side fiscal policy.

Along with other supply-side policies described in the next section, supply-side fiscal policy is used to try and shift the economy's long-run aggregate supply (*LRAS*) curve to the right, thereby increasing the economy's potential and normal capacity level of output. The effect of successful supply-side fiscal policy on the *LRAS* curve is shown in Figure 9.9. The *LRAS* curve shifts rightward from $LRAS_1$ to $LRAS_2$, with the normal capacity level of output increasing from y_1 to y_2. (Note that an outward movement of the economy's production possibility frontier can also illustrate the intended effect of supply-side policies.) Supply-side policy is explained in rather more detail in section 9.3.

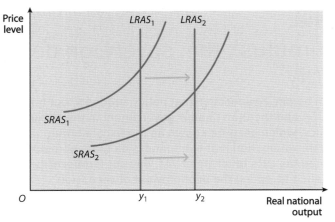

Figure 9.9 The intended effect of supply-side fiscal policy

The Office for Budget Responsibility

The Office for Budget Responsibility (OBR) was created in 2010 to provide independent analysis of the UK's public sector finances. The OBR produces forecasts for the economy and public finances. The Treasury still produces the bulk of the forecasting but, instead of the chancellor making judgements based on these data, the OBR rules on whether the government's policy has a better than 50% chance of meeting fiscal targets.

The OBR's spring forecast is published at the same time as the budget and incorporates the impact of any tax and spending policy measures announced in the budget.

The OBR also judges progress made towards achieving the two fiscal targets that the government aims to 'hit' in the medium term: that is, up to about 5 years ahead. The first target is to balance the cyclically adjusted current budget over a 5-year period. Budget deficits tend to rise during recessions and fall during the recovery and boom phases of the economic cycle. The cyclically adjusted budget balance is an estimate of what the budget balance would be if actual GDP were equal to potential (full-employment) GDP. Given that there has been a budget deficit in all recent years, the aim stated in 2010 of eliminating the deficit over the period extending to 2015/16 never seemed likely to be achieved.

The second target, announced when the OBR was set up in 2010, was a reduction by 2015/16 in the size of the national debt as a percentage of GDP. At the time of writing in February 2015, it is almost certain this will not be achieved. The budget *deficit* may indeed continue to fall, but as long as the deficit exists, the government has to undertake new *borrowing* to finance the deficit. The new borrowing adds to the stock of accumulated government borrowing, which is of course the national debt. (But although the national debt always increases when there is a budget deficit, the national debt could of course *fall as a percentage of GDP*, if economic growth, and possibly inflation, cause nominal GDP to increase at a faster rate than the nominal national debt.)

Cyclical and structural budget deficits

To understand fully the links between the government's budgetary position and the wider economy, it is useful to distinguish between the cyclical and the structural components of the budget deficit and borrowing requirement. The cyclical budget deficit is the part of the overall budget deficit that rises

> **KEY TERM**
> **national debt** the stock of all past central government borrowing that has not been paid back.

> **KEY TERM**
> **cyclical budget deficit** the part of the budget deficit which rises in the downswing of the economic cycle and falls in the upswing of the cycle.

and falls with the downswings and upswings of the economic cycle. In the downswing of the economic cycle, tax revenues fall but public spending on unemployment and poverty-related welfare benefits increases. As a result, the government's finances deteriorate. Conversely, in the recovery and boom periods, tax revenues rise and spending on benefits falls.

A cyclical deficit occurs in a downswing in the economic cycle (especially in a recession), to be followed by a cyclical budget surplus in the subsequent recovery and boom periods — providing they are sufficiently sustained.

By contrast, as the name suggests, growth in the structural component of the budget deficit and borrowing requirement relates in part to the changing structure of the UK economy. (It also relates to government policy decisions, for example those related to defence expenditure.) In recent years, a number of factors and trends have contributed to the growth of the structural budget deficit. These range from deindustrialisation and globalisation eroding the tax base, via the movement of industries to central Europe and Asia, through to an ageing population and the growth of single-parent families dependent on welfare benefits.

The growing structural deficit carries the rather dispiriting message that a government that seriously wishes to improve public sector finances will need to introduce significant tax increases or public spending cuts, or possibly both. Check whether public spending cuts continue after the 2015 general election.

The reasons for taxation and government spending

A first reason for taxation is to raise the revenue required to finance government spending. Second, taxes and subsidies (which are a part of government spending) can be used to alter the relative prices of goods and services in order to change consumption patterns.

However, ultimately, the reasons for and aims of both taxation and public spending depend on the underlying philosophy and ideology of the government in power. They differ significantly, for example, between Keynesian and free-market or supply-side inspired governments.

Governments use taxation and government spending in the macroeconomic management of the economy. It is the fiscal policy element of macroeconomic management that we cover in this section of the chapter. Within fiscal policy, two of the main reasons for public spending and taxation fall into two categories: allocation and distribution:

- **Allocation.** As we have just noted, taxes are used to alter relative prices and patterns of consumption. Demerit goods, such as alcohol and tobacco, are taxed in order to discourage consumption, while merit goods, such as museums, are untaxed and subsidised and sometimes directly provided by the state. In a similar way, taxes are used to finance the provision of public goods, such as defence, police and roads. Also, under the 'polluter must pay' principle, taxes are used to discourage and reduce the production and consumption of negative externalities, such as pollution and congestion. Likewise, subsidies are used to encourage the production or provision of external benefits or positive externalities. In some countries, for example, governments give grants to householders to pay for maintaining the external appearance of properties and gardens. Taxation can be used to deter monopoly by taxing monopoly profit through removing the windfall gain accruing to a monopolist as a result of barriers to entry and inelastic supply.

KEY TERMS

progressive taxation a tax is progressive if, as income rises, a larger proportion of income is paid in tax.

principle of taxation a criterion used for judging whether a tax is good or bad. Also known as a **canon of taxation.**

economy the principle of taxation which requires a tax to be cheap to collect in relation to the revenue it yields.

convenience the principle of taxation which requires a tax to be convenient for taxpayers to pay.

certainty one of the principles of taxation. Tax payers should be reasonably certain of the amount of tax they will be expected to pay.

equity (as a principle of taxation) requires a tax to be fair.

efficiency (as a principle of taxation) a tax should achieve its desired objective(s) with minimum unintended consequences.

flexibility the principle of taxation that requires a tax to be easy to change to meet new circumstances.

● **Distribution.** The price mechanism is value-neutral with regard to the equity or social fairness of the distributions of income and wealth in the economy. For example, wage and salary levels, determined by the market, do not reflect the social value of activities such as investment banking and nursing. If the government decides that the distributions of income and wealth produced by free market forces are undesirable, taxation and transfers in its public spending programme can be used to modify these distributions and reduce the alleged market failure resulting from inequity.

In the past, UK governments of all political complexions used progressive taxation and a policy of transfers of income to the less well off in a deliberate attempt — albeit with limited success — to reduce inequalities in the distribution of income. Governments also extended the provision of merit goods such as free state education and healthcare, in order to improve the social wage of lower-income groups. The social wage is the part of a worker's standard of living received as goods and services provided at zero price or as income in kind by the state, being financed collectively out of taxation.

The principles of taxation

Taxpayers commonly view all taxes as 'bad', in the sense that they do not enjoy paying them, although most realise that taxation is necessary in order to provide for the useful goods and services provided by the government. A starting point for analysing and evaluating whether a tax is 'good' or 'bad' is Adam Smith's four principles of taxation, which are also known as the canons of taxation. Adam Smith suggested that taxation should be equitable, economical, convenient and certain, and to these we may add the principles of efficiency and flexibility. A 'good' tax meets as many of these principles as possible, although because of conflicts and trade-offs, it is usually impossible for a tax to meet them all at the same time. A 'bad' tax meets few if any of the guiding principles of taxation.

Economy means a tax should be cheap to collect in relation to the revenue it yields. Convenience and certainty mean that a tax should be convenient for taxpayers to pay and that taxpayers should be reasonably sure of the amount of tax they will be required to pay to the government. Equity means a tax system should be fair, although there may be different and possibly conflicting interpretations of what is fair or equitable. Specifically, a particular tax should be based on the taxpayer's *ability to pay*. This principle is one of the justifications of progressive taxation, since the rich have a greater ability to pay than the poor. Efficiency requires a tax to achieve its desired objective(s) with minimum undesired side effects or unintended consequences. The disincentive effect on effort can be thought of as an unintended consequence of high rates of income tax. Finally, to comply with the principle of flexibility, a tax must be easy to change to meet new circumstances.

How government spending affects the pattern of economic activity

As Figure 9.10 shows, at the time of the March 2014 budget, total UK government expenditure was expected to be £732 billion during the financial year 2014/15. (Taking account of tax revenue and other government receipts which are shown in Figure 9.12, this means that the budget deficit for 2014/15 was expected to be £84 billion.)

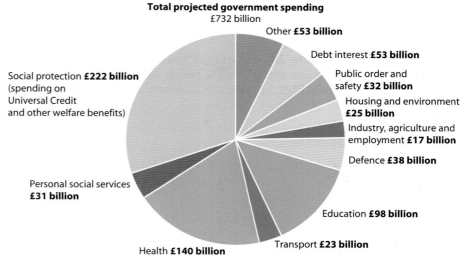

Figure 9.10 Treasury estimates of government spending, 2014–15

Perhaps more significant than the absolute totals of public expenditure is the ratio of public expenditure to national income or GDP, which indicates the share of the nation's resources taken by the government. Apart from the periods 1914–18 and 1939–45, which saw rapid, but temporary, increases in government spending to pay for the First and Second World Wars, the twentieth century witnessed a steady but relatively slow increase in government expenditure from around 10% to over 40% of GDP, reaching 46.75% in 1982/83. The ratio continued to rise in the early 1980s and fell in the late 1980s, before rising and falling again in the 1990s. By 2014/15, as Figure 9.10 shows, the ratio had increased again to nearly 48% in the depths of the recession. At the same time, tax revenues had fallen to about 36.5% of GDP. The spending figure fell to about 43.5% of GDP at the end of the 2011/12 financial year and tax revenues rose to about 37.6% of GDP. The forecast data up to the year 2018/19 may seem very optimistic. However, if the economic recovery not only continues but gathers steam, a fall in the cyclical deficit may lead to government finances moving into surplus. When you read this chapter, check whether this optimism was justified.

QUANTITATIVE SKILLS 9.2

Worked example: calculating government spending percentages (1)

Calculate the percentage shares of spending on social protection and education in the estimates for total government spending in 2014/15.

According to the pie graph in Figure 9.10, the estimate for spending on social protection was £222 billion out of estimated total government spending of £732 billion. As a percentage, this is:

$$\frac{£222 \text{ billion}}{£732 \text{ billion}} \times 100 = \text{approx. } 30.3\%$$

The estimate for spending on education was £98 billion out of estimated total government spending of £732 billion. As a percentage, this is:

$$\frac{£98 \text{ billion}}{£732 \text{ billion}} \times 100 = \text{approx. } 13.4\%$$

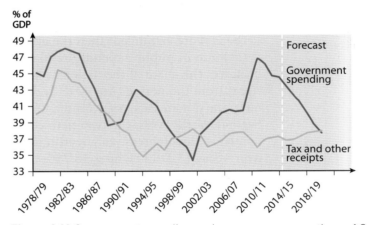

Figure 9.11 Government spending and revenue as proportions of GDP, 1978/79 to 2018/19

One reason for the changes in the ratios of government spending and taxation as ratios of GDP lies in changes taking place in employment and unemployment, which in turn relate to the economic cycle. As Figure 9.10 shows, spending on social security (under the heading 'Social protection'), which includes unemployment-related benefits, is by far the largest single category of public spending. When the economy booms, unemployment falls, so spending on social security also falls. As a result, the cyclical component of the budget deficit becomes smaller. The reverse is true in a recession.

Transfer payments made by the government

A large part of government expenditure takes the form of transfer payments: for example, the state pension and unemployment-related benefits. As the name indicates, in this context (though not in the way the term 'transfers' is used in the current account of the balance of payments), transfer payments are a redistribution of spending power from taxpayers in general to those receiving welfare benefits and also to holders of the national debt. By contrast, government spending on new hospitals or schools directly increases national output. As a generalisation, income taxes and transfers reduce the disposable incomes of those in work and increase the disposable incomes and spending power of those living on welfare benefits, some of whom are out of work, and to holders of the national debt.

In Figure 9.10, transfers are the major part of the item 'Social protection', which at £222 billion in 2014/15 dwarfed all other types of public spending, including health and education. When transfers, including debt interest, are excluded, government spending falls from around 45.0% of GDP in 2014/5 to close to 25.0%. This figure is a more accurate measure of the share of national output directly commanded by the state (and thus unavailable for use in the private sector) to produce the hospitals, roads and other goods and services which government collectively provides and finances, for the most part, out of taxation.

Debt interest is made up of payments by the government to people who have lent to the state (i.e. to holders of the national debt). In 2014/15, interest payments on the national debt were expected to be £53 billion, or over 7% of public spending. This item of public spending, which rises when interest rates rise and falls when interest rates are cut, is a transfer from taxpayers in general to people who lend their savings to the government. Total interest payments are affected by the general level of interest rates, which are heavily influenced by the level of Bank Rate set by monetary policy. In terms of fiscal policy, if the national debt (relative to nominal GDP) can be reduced, debt interest as a fraction of nominal GDP also falls — providing interest rates don't rise. Conversely, if the national debt rises faster than nominal GDP, debt interest rises as a fraction of real GDP — providing interest rates don't fall.

The relationship between the budget balance and the national debt

In recent decades, UK governments have usually run budget deficits. In this situation, the *flow* of public sector borrowing which finances the budget deficit builds up a *stock* of accumulated debt. The central government's accumulated debt is the national debt.

Government ministers as high as the prime minister — the formal Head of the Treasury — sometimes confuse the two 'D' words: Deficit and Debt. In the depths of recession before 2010, both the budget deficit and the national debt (and the wider public sector debt) were growing. More recently, the deficit fell by a third (a fact much trumpeted by the Treasury), but the national debt continued to grow. To understand the reason for this, you must first understand the difference between stocks and flows. A budget deficit is an example of an economic flow. This means that even when the deficit is falling, providing it is still positive (i.e. not a budget surplus), the flow of new borrowing that finances the budget deficit adds to the stock of the national debt.

It is useful also to distinguish between the *nominal* or *money* values of the budget deficit and the national debt as a percentage of nominal GDP — the 'debt to GDP' ratio. The debt to GDP ratio is an indicator of the burden of the national debt on the economy. With an understanding of these differences, you can appreciate that while the nominal national debt may be rising, the national debt as a percentage of nominal GDP may be falling. This happens when nominal GDP rises faster than the nominal debt, either because of economic growth (which is good) or inflation (which may be bad), or both.

Because it increases the national debt, a budget deficit generally increases the total interest payments the government has to pay to savers who have lent to the government. Conversely, a budget surplus allows the government to reduce the national debt by paying back a fraction of past borrowing. As mentioned already, changes in interest rates will also affect the outcome.

STUDY TIP
Make sure you don't confuse the national debt with the budget deficit, but understand the links between the two.

255

How taxation affects the pattern of economic activity

Figure 9.12 shows the total amount of revenue the UK government expected to collect from different taxes in 2014/15. By studying the pie graph, you can calculate the relative or proportionate importance of each tax. The three main categories of tax are taxes on income, taxes on spending or expenditure, and taxes on capital.

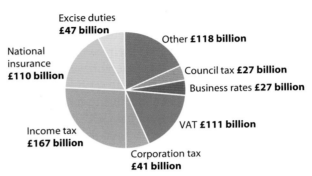

Total projected government tax revenues and other receipts
£648 billion

Figure 9.12 Treasury estimates of government tax revenues and other receipts, 2014–15

Taxes on income include not only personal income tax (income tax in Figure 9.12) but also national insurance contributions and corporation tax. National insurance contributions (which in legal terms are not strictly a tax) are a second type of personal income tax, which may eventually be merged into personal income tax. Corporation tax is a tax paid by companies on their profits.

The two main indirect taxes are value added tax (VAT) and excise duties on goods such as motor fuels, alcohol drinks and tobacco. In 2014/15 these were expected to raise £111 billion and £47 billion in tax revenues.

Taxes on wealth and capital are not very important in the UK. Council tax, which is a tax on property, and business rates are the only wealth taxes shown in Figure 9.12. Inheritance tax, which is a tax on wealth given from the dead to the living, is included in the category 'Other' in the pie graph. Much of income tax revenue is of course paid when people work for a living, producing useful goods and services. Wealth taxes, which by contrast stem from the ownership of assets such as houses and stocks and shares, reflect the accumulation or build-up of personal and household wealth in the economy.

TEST YOURSELF 9.2
Calculate the percentage shares of estimated total government revenue in 2014/15 of income tax and corporation tax.

Progressive, regressive and proportional taxation

If the government decides that the distributions of income and wealth produced by free-market forces are undesirable, taxation and transfers in its public spending programme can be used to modify these distributions and to try to reduce this market failure resulting from 'inequity'.

Until quite recently, British governments of all political complexions used **progressive taxation** and a policy of transfers of income to the less well-off, in a deliberate attempt — albeit with limited success — to reduce inequalities in the distribution of income. A tax is progressive when the proportion of income paid in tax rises as income increases. Progressive taxation, combined with transfers to lower-income groups, reduces the spending power of the rich, while increasing that of the poor. However, some taxes, particularly those designed to reduce consumption of the demerit goods alcohol and tobacco, are regressive and fall more heavily on the poor. These taxes are regressive. **Regressive taxation** means that the proportion of income paid in tax falls as income increases. In recent years, many economists and politicians, usually of a pro-free market persuasion, have advocated the introduction of **proportional taxation**, which in the case of a proportional income tax is sometimes called a 'flat tax'.

The word 'progressive' is value-neutral, implying nothing about how the revenue raised by the government is spent.

Capital gains tax, council tax and inheritance tax are the UK taxes imposed on capital and wealth. However, wealth is lightly taxed in the UK. For many decades in the twentieth century, inequalities in the distribution of wealth were substantially reduced, but since 1979 they have risen again. In 2014, the ONS estimated that the wealthiest 20% of UK households owned 63% of total aggregate household wealth in 2010/12; a share which has increased slightly from 62% in 2006/08 and 2008/10. At the other extreme, the poorest 20% owned less than 1% of total household wealth.

Nevertheless, many people believe wrongly that income taxes are strongly progressive in the UK. Personal income tax is only slightly progressive for most income groups, becoming rather more progressive for the richest fifth of households. The progressivity of income tax was reduced by the abolition in 2013 of the highest 50% marginal rate of income tax, which was levied on those with taxable incomes over £150,000. However, the 50% rate of income tax only remained in place for 2 years. It is also the case that fewer low-paid people now pay income tax. This is because the basic **tax threshold** has been increased by more than the rate of inflation. The marginal tax rate is the amount of tax paid on an additional pound of income, while the tax threshold is the income level at which a person begins paying income tax.

Because the council tax and indirect taxes (mostly expenditure taxes) are regressive, taking a declining proportion of the income of rich households, overall the UK tax system is at best only slightly progressive, and it may even be regressive.

Direct and indirect taxation

Income tax is an example of a **direct tax** because the person who receives and benefits from the income is liable in law to have to pay the tax to the government; they cannot pass the tax on to someone else. Corporation tax and national insurance contributions are other examples of direct taxes.

By contrast, *most* taxes on spending, such as value added tax (VAT) and excise duties, are **indirect taxes**. This is because the seller of the good, and not the buyer who benefits from its consumption, is liable to pay the tax. Nevertheless, as we explained in Chapter 2 (section 2.3), firms try to raise the prices they charge customers in order to recoup the tax revenue they pay to the government. When this happens, the buyers of the good *indirectly* pay some or all of the tax, via the higher prices the sellers now charge.

Microeconomic ways in which taxes and government spending affect the pattern of economic activity

As we have already mentioned, taxes and subsidies are used to alter the relative prices of goods and services in order to change consumption patterns. Demerit goods such as alcohol and tobacco are taxed in order to discourage consumption, while merit goods such as healthcare and education are subsidised and often publicly provided. Taxes are also used to finance the provision of public goods such as defence, police and roads. Under the 'polluter must pay' principle, taxes are also used to discourage and reduce the production and consumption of negative externalities such as pollution and congestion.

The influence of supply-side theory on government spending, taxation and the pattern of economic activity

Between 1979 and 1997, and under the influence of supply-side theory, Conservative governments changed the structure of both taxation and public spending to widen rather than reduce inequalities in the distributions of income and wealth. The Conservatives believed that greater incentives for work and enterprise were necessary in order to increase the UK's growth rate. For the Conservatives, progressive taxation and transfers to the poor meant that people had less incentive to work harder and to engage in entrepreneurial risk. The ease with which the poor could claim welfare benefits and the level at which they were available created a situation in which the poor rationally chose unemployment and state benefits in preference to wages and work. In this dependency culture, the unwaged were effectively married to the state.

From 1997 until losing office in 2010, Labour governments tried to use fiscal policy both to improve the economy's supply-side performance and to make the distribution of income once again more equal. The policy had only limited success. Although the real incomes of most of the poor increased in these years, income inequalities continued to grow, largely because high incomes grew at a much faster rate than low incomes. Since the 2008/09 recession, however, and at least until 2014, average real incomes fell by near-record amounts, and, according to the Institute of Fiscal Studies, inequality fell back to levels last seen in the mid-1990s.

KEY TERMS
supply-side policies aim to improve national economic performance by creating competitive and more efficient markets and through interventionist policies such as government finance of labour retraining schemes. (See also **supply-side fiscal policy**.)

supply-side economics a branch of free-market economics arguing that government policy should be used to improve the competitiveness and efficiency of markets and, through this, the performance of the economy.

TEST YOURSELF 9.3
In which one of the following situations is a government most likely to pursue a contractionary fiscal policy in order to decrease aggregate demand?

A When there is a negative output gap

B When the long-run trend rate of economic growth is too high

C When there is a low level of structural unemployment

D When inflationary pressures are operating in the economy

Explain why D provides the correct answer and why A, B and C do not.

ACTIVITY
Access the website of Her Majesty's Revenue and Customs on **www.hmrc.gov.uk/vat/start/introduction.htm** and on **www.hmrc.gov.uk/incometax/basics.htm** and read the advice HRMC gives to taxpayers on income tax and VAT. Write a short report to summarise your findings.

9.3 Supply-side policies

The meaning of supply-side economics

Supply-side policies can best be understood if you first understand the meaning of **supply-side economics**. Back in 1983, Arthur Laffer, an eminent supply-side economist, wrote:

> Supply-side economics provides a framework of analysis which relies on personal and private incentives. When incentives change, people's behaviour changes in response. People are attracted towards positive incentives and repelled by the negative. The role of government in such a framework is carried out by the ability of government to alter incentives and thereby affect society's behaviour.

Supply-side economics and the free-market revival

Supply-side economics grew in significance in the 1980s as a part of the free-market revival. Free-market economists believe in the virtues of capitalism and competitive markets — a belief which is matched by a distrust and dislike of 'big government' and state intervention in the economy.

STUDY TIP
It is important to understand that, originally, supply-side economics was part of the free-market revival.

The original meaning of supply-side economic policy

259

When supply-side economics first came to prominence around 1980, it focused narrowly on the effects of fiscal policy on the economy. (Soon after, other supply-side policies were started, including privatisation and trade union reform.) As we have seen, during the Keynesian era most economists regarded fiscal policy — and especially taxation — as a demand management tool. In Keynesian economics, the government's budget deficit lay at the centre of fiscal policy. The Keynesians largely ignored the impact of public spending and tax changes on the supply side of the economy, focusing instead on how changes in government spending and taxation affect aggregate demand.

By contrast, supply-side economics initially grew out of the concern expressed by free-market economists about the microeconomic effects of demand-side Keynesian fiscal policy. Indeed, in many respects, supply-side economics is a revival of the old pro-free market theory that largely disappeared from view during the Keynesian era. The central idea of supply-side economics is that a tax cut should be used, not to stimulate aggregate demand Keynesian-style, but to create incentives by altering relative prices, particularly those of labour and leisure, in favour of work, saving and investment, and entrepreneurship, and against the voluntary choice of unemployment.

The wider meaning of supply-side economic policy

Supply-side economic policy now encompasses more than just fiscal policy; it is the set of government policies which aim to change the underlying structure of the economy and improve the economic performance of markets and industries, and of individual firms and workers within markets. For the most part, supply-side policies are also *microeconomic* rather than simply *macroeconomic*, since, by acting on the motivation and efficiency of individual consumers, workers and entrepreneurs within the economy, the policies aim to enhance general economic performance and the economy's underlying production potential by improving microeconomic incentives.

Supply-side economists, and free-market economists in general, believe that if markets are allowed to function competitively, the economy is usually close to full employment. However, due to distortions and inefficiencies resulting from Keynesian neglect of the supply side, toward the end of the Keynesian era economic growth and full employment were not achieved. To increase levels of output and employment (and to reduce unemployment), supply-side economists recommend the use of appropriate *microeconomic* policies to remove distortions, improve incentives and generally make markets more competitive.

During the Keynesian era, government microeconomic policy in the UK was generally interventionist, extending the roles of the state and of the planning mechanism. **Interventionist supply-side policies**, such as regional policy, competition policy and industrial relations policy (which were known collectively as industrial policy), generally increased the role of the state and limited the role of markets.

By contrast, pro-free market supply-side microeconomic policy is *anti-interventionist*, attempting to roll back government interference in the activities of markets and of private economic agents, and to change the economic function of government from *provider* to *enabler*. **Non-interventionist supply-side policies** include tax cuts to create incentives to work, save and invest, cuts in welfare benefits to reduce the incentive to choose unemployment rather than a low-paid work alternative, **privatisation**, **marketisation** (**commercialisation**) and **deregulation**. (The main interventionist supply-side policies supported by free-market economists are government provision of external economies that benefit private sector firms. These policies include government provision of education and training and investment in infrastructure projects such as motorways and high-speed trains.)

In essence, the supply-siders, together with the other free-market economists, wish to create an enterprise culture. In this broad interpretation, supply-side policies aim to promote entrepreneurship and popular capitalism and to replace the dependency culture and statism that supply-side economists argue had been part of the Keynesian mixed economy. Successful supply-side policies can also

---

STUDY TIP
You should appreciate that many supply-side policies are microeconomic rather than macroeconomic.

KEY TERM
interventionist policies occur when the government intervenes in, and sometimes replaces, free markets. Interventionist supply-side policies include government funding of research and development.

SYNOPTIC LINK
Interventionist supply-side policies are used to correct many of the market failures described in Chapter 5.

KEY TERMS
non-interventionist supply-side policies free up markets, promote competition and greater efficiency, and reduce the economic role of the state.

privatisation involves shifting ownership of state-owned assets to the private sector.

marketisation involves shifting provision of goods or services from the non-market sector to the market sector. Also known as **commercialisation**.

deregulation involves removing previously imposed regulations. It is the opposite of regulation.

reduce both unemployment and inflation in the long term, and improve UK external performance, as reflected in the balance of payments on current account. This is because the supply-side reform produced by liberating markets is expected to produce conditions in which domestically produced goods are both price competitive and quality competitive in overseas markets.

However, to bring about the long-run improvements in economic performance required to achieve these ends, substantial and sustainable increases in labour productivity are required. This in turn requires successful reform of the supply side of the economy.

Supply-side improvements and supply-side policies

Economics students often confuse **supply-side improvement** (or supply-side reform) with supply-side policies. While the two are linked, they do not mean exactly the same thing. For the most part, supply-side improvements are undertaken by the private sector itself as a result of entrepreneurs realising they must make their firms more efficient and competitive, first to survive in the modern global economy, and second to make profits. By contrast, the government's supply-side policies are part of the means of achieving this desirable outcome. In the free-market view, by financially propping up uncompetitive firms, interventionist supply-side policies are often counterproductive in bringing about supply-side improvements. This is not necessarily true, however, in the case of interventionist policies which provide training, infrastructure and other external economies that reduce firms' costs. Nevertheless, as already mentioned, pro-free market economists generally prefer non-interventionist supply-side policies. By liberalising markets and setting them free, the government pursues the role of *enabler* rather than *provider*. They are also against interventionist policies, because, to finance them, higher taxes are required, which damage incentives. They also question the quality of government provision.

The Laffer curve

Supply-side economists believe that high rates of income tax and the overall tax burden create disincentives, which, by reducing national income as taxation increases, also reduce the government's total tax revenue. This effect is illustrated by a Laffer curve, such as the one in Figure 9.13.

The Laffer curve, named after the leading supply-side economist Arthur Laffer, quoted at the beginning of this section, shows how the government's total tax revenue changes as the average tax rate increases from 0% to 100%. Tax revenue must be zero when the average tax rate is 0%, but Figure 9.13 also shows that total tax revenue is assumed to be zero when the tax rate is 100%. With the average tax rate set at 100%, all income must be paid as tax to the government. In this situation, there is no incentive to produce output other than for subsistence, so with no output produced, the government ends up collecting no tax revenue.

Between the limiting tax rates of 0% and 100%, the Laffer curve shows tax revenue first rising and then falling as the average rate of taxation increases. Tax revenue is maximised at the highest point on the Laffer curve, which in Figure 9.13 occurs at an average

261

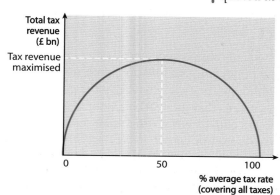

Figure 9.13 A Laffer curve

tax rate of 50%. Beyond this point, any further increase in the average tax rate becomes counterproductive, causing total tax revenue to fall. (The tax rate which maximises total tax revenue isn't necessarily 50%. It can vary through time.)

Supply-side economists argue that the increase in the tax burden in the Keynesian era, needed to finance the growth of the government and the public sector, raised the average tax rate towards or beyond the critical point on the Laffer curve at which tax revenue is maximised. In this situation, any further tax increase has the perverse effect of reducing the government's total tax revenue. Indeed, according to supply-side theory, if the government wishes to increase total tax revenue, it must cut tax rates rather than increase them.

A reduction in tax rates creates the incentives needed to stimulate economic growth. Faster growth means that total tax revenue increases despite the fact that tax rates are lower. Arguably, the effect is reinforced by a decline in tax evasion and avoidance, as the incentive to engage in these activities reduces at lower tax rates.

CASE STUDY 9.4

Have UK politicians been influenced by supply-side theory?

On 18 December 2012, Chancellor George Osborne spoke to a gathering of American supply-side economists at the Manhattan Institute for Policy Research in New York City. In answer to a question about the division between American Republicans and British Conservatives on the power of tax rate cuts to generate tax revenue, George Osborne replied:

Well I'm a fiscal Conservative, and I don't want to take risks with my public finances on an assumption that we are at some point on the Laffer curve. What I would say is, let's see the proof in the pudding: in other words, I'm a low-tax Conservative, I want to reduce taxes, but I basically think you have to do the hard work of reducing government spending to pay for those lower taxes. If you want to cut taxes, cut welfare and cut spending, and that's what I'm doing.

Osborne seemed to be rejecting the 'extreme' supply-side argument, based on the Laffer curve, that tax cuts can be self-financing and that they are all that is needed for growth generation. Osborne, along with other Conservative members of the UK government (in early 2015), is best regarded as a 'moderate' rather than an 'extreme' supply-sider.

Many Labour and Lib Dem politicians now also accept moderate supply-side arguments, though they continue to reject extreme supply-side calls for swingeing tax cuts and greater income inequality in order to incentivise the population. Especially since the emergence of the sovereign debt problem, few politicians now call for continuous large budget deficits as the way to achieve growth and full employment, and there is general agreement that the tax structure should be used in a supply-side way to create incentives for work, entrepreneurship, saving and investment.

Follow-up questions

1 Describe the difference between 'extreme' and 'moderate' supply-side views on the role of tax cuts.
2 How has the emergence of the sovereign debt problem affected fiscal policy?

The 'trickle-down' effect

Along with other free-market economists, supply-side economists believe that, in the long run, expansionary fiscal policy leads to inflation, with no increase in real output. Some believe that although the rich benefit most from supply-side tax cuts, a 'trickle-down' effect means that the working poor also benefit. This is because the rich respond to tax cuts by employing more servants, nannies and gardeners, albeit generally on low wages.

But other economists question the strength and even the existence of trickle-down effects. J.K. Galbraith, for example, caustically quipped the less than elegant metaphor that if one feeds the horse enough oats, some will pass through to the road for the sparrows. Galbraith went on to state, 'We can safely abandon the doctrine that the rich are not working because they have too little money and the poor because they have too much.' And even if a trickle-down effect does operate, the widening income inequalities that are responsible for more of the poor being employed by the rich are viewed by Keynesian economists as far too inequitable or unfair.

Microeconomic theory and the effects of supply-side fiscal policy

The supply-side theory of the effects of taxation on labour market incentives, which lies at the heart of free-market supply-side economics, depends on the shape of the supply curve of labour.

Supply-side economists usually assume a conventional upward-sloping supply curve of labour. Such a curve, which is illustrated in Figure 9.14(a), shows that workers respond to higher wage rates by supplying more labour.

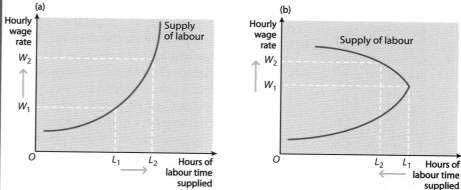

Figure 9.14 Microeconomic labour supply curves

Since a cut in the rate at which income tax rates are levied is equivalent to an increase in the wage rate, the upward-sloping supply curve implies that workers respond to cuts in the marginal rate of income tax by working harder. (The marginal rate of income tax is the percentage of the last pound of income paid in tax.) If this is the case, a reduction in income tax rates creates the incentive for workers to supply more labour (and for entrepreneurs to become more enterprising), while an increase in income tax rates has a disincentive effect on effort and the supply of labour.

However, the supply curve of labour need not necessarily slope upward throughout its length. The backward-bending labour supply curve in Figure 9.14(b) is another possibility. It shows that, above the hourly wage rate W_1, any further wage rate increase (or income tax decrease) causes workers to supply *less* rather than *more* labour. In this situation, workers prefer to enjoy extra leisure time rather than to work. Following an increase in the hourly wage rate from W_1 to W_2, the hours of labour time supplied fall from L_1 to L_2.

It is important to note that, if supply curves of labour bend backward, the supply-side argument — that tax reductions increase national output and efficiency through their effect on labour market incentives — becomes much weaker. Far from encouraging people to work harder, a wage rise or income tax cut might have the opposite effect, causing people to work fewer hours and to enjoy more leisure time instead.

Examples of supply-side economic policies

We conclude the chapter by outlining examples of supply-side policies other than those that relate to the effect of fiscal policy on personal incentives. Some of these have already been mentioned. It is also worth noting that supply-side policies include measures such as government spending on education and training, cuts in income and corporation tax, welfare reform, and industrial policy.

All the policies listed below have been implemented in the UK over approximately the last 30 years. However, some policies, such as creating internal markets in the provision of state healthcare and education, have been partially implemented and then largely withdrawn.

Industrial policy measures

- **Privatisation** The sale or transfer of assets such as nationalised industries from the public sector to the private sector
- **Marketisation (or commercialisation)** Shifting economic activity from non-market provision (financed by taxation) to commercial or market provision for which the customer pays
- **Deregulation** The removal of previously imposed regulations in order to promote competition. Deregulation removes barriers to market entry to make markets contestable, and gets rid of unnecessary 'red tape' or bureaucracy, which had increased firms' costs of production
- **Internal markets** In the National Health Service and education, where the state continues to be a major producer and provider of services, internal markets can be introduced to provide a form of commercial discipline and to improve efficiency. In an internal market, which is a substitute for privatisation, the taxpayer continues to finance hospitals and schools, but hospitals and schools 'earn' the money according to how many patients and pupils they attract

Labour market measures

- **Lower rates of income tax** Reducing marginal rates of income tax to create labour market incentives, and raising tax thresholds or personal tax allowances to remove the low-paid from the tax net
- **Reducing state welfare benefits relative to average earnings** Lower benefit levels create incentives to choose low-paid employment in preference to claiming unemployment-related benefits. In addition, welfare benefits can be made more difficult to claim, and available only to claimants genuinely looking for work.
- **Changing employment law to reduce the power of trade unions** Removing trade unions' legal protection, restricting their rights, and extending the freedom for workers not to belong to unions, and for employers not to recognise and negotiate with unions. Replacing collective bargaining with individual wage negotiation and employer determination of pay. Restricting the right to strike and to undertake industrial action
- **Repealing legislation which limits employers' freedom to employ** This makes it easier for employers to 'hire and fire' workers
- **More flexible pension arrangements** Encouraging workers to 'opt out' of state pensions and to arrange private pension plans so as to reduce the burden on taxpayers. Allowing workers to transfer private sector pensions between employers when changing jobs

- **Improving the training of labour** Establishing training agencies and academies to develop vocational technical education. However, UK governments have rejected the proposal to impose a 'training tax' on all employers to prevent free-riding by firms with no training schemes, which poach trained workers from firms that do train their workers

Though not a government policy, the introduction of short-term employment contracts in labour markets replaced 'jobs for life' with short-term labour contracts. This, together with the promotion of profit-related and performance-related pay, has had a supply-side effect. Also, 'zero hours' employment contracts have recently been introduced by a large number of employers. Critics of these policies believe they lead to even greater poverty and inequality for ordinary workers in an increasingly casualised and exploited part-time labour force.

Financial and capital market measures

- **Deregulating financial markets** Creating greater competition among banks and building societies, and opening up the UK financial markets to overseas banks and financial institutions. These reforms increase the supply of funds and reduce the cost of borrowing for UK firms. Financial deregulation and the removal of foreign exchange controls also encourage 'inward' investment by overseas firms such as Samsung and Nissan. However, very lightly regulated banks created by financial deregulation contributed significantly to the financial crisis which began in 2007 and then ushered in the 2008/09 recession
- **Encouraging saving** Governments have created special tax privileges for saving. They also encouraged saving by giving individual shareholders first preference in the market for shares issued when former nationalised industries such as British Gas were privatised. However, most individual shareholders quickly sold their shares to institutional shareholders, which negated one of the main reasons for privatisation. It is also worth noting that in recent years, very low interest rates, brought about by the government's monetary policy, have discouraged saving
- **Promoting entrepreneurship** Governments have encouraged the growth of popular capitalism and an enterprise culture. Company taxation has been reduced and markets have been deregulated to encourage risk taking
- **Reducing public spending and public sector borrowing** This was intended to free resources for private sector use and avoid crowding out

---

TEST YOURSELF 9.4

The chancellor of the exchequer recently announced plans to increase government spending on construction projects, such roads and high-speed train lines. Which of the following three policies is this an example of?

(a) Expansionary monetary policy

(b) Interventionist supply-side policy

(c) Contractionary fiscal policy

Explain your answer.

- Along with fiscal policy and supply-side policy, monetary policy provides a way of managing the national economy.
- In the UK, monetary policy is implemented by the country's central bank, the Bank of England.
- Control of inflation is the main monetary policy objective, but there are other objectives.
- Central government sets the inflation rate target, which was 2% between 2003 and 2015, measured by the CPI. In future years the target may be changed by the government.
- The Bank of England's Monetary Policy Committee (MPC) implements monetary policy to try to hit the 2% inflation rate target, but it is less effective at controlling cost-push inflation.
- Bank Rate is the main monetary policy instrument, but other instruments such as quantitative easing (QE) are now sometimes used.
- Monetary policy is used to manage the level of aggregate demand.
- Changes in interest rates affect consumption, investment and net export demand, and shift the position of the AD curve.
- Monetary policy can be effective in controlling demand-pull inflation, but it is less effective at controlling cost-push inflation.
- Monetary policy was successful in controlling inflation in the UK in the 1990s and early 2000s. After two bouts of relatively high inflation in 2008 and 2011, the inflation rate has been around the 2% rate or lower since then — at least up to 2015.
- Fiscal policy uses government spending, taxation and the budgetary position to try to achieve the government's economic policy objectives.
- Keynesian fiscal policy (or demand-side fiscal policy) manages the level of aggregate demand.
- Changes in the government's budget deficit or surplus are important in Keynesian fiscal policy.
- Budget deficits and surpluses are *flow* concepts, and are the difference between the *flows* of government spending and tax revenue.
- The national debt is a *stock* concept, and is the historical accumulation of central government borrowing which has not as yet been paid back or redeemed.
- The size of the government spending multiplier affects the power of Keynesian fiscal policy.
- Government spending is a component of aggregate demand.
- Changes in government spending and/or taxation shift the AD curve.
- The effect on real output and employment depends on the shape and slope of the SRAS curve, i.e. the amount of spare capacity in the economy.
- Supply-side fiscal policy affects the position of the LRAS curve.
- In supply-side fiscal policy, tax changes are used to try to change incentives in the economy.
- A significant proportion of government spending takes the forms of transfers and debt interest payments.
- Progressive taxation and transfers are used to redistribute income from higher-income groups to lower-income groups, but income inequalities have widened since the 2008/09 recession.
- Free-market supply-side economists argue that government policy should be used to improve incentives and the competitiveness and efficiency of markets.
- In its early years, supply-side economics focused on how, via increased incentives, tax cuts promote economic growth and are self-financing.
- The growth of supply-side economics has been part of the free-market revival.
- Supply-side economists are generally anti-interventionist and wish to reduce the economic role of the state. However, some supply-side policies, such as government financing of retraining schemes in labour markets, are interventionist.
- Supply-side policies contribute to supply-side reform and supply-side improvements.
- Most economists now accept the argument that the supply side of the economy is just as important as the demand side.
- Many supply-side policies are microeconomic rather than macroeconomic.

Questions

1 Explain how changes in Bank Rate affect aggregate demand.

2 Discuss the view that monetary policy is inappropriate for controlling cost-push inflation.

3 Evaluate the Bank of England's success since 2008 in controlling the rate of inflation.

4 Explain the relationship between a budget deficit and the national debt.

5 Evaluate the view that cuts in the higher rates of income tax are required in order to create the incentives necessary for stimulating economic growth.

6 Explain the role of fiscal policy in supply-side economic policy.

7 To what extent do you agree that supply-side improvements are needed if UK macroeconomic performance is to improve? Justify your answer.

8 Assess the view that a cut in income tax rates inevitably leads to an increase in total tax revenue.

9 With the help of *AD/AS* diagrams, explain the difference between supply-side and Keynesian views on the effect of an increase in aggregate demand on the economy.

Macroeconomic key terms

accelerator a change in the level of investment in new capital goods is induced by a change in the rate of growth of national income or aggregate demand.

actual output level of real output produced in the economy in a particular year, not to be confused with the trend level of output. The trend level of output is what the economy is capable of producing when working at full capacity. Actual output differs from the trend level of output when there are output gaps.

aggregate demand the total planned spending on real output produced within the economy.

aggregate supply the level of real national output that producers are prepared to supply at different average price levels.

availability of credit funds available for households and firms to borrow.

balance of payments a record of all the currency flows into and out of a country in a particular time period.

balance of payments equilibrium (or current account equilibrium) occurs when the current account more or less balances over a period of years.

balance of trade the difference between the money value of a country's imports and its exports. Balance of trade is the largest component of a country's balance of payments on current account.

balance of trade deficit the money value of a country's imports exceeds the money value of its exports.

balance of trade in goods the part of the current account measuring payments for exports and imports of goods. The difference between the total value of exports and the total value of imports of goods is

sometimes called the 'balance of visible trade'.

balance of trade in services is part of the current account and is the difference between the payments for the exports of services and the payments for the imports of services.

balance of trade surplus the money value of a country's exports exceeds the money value of its imports.

balanced budget achieved when government spending equals government revenue ($G = T$).

Bank of England the central bank in the UK economy which is in charge of monetary policy.

Bank Rate the rate of interest the Bank of England pays to commercial banks on their deposits held at the Bank of England.

budget deficit occurs when government spending exceeds government revenue ($G > T$). This represents a net injection of demand into the circular flow of income and hence a budget deficit is expansionary.

budget surplus occurs when government spending is less than government revenue ($G < T$). This represents a net withdrawal from the circular flow of income and hence a budget surplus is contractionary.

central bank controls the banking system and implements monetary policy on behalf of the government.

certainty one of the principles of taxation. Tax payers should be reasonably certain of the amount of tax they will be expected to pay.

claimant count the method of measuring unemployment according to those people who are claiming unemployment-related benefits (Jobseeker's Allowance).

closed economy an economy with no international trade.

consumer prices index (CPI) the official measure used to calculate the rate of consumer price inflation in the UK. The CPI calculates the average price increase of a basket of 700 different consumer goods and services.

consumption total planned spending by households on consumer goods and services produced within the economy.

contractionary fiscal policy uses fiscal policy to decrease aggregate demand and to shift the AD curve to the left.

contractionary monetary policy uses higher interest rates and other monetary tools to decrease aggregate demand and to shift the AD curve to the left.

convenience the principle of taxation which requires a tax to be convenient for taxpayers to pay.

cost-push inflation a rising price level caused by an increase in the costs of production, shown by a shift of the $SRAS$ curve to the left. Also known as **cost inflation**.

credit crunch occurs when there is a lack of funds available in the credit market, making it difficult for borrowers to obtain financing, and leads to a rise in the cost of borrowing.

crowding out a situation in which an increase in government or public sector spending displaces private sector spending, with little or no increase in aggregate demand.

current account deficit occurs when currency outflows in the current account exceed currency inflows. It is often shortened to 'exports less than imports'.

current account of the balance of payments measures all the currency flows into and out of a country in a particular time period in payment for exports and imports, together with income and transfer flows (primary income and secondary income flows).

current account surplus occurs when currency inflows in the current account exceed currency outflows. It is often shortened to 'exports greater than imports'.

cyclical budget deficit the part of the budget deficit which rises in the downswing of the economic cycle and falls in the upswing of the cycle.

cyclical budget surplus if the structural deficit were zero, a cyclical surplus would probably emerge in the upswing of the economic cycle.

cyclical unemployment also known as **Keynesian unemployment** and **demand-deficient unemployment**. As the latter name suggests, it is unemployment caused by a lack of aggregate demand in the economy and occurs when the economy goes into a recession or depression.

deficit financing deliberately running a budget deficit and borrowing to finance the deficit.

deflation a persistent or continuing fall in the average price level.

deindustrialisation the decline of manufacturing industries, together with coal mining.

demand-side relates to the impact of changes in aggregate demand on the economy. Associated with Keynesian economics.

demand-pull inflation a rising price level caused by an increase in aggregate demand, shown by a shift of the *AD* curve to the right. Also known as **demand inflation**.

demand-side fiscal policy used to increase or decrease the level of aggregate demand (and to shift the *AD* curve right or left) through changes in government spending, taxation and the budget balance.

deregulation involves removing previously imposed regulations. It is the opposite of regulation.

direct tax a tax which cannot be shifted by the person legally liable to pay the tax onto someone else. Direct taxes are levied on income and wealth.

discretionary fiscal policy involves making discrete changes to *G*, *T* and the budget deficit to manage the level of aggregate demand.

disinflation when the rate of inflation is falling, but still positive and the price level is rising more slowly than previously.

distribution of income the spread of different incomes among individuals and different income groups in the economy.

economic cycle upswing and downside in aggregate economic activity taking place over 4 to 12 years. Also known as a **business cycle** or a **trade cycle**.

economic performance success or failure in achieving economic policy objectives.

economic recovery when short-run economic growth takes place after a recession.

economic shock an unexpected event hitting the economy. Economic shocks can be demand-side or supply-side shocks (and sometimes both) and unfavourable or favourable.

economy the principle of taxation which requires a tax to be cheap to collect in relation to the revenue it yields.

efficiency (as a principle of taxation) a tax should achieve its desired objective(s) with minimum unintended consequences.

emerging-market country a country that is progressing towards becoming more economically advanced, by means of rapid growth and industrialisation.

equation of exchange the stock of money in the economy multiplied by the velocity of circulation of money equals the price level multiplied by the quantity of real output in the economy. ($MV = PQ$)

equilibrium unemployment exists when the economy's aggregate labour market is in equilibrium. It is the same as the natural level of unemployment.

equilibrium national income the level of real output at which aggregate demand equals aggregate supply ($AD = AS$). Alternatively, it is the level of income at which withdrawals from the circular flow of income equal injections into the flow. Also known as macroeconomic equilibrium.

equity (as a principle of taxation) requires a tax to be fair.

exchange rate the price of a currency, e.g. the pound, measured in terms of another currency such as the US dollar or the euro.

expansionary fiscal policy uses fiscal policy to increase aggregate demand and to shift the *AD* curve to the right.

expansionary monetary policy uses lower interest rates and other monetary instruments, such as quantitative easing, to increase aggregate demand and to shift the *AD* curve to the right.

export-led growth in the short run, economic growth resulting from the increase in exports as a component of aggregate demand. In the long run, economic growth resulting from the growth and increased international competitiveness of exporting industries.

exports domestically produced goods or services sold to residents of other countries.

fiscal policy the use by the government of government spending and taxation to try to achieve the government's policy objectives.

flexibility the principle of taxation that requires a tax to be easy to change to meet new circumstances.

frictional unemployment unemployment that is usually short term and occurs when a worker switches between jobs.

Also known as transitional unemployment.

full employment according to Beveridge's definition, full employment means 3% or less of the labour force unemployed. According to the free-market definition, it is the level of employment occurring at the market-clearing real-wage rate, where the number of workers whom employers wish to hire equals the number of workers wanting to work.

geographical immobility of labour when workers are unwilling or unable to move from one area to another in search of work.

gross domestic product (GDP) the sum of all goods and services, or level of output, produced in the economy over a period of time, e.g. one year.

import-cost inflation a rising price level caused by an increase in the cost of imported energy, food, raw materials and manufactured goods, shown by a shift of the *SRAS* curve to the left.

imports goods or services produced in other countries and sold to residents of this country.

index number a number used in an index, such as the consumer prices index, to enable accurate comparisons over time to be made. The base year index number is typically 100. In subsequent years, percentage increases cause the index number to rise above the index number recorded for the previous year, and percentage decreases cause the index number to fall below the index number recorded for the previous year.

indexation the automatic adjustment of items such as pensions and welfare benefits to changes in the price level, through the use of a price index.

indirect tax a tax which can be shifted by the person legally liable to pay the tax onto someone else, for example through raising the price of a good being sold by the taxpayer. Indirect taxes are levied on spending.

inflation a persistent or continuing rise in the average price level.

inflation rate target the CPI inflation rate target set by the government for the Bank of England to try to achieve. The target is currently 2%.

injection spending entering the circular flow of income as a result of investment, government spending and exports.

interventionist policies occur when the government intervenes in, and sometimes replaces, free markets. Interventionist supply-side policies include government funding of research and development.

investment total planned spending by firms on capital goods produced within the economy.

involuntary unemployment when workers are willing to work at current market wage rates but there are no jobs available.

Keynesian economists followers of the economist John Maynard Keynes, who generally believe that governments should manage the economy, particularly through the use of fiscal policy.

Labour Force Survey a quarterly sample survey of households in the UK. Its purpose is to provide information on the UK labour market. The survey seeks information on respondents' personal circumstances and their labour market status during a period of 1–4 weeks.

life-cycle theory of consumption a theory that explains consumption and saving in terms of how people expect their incomes to change over the whole of their life cycles.

liquidity measures the ease with which assets can be turned into cash quickly without a loss in value. Cash is the most liquid of all assets.

long-run aggregate supply (LRAS) aggregate supply when the economy is producing at its production potential. If more factors of production become available or productivity rises, the *LRAS* curve shifts to the right.

long-run economic growth an increase in the economy's potential level of real output, and an outward movement of the economy's production possibility frontier.

long-run Phillips curve a vertical curve located at the natural rate of unemployment (NRU). It differs from the short-run Phillips curve in that its vertical shape takes account of the role of expectations in the inflationary process.

macroeconomics involves the study of the whole economy at the aggregate level.

marginal propensity to consume (MPC) the fraction of an increase in disposable income (after tax) that people plan to spend on domestically produced consumer goods.

marketisation involves shifting provision of goods or services from the non-market sector to the market sector. Also known as **commercialisation**.

monetarists economists who argue that a prior increase in the money supply is the cause of inflation.

monetary policy the use by the government and its agent, the Bank of England, of interest rates and other monetary instruments to try to achieve the government's policy objectives.

Monetary Policy Committee (MPC) nine economists, chaired by the governor of the Bank of England, who meet once a month to set Bank Rate, the Bank of England's key interest rate, and also decide whether other aspects of monetary policy need changing.

money an asset that can be used as a medium of exchange; it is used to buy things.

money supply the stock of money in the economy, made up of cash and bank deposits.

multiplier the relationship between a change in aggregate demand and the resulting usually larger change in national income.

national capital stock the stock of capital goods, such as buildings and machinery, in the economy that has accumulated over time and is measured at a point in time.

national debt the stock of all past central government borrowing that has not been paid back.

national income the *flow* of new output produced by the economy in a particular period (e.g. a year).

national output the same as national income, namely the *flow* of new output produced by the economy in a particular period (e.g. a year).

national product another name for national income and national output.

national wealth the stock of all goods that exist at a point in time that have value in the economy.

natural rate of unemployment (NRU) the rate of unemployment when the aggregate labour market is in equilibrium.

negative output gap the level of *actual* real output in the economy is lower than the *trend* output level.

net investment income the difference between inward and outward flows of investment income. When net investment income is positive, the UK is earning more income generated by the direct and portfolio investments held abroad than it is paying to overseas owners of capital assets in the UK. Investment income is the main component of primary income flows in the current account of the balance of payments.

nominal GDP GDP measured at the current market prices, without removing the effects of inflation.

non-interventionist supply-side policies free up markets, promote competition and greater efficiency, and reduce the economic role of the state.

occupational immobility of labour when workers are unwilling or unable to move from one type of job to another, for example because different skills are needed.

open economy an economy open to international trade.

output gap the level of *actual* real output in the economy is greater or lower than the *trend* output level.

performance indicator provides information for judging the success or failure of a particular type of government policy such as fiscal policy or monetary policy.

Phillips curve based on evidence from the economy, showing the apparent relationship between the rate of inflation and the rate of unemployment. Now known as the short-run Phillips curve.

policy conflict occurs when two policy objectives cannot both be achieved at the same time: the better the performance in achieving one objective, the worse the performance in achieving the other.

policy instrument a tool or set of tools used to try to achieve a policy objective.

policy objective a target or goal that policy-makers aim to 'hit'.

positive output gap the level of *actual* real output in the economy is greater than the *trend* output level.

price index an index number showing the extent to which a price, or a 'basket' of prices, has changed over a month, quarter or year, in comparison with the price(s) in a base year.

principle of taxation a criterion used for judging whether a tax is good or bad. Also known as a **canon of taxation**.

privatisation involves shifting ownership of state-owned assets to the private sector.

pro-free market economists opponents of Keynesian economists, who dislike government intervention in the economy and who much prefer the operation of free markets.

progressive taxation a tax is progressive if, as income rises, a larger proportion of income is paid in tax.

proportional taxation when the proportion of income paid in tax stays the same as income increases.

public sector borrowing borrowing by the government and other parts of the public sector to finance a budget deficit.

quantity theory of money oldest theory of inflation, incorporated into monetarism, which states that inflation is caused by a persistent increase in the supply of money.

rate of interest the reward for lending savings to somebody else (e.g. a bank) and the cost of borrowing.

real GDP a measure of all the goods and services produced in an economy, adjusted for price changes or inflation. The adjustment transforms changes in nominal GDP, which is measured in money terms, into a measure that reflects changes in the total output of the economy.

real wage the purchasing power of the nominal (or money) wage; for example, real wages fall when inflation is higher than the rise in the nominal wage rate and real wages rise when the nominal wage rate increases more rapidly than inflation.

real-wage unemployment unemployment caused by real wages being stuck above the equilibrium real wage.

recession a fall in real GDP for 6 months or more.

reflationary policies policies that increase aggregate demand with the intention of increasing real output and employment.

regressive taxation when the proportion of income paid in tax falls as income increases.

reindustrialise growth of manufacturing industries to replace industries which have disappeared or declined significantly in size. Reindustrialisation is the opposite of deindustrialisation.

retail prices index (RPI) the RPI is an older measure used to calculate the rate of consumer price inflation in the UK. Currently, the UK government uses the CPI for the indexation of state pensions and welfare benefits and for setting a monetary policy target, and the RPI for uprating each year the cost of TV and motor vehicle licences, together sometimes with taxes on goods such as alcoholic drinks.

saving income which is not spent.

seasonal fluctuation variation of economic activity resulting from seasonal changes in the economy.

seasonal unemployment unemployment arising in different seasons of the year, caused by factors such as the weather and the end of the Christmas shopping period.

short-run aggregate supply (SRAS) aggregate supply when the level of capital is fixed, though the utilisation of existing factors of production can be altered so as to change the level of real output.

short-run economic growth growth of real output resulting from using idle resources, including labour, thereby taking up the slack in the economy.

sovereign debt problem sovereign debt is the part of the national debt owned by people or institutions outside the country that has sold the debt to them. The sovereign debt problem stems from the difficulties governments face when trying to finance budget deficits by borrowing on international financial markets.

structural budget deficit the part of the budget deficit which is not affected by the economic cycle but results from structural change in the economy affecting the government's finances, and also from long-term government policy decisions.

structural unemployment long-term unemployment occurring when some industries are declining, even though other industries may be growing. Also occurs within a growing industry if automation reduces the demand for labour, and when production requires new skills not possessed by the workers who lose their jobs. Structural unemployment is associated with the occupational and geographical immobility of labour.

supply-side relates to changes in the potential output of the economy which is affected by the available factors of production, e.g. changes in the size of the labour force, and the productivity of the economy.

supply-side economics a branch of free-market economics arguing that government policy should be used to improve the competitiveness and efficiency of markets and, through this, the performance of the economy.

supply-side fiscal policy used to increase the economy's ability to produce and supply goods, through creating incentives to work, save, invest, and be entrepreneurial. Interventionist supply-side fiscal policies, such as the financing of retraining schemes for unemployed workers, are also designed to improve supply-side performance.

supply-side improvement reforms undertaken by the private sector to reduce costs to enable firms to become more productively efficient and competitive. Supply-side improvement often results from more investment and innovation, often undertaken by firms without prompting from the government.

supply-side policies aim to improve national economic performance by creating competitive and more efficient markets and through interventionist policies such as government finance of labour retraining schemes. (See also supply-side fiscal policy.)

tax threshold the basic tax threshold is the level of income above which people pay income tax. Income below the basic tax threshold is untaxed.

technical progress new and better ways of doing things.

trade-off between policy objectives the extent to which one policy objective has to be sacrificed in order to achieve another objective.

transfers payments flowing between countries in forms such as foreign aid, grants, private transfers and gifts and payments to or from the EU budget. They are payments that are made without anything of economic value being received in return. Not to be confused in this context with the part of government spending in which tax revenues are paid to people such as pensioners, without any output being produced in return.

trend growth rate the rate at which output can grow, on a sustained basis, without putting upward or downward pressure on inflation. It reflects the annual average percentage increase in the productive capacity of the economy.

voluntary unemployment occurs when workers choose to remain unemployed and refuse job offers at current market wage rates.

wage-cost inflation a rising price level caused by an increase in wages and salaries, shown by a shift of the *SRAS* curve to the left.

wealth the *stock* of assets which have value at a point in time, as distinct from income which is a *flow* generated over a period of time.

withdrawal a leakage of spending power out of the circular flow of income into savings, taxation or imports.

Macroeconomic practice questions

In this section you will find a set of objective test questions, followed by a context question for AS.

Objective test questions

1 What are the three leakages from the circular flow of income?

  A Investment, taxes and spending on imports

  B Saving, taxes and spending on imports

  C Saving, government spending, spending on imports

  D Saving, taxes, spending on exports

2 Real national income may be defined as:

  A the sum of all the incomes earned over a given time period

  B national income expressed in constant prices

  C national income expressed in current prices

  D national income net of all tax payments

3 The diagram below illustrates two aggregate demand curves (AD_1 and AD_2), the long-run aggregate supply curve (*LRAS*) and the short-run aggregate supply curve (*SRAS*) for an economy.

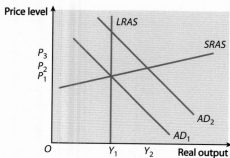

The shift of the AD curve from AD_1 to AD_2 will:

A increase both real output and average prices in the short run

B leave average prices and real output unchanged in the short run

C increase real output but not average prices in the long run

D leave average prices and real output unchanged in the long run

4 Supply-side policies are said to be more effective than demand-side policies at reducing:

A demand-pull inflation

B interest rates

C frictional unemployment

D labour productivity

5 An increase in interest rates is most likely to lead to:

A an increase in inflation

B a reduction in new housing loans

C a decrease in the level of unemployment

D a rise in investment spending

6 An expansionary fiscal policy may include which **one** of the following?

A Lower rates of taxation and increased government spending

B Lower interest rates and a fall in the exchange rate

C An increase in money supply and higher interest rates

D Lower government spending and higher rates of taxation

7 The table below shows the changes in money wages and the price level in a certain economy.

	Index of money wages	Index of prices
Year 1	100	100
Year 2	120	110

From this information, we can conclude that there has been an increase in real wages of:

A just over 120%

B exactly 20%

C exactly 19%

D about 10%

8 The diagram below shows the weekly gains and losses of income experienced by households in a country as a result of the government's budget.

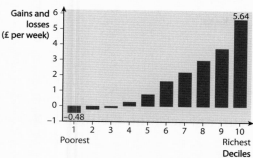

Which of the following can be concluded from the data?

A Every household in the top decile gained £5.64 a week as a result of the budget.

B The distribution of income was most equal for the households in the third decile.

C For the population as a whole, the distribution of income was highly unequal.

D Most decile groups benefited from an increase in income as a result of the budget.

9 The table below shows the consumer prices index for a particular country over a time period.

Year	Consumer prices index
2011	96
2012	100
2013	103
2014	111

It can be concluded from the data that:

A deflation occurred in 2011

B 2012 is the base year for the data series

C the price level facing consumers increased in every year in the data series

D over the whole period, the price level increased by 15%

10 The figures below are a selection of national income statistics for a given economy.

GDP	£6847 bn
Consumption	£5528 bn
Government spending	£942 bn
Investment	£529 bn

Given the amounts above, net exports are:

A −£319 billion

B −£152 billion

C £6,999 billion

D £413 billion

AS context question

Context 1

Total for this context: 50 marks

The UK trade gap

Study **Extracts A, B and C** and then answer **all** parts of Context 1 which follow.

Extract A: The balance of payments deficit on current account, £ billion, 2003–13

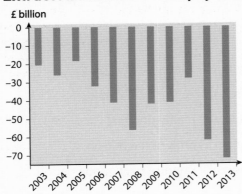

Source contains public sector information licensed under the Open Government Licence v. 1.0

Extract B: UK trade deficit hits record high

1 Whatever happened to the UK's promised export boom? For several years after 2008 the pound's exchange rate fell, making Britain's exports more price competitive in world markets. At the same time, the falling exchange rate increased the price of imports, making them less price competitive in the UK market.

Well, exports certainly increased. However, 10 despite a 25% fall in the value of the pound in 2008 and 2009, the rise was only slight. There were plenty of competing explanations as to why. Our reliance on the EU, which apart from Germany has struggled to grow since 2008, was one of them. The propensity for exporters to jack up their prices rather than increase production in response to higher demand was another factor.

Then in 2013, the pound's exchange rate began 20 to rise – exactly the opposite of what textbooks tell us is likely to happen when a country's exports cannot match the prices charged by overseas competitors. One of the factors which led to a rising pound was the strength of the recovery in the British economy. Overseas owners of funds believed that the 'only way was up' for UK interest rates and that higher interest rates would reward them for holding their funds in the pound.

30 Allied to this was the view taken by foreign investors that the UK is a 'safe haven' in which to deposit funds in a troubled world. Factors such as these overrode the textbook view that with a current account deficit close to a record high of 5% of GDP, the exchange rate should be falling and not rising.

Source: News reports, August 2014

Extract C: Export-led growth

1 Over several decades, one of the most deep-rooted problems facing the UK economy has been the weak performance of British industries in the competitive world market for manufactured goods.

When recession hits the UK economy, both exports and imports fall. What happens next in a recession depends on which falls faster. In 2008, the fall in the overseas demand for 10 UK exports, particularly US demand, was one of the most important causes of the collapse of aggregate demand and the contractionary multiplier effect, which brought about the recession which started in that year.

During the more recent period of recovery and positive economic growth, UK households have directed much of their extra income to spending on imports. Unfortunately, people living in other countries have been much less 20 willing to buy British goods. As a result, the gap between exports and imports in the UK current account of the balance of payments has generally widened.

Economists have often said that export-led growth is the way forward for stabilising the UK economy. But achieving this is much easier

said than done. Fundamental supply-side reforms and investment in the modernisation of British industry are necessary for export-led 30 growth to take place. Aggregate demand must also expand in the countries to which the UK wishes to sell manufactured goods.

Although lip service will continue to be given to the need for export-led growth, the reality is that the current economic recovery is once again being left to consumption-led growth. But this means that all the 'boom and bust' problems of the past will again resurface. Export-led growth is needed, together with 40 investment-led growth, but many economists doubt whether either growth path can be achieved and sustained.

Source: News reports, August 2014

01 Define the term 'exports' (**Extract B**, line 4).

(3 marks)

02 The ONS has estimated that UK money GDP in 2013 was approximately £1.6 billion.

Using the data in **Extract A**, estimate the size of the UK's current account deficit in 2013 as a percentage of UK GDP.

(4 marks)

03 Using **Extract A**, identify **two** significant features of the changes in the UK's balance of payments on current account over the period shown.

(4 marks)

04 **Extract B** (lines 2–3) state that for several years after 2008 the pound's exchange rate fell, making Britain's exports more price competitive in world markets.

Draw an *AD/AS* diagram to illustrate how a fall in the exchange rate is likely to affect national output.

(4 marks)

05 Lines 11 and 12 of **Extract C** mention 'the collapse of aggregate demand and the contractionary multiplier effect'. Explain how a collapse of aggregate demand and a contractionary multiplier effect are likely to affect unemployment in an economy.

(10 marks)

06 **Extract C** (lines 35–36) state 'that the current economic recovery is once again being left to consumption-led growth'.

Assess the view that relying on consumption-led growth will mean that the economic recovery in the UK is unsustainable.

(25 marks)

Index

Note: **bold** page numbers indicate key terms.